AVIATION CENTURY

WINGS OF CHANGE

AVIATION CENTURY

WINGS OF CHANGE

RON DICK AND DAN PATTERSON

The BOSTON
MILLS PRESS

A BOSTON MILLS PRESS BOOK

First printing

National Library of Canada Cataloguing in Publication

Dick, Ron, 1931–
Aviation century wings of change / Ron Dick and Dan Patterson.

Includes bibliographical references and index.

ISBN 1-55046-428-0

1. Aeronautics — History.
I. Patterson, Dan, 1953–
II. Title.

TL600.D53 2005   629.13'009   C2005-901131-9

Publisher Cataloging-in-Publication Data   (U.S.)

Dick, Ron, 1931–
Aviation century wings of change / Ron Dick ; and Dan Patterson. — 1st ed.

[288] p.: ill. , photos. (chiefly col.) ; cm. (Aviation Century)

Includes bibliographical references and index.

Summary: Comprehensive resource to aeronautical developments in the 20th
century, including: commercial aviation, private flying, sailplanes, lighter-than
air flight (balloons, dirigibles), rotary wings (helicopters), research and
development, and test pilots.

ISBN 1-55046-428-0

1. Airplanes — History – 20th century.
2. Aircraft industry — History – 20th century. 3. Aeronautics—History – 20th
century. I. Patterson, Dan, 1953– II. Title. III. Series.

629.13'009 22   TL600.D52 2005

Published in 2005 by BOSTON MILLS PRESS
132 Main Street,
Erin, Ontario N0B 1T0
Tel 519-833-2407
Fax 519-833-2195

IN CANADA:
Distributed by Firefly Books Ltd.
66 Leek Crescent
Richmond Hill, Ontario L4B 1H1

IN THE UNITED STATES:
Distributed by Firefly Books (U.S.) Inc.
P.O. Box 1338, Ellicott Station
Buffalo, New York 14205

books@bostonmillspress.com
www.bostonmillspress.com

Aviation Century series editor: Kathleen Fraser
Design: PageWave Graphics Inc.

Printed in China by SNP Leefung Printers Limited

The publisher gratefully acknowledges the financial support for our publishing program by the Canada Council for the Arts,
the Ontario Arts Council and the Government of Canada through the Book Publishing Industry Development Program.

FRONT JACKET MAIN IMAGE *Boeing 747 on the United Parcel Service ramp,
Louisville, Kentucky. The combination of widebody Jumbo jets and turbofan
engines made possible the rapid growth in the carriage of passengers and freight
worldwide from the 1970s on. Intercontinental travel became commonplace and
overnight freight delivery to almost anywhere became feasible. This Boeing 747,
powered by Pratt & Whitney turbofans producing close to 50,000 pounds of
thrust each, is capable of lifting up to a quarter of a million pounds of freight.*
FRONT JACKET BOTTOM ROW
FAR LEFT *Piasecki H-21 at the American Helicopter Museum.*
CENTER LEFT *Howard Steele lights the propane burner and fills his hot-air
balloon.*
CENTER RIGHT *The Bell X-1B at the National Museum of the United States Air
Force.*
FAR RIGHT *Schweizer 1-26 soaring over October trees.*
BACK JACKET *Jerry Kemp and grandson in his immaculate Globe Swift, near
Covington, Ohio, 2003.*

HALF-TITLE PAGE *The North American XB-70 on final approach for its last
landing at Wright-Patterson AFB, spring of 1968.*
PAGE 2 *De Havilland Hornet Moth.*
TITLE PAGE *A newly built Waco Classic on floats.*
PAGE 4 *The Nord 1500-02 Griffon II preserved by the Musée del l'Air et de
l'Espace at Le Bourget.*
PAGE 6 *Transforming the 20th century: an exact replica of the Wright brothers
wind tunnel balance, copies of their letters and graphic results of their
experiments; an air foil wing rib shaped by their findings, and a late-century
wind tunnel model.*

Dedicated to aviators,
past, present
and of the future.

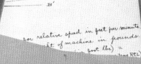

Contents

ACKNOWLEDGMENTS

THIS FOURTH VOLUME OF the Aviation Century series takes the story of commercial aviation into the jet age, but it also deals with many facets of aviation hardly mentioned in previous volumes. Many of those who had helped with earlier books were once more generous in offering assistance for this one. However, in seeking to widen their horizons to cover rotary-winged and lighter-than-air flight, and to introduce the world of aeronautical research and development, the authors found that they needed to add considerably to the list of those to whom they are indebted. Thanks are now due to an impressive number of organizations and individuals, representing a sizeable proportion of the world's leading aviation museums, industries and practitioners. Many names on this page are appearing for the fourth time in the series, and some are being welcomed as new contributors. The work on this book could not have been completed without their willing help. The authors are sincerely grateful to them all for their unfailing support. It is earnestly hoped that every one will be remembered in our acknowledgments, but we are only too well aware that we are less than perfect. With the best of intentions, it is still possible that a person or organization will be overlooked, or that mistakes will be made and credit perhaps given incorrectly. If that occurs, the authors would be glad to have the errors brought to their attention so that apologies can be offered and corrections made in future editions.

As was the case for the previous books in this series, the help of the aviation museums and archives of North America and Europe was indispensable in the preparation of this volume. The authors are particularly grateful to the directors and staffs of the Smithsonian's National Air & Space Museum, Washington, D.C.; the Museum of Flight, Seattle, Washington; the Virginia Aviation Museum, Richmond, Virginia; the EAA's Air Venture Museum, Oshkosh, Wisconsin; the USAF History Office; the National Museum of the United States Air Force, Dayton, Ohio; the Air Force Flight Test Center Museum, Edwards AFB, California; the Museum of Naval Aviation, Pensacola, Florida; the U.S. Marine Corps Museum, Quantico, Virginia; the American Helicopter Museum, West Chester, Pennsylvania; the National Aviation Hall of Fame; the International Association of Eagles; the Canada Aviation Museum, Ottawa; the Canadian Warplane Heritage Museum, Hamilton, Ontario; the Royal Aeronautical Society, London; the Imperial War Museum, Duxford, U.K.; the Royal Air Force Museum, Hendon and Cosford, U.K.; the Fleet Air Arm Museum, Yeovilton, U.K.; the Shuttleworth Trust; the Musée de l'Air et de l'Espace, Le Bourget, France; the Museo Storico Aeronautica Militare, Vigna di Valle, Italy; the Museo Caproni, Trento, Italy; the Flygvapenmuseum, Linköping, Sweden; and the Muzeum Lotnictwa Polskiego, Krakow, Poland.

Archive photographs in *Aviation Century Wings of Change* came from the collections of Wright State University; the Smithsonian National Air & Space Museum; the Museum of Flight, Seattle; the National Museum of the United States Air Force; the National Museum of Naval Aviation, Pensacola; and from the private collections of the authors. In the United Kingdom, the staffs of Key Publishing (including *FlyPast* and *Air International* magazines) and *Aeroplane Monthly* magazine were kind enough to give us access to their unrivaled archives of aviation photography.

Particular thanks go to a number of individuals for their encouragement of our efforts and for finding and providing material for this volume: Fred Smith, Tom Poborezny, Richard Hallion, Dennis Parks, Katherine Williams, Bob Rasmussen, Hill Goodspeed, David McFarland, Floyd McGowin, Donald Nijboer, Michael Oakey, Tony Harmsworth, Tanya Caffrey, Nick Stroud, Lydia Matharu, Phil Jarrett, Ken Ellis, Malcolm English, Ted Inman, Lieutenant General Antonino Lenzo, Colonel Marco Scarlatti, and Lieutenant Egidi.

Aviation Century Wings of Change benefited hugely from the generosity of a number of distinguished aviation artists, whose work decorates many of the pages in the book: Gil Cohen, Don Connolly, Hélène Croft, Jim Dietz, Ron Hart, Paul Rendel, Malcolm Root, Robert Taylor and Michael Turner.

We also want to make note of Boston Mills Press, whose belief in our project has been resolute. Our editor, Kathy Fraser, has taken on this project and believed in its value, reading every word and sharing the wonder and fascination we have discovered through the long process of creating this series. Publisher John Denison and managing editor Noel Hudson complete the small but dedicated staff that makes Boston Mills a large force in quality publishing. Thanks also to the designers at PageWave Graphics, especially Andrew Smith, for all of their hard work.

Four down and one to go. Work on the Aviation Century series is almost at an end, and the authors again acknowledge the continuing tolerance and resilience of their wives, Paul and Cheryl, in the face of what must at times have seemed an unending task. Without their capacity to calm us down in times of stress, find encouraging words when progress was slow, apply restraint when ebullience threatened judgment, counter despair with patient counsel, and ease exhaustion with pleasant companionship, this book (and its predecessors) could not have been completed. Once again, we offer them our gratitude and love for everything they do to keep us healthy, happy and pointed in the right direction.

RON DICK AND DAN PATTERSON

FOREWORD
Fred Smith

THIS BOOK TELLS the dramatic story of the world-shrinking developments in commercial aviation after World War II, and goes on to cover many other aspects of the aeronautical world. Painstaking research has produced a comprehensive and well-illustrated text, and the original color photography offers new perspectives on the machines that have transformed our civilization.

Since time immemorial, history records the desire of people to travel and trade. Until the 20th century, the difficulties, dangers and discomforts attendant to such activities are well chronicled. Time and distance were immutable barriers to economic growth until the recent past.

With the beginning of powered flight in 1903, these age-old constraints began to fall away. For over 100 years now, a worldwide assemblage of aviators, engineers, entrepreneurs, scientists and dreamers have shrunk the world so one can fly from any point to any other in less than a day. High-tech and high-value-added goods can be picked up, transported and delivered economically, anywhere, in a matter of hours.

This state of affairs did not come easily or without great cost and loss of life, as technical problems were met and conquered during the early decades of flight. But the very attribute of aviation that most appeals to people — speed of travel — permitted an iterative, worldwide development of new aircraft, engines and instruments that transformed flying from daunting to routine.

In 1944, as World War II wound down, a new civil aviation regulatory regime was created in Chicago by a treaty among fifty-two countries, and the fantastic technologies of flight developed during the conflict soon spawned airline systems that now cover the world like a tightly woven net. Of particular importance were conceptual breakthroughs in aerodynamics, propulsion, and weather capabilities that led to early commercial jets in the decade after the war. Swept wings, jet engines, radar and all-weather landing systems were developed to meet military needs, but combined in the 1960s to produce aircraft of great utility and increasing efficiency for various needs.

Turbofan passenger transports and business jets and turboprops allowed the development of trading and personal relationships impossible to imagine only a few years before. Roughly nine million people flew the year of the Chicago convention, rising to an estimated 1.6 billion passenger trips in 2004. During that sixty-year span, each generation of new transports offered greater reliability, economy and safety. In fact, aviation technology evolved at the end of the 20th century to become by far the safest mode of travel — a feat that would have amazed the intrepid travelers of the prewar era.

Only tiny amounts of cargo were flown in the 1940s and 1950s, but by the 100th anniversary of flight, millions of shipments per day were being moved in worldwide air cargo and air express systems that carry almost half the total value of all trade between continents. Jumbo air freighters now serve as the "clipper ships of the computer age," bringing the products of modern life to any country or consumer. Businesses large and small, in remote locations and in the biggest cities, can sell and source products with little regard to geography or distance.

Perhaps even more incredible than the technological achievements of the aviation century has been the unparalleled cooperation of people from all corners and cultures of the world to create today's airplanes, airports, and air traffic systems. Without ICAO, IATA and other global organizations similarly devoted to the harmonious and progressive development of aviation, our lives today would be radically different.

In many instances, this dedication has led to remarkable levels of unselfish collaboration among disparate individuals, firms and governments. We can hope that this demonstration of the very best in human endeavor might serve as a guide for a future devoid of war and misery in a world made small by flight.

FREDERICK W. SMITH
FOUNDER AND CEO, FEDEX CORPORATION
MEMPHIS, TENNESSEE, SEPTEMBER 2004

FOREWORD
Michael Oakey

WATCH A BOEING 747 sail past, a few hundred feet up, on final approach on a damp morning: fleeting clouds of condensation flicker over its wing, and thick tubular vortices stream off its wingtips as the 300-ton airliner squeezes moisture out of the surrounding air. Who could possibly fail to be fascinated, impressed, awestruck?

Well, quite a lot of people, apparently, judging by the reaction of my fellow commuters on the 7:20 train from Sussex to London as we rattle past the runway threshold of Gatwick Airport every morning. As the editor of *Aeroplane* magazine, I instinctively crane my neck to see what's on the runway, what's taxiing in or out, what's on the glide slope; but the travelers around me remain mostly stolid behind their newspapers, oblivious to the manmade miracle happening above their heads. And this neatly illustrates the paradox of aviation today: it has never been more advanced, yet never more thoroughly commonplace.

In the decades since World War II, flying has stopped being the preserve of the elite few, and has opened up to everyone, most of all through the rise of jet airline travel. Millions of people fly off every year on holiday or on business, with little more sense of occasion than if they were catching a bus. Many airports give passengers barely a glimpse of the aircraft as they walk from departure lounge to gate, to airbridge, to cabin. Once aboard, they are offered magazines and movies and, I note despairingly, are actively encouraged to close the blinds. Thus they are insulated from the rich experience of flying — the lofty perspectives, the cloudscapes, the brilliant sun and deep blue sky above, the tiny ice crystals forming inside the window-glazing as a reminder that they really are traveling at 500 mph at 35,000 feet, through thin air chilled to minus 50 degrees Celsius.

It was not always so mundane, and this fourth volume of *Aviation Century* charts the amazing changes over the past fifty years or so that have made flying part of everyday life for such a large chunk of the world's population. It's not just airline travel: airfreight services enable us to buy cheap fresh fruit and vegetables from every corner of the globe year-round in our local supermarket; helicopters provide emergency services, traffic surveillance and taxicab rides; and the blossoming of general aviation, gliding, air shows, ultralights and ballooning have turned aviation into recreation for many.

Such progress has come at a cost, however, not just in money and effort, but in human life — especially the lives of gallant test pilots who pioneered high-speed flight from the 1940s to the 1970s. Many, such as John Derry, George Welch and Mike Lithgow, paid the ultimate price for pushing at aviation's boundaries. Along with many more who survived, including Roland Beamont and Tony Le Vier, Peter Twiss, Chuck Yeager, Jacqueline Auriol, Neville Duke and John Cunningham, they all became national heroes at a time when to be a test pilot was to reach the pinnacle of human endeavor. A whole chapter of this book is rightly devoted to test pilots and test flying.

Now that flying is, in one way or another, part of all our lives, can we expect it to become ever more integrated into our lifestyles? While writing this foreword, I read a survey in *Aeroplane*'s one-time rival sister magazine *Flight International* about PAVs — Personal Air Vehicles. Once again history has come full circle, with the prospect, first offered in the 1920s, of "an aircraft in every back yard," compact single-seat machines for pleasure and commuting. I don't know if it will ever happen, but if it does I would gladly fly a PAV and relinquish my grubby seat on the 7:20 train to London. I would miss my close-up view of big airliners sailing overhead into Gatwick, though.

MICHAEL OAKEY
EDITOR, *AEROPLANE* MAGAZINE,
LONDON, ENGLAND, FEBRUARY 9, 2005

PHOTOGRAPHER'S PREFACE
Dan Patterson

WHEN RON AND I BEGAN this project, we started with an outline, lots of ideas, and a three-page typed list of all the locations in the world that we thought had the best options for research, artifacts and icons of aviation history. We decided that we should attempt to go wherever we could, and try to find original sources as well as researching through photo archives for those "treasures" that have rarely been seen or published. Of course, we had no money and the scale of the list was, to say the least, intimidating.

We found support from Boston Mills Press and decided to just whack away at the list a piece at a time, because if you looked at it as a whole it seemed an insurmountable mountain to climb. That was in 1998, and now that we have crossed the mountain, the view from the other side is good. Most of the items on that list have been checked off. There are lots of penciled-in additions, which also eventually were crossed off, but for the most part we accomplished our goal. There are a few places we just didn't make it to. However, our intent is to not give up on those, as we have discovered that we have created an enormous library and resource of aviation history. Ron has written nearly 500,000 words, and the new photographs I have made for this project have become a collection that covers nine countries and well over 50,000 images. We're not going to stop accumulating materials or stories just because this part of our project is approaching a conclusion, with only one more volume to go. The Aviation Century project will continue.

As we talked with the global aviation community, pilots, mechanics, historians, museum directors and staff, famous aviators and regular people simply fascinated by airplanes, I noticed a common thread that crossed over the entire spectrum. Nearly all have had some experience with model airplanes. Models that fly, models that sit on desks and bookshelves. Models that proved a theory in a wind tunnel, or sold a concept that became a full-size airplane that has become a part of this history. Small and not-so-small flying creations made from wood, plastic, foam, paper, metal and all of the combinations of those and other elements that the imagination can combine. This thread is unbroken, from Leonardo da Vinci to Orville and Wilbur Wright, to Francis Rogallo, to Neil Armstrong, and it continues to this day.

I began early with a fascination for flying machines. Not long after that, I discovered the hobby shops, and since I couldn't actually get into a World War II airplane, I figured I could make models of them. The process was bumpy at first, as I discovered that the glue actually did melt the plastic if you put too much on, and the clear pieces for the canopies and windows would be sort of cloudy with the gluey fingerprints of a twelve-year-old boy. I also discovered, to my mother's dismay, what happened when you poured a whole bottle of black enamel paint into the porcelain toilet, and how long it took to scrape it all off with a single-edged razor blade. Something I had time for, since the models and the paints were off limits for a while after that.

Eventually my plastic Air Force expanded beyond the available flat spaces in my room and I started to look upward and imagine my armada in the air. My friend Paul Perkins had suspended his models from a fishing-line web that offered the possibility of formations slowly turning in the air currents. I just had to have that. Our house on Harvard Boulevard, however, did not have moldings around the ceilings like Paul's did to tack the line into. I was crushed. My ever-innovative grandfather came to the rescue, and soon the plaster walls had several eye-bolts securely anchored into them and a triangle of 20-pound-test fishing line ran across the room just a few inches below the ceiling. Soon the B-17s were in formation with their fighter escorts and fighting off the Luftwaffe on the other line. Young boys have the ability to mimic all of the sounds of guns and machinery heard in the war movies, and I was no exception. In my mind, I was inside my warplanes and it was going to sound right.

Of course, this adventuring also came with some huge aerial tragedies, as I didn't know a lot about tying knots, and one hurried rush to get dressed for school and put on a sweater brought down a whole division of airplanes. This is when I learned about dealing with things that cannot under any circumstances be fixed and when it's best to start over.

I also found, as I became a father, that the opportunity to pass on this fascination to my kids was a great rationalization to go to the hobby shop and continue my enjoyment of model airplanes. We came to find that the Christmas break from school was our time to work on models together, and now, even though they've moved out, I look forward to the holidays when I will have the time to build a model.

I went to the hobby shop today and found one that I've been looking for.

Dan Patterson
Dayton, Ohio
November 2004

INTRODUCTION
Air Vice-Marshal Ron Dick

THE FIRST THREE volumes of the Aviation Century series deal principally with developments in military and commercial fixed-wing aviation from 1900 to the end of World War II. Chapter 1 of this volume, *Aviation Century Wings of Change*, takes the story of commercial aviation through the end of the 20th century, completing 100 years in which airliners grew from frail biplanes used by a few daring and hardy passengers to huge Jumbos capable of carrying hundreds of people halfway round the world in air-conditioned comfort. In the process, the airlines brought irrevocable political, economic and social change to the world we live in. Paradoxically, although commercial aircraft affect the lives of everyone on the planet in some way, they are largely taken for granted, their significance obscured by their everyday familiarity.

> *"The aeroplane is the nearest thing to animate life that man has created. In the air a machine ceases indeed to be a mere piece of mechanism; it becomes animate and is capable not only of primary guidance and control, but actually of expressing a pilot's temperament."*
>
> SIR ROSS SMITH, K.B.E.,
> *NATIONAL GEOGRAPHIC* MAGAZINE, MARCH 1921

The remaining chapters of *Aviation Century Wings of Change* examine the wider world of aeronautics, covering private flying, lighter-than-air flight, rotary wings, and the challenges of research and development.

In the beginning, all aviation was private. Chapter 2 shows that private flyers were always active between the wars, founding flying clubs and offering those who could afford it the chance to experience life in the third dimension. It was not until after WWII, however, that private aviation became truly widespread, military surplus light aircraft igniting a period of explosive growth in the use of flying machines for leisure or as personal transport. The wish for even smaller and cheaper aircraft led to ultralights, and those who yearned for quiet fixed-wing flight produced elegant sailplanes that could ride thermals for hours, covering hundreds of miles and reaching great altitudes. Less ambitious but perhaps more thrilling flight is offered to the pilot who is prepared to strap on a harness and take to the air suspended beneath the simple wing of a hang glider or parasail.

Man first flew with the help of balloons, and in the early years of the 20th century, it seemed that airships (large, steerable balloons, known as dirigibles) would be the most practical means of transporting passengers and freight by air. The great German Zeppelins also appeared to make strategic bombing a practical proposition. Chapter 3 tells how, in both commercial and military terms, large airships failed to live up to their early promise and were discarded after compiling disastrous records in both peace and war. However, their smaller cousins, the "blimps," survived to become common sights at fairs and sporting events, and 21st-century technology may yet resurrect massive airships capable of carrying payloads of thousands of tons. Even as the airships faded, lighter-than-air enthusiasts remained faithful to balloons. Festivals gathering together imaginative creations of every shape and color are now frequent events. Most balloons float quietly over the countryside, giving their passengers the opportunity to observe wildlife or get a different perspective on the world. Others have been developed that are capable of reaching the stratosphere and crossing oceans on spectacular intercontinental flights.

Chapter 4 shows that the complexities of rotary wings proved more difficult to master than those of fixed wings. Inventors recorded failure after failure in rotary flight during the half century after the Wright brothers' achievements at

Kittyhawk, and real success only followed from the dogged persistence of such determined men as Igor Sikorsky and Frank Piasecki. In their own way, helicopters have revolutionized many aspects of our daily lives. They have matured into reliable workhorses, taking human flight into regions impossible for conventional aircraft. The roofs of buildings can be airports for businessmen in a hurry, and clearings in jungles or offshore oil rigs can be landing sites. For the military, helicopters revive the cavalry tradition, providing fast-moving units for rapid troop deployment, reconnaissance, airborne attack and rescue. Law enforcement, too, has moved into the third dimension, using helicopters for a variety of tasks, from the pursuit of criminals to traffic control. The

versatility of the helicopter in reaching previously inaccessible places makes it particularly valuable in times of disaster. Earthquakes, forest fires and motorway accidents are all events at which rotary wings can prove their worth.

The final chapter of *Aviation Century Wings of Change* gives a brief introduction to the challenges of aeronautical research and development. These activities are the foundations on which the aeronautical world is built. From the beginning, painstaking preparation has been the key to producing machines capable of flying. The Wright brothers showed the way with their methodical approach to solving the problems of flight. Although the technology has become infinitely more complex, the principle has remained the same. Thorough research and careful development are essential prerequisites to aeronautical success. With the possible exception of Louis Blériot, who was fortunate to survive the crashes that followed his preference for the trial-and-error method, the great names of aviation were individuals well aware of the need to be meticulous in the process of designing and producing aircraft. They also knew that when the designers and builders had done their work, a pilot would have to test their product by taking it into the air. In earlier days, considerable risk was an inherent element in the role of the test pilot. Even now, in the computer age, when most problems can be overcome (or at least predicted) before the machine ever leaves the ground, risk has not been completely eliminated. Test pilots may no longer be the glamorous figures of the early days, but they are the elite of the aviation world — highly trained, competent professionals who lead the way to the future of flight. Chapter 5 pays tribute to a few of those who have graced this unique profession and made possible the achievements of the Aviation Century.

Ron Dick
Fredericksburg, Virginia
September 2004

CHAPTER 1

The Safest Way to Travel

For most of the world's leading aeronautical nations, World War II ended or severely restricted civil air operations and brought the development of transport aircraft to a halt. In Europe, Lufthansa flew routes within the German-occupied territories and established a few links with neutral countries, using mostly the ageing but reliable Junkers 52/3m. For the United Kingdom, the principal tasks of the British Overseas Airways Corporation (successor to Imperial Airways) were to maintain communications between the countries of the Commonwealth and to operate a North Atlantic service. Even before the Japanese interposed themselves in 1942, the U.K.–Australia link was tortuous, with BOAC landplanes flying from the United Kingdom to the Sudan via West Africa, and then handing over to C class flying boats operating the Horseshoe route from Durban through the Middle East to Sydney. After the fall of Singapore, Calcutta became the Horseshoe terminus until July 1943, when Qantas opened a challenging Catalina service from Perth to Ceylon, taking 28 to 30 hours to cross more than 3,500 miles of the Indian Ocean. Across the North Atlantic, BOAC used ex-Pan American Boeing 314s, and the airline's crews also flew between Scotland and Sweden for supplies of high-grade ball bearings, following a route over occupied Norway. Initially this hazardous enterprise was accomplished with a series of Lockheed aircraft — Super Electra, Hudson, Lodestar   but when the Luftwaffe began making serious attempts to interrupt the flights with night fighters, the high-speed Mosquito was introduced. (The first aircraft used on the flights to Sweden was a Lockheed 14 Super Electra, registration G-AGBG, which became known to its crews as "Bashful Gertie, the terror of the Skaggerack.")

Britain's wartime aircraft industry necessarily concentrated on armed combat aircraft, and there was no spare capacity for designing and producing new transports. BOAC mostly had to use what was already available. Even in the darkest hours of the war, however, the British government was aware of the need to consider what might be required in the postwar civil aviation world. In December 1942, and again in May 1943, committees were set up under Lord Brabazon to examine the problem. In general, the committee members built upon their experience of the prewar era, and some of their recommendations led to such unsuccessful postwar aircraft as the lumbering Bristol Brabazon and the huge Saunders Roe Princess flying boat, both overtaken by events before they entered service. However, one conclusion was reached that had a significant long-term effect. It was agreed

Opposite Page
Boeing 747 over Manhattan, *by Michael Turner.*

The B&W was the first aircraft designed and built by timberman William E. Boeing and a U.S. Navy engineer named Conrad Westervelt. On June 15, 1916, William Boeing himself flew the B&W on its first flight. The aircraft displayed at the Museum of Flight in Seattle is a 1966 B&W replica built for the Boeing Company's 50th anniversary by Clayton Scott.

LEFT Clayton Scott, "Scotty," was born less than two years after the Wright brothers first flew. He gained his pilot's license in 1927, and he was still flying as the 21st century dawned. In the late 1920s, he flew Keystone-Loening Air Yachts on the first air passenger service between Seattle and Bremerton, and in the 1930s served as William Boeing's personal pilot. During WWII, "Scotty" became the chief production test pilot for Boeing, a position he held until 1966. In that time, he flight-tested thousands of aircraft, from B-17s to B-52s and 727s. Retired from Boeing, he went on working, bringing a lifetime's aeronautical experience to bear on the task of converting landplanes to floatplanes before flying them from Renton Municipal Airport, near Seattle.

that Britain could benefit from having led the world in turbojet development by becoming the first nation to produce airliners powered by jet or turboprop engines.

The situation was different for the United States. Having established a lead in airliner design before WWII, American aircraft manufacturers entered the postwar world well placed to consolidate their dominance. A significant proportion of the wartime American aircraft industry was devoted to the production of excellent transports, and the transcontinental requirements of both the U.S. domestic airlines and the military pointed the way to the development of larger, longer range aircraft. Far removed from the active theaters of war and with a continent to cover, the national airlines found that the conflict actually stimulated their growth. Domestic services developed and in addition the airlines were contracted by the U.S. government to assist the military transport commands in the movement of personnel and cargo. Until the U.S. entry into the war, the only American airline to operate outside North America was Pan American, but that soon changed, with TWA flying pressurized Boeing Stratoliners and Douglas C-54s across

the Atlantic, and American Export Airlines joining in with Sikorsky VS-44 flying boats between New York and Foynes, Ireland. Other airline crews were seconded to fly military C-54s wherever they were needed. As a result, the United States ended the war with thousands of air and ground crews experienced in meeting the demands of long-distance air travel. Other postwar benefits included the availability of hundreds of new airfields capable of handling large aircraft, and a population that had become accustomed to thinking of air travel as an everyday (and relatively safe) occurrence.

Conference in Chicago

Differences of opinion can occur between even the closest of allies, and that was certainly true of Britain and America when it came to considering international agreements for the conduct of civil aviation after WWII. In an attempt to settle issues of transit and landing rights, route allocations, flight safety and general air navigation, the United States hosted an International Conference on Civil Aviation in Chicago during November and December 1944. Wartime

The Bristol Brabazon. *An elephantine anachronism when it finally flew in 1949, the* Brabazon *idea was overtaken by events. Conceived as an aerial transport for the wealthy, it provided a minimum of 200 cubic feet of space for every passenger, including sleeping berths, a dining room, a movie theater, promenade and bar. The* Brabazon *was the first aircraft with 100-percent powered flying controls, the first with electric engine controls, the first with high-pressure hydraulics, and the first with A.C. electrics. It even had a system of gust alleviation, using servos triggered from a probe in the aircraft's nose. Only one was ever built.*

difficulties notwithstanding, representatives of fifty-two countries took part in the conference; the Soviet Union was a notable absentee. Prominent on the agenda were proposals for five freedoms of the air:

1. Freedom to fly over foreign territory without landing.
2. Freedom to land for technical, non-traffic, non-commercial reasons.
3. Freedom to load passengers, mail and cargo in an airline's country of origin and deliver them to a foreign country.
4. Freedom to load passengers, mail and cargo in a foreign country and transport them to an airline's country of origin.
5. Freedom to transport passengers, mail and cargo from one foreign country to another.

Agreement was reached on the first two of these freedoms (right of transit and technical stop), but the remaining three proved intractable. The United States wanted all five freedoms agreed, but Britain was wary of American postwar domination of international air routes, including those in Europe and between Britain and the countries of the British Commonwealth. The U.S. possession of thousands of modern transports and a large aircraft industry capable of converting quickly to civil production seemed to guarantee the Americans the upper hand in the negotiations, but those advantages were offset to some extent by the U.S. lack of a worldwide network of bases, something that the British Commonwealth already had in place. While the three "commercial" freedoms could not be agreed at Chicago, the United States and Britain reconsidered them bilaterally at Bermuda in 1946 and managed to reach an acceptable compromise, allowing both countries to go forward with their development of civil aviation.

Organization

Although the Chicago Conference did not produce much in the way of international accord on most of the topics discussed, it did result in an agreement to establish the International Civil Aviation Organization. The ICAO was to be an agency of the United Nations concerned with a wide range of civil aviation matters: regulations for training and licensing aeronautical personnel in the air and on the ground; communication systems and procedures; rules of the air and air traffic control systems and practices; the airworthiness, registration and identification of aircraft engaged in international air navigation; maps and charts; and meteorology.

The lack of general agreement in Chicago on such things as routes or fare structures generated a further meeting between airlines at Havana in April 1945. This led to the founding of the International Air Transport Association (IATA), initially an organization of fifty-seven airlines from thirty-one countries and the natural successor to the much smaller International Air Traffic Association founded at the Hague in 1919. The explosive growth of commercial aviation in the second half of the 20th century saw IATA's membership climb to over 230 members from more than 130 nations. IATA's stated aims were to promote safe, regular and economical air transport for the benefit of the peoples of the world, to foster air commerce, and to study any associated problems. Among the early questions needing answers were who could fly where, at what cost, how were the proceeds from multi-airline journeys to be divided up, and how did airlines settle their accounts? IATA was behind the creation of a coherent fares and rates pattern, enabling passengers to pay for their ticket in one place, in one currency, but complete their journey using two or more airlines from different countries using different currencies. The predictability of fares and rates allowed airlines to accept each others' tickets on multisector journeys. The IATA Clearing House, which settles debts between airlines, cleared $17 million in 1947; by the mid-1990s the sum approached $23 billion.

AMERICAN SUPREMACY

In 1941, the commercial airlines of the United States managed to carry a total of over four million passengers. Growth then slowed for a while, but in 1945 the total rose above six million. In an impressive postwar acceleration, internal U.S. passenger traffic reached sixteen million by 1951, with the "big four" (American, Eastern, United, TWA) between them accounting for more than thirteen million in that year. The competition was fierce as airlines and aircraft manufacturers fought for slices of what was a rapidly and continually expanding civil aviation pie.

With the end of WWII, thousands of military transport aircraft became surplus and many were converted to civil standards to meet growing passenger demand. Most of the short-haul operations, both in the United States and elsewhere, were flown by Douglas DC-3s, and the majority of those were converted C-47s. Rugged and dependable, the DC-3 was inexpensive to operate and could be used in areas that lacked sophisticated facilities. To a DC-3, a hard-surfaced runway was almost a luxury. No aircraft played a greater part in introducing the American public to aviation as a means of travel, but it was inevitable that people would soon demand more than the simple DC-3 could offer. As airline passengers became more experienced and discerning, they adopted the "faster, further, higher" credo of the pioneers. They wanted an aircraft that could fly above the worst of the weather, and get to distant destinations with greater speed and without having to refuel. The first steps in this direction had been taken before the war.

Competition in the United States

The four-engined Boeing 307 Stratoliner, which first flew at the end of 1938, was the first airliner to have a pressurized fuselage, allowing it to operate with passengers at altitudes well above 10,000 feet. With a cruising speed of 220 mph and a range of more than 2,000 miles, it attracted orders from Pan American and TWA and promised Boeing considerable commercial success, but the company's wartime

The Boeing 307 Stratoliner was the first fully pressurized airliner to enter service anywhere in the world. When it first flew in 1938, the Stratoliner's cockpit was state-of-the-art — roomy, comfortable and functional. The airliner entered service with TWA in July 1940, but its subsequent development was curtailed by WWII. Only ten were built. One survives and is on display at the Steven F. Udvar-Hazy Center of the National Air & Space Museum, Dulles Airport, Washington, D.C.

More than 700 DC-6s were built by Douglas between 1946 and 1959. Originally planned as a WWII military transport, it was redesigned to compete with the Lockheed Constellation as a long-range pressurized airliner. In 1952, Pan Am used the DC-6 to inaugurate transatlantic tourist class flights, and in 1954 the New Zealand airline TEAL (Tasman Empire Airways Ltd.) bought three Douglas DC-6s. They were used on routes to Australia and on the Hibiscus service to Fiji.

concentration on bombers brought the Stratoliner's production run to an end after only ten had been built. Leadership in the postwar business of building airliners passed to the rival companies of Douglas and Lockheed, whose designers developed two competing series of outstanding four-engined aircraft that dominated the commercial aviation world for well over a decade.

The original Douglas DC-4 was developed in the late 1930s after discussions with five U.S. airlines (American, TWA, Eastern, United, Pan Am) established a requirement for a long-range airliner. Each airline contributed $100,000 toward the cost of development. The result was a complex, pressurized machine with three fins that had a disappointing performance and a host of maintenance problems. Douglas went back to the drawing board and came up with a simpler, unpressurized aircraft, also designated DC-4, in what came to be seen as the classic airliner form — four engines mounted on a low wing, a long tubular fuselage, a tall single fin, and a retractable nose-wheel undercarriage. (The original three-finned aircraft became DC-4E for experimental.) By the time the DC-4 was ready for service

in 1942, the United States was at war, so it was produced for the USAAF as the C-54 Skymaster (USN R5D). Although they could not manage the jump nonstop, C-54s established the first regular transport service across the Atlantic, sometimes completing as many as twenty crossings each way per day. One (a VC-54C named *Sacred Cow*) was used by President Roosevelt to attend the Yalta Conference in 1945, and later became President Truman's official aircraft. Almost 1,300 C-54s/DC-4s were built, and after the war they continued to prove themselves invaluable. They were indefatigable workhorses during the Berlin Airlift, and many surplus military versions were made available to airlines, eventually being operated by companies in every part of the world. (See the fifth volume of *Aviation Century*, Chapter 1, "American Independence," and "Operation Vittles.") American Overseas Airlines became the first to introduce a commercial landplane transatlantic service with an inaugural DC-4 flight from New York to Hurn, England, on October 23, 1945, and on March 7, 1946, American Airlines began a transcontinental DC-4 service between New York and Los Angeles, averaging fourteen and a half hours westbound and just over an hour less eastbound. These times were some three hours better than those of the DC-3.

The Lockheed Constellation was conceived in 1939 by Howard Hughes and designed by Kelly Johnson. The result was one of the most distinctive aircraft ever built. The DC-4 had an essentially practical, no-nonsense appearance, but the Constellation was a beauty of subtly blending curves. Its nose drooped to shorten the nose-wheel leg, and the dolphinlike fuselage tapered gracefully toward the rear, sweeping upward to carry the triple-finned tail. Beneath its attractive exterior the "Connie" hid many innovative features, including powered flying controls and the first reversible-pitch propellers used to shorten the landing run of a civil airliner. It was pressurized to allow operations above 20,000 feet and its four 2,200-horsepower supercharged engines gave it a cruising speed of 280 mph, thus stealing a considerable march on the competition. It was intended to give Hughes' TWA a marked advantage over the DC-4s of American and United, and in 1943 the early flights of the first Constellation confirmed its promise. However, the demands of the war being paramount, the production models followed the DC-4 into military service as C-69s. With a flash of showmanship, Hughes delivered the prototype to the USAAF himself, painting it in TWA red and flying it from Burbank to Washington in under seven hours, half an hour less than Hughes' own transcontinental record set in 1937. (See *Aviation Century The Golden Age,* Chapter 2, "In Wiley's Wake.")

TWA finally took delivery of ten Model L-049 Constellations toward the end of 1945 and, on February 15, 1946, advertised the opening of its transcontinental service with another theatrical flourish from Hughes. Gathering together a bevy of Hollywood's famous, including such luminaries as Paulette Goddard, Veronica Lake, Virginia Mayo, Linda Darnell, William Powell, Walter Pidgeon and Edward G. Robinson, he flew them from Los Angeles to New York. That month also saw Pan American flying Constellations to Bermuda and TWA taking them across the Atlantic to Paris. Over the next five years, Lockheed improved the breed until, in 1951, the Super Constellation appeared. With its fuselage lengthened by 18 feet, the Super Connie's graceful lines were even more elegant. When powered by four Wright R-3350 Turbo-Compound double-row radials of 3,250 horsepower and fitted with tip tanks, the Model L1049G could cruise at 330 mph and had a maximum range of 4,800 miles. Various seating arrangements could accommodate up to 100 passengers, and its all-up weight reached 140,000 pounds, compared to the 86,000 pounds of the L049. One more variation on the theme, the L1649 Starliner, flew in 1956. It had a new, much longer wing and an increased range, but it was by then being overtaken by events as jet-powered designs made themselves felt. The Starliner was the last of a distinguished line and had a claim to being the ultimate expression of the piston-powered airliner.

Often described as the most beautiful and elegant airliner ever designed, the Lockheed Constellation first flew in 1943 and was produced in a steadily improving series of models until 1958, a total of 856 being built. Chicago and Southern flew Constellation 649s (including N86521, seen here) from 1950 until the airline merged with Delta in May 1953.

The Douglas Response

Douglas reacted to the challenge of the early Constellations by redesigning the DC-4. The result was the DC-6, which was itself improved in several variants. (Another variation on the Douglas theme was the Canadair Four, built in Canada and embodying features of both the DC-4 and 6. It was powered by Rolls-Royce Merlins and flown principally by the RCAF, Trans-Canada Airlines [as the North Star], and BOAC [as the Argonaut.]) In its definitive form, the DC-6B, the fuselage was pressurized and lengthened to accommodate up to 102 passengers, and power came from four Pratt & Whitney R-2800s of 2,400 horsepower each, allowing it to match the performance of the Constellation. The DC-6B proved to be one of the most efficient piston-engined transports ever made: 288 were built and many continued to serve airlines all over the world for years after the advent of the jets. If the DC-6B had a shortcoming, it was that it lacked transcontinental range. This was corrected when the design was stretched still further to accept the Wright Turbo-Compound engines used by the Super Constellation. The DC-7 was the first airliner to have the capacity to cross the United States continent nonstop in both directions. It inaugurated the American Airlines service between New York and Los Angeles on November 29, 1953, with a scheduled time of 8 hours, 45 minutes westbound and 8 hours eastbound. In its ultimate DC-7C Seven Seas form, its range increased to over 4,000 miles to give it a transatlantic nonstop capability. The DC-7C also made possible one-stop services between Europe and Japan, with airlines flying the polar route and refueling at Anchorage.

THE OUTSIDER

There was one other American four-engined transport available after WWII. Larger than either of the competing products from Douglas and Lockheed, the Boeing 377 Stratocruiser mated a capacious double-bubble fuselage to the wings, engines, undercarriage and tail of the B-29 Superfortress. When it first flew in July 1947, it seemed that

TOP *Designed to meet an American Airlines requirement for a DC-3 replacement, the Convair 240 was the first pressurized twin-engined airliner. It entered service with American in 1948, and over 1,000 240s (and improved 340/440 models) were built before production ended in 1956.* VFR on Top *by Ron Hart.*
BOTTOM *The DC-7 was the last of the Douglas propeller-powered transports. It entered service with American Airlines in November 1953, and was the first commercial aircraft capable of flying nonstop westbound across the United States against the prevailing winds.* Flagship Missouri *was one of thirty-four DC-7s flown by American Airlines.*

Pan American's Boeing 377 Stratocruiser Clipper Morning Star *(capacity up to 100 passengers and crew) flies by Cunard's* Queen Elizabeth *(over 3,000 passengers and crew). In the 1950s, it seemed unlikely that aircraft could destroy the transatlantic ocean liner trade. However, between 1957 and 1965, shipping traffic plummeted from more than one million passengers to only 650,000, while the airline passenger figure quadrupled to four million and went on rising.*

Boeing's new airliner would lead the field. It could fly higher, faster and further than its competitors, and could seat more passengers. It even boasted the luxury of a lower deck lounge reached by a spiral staircase. However, the 377 had not been designed from the outset as a civil airliner. It was an adaptation of the USAF's C-97 transport/tanker, and military requirements had shaped the original design, producing a heavy airframe that needed the power of four 3,500-horsepower Pratt and Whitney Double Wasps. In airline service, the engines had a poor reputation for reliability, and the Stratocruiser was costly both to operate and to buy. Popular though it was with the passengers of Pan Am and BOAC, the Stratocruiser was not an economic success, and, although the USAF took nearly 900 C/KC-97s, only 56 of the civil version were built. By the 1950s, it seemed that Boeing's future lay firmly in the military sphere, and that the odds were heavily against anyone mounting a serious challenge to the grip held by Douglas and Lockheed on the production of civil airliners.

American Twins

While the big four-engined transports served the airlines well on the long-distance routes, it was soon clear that the postwar short-haul duties could not be left forever to the ubiquitous DC-3. Two companies offered solutions, both of them flying prototypes in 1946. Convair produced their Model 110, a twin-engined, unpressurized thirty-seater, but quickly moved on to a larger pressurized version capable of carrying forty passengers, the Convair 240. This entered service with American Airlines in June 1948, and was then supplied to Pan American, Western, Aerolineas Argentinas, KLM, Sabena, Swissair, and other customers worldwide. Two Ethiopian Airlines 240s were fitted with JATO (Jet Assisted Take-Off) to ease operation from East Africa's hot and high airfields, a feature that offered an unusual thrill to civilian passengers. (In the 1970s, Ethiopian DC-3s were still thrilling passengers in their own way, flying from grass strips and using internal routes that went through, rather than over, Ethiopia's

TOP *The Lancastrian was a civil transport conversion of the Avro Lancaster bomber. It was first used in 1943 by Trans-Canada Airlines on the Montreal-to-Prestwick route. British Overseas Airways, British South American Airways, Qantas and Flota Aerea Mercante Argentina also used Lancastrians after WWII. However, since there was accommodation for only nine passengers, the Lancastrian was never more than an interim response to the postwar demand for commercial aircraft.*

BOTTOM *The de Havilland Dove was developed for a small feeder-liner for U.K. and Commonwealth domestic services. The Series 1 could seat eight passengers but the Series 2, introduced in 1948, accommodated six in an executive layout. This version soon proved popular with major companies. The Dove was Britain's best-selling civil transport in the years after WWII, and 542 were built between 1945 and 1967, by which time it had become a Hawker Siddeley product.*

mountains.) By 1952, the Model 340, with a greater span and longer fuselage to raise passenger capacity to fifty-two, was joining United and Braniff, and four years later the Convair 440 Metropolitan appeared, modified to increase cruising speed, reduce cabin noise, and carry weather radar. Lufthansa, Iberia, Alitalia and SAS were among Metropolitan operators. Together with military sales, the production of all models of Convair's twin reached well over a thousand. They were too good to waste, so even as the jet age dawned, more than two hundred Convairliners were later converted to turboprop power, most of them fitted with Rolls-Royce Darts.

A less successful effort to replace the DC-3 was the Martin 2-0-2. Similar to the Convairliner, the 2-0-2 had less appeal because it was left unpressurized. The type also earned a poor safety record. Five Northwest Airlines 2-0-2s were written off between August 1948 and January 1951, including a major fatal accident in 1948 when one aircraft suffered a structural failure of the wing in flight. The 2-0-2 was withdrawn from service and it was two years before it returned to flying with TWA as the 2-0-2A. TWA stayed loyal to the design and also operated the much improved 4-0-4 from 1951, but Martin's twin never achieved the success of its Convair competitor, and only about 150 of all variants were built.

Le Bourget airport started life in 1914 as a fortified camp defending Paris against the Zeppelins. After WWI, it was developed as one of the world's first international airports, and was also one of the first airfields to have a hard surface runway. By the 1930s, Le Bourget had acquired impressive terminal buildings, and in 1937 the airport was capable of handling 131,000 passengers and more than 18,000 tons of freight per year. Le Bourget retained a leading role in commercial aviation until the 1970s, after which it became the site for one of the world's premier aviation museums. The original terminal building has been preserved (top) and a sculpture symbolizing air travel has been placed in front (bottom). The post-WWII flights of Air France to the Far East are recalled in colorful posters.

Britain Turns from War to Peace

Lacking the solid foundation of a large domestic market and without an industry already involved in the production of modern transport aircraft, Britain entered the postwar world ill-equipped to offer a serious challenge to the dominance of Douglas and Lockheed. Interim, and inadequate, solutions were found by converting wartime bomber types for civilian use. The Avro Lancastrian was a thinly disguised Lancaster, minus such military accoutrements as bomb doors and gun turrets, but fitted with nine sideways-facing seats in the narrow bomber fuselage. A similar conversion of the Handley Page Halifax, known as the Halton, offered ten seats. Both types were used by BOAC on routes to Australia (66 hours to Sydney) and Africa, and a new state airline, British South American Airways (BSAA), used Lancastrians across the South Atlantic. Given the ratio of fare-paying passengers to thirsty engines, it is hardly surprising that these operations were considerably less than economically viable.

An attempted improvement was the Avro Tudor, the first postwar British airliner type to fly, and even that was based on Avro's Lincoln bomber, a scaled-up version of the Lancaster. It retained the bomber's tailwheel configuration and Merlin engines, but did take a step toward the future with a pressurized fuselage. In its Tudor 1 form, only twelve passengers were provided for, and the intended customer, BOAC, was dissatisfied with the design, perpetually submitting requests for modification and finally deciding not to operate the aircraft. The Tudor story was then marked by a tragic series of misadventures. The first stretched Tudor 2 (capacity, sixty passengers) was lost on a test flight in 1947 because the aileron controls had been connected round the wrong way; a BSAA Tudor 4 disappeared over the Andes in 1947 and two more vanished without trace near Bermuda, to the excitement of people convinced of the Bermuda Triangle's dark secrets; and in March 1950 a Tudor 5 crashed in Wales, killing eighty passengers and crew in the worst civil aviation disaster to that date. Several Tudors continued to fly as freighters for a while, but the airlines looked

"Greater cruising speeds are possible, but the size of the earth does not warrant greater speeds. The progress of air transportation will benefit more if designers will give more attention to increased passenger comfort and ways and means to lower transportation costs rather than greater speed."

IGOR SIKORSKY IN A LECTURE
TO THE ROYAL AERONAUTICAL SOCIETY,
LONDON, NOVEMBER 15, 1934

elsewhere for passenger aircraft. BOAC chose the Handley Page Hermes 4, but even this failed to match its American contemporaries and was regarded as no more than a stopgap on the way to better things. After a protracted period of development, the Hermes entered service in 1950. Only twenty-five were delivered, and they were used on BOAC's routes to Africa before being handed on to charter operators.

The British aircraft industry was more successful when it came to producing short-haul aircraft. Among the postwar crop were the Vickers Viking, Miles Marathon, Airspeed Ambassador, de Havilland Dove and Heron, and two uncompromisingly boxy cargo carriers, the Bristol Freighter and Miles Aerovan. The Freighter first flew in December 1945 and six months later was the first postwar British transport aircraft to be given a Certificate of Airworthiness. Over 200 were built and in various forms saw service with operators all over the world, but they are probably best remembered for their pioneering use by Silver City Airways as an airborne car ferry across the English Channel. If the slab-sided Freighter could best be described as utilitarian, the Airspeed and de Havilland designs were undeniably elegant. The graceful lines of the Ambassador rivaled those of the larger Constellation, and the aircraft performed well in service with British European Airways (BEA) but was denied a large production run by the turn to turboprop airliners. The eight/eleven-seat Dove and its four-engined cousin, the fourteen/seventeen-seat Heron, proved to be extremely popular at the lower end of the passenger-carrying range. Powered by Gipsy Queen engines, the two light transports were reliable and reasonably economical, and in their various forms were operated all over the world, notably by the small local airlines of Europe and Africa. Over 500 Doves and some 150 Herons were built.

Not all of the commercial aircraft flying after WWII were new. Many were survivors from an earlier age. Typical were the de Havilland Dragon Rapides that for many years were used to connect the British mainland with its outer islands. The pilots of these delightful biplanes were often great characters, free spirits in the tradition of flying's Golden Age. Among them was Captain Johnny Tempest, a large man with a black beard and a devilish sense of humor. He was the pilot of a Dragon Rapide scheduled to fly from Aberdeen to Orkney in the early 1950s. When the passengers began to board the aircraft, Captain Tempest was already sitting in the rearmost seat near the cabin door dressed in a Scottish cape. The passengers were surprised to find that their pilot was apparently still not on board, but they settled down to await his arrival. The man with the black beard was not so ready to be patient. After voicing several complaints, he burst out: "Five more minutes and if he hasn't turned up by then, I'll fly this thing myself." Five minutes later, the man rose from his seat and shouted: "That's it! I'll fly the bloody thing!" He then stormed into the cockpit, started the engines and took off.

French Revival

To hasten the transition to peacetime production in 1945, the French aviation industry relied initially on design specifications first issued in 1936. The giant six-engined Latécoère 631 flying boat was conceived for transatlantic service. The prototype flew in 1942, but was destroyed on the Bodensee during a raid by RAF Mosquitos in 1944. Air France acquired three 631s and in 1947 set about flying them in their intended role between Biscarosse on the Bay of Biscay and Martinique. One crashed on its delivery flight and, in 1948, another was lost over the Atlantic, after which the type was withdrawn from passenger service. Better fortune favored the Sud-Est 161 Languedoc, a conventional four-engined airliner with a tailwheel undercarriage that started life as the Bloch 161 and first flew in 1939. Some 100 were built, most of which, with their original Gnome-Rhône engines replaced by Pratt & Whitneys, served Air France as interim airliners until the early 1950s.

An ambitious French attempt to match the success of the DC-4 was made with the Sud-Est Armagnac, but teething troubles delayed its introduction until 1952, after which it was found to be reliable but uneconomic. Only eight saw service, flying between Toulouse and Saigon until the French withdrawal from Indo-China. A more original aircraft was the portly Breguet 763 Provence (commonly known as Deux-Ponts), a double-deck, triple-finned, mid-wing transport that began flying from Marseilles to Algiers and Tunis in March 1953 and operated between Paris and other European capitals during the 1950s. The imaginative Deux-Ponts design included an upper deck with fifty-nine seats and a lower cargo deck, the two being connected by front and rear staircases. Alternatively, seating for forty-eight more passengers could be added instead of cargo, and this configuration was used between Paris and Nice. After it was replaced on passenger services, the Deux-Ponts continued as a freighter until 1971.

After WWII, there was a brief flirtation with the idea of a return to the era of the great flying boats. Several six-engined Latécoère 631 flying boats were built and Air France began using them on a transatlantic service to Martinique, but after one disappeared into the Atlantic in August 1948 they were withdrawn. One survived flying charters in Africa, but that aircraft broke up in midair over Cameroon in 1955.

THE AN-2

The An-2 was originally designed to a USSR Ministry of
Agriculture and Forestry requirement but it became one
of the most versatile aircraft ever produced. The prototype
flew on August 31, 1947, and the An-2 entered service the
following year. The biplane configuration gave good
takeoff performance, docile low-speed handling and
excellent climb rate, and handling was further improved
by wings fitted with leading-edge slats and double slotted
flaps. The An-2 was produced in the Soviet Union, Poland
and China, and a remarkable range of variants was
developed, including crop sprayers, water bombers,
floatplanes, VIP transports, air ambulances, and aircraft
for high-altitude meteorological research, TV relay work,
and geophysical survey. In military service, the An-2 could
be used in many roles — navigation trainer, paratroop
transport, special forces insertion, and general utility
duties. No aircraft has done more than the An-2 to open
up and serve the needs of the remote regions of Siberia.

Seen here are the An-2 flown by the "Utterly
Butterly" display team in the United Kingdom (below),
and details of two aircraft photographed by Dan Patterson
in Warsaw, Poland, and at La Ferté Alais, near Paris.

The Breguet 763 Provence (more commonly known as the Deux-Ponts) was a two-deck convertible passenger/cargo airliner. When flown in the passengers-only role, it had seating for fifty-nine on the upper deck and forty-eight below. The Deux-Ponts was introduced on Air France routes to Algiers in 1953, and cargo versions continued in service until 1971.

Other Europeans

The Italian aviation industry began a slow postwar recovery with two established designs. The Fiat G.212 was the last of the big trimotors to be produced. Only nine of the commercial variant were built, and they were operated by ALI (Avia Linee Italiane) and SAIDE (Services Aérien Internationaux d'Egypte) until the early 1950s. The four-engined Savoia Marchetti 95 entered commercial service with a newly formed airline, Alitalia, in 1947. An S.M.95 named *Marco Polo* inaugurated Alitalia's first international route between Rome and Oslo on August 6, 1947, and eight months later the airline added flights to London. In 1949, LATI (Linee Aeree Transcontinentali Italiane) opened a short-lived S.M.95 service across the South Atlantic, with the final leg into Caracas measuring some 2,500 miles. By 1951, the S.M.95s were outdated and were already being retired. Far more successful was a much smaller Piaggio design. The P.136 gull-winged amphibian was a five-seater powered by Lycoming GO-480 engines driving pusher propellers, variants of which appeared in the United States under the name Royal Gull. A later development, the P.166, was an attractive twelve-seat landplane that gained many export orders. Eighty-five were built and were used by operators as far afield as Australia and New Guinea.

The only Swedish airliner produced after WWII was the SAAB Scandia, another aircraft designed in the search for a DC-3 replacement. In its final form it was powered by two Pratt & Whitney R-2180s of 1,825 horsepower and could accommodate up to thirty-six passengers. The Scandia first flew in 1946 but did not enter service with SAS (Scandinavian Airlines System) until 1951. Promising though it was, the Scandia failed to attract customer, and only eighteen were built (six in the Netherlands by Fokker), eight flying with SAS and ten with two Brazilian airlines, Aerovias Brazil and VASP (Viacao Aérea Sao Paulo). Eventually VASP bought up all the available Scandias and became the only operator, keeping them in service until 1969. Comfortable and reliable, the Scandia had one minor fault that could be disturbing during night flights. Its high-mounted exhausts blazed so brightly in the dark that SAS had to put leaflets on board explaining that such fireworks were normal and passengers need not be alarmed.

Self-Sufficient Soviets

After WWII, the Soviet Union's air services depended heavily on the Li-2, a version of the DC-3 constructed under licence by Lisunov. (There were 6,157 Li-2s manufactured in the Soviet Union.) Li-2s continued in production until the early 1950s, but Aeroflot decided that there was a need for a more modern transport of Soviet design to supplement the Li-2s and cope with the airline's postwar expansion. The result was the Ilyushin 12 (NATO Coach), a twin-engined aircraft

LEFT *Initially ordered by the Italian military in 1950 as an air-sea rescue aircraft, the gull-winged Piaggio 136 amphibian was powered by two Lycoming engines driving pusher propellers. It was attractive and economical, and soon found favor as an executive aircraft; more than twenty, known as Royal Gulls, were exported to the United States. Here a Royal Gull is moored on the River Thames, near London's Tower Bridge.*
BELOW *The last large Italian airliners to be built were the Savoia Marchetti S.M.95s operated in small numbers by Alitalia, LATI, and the Egyptian airline SAIDE in the late 1940s. The S.M.95 was unusual among four-engined airliners of the period in having wooden wings. Alitalia's aircraft were named after famous explorers and navigators, including I-DALN* Sebastiano Caboto, *seen here.*

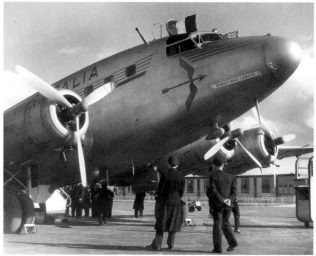

BELOW *The SAAB 90 Scandia prototype (SE-BCA) made its first flight in November 1946, but development of this twin-engined DC-3 replacement was protracted and it did not enter service with SAS until November 1950. Efficient though it was, the Scandia did not attract many orders and only seventeen were built. They were operated by SAS and two Brazilian airlines, Aerovias Brasil and VASP. VASP kept flying Scandias until the mid-1960s.*

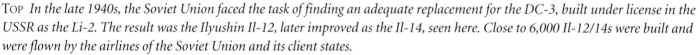

TOP *In the late 1940s, the Soviet Union faced the task of finding an adequate replacement for the DC-3, built under license in the USSR as the Li-2. The result was the Ilyushin Il-12, later improved as the Il-14, seen here. Close to 6,000 Il-12/14s were built and were flown by the airlines of the Soviet Union and its client states.*

BOTTOM *The Ilyushin Il-18 enjoyed one of the longest production runs of any turboprop airliner: 565 were built. The Il-18 entered Aeroflot service in April 1959 and played a significant role in developing air services to Russia's remote regions in the 1960s and 1970s. The Il-18V could seat 90 to 100 passengers and became the standard Aeroflot version.*

with a nose-wheel that proved to be somewhat underpowered for its weight. Nevertheless, it was produced in large numbers and saw service with Aeroflot and with the airlines of Czechoslovakia (CSA) and Poland (LOT). Not nearly so successful was Ilyushin's attempt to produce a much larger four-engined airliner, the sixty-seat Il-18. It was used on selected routes from 1948, but it was not a stellar performer and the rustic airports of the time in the Soviet Union found it difficult to handle, so only a few were built. By 1950, they had been withdrawn from service. Many lessons were learned by Ilyushin from the Il-12 and

Il-18, as his subsequent designs showed. The Il-14 (NATO Crate), a much improved version of the Il-12, capable of seating thirty-two passengers, entered service in November 1954. A more efficient wing carried Shvetsov engines with thrust augmentation exhausts, new slotted flaps were fitted, and a square-topped fin replaced the triangle of the Il-12. Over 1,000 Il-14s were built in the factories of the Soviet Union, East Germany and Czechoslovakia.

While Ilyushin worked to produce an efficient airliner, Antonov took what looked like a backward step. He designed a large single-engined biplane. With no concessions to grace or elegance, the An-2 (NATO Colt) was a utilitarian masterpiece, just what was needed in the vast undeveloped lands of the Soviet Union. When it first flew in August 1947, the prototype An-2 attracted little attention and its unprepossessing appearance offered few hints of its inherent versatility. Originally built to satisfy a requirement of the Soviet Ministry of Agriculture and Forestry, the An-2 soon showed that it was an adaptable thoroughbred capable of taking on many different roles. By the mid-1950s, An-2s had transported freight, dusted crops, patrolled power lines, gathered meteorological information, carried paying passengers, flown as school buses, served as ambulances, dropped parachutists, conducted aerial surveys, supported fisheries, fought fires and joined the military. They had become indispensable to thousands of isolated communities scattered across the vastness of the Soviet Union. Lacking even rudimentary surface communications, the people who choose to live in the remote regions of Siberia rely on the An-2 as their lifeline to the wider world, a means of ensuring supplies, getting education for their children, and reaching out for help in medical emergencies. In many of the most forbidding areas, settled life would be all but impossible without Antonov's rugged biplane. It is a mark of the An-2's value that more of them have been built than any other transport aircraft. By the end of the 1980s, at least 16,000 had been produced — more than 5,000 by Antonov, over 11,000 by the PZL-Mielec factory in Poland, and some in China. Thousands were still in use in dozens of countries at the end of the century.

Award-winning artist Hélène Croft lives in Fort Smith in the Northwest Territories of Canada, and each year, three of Kenn Borek Air's de Havilland Twin Otters fly from Calgary, Alberta, to Antarctica to support the American and Italian research programs. In her painting Change of Crew, *Hélène Croft captures a moment when inquisitive (but flightless) penguins examine an airborne intruder.*

KENMORE AIR, SEATTLE

In a world where commercial aviation is dominated by automation and controlled procedures, it is refreshing to experience flight with an airline that relies primarily on the skill and judgment of pilots using maps and a compass. Kenmore Air flies from Seattle to destinations throughout British Columbia and the San Juan Islands. Cruising altitudes vary between 1,500 and 4,000 feet, allowing passengers to enjoy close-up views of mountains, evergreen forests and rugged inlets that can only be imagined from the cocoon of a jet airliner at 30,000 feet.

To quote from Kenmore's brochure: "Once you've experienced the exhilaration of journeying between sea and sky on the same flight, other types of aircraft will seem rather ordinary. Kenmore Air's planes are smaller and noisier than you're probably used to. Pilots pass out earplugs, not peanuts. Seating can be cozy, but flights are short and everyone is friendly. If a pod of whales or a Trident sub is spotted, you may divert for a better view. Pilots fly our planes, not computers."

Kenmore Air Harbor opened in 1946 on Seattle's Lake Washington. The single Aeronca Model K floatplane with which Kenmore Air began was soon joined by two Taylorcrafts and an Aeronca Champ. From these modest origins has grown a fleet of twenty-two floatplanes, which annually log more than 2 million miles and carry more than 60,000 passengers. The original small dock has been developed into a major operating and maintenance facility known worldwide for the quality of its service. Specialists in upholstery, avionics, metal fabrication, painting, engine overhaul and airframe rebuild form a team that is the pride of the industry. The last Beaver came off the production line in 1967, but Kenmore's remanufacturing team strips them down and rebuilds them to "better than new" condition, incorporating many improvements the team has designed.

Seen here: A turbo-powered Otter arrives at Kenmore's downtown Seattle terminal on Lake Union (above); an Otter surges away from downtown (below). Opposite, clockwise starting top left: an Otter at the Lake Washington dock; the floats hiss as a Beaver feathers onto the water of Lake Washington; a Beaver cruises in the sunset over Seattle; one of Kenmore's happy pilots.

The seven-passenger piston-engined de Havilland Beaver is one of the most successful bush aircraft ever built. It has been the mainstay of the Kenmore fleet since the early 1960s. The Beavers on these pages are seen in their natural elements of the air and water of Washington State. The view of the throttle quadrant (opposite page, top left) offers a sharp contrast with the sophisticated glass cockpits of modern jet airliners.

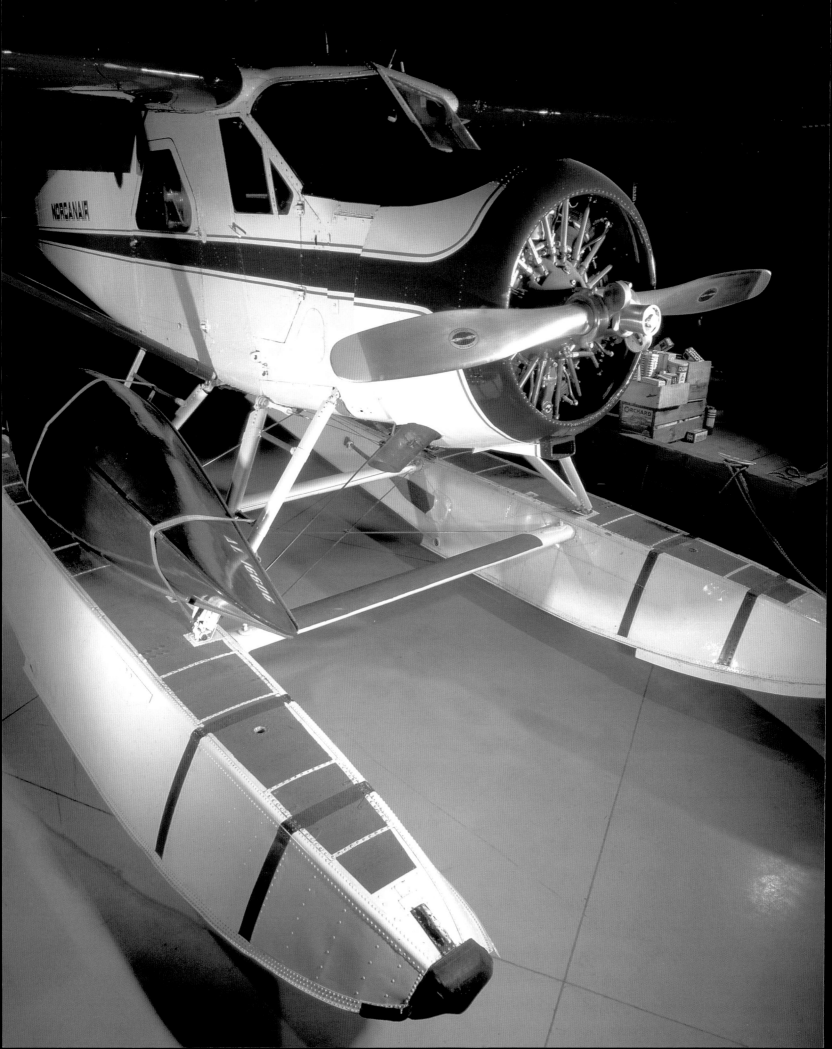

Capable Canadians

The problems of Siberian communities are also those of the people who live outside the metropolitan areas of Canada and Alaska. Similarly, ways of solving them came by air. A de Havilland Canada (DHC) questionnaire of November 1946 asked Canadian pilots for their ideas about an ideal bush plane. From the feedback came the DHC-2 Beaver, the prototype of which flew in August 1947. Specifically designed to meet the challenges of remote, undeveloped regions, it came to be regarded with great affection by the people it served. Like the An-2, the Beaver is a tough, relatively simple aircraft powered by a single radial engine and equipped with high-lift devices to allow it to operate from small, unsophisticated airstrips. It converts rapidly from carrying freight to seating seven passengers, and can be fitted with a conventional tailwheel undercarriage, skis, floats, or amphibious pontoons. It is the quintessential bush pilot's aircraft, and has been a common sight on the lakes, rivers, and icefields of the northernmost reaches of the American continent for over half a century.

> *"There are no distant places any longer; the world is small and the world is one."*
> WENDELL WILKIE, 1943

Having established a reputation for building capable bush aircraft, DHC went on to produce the Beaver's larger cousin, the DHC-3 Otter, a ten-seater with comparable short takeoff and landing (STOL) qualities. Almost 500 Otters were added to the more than 1,600 Beavers produced, and hundreds of these remarkable aircraft remained in operation into the 21st century, with little sign that their usefulness was in any way diminished. South of the border,

The de Havilland Canada Beaver exhibited on floats at the Canada Aviation Museum in Ottawa is CF-FHB, the prototype, which first flew on August 16, 1947. The Beaver was designed and built in response to the demands of Canadian bush operators. With its all-metal construction and high-lift wing, the Beaver was a robust aircraft with excellent short takeoff and landing characteristics even with heavy loads. The Beaver was such a success that more were built than any other aircraft designed and manufactured in Canada. More than sixty countries bought the Beaver in its various forms, and almost 1,000 of the 1,600 made were flown by the U.S. military. Many were used in Korea, where it was known as the general's jeep.

in the United States, Cessna was notable in grasping the opportunity to design a rugged "go anywhere" aircraft. The company described its high-winged Caravan as having "big wheels, short-field performance, and a Herculean load capacity — the ideal aircraft for reaching runways in places other airplanes wouldn't dream of going." That the design lived up to the claims is evident from the fact that more than 1,100 Caravans are operating in over sixty countries.

WORLD SHRINKERS

While their postwar large piston-engined airliners were generally abject failures, the United Kingdom's aircraft and engine manufacturers hoped for better things as they sought to take advantage of the running start Frank Whittle's genius had given them in the development of gas turbine technology. The first jet airliner to fly was the Vickers Nene-Viking, a test-bed conversion of the standard Viking that took to the air on April 6, 1948, and flew a trial from London to Paris and back three months later. Interesting though it was, the Nene-Viking was not the aircraft on which Vickers was prepared to bank its future. At this early stage in the history of the jet engine, neither the manufacturers nor the operators were entirely comfortable with the idea that pure jets were likely to be economically successful. The more cautious move toward adopting the new technology was to try the turboprop, in which the reassuring propeller was retained but was driven by a turbine. As passengers soon found, one advantage of this arrangement is that there are no reciprocating parts and therefore far less vibration than is produced by a piston engine.

The Turbine Propped

The first turboprop to be used commercially was the Rolls-Royce Dart; four of them powered the aircraft on which Vickers did bank its future, the Viscount. When the prototype Viscount 630 first flew in July 1948, British European Airways, the principal intended customer, remained unconvinced of its economics and ordered twenty piston-engined Airspeed Ambassadors. However, BEA used the thirty-two-seat Viscount 630 for route-proving trials, including the

The Vickers Viscount was one of the most successful of the first-generation post-WWII commercial aircraft. The Viscount 630 was first introduced to service by British European Airways in 1950, but was deemed too small and slow. The larger and faster Viscount 700 joined BEA in 1953 and began to fly the world's first scheduled turboprop services. By the time the last 800 series aircraft left the production line in 1964, 459 Viscounts had been built. Seen here, in the colors of Capital Airlines, is G-AMAV, the third prototype and first Viscount 700, manufactured in 1950.

world's first scheduled turbine-powered service, which ran for a month between London and Paris from July 29, 1950. Passenger reaction was such that, when the stretched Viscount 701 arrived with more powerful Darts and fifty-two seats, BEA ordered twenty. These entered regular airline service in April 1953, by which time Vickers was filling its order book. Sales started with Aer Lingus, Trans-Canada, Trans Australia, and Air France. Significant sales were made in the United States, too, with sixty Viscounts going to Capital Airlines and another fifteen to Continental. The final delivery, a series 800 aircraft and the 445th Viscount made, went to All Nippon Airways in February 1963. By any standards, the Viscount was a success and was the aircraft that, more than any other, changed postwar air travel. Vickers tried to follow up this achievement with the larger Vanguard in 1959, but by then interest in large turboprops was waning and only two buyers, BEA and Trans-Canada, could be found. Just forty-four Vanguards were built. (One Viscount found out the hard way that large birds fly

in darkness. On November 23, 1962, a United Airlines Viscount 745D flew into a flock of whistling swans at night, 6,000 feet above Ellicott, Maryland. One swan, estimated at about 13 pounds, struck the leading edge of the tailplane, which collapsed and broke away. Control was lost and the Viscount crashed, killing all eighteen persons aboard.)

In the United States, manufacturers and airlines were in no hurry to adopt turbine power. The dominance of American piston-engined airliners was established, their economics were favorable, and they offered transcontinental range while carrying up to 100 passengers. Constellations and DC-7s were still being delivered in 1958. Apart from the flirtation with imported Viscounts, there was little enthusiasm in the United States for large turboprop airliners. Lockheed produced the L-188 Electra, which entered service with Eastern Airlines in January 1959, but two serious accidents revealed a structural weakness. Although the fault was corrected and the Electra performed well for years on the east coast routes of the United States and with several overseas operators, both as an airliner and a freighter, no further orders were placed. (Suitably strengthened, the military version of the Electra, the P-3 Orion maritime patrol aircraft, was built in large numbers and continued to serve into the 21st century.)

Several other European manufacturers produced turboprop airliners with varying degrees of success. In Britain, Handley Page flew the Herald with four piston engines in 1955 before changing to twin Dart turboprops in 1958, but by then it was too late to attract customers already committed elsewhere. The Bristol Britannia was a larger four-engined airliner designed to meet the long-range needs of BOAC. Bedeviled by development problems, it did not enter service until 1957, so was overtaken by the introduction of pure jets, and fewer than ninety were built. (The Britannia design was the basis for the Canadair CL-44 freighter flown by, among others, the Flying Tiger Line.) A more successful British aircraft, the Avro (later Hawker Siddeley) 748, did not appear until 1960 but was flown by a host of major operators, including Varig, South African Airways, Indian Airlines, Philippine Airlines, LIAT, Dan-Air, and British Airways. The 748 led to a series that, in the form of the British Aerospace ATP (Advanced Turbo-Prop), was still being delivered in the 1990s, with over 500 of all variants built. However, by far the most prolific short-haul

design was the Fokker F-27 Friendship from the Schipol factory in the Netherlands. Launched into service by Aer Lingus in 1958, more than 800 F-27s (in all forms and successive F-50 variants) were built, and over 200 more were manufactured by Fairchild in the United States for use by carriers such as Piedmont, Bonanza and West Coast.

The crowded mid-size turboprop market was further complicated in the 1970 and 1980s by aircraft from Canada and Sweden, plus a Franco-Italian effort. In Canada, the four-engined DHC-7 flew in 1975. Its double-slotted flaps and multiple spoilers gave it short-field capabilities attractive to commuter airlines worldwide, notably those who wished to fly out of the challenging City Airport in what had been the London docks. The DHC-8 twin followed in 1983, embodying all the Dash 7's advantages with improved economy. The Dash 8-400, introduced in 1998, was powered by two 5071-shaft-horsepower PW120 turboprops driving six-bladed propellers, and was stretched to accommodate seventy-eight passengers. Over 500 Dash 8s were delivered by the end of the century. In the 1980s, Sweden's SAAB took its share of the market with the SAAB 340, sharing production with Fairchild in the United States. Nearly 500 examples of the 340 and its successor, the SAAB 2000, were sold worldwide, but production ceased in 1999 as sales slowed. The early 1980s also saw a Franco-Italian

The de Havilland Canada DHC-8 (commonly known as the Dash 8) is a twin-turboprop airliner designed in the early 1980s. It is now made by Bombardier Aerospace, which purchased DHC from Boeing in 1992, and since 1996 has been known as the Q Series turboprop. From the second quarter of 1996, all Dash 8s have been fitted with a computer-controlled noise and vibration suppression system (or NVS), which explains the Q (for "quiet") designation.

Good Morning London, *by Ron Hart.*

short-haul competitor. Aérospatiale and Alenia joined forces, forming Avions de Transport Regional (ATR) to produce a mid-size turboprop airliner. The ATR-42 flew in 1984, the result of regional component manufacture (the fuselage and tail from Naples, the landing gear from Capodichino, the wings and nacelles from Nantes) and final assembly at Toulouse. Early operators included Finnair, Air Queensland, Air Calédonie, and both Simmons Airlines and Continental Express in the United States. In 1988, the stretched and improved ATR-72 followed, and both models attracted orders for well over 200, despite some concern about their ability to cope with flight in freezing conditions, especially after the crash of an ATR-72 in the United States in 1994. (See the fifth volume of *Aviation Century*, Chapter 2, "Fear of Freezing.") However, by the late 1990s, ATR sales were slowing as the principal operators began to show a preference for short-haul jets.

Another short-haul turboprop was the only airliner produced in postwar Japan. The NAMC YS-11 (Nihon Aircraft Manufacturing Company, a consortium including Kawasaki, Mitsubishi, Fuji, Showa, and Shin Meiwa) was similar to the HS 748 in having its twin Rolls-Royce Darts mounted above the wing, but it was some 25 percent longer and heavier than the British aircraft. Over 180 were built, principally for domestic routes, but a number found their

way into the United States market with operators such as Piedmont and Mid-Pacific Airlines. First flown in 1962, the NAMC-11 was still being flown by many carriers in the late 1990s, including Air Express, by which time Indonesia was trying to enter the market with the IPTN N-250, a high-wing seventy-seater that is the first in its class to be equipped with fly-by-wire controls. (In a fly-by-wire system, the pilot's control inputs are fed to a computer that then selects the control surfaces to operate. Normally the control surfaces will move as the pilot commands, but in some cases the fly-by-wire system may modify the response, depending on the circumstances. If the pilot's control input is considered unsafe, it may not be carried out at all. In this respect, fly-by-wire represents a major departure from all that has gone before, since it takes the ultimate authority from the pilot and gives it to the system designers.)

Soviet Growth

If large turboprop airliners prospered anywhere, it was in the Soviet Union. Sergei Ilyushin's rugged and reliable Il-18 (NATO Coot; nothing like the earlier piston-engined Il-18), a 100-seater similar to the Britannia, went into service with Aeroflot in 1959, meeting the requirements of Muscovites seeking the sun in Black Sea resorts and later proving invaluable both for services to central Asia and north of the Arctic Circle. Including 100 maritime reconnaissance versions, 670 were manufactured, and export customers included Bulgaria, Rumania, Poland, Czechoslovakia, East Germany, and China. In 1961, an Il-18 was the first commercial airliner to touch down in Antarctica. The astonishing Tupolev 114 (NATO Cleat, adapted from the Tu-95 Bear bomber) was the largest commercial aircraft in the world when it appeared in 1957 and for many years thereafter. Powered by four 12,000-horsepower Kuznetsov engines driving contra-rotating propellers, it spanned 168 feet and was almost 178 feet long. It could carry 170 passengers and had a maximum takeoff weight of 386,000 pounds. Among the long distance routes the Tu-114 operated in the 1960s were those from Moscow to Khabarovsk, Havana, Accra, Montreal and Delhi. Remarkably, it also featured in a 1967 arrangement with Japan in which a nonstop service between Moscow and Tokyo (4,653 miles in 11½ hours) was flown by Soviet and Japanese crews, with the Tu-114s bearing the insignia of Japan Air Lines.

The most prolific Soviet turboprop designer was Oleg Antonov. The An-8 (Camp) military transport of the 1950s established his pattern for freighter aircraft capable of operating from basic airstrips. The high wing carried a bulbous fuselage with low ground clearance, allowing for a wide

loading ramp under an upswept tail. He repeated these features in the An-10 (Cat), a four-engined transport that Aeroflot began flying in 1959. The 100-seat An-10A followed in 1960 and was used extensively on Aeroflot's internal services, proving especially valuable on polar routes. The An-12B was a civil freighter version of the An-10 and its success encouraged the Antonov team to think on an even grander scale. The huge An-22 *Antheus* (NATO Cock) was made to accept large, awkwardly shaped loads such as a mobile missile unit, and could carry payloads of close to 100 tons. Its surprise appearance at the 1965 Paris Air Show confirmed that the Soviet aircraft industry was capable of producing remarkably original, world-beating designs, and in 1966 an An-22 emphasized the fact by setting eleven payload-to-height records, including one of 85,000 kilograms (187,393 pounds) to 6,600 meters (21,654 feet).

While Aeroflot's large, long-range aircraft caught the eye and attracted international comment, not much was heard about the far smaller workhorse airliner that flew the hundreds of routes serving communities all over the vast reaches of the Soviet Union. Antonov's An-24 (Coke) was an F-27 lookalike that first flew in 1959. It proved to be a very reliable machine, easy to maintain and simple to operate. By the time production ceased in 1978, over 1,300 An-24s had been built. Even after that, production of an improved

The Antonov An-24 entered service with Aeroflot in 1962 as a replacement for the Ilyushin Il-14. A typical Antonov high-wing design, the An-24 had to be able to operate effectively in sub-zero or tropical temperatures and from paved runways or rough fields. It was fitted with a system for adjusting the tire pressures in flight to allow for different surfaces. Over 1,100 were built and many continue to be used in Russia, and in several Asian and African countries.

version was continued in China as the Xian Y-7. A further 1,400-plus An-26s (Curl), a cargo version of the An-24, were also built. Other developments were the An-30 (Clank) for photographic survey (130 built), and the An-32 (Cline) for operations from rudimentary "hot and high" airstrips (350 built).

An-24s were still flying their routes at the end of the century, long after their larger contemporaries had been retired. Their service has not been trouble free. In their forty years of operation, over 120 An-24s (military and civil) have been lost or damaged beyond repair. (If the An-24 loss number seems high, it should be noted that, during the same period, the worldwide losses for the F-27 and its derivatives exceeded 200.)

As the An-24s aged and the need for a replacement became readily apparent, Ilyushin entered the commuter field with the Il-114. Admirable though it seemed when it flew in 1990, the Il-114 suffered a series of problems, including engine faults that led to aircraft losses. Antonov's An-24 successor, the fifty-two-seat An-140, did not fly until 1997, but was much more successful, attracting Aeroflot and other CIS customers immediately. It is faster, quieter, and twice as fuel efficient as the An-24, and improves on its predecessor's capability to operate from short unprepared runways at high altitudes under VFR and IFR conditions. A contract with Iran for licensed production of 100 An-140s underlined the success of the design, which seems set to maintain Antonov's eminence in the short-haul turboprop market.

Minor Movers

At the lower end of the scale in terms of size, a host of small turboprops jostled for niches in the under-forty-seat category. They included, in order of their country of origin: Australia, GAF Nomad (first flight, 1971); Brazil, Embraer Bandeirante (1972); Canada, DHC-6 Twin Otter (1965); China, Harbin Y-12 (1982); Czech Republic, LET 410 (1969); France, Nord 262 (1962); Germany, Dornier 228 (1981), Dornier 328 (1991); Japan, Mitsubishi MU-2 (1963); Soviet Union, An-28 (1969), An-38 (1994); Spain, CASA 212/235 (1971/83); Switzerland/U.K., Pilatus-Britten Norman Turbine Islander; U.K., Short Skyvan (1963), Short 330 (1974), BAe Jetstream 31 (1980), Short 360 (1981); U.S., Swearingen Metro (1969), Beech 1900 (1982), Cessna F406 Caravan II (1983).

Impressive turboprop production runs of several hundred have been recorded by the Embraer Bandeirante, DHC Twin Otter, LET 410, Mitsubishi MU-2, An-28, CASA 212, Swearingen Metro, Beech 1900, and the Short series. The small turboprop airliner market was generally not one that held much appeal for the U.S. aircraft industry even though demand was considerable. By the late 1990s there were almost fifty U.S. airlines operating well over 1,000 turboprop aircraft imported from Brazil, Canada, France, Germany, Sweden and the United Kingdom. Among them were more than 200 from both de Havilland Canada and Embraer, and some 150 from both ATR and British Aerospace.

Developed in the 1960s as an aircraft to fill the gap once occupied by the D.H. Dragon Rapide, the Britten Norman Islander was designed to be rugged, durable and cheap to operate. Over 1,200 have been delivered. The Islander lives up to its name, being particularly popular for getting small numbers of passengers in and out of small islands all over the world. Wakaya is a typical destination, a lush speck of land only 6 miles long that is home to an exclusive resort. It is 50 minutes from Fiji aboard the Islander that constitutes the entire fleet of Air Wakaya.

The revolutionary de Havilland 106 Comet first flew in July 1949. The crew members were test pilot John Cunningham, copilot John Wilson and flight test observer Tony Fairbrother. In Aeroplane Monthly 8/89, *Fairbrother was quoted as saying of the Comet: "I don't think it is too much to say that the world changed from the moment its wheels left the ground." First public view of the Comet was at the 1949 Farnborough Air Show, seen here.*

Pure Jet Revolution

A specific recommendation of Britain's wartime Brabazon Committee was for the development of a jet mailplane capable of carrying a ton of cargo across the Atlantic at 400 mph. The initial proposal did not envisage the carriage of any passengers. However, by 1944 the parameters had changed to give priority to the provision of air services to the countries of Europe and the British Commonwealth. The range requirement was reduced to only 800 miles, and it was thought that the aircraft should have seats for fourteen passengers. The company that took up the challenge of leading the way into the unknowns of the jet age for commercial aircraft, and then took several steps beyond the conservative concepts arising from the deliberations of the Brabazon Committee, was led by Sir Geoffrey de Havilland.

In 1946, de Havilland settled on a design for a four-jet, thirty-two-seat airliner with gently swept wings. By the time of its first flight on July 27, 1949, the sleek D.H.106 Comet 1 had become a breathtaking leap into aviation's future. It offered a cruising speed of 500 mph at 40,000 feet, a range of 1,750 miles, and could seat up to forty-four pas-

sengers. The skepticism of many in the airline industry about the economics of such an aircraft was swept aside soon after BOAC started flying the world's first jet passenger services between London and Johannesburg on May 2, 1952. Passengers loved the Comet for its smooth, quiet ride and for cutting journey times in half. The world's airlines paid attention and began lining up to place orders with de Havilland. The prestige of the British aircraft industry reached new heights, only to be dragged down by a series of horrific accidents.

In 1953/54, three Comets broke up in the air, killing all the passengers and crew. The Comets were grounded and de Havilland's prospective customers fell silent. Exhaustive investigations followed, revealing that de Havilland's trailblazer had fallen victim to metal fatigue. Repeated pressurizations had caused cracks to appear at the corners of the Comet's square windows, and eventually these had spread, causing the fuselage to fail and explode with great violence. (See the fifth volume of *Aviation Century,* Chapter 2, "Machines Can Be Fragile.") A complete redesign, occupying some four years, led to the Comet 4, a much improved aircraft that could seat up to eighty passengers and had a range of 3,000 miles. It became the first jet airliner to fly a scheduled transatlantic service when BOAC inaugurated flights to New York on October 4, 1958, three weeks before Pan Am began flying Boeing 707s to Paris. By then, however, it was too late for de Havilland to continue as the world's leader in jet travel. The experience of the Wright brothers was paralleled, in that once the concept was shown to be feasible, the baton of leadership slipped from the grasp of the pioneers and crossed the Atlantic, but this time in the opposite direction. Boeing was on the way to becoming the dominant force in the jet airliner industry.

Before Boeing

The Comet was the first jet airliner designed as such to fly, but it beat the second into the air by only two weeks. Avro Canada's C-102 Jetliner flew in August 1949. A good-looking fifty-seater, it failed to attract any orders and only one was built. The Soviet Union was not too far behind,

avoiding the risks of new design by basing its first jet airliner on the Tupolev 16 bomber. The resulting Tu-104 first flew in 1955 and was revealed to a surprised Western world on March 22, 1956, when the KGB chief arrived in London to make arrangements for a visit by Soviet leaders the following month. Its appearance caused a considerable stir and Western journalists were not slow to point out that Aeroflot's new flagship was flying while the Comet was grounded and the Boeing team still had many months of work to do before their jet airliner could enter service. The Tu-104 began its commercial life on September 15, 1956, and immediately showed how it would transform Aeroflot's operations, covering the Moscow–Omsk–Irkutsk route in seven hours instead of the eighteen taken by the Il-14s. In the next two years, the Tu-104 was introduced on routes to Peking, Tashkent, Delhi, Prague, Copenhagen, Amsterdam, Brussels, Paris and Cairo, and during that period was the only jet airliner in the world flying scheduled services.

The first D.H. Comet prototype was eventually given the registration G-ALVG and appeared in BOAC's Speedbird markings. The Comet in this photograph has the original single-wheel main undercarriage, replaced on later aircraft with four-wheel bogies. John Cunningham was chief test pilot for de Havilland and was responsible for test-flying the Comet. Here he is seen climbing aboard the specially prepared D.H. Vampire in which he set an altitude record of 59,446 feet in 1948.

The world's first pure jet flight with fare-paying passengers was made on May 2, 1952, in Comet 1 G-ALYP, seen here in company with G-ALVG and G-ALZK, the first and second Comet prototypes. G-ALYP was the Comet that disintegrated and fell into the sea off the Italian coast, near Elba, in January 1954. The scattered pieces of the aircraft were recovered by the Royal Navy and painstakingly assembled by investigators at Farnborough, U.K. The techniques developed during that process have influenced accident investigation ever since.

Brilliant Boeings

Unable to make significant inroads into a post-WWII civil airliner market dominated by Douglas and Lockheed, Boeing was kept alive by its military sales. Among the most significant of these was the B-47, a revolutionary jet bomber with sharply swept wings and podded engines. (See the fifth volume of *Aviation Century,* Chapter 1, "Reach and Power for the USAF.") The experience gained in designing the B-47 was to prove invaluable in laying the foundations for commercial success. Boeing's executives took note of the ecstatic reaction to the Comet when it appeared and decided that if the company were to have a future in the commercial field it would have to be based on a jet transport with transatlantic range. With an eye on a possible

military requirement, and a concession to corporate secrecy, the new Boeing was given the model number 367-80. This misleading designation suggested that it was the eightieth design study based on the Model 367, the USAF's piston-engined KC-97. Forever after, the prototype was known as the Dash 80.

Try as they might, Boeing could not attract advance orders for an aircraft based on the Dash 80. With the Comet experience fresh in their minds, airline executives were wary, and the USAF at first seemed happy to have their tanker needs taken care of for the foreseeable future by the KC-97 fleet. Boeing therefore took a gamble and invested $16 million of company money in the construction of the Dash 80. It was rolled out in May 1954 and flown two months later. A month after that the USAF signed a contract for an initial batch of twenty-nine jet tankers, which were given the Boeing model number 717 and the air force designation KC-135. Boeing thereby gained some breathing space, but the civil carriers remained aloof for several more months. Nevertheless, it was evident that U.S. airlines were now showing some interest in a civil development of the Dash 80 (Model 707), no doubt energized by the news that BOAC would introduce the Comet 4 on the Atlantic route in 1958, and encouraged by the thought that any teething troubles with the Boeing design would be overcome at the USAF's expense.

The cork finally came out of Boeing's airliner bottle in October 1955 when Juan Trippe ordered twenty 707s for Pan American, although for a while the success must have tasted bittersweet. By now, Douglas had realized that it would be a mistake to ignore public excitement over the possibilities of jet travel. In an effort to make up for lost time, Douglas proposed building a jet airliner that would be larger and go further than the 707. It might be in service a year later but it would be better. Banking on the reputation of earlier Douglas products, Juan Trippe backed the gamble and ordered twenty-five DC-8s at the same time that he ordered the Boeings. Glad though he was that Pan Am had ordered the 707, Boeing's president, Bill Allen, was not too happy about finding that Douglas had attracted more orders for an aircraft that existed only on the drawing board. The situation was exacerbated a month later when United Airlines announced its intention to buy thirty DC-8s. Competition between the two companies intensified, with

Boeing showing great flexibility, offering variants of the original 707 that would more than match the DC-8 for seating capacity and range. By 1956, there had been a flood of orders for the two airliners, with United, KLM, SAS, Swissair, Trans-Canada, Japan Air Lines, and Eastern opting for the DC-8, and Qantas, Lufthansa, Air France, Air India, Sabena, TWA, American, Western, and Continental choosing the 707. Douglas had done well in coming from behind, and there was a late (and ineffective) challenge from Convair with its 880 and 990 models, but in terms of numbers Boeing had gained the upper hand. It was a decisive advantage that would never be relinquished.

Douglas did return to the charge, installing turbofans and eventually stretching the DC-8's fuselage in the Super Sixty series to an incredible 187 feet. The long, narrow-bodied aircraft, overtaken in passenger appeal by the spacious Jumbos in the 1970s, was nonetheless efficient and continued to serve as a freighter for carriers such as United Parcel Service and Airborne Express. On the other side of the Atlantic, large four-jets appeared in Britain and the Soviet Union. Vickers produced the VC-10, an elegant airliner similar to the 707 in size but with engines in pods at the rear of the fuselage. It was popular with passengers and managed better than average load factors, but it did not sell beyond British airlines and traditional British markets in Africa. In time, many of the fifty-four VC-10s built were transferred to the RAF to serve as military transport/tankers. Bearing close resemblance to the VC-10, with a high T-tail and four engines at the back, the Ilyushin 62 first flew in January 1963, just three months after

Excellent airliner though it was, the Douglas DC-8 suffered the handicap of entering service in September 1959, a year behind the Boeing 707. That delay cost Douglas the dominance it once held in the commercial airliner market. Launch customers for the DC-8 were United and Delta. The jet age for Air Canada began in April 1960 with the first deliveries of DC-8s to replace the Super Constellations as the airline's principal aircraft.

TOP *The Boeing Type 367-80 (thereafter usually referred to as the Dash 80) was rolled out of its Renton hangar, near Seattle, for the first time on May 14, 1954, in the presence of a large and admiring crowd. First flight took place on July 15, 1954, with Tex Johnston at the controls. The following month, Tex Johnston gained great publicity for the Dash 80 by doing two barrel rolls over Lake Washington in front of the world's press. Boeing president William Allen bet the future of his company on this aircraft, the prototype of the outstanding Boeing 707.*

BOTTOM *The Boeing 707 was the airliner that led the way in exploiting jet power for commercial aviation and established Boeing's long-lived dominance as a manufacturer of civil airliners. The first order for the 707 was placed by Pan American World Airways, and the first 707-121 for Pan Am was rolled out on October 28, 1957. Pan Am's fifth 707 aircraft (N711PA) inaugurated the first revenue-earning 707 flight on October 26, 1958. The final variant of the 707 built (a 720 delivered to Western Airlines on September 20, 1967) was the 837th aircraft manufactured.*

the Vickers aircraft. Once difficulties with its Kuznetsov engines had been overcome, the Il-62 became Aeroflot's flag carrier when the Cold War was at its most icy, flying routes to the capitals of Western Europe and Japan, and inaugurating services to Montreal (1967) and New York (1968).

David and the Marine Goliath

In the 1930s, anyone suggesting that small machines such as aircraft would eventually drive the mighty ocean liners from the seas would have been thought stupid. The post-WWII decade continued to be profitable for the big ships, notably the transatlantic service operated by Cunard Line's *Queen Mary* and *Queen Elizabeth*. By the end of the 1950s, however, air travel had completely changed the situation. In 1954, one million people crossed the Atlantic by sea and some 600,000 by air. When asked if this was worrying, a Cunard Line director replied: "Flying is but a fad. There will always be passengers to fill ships like the *Queens*." Cyrus R. Smith, president of American Airlines, disagreed. He pointed out that "one great effect of the war was that people became accustomed to traveling in air-

planes. We had carried some seven million soldiers and we had taken the newness out of traveling by air. The people were pretty well used to flying and they acquainted their families with the fact that it was a good way to travel." Just three years later, even before the advent of the revolutionary jets, the rival systems carried one million passengers each, and by 1961 the ships were in irreversible decline, attracting only 750,000, compared to the two million who preferred a crossing of a few hours to one of four or five days. On one crossing, the *Queen Elizabeth* carried only 200 passengers and 1,200 crew. The *Queen Mary* was finally retired in 1967, and the *Queen Elizabeth* in 1968. They were followed in later years by other great liners such as the *United States* and the *France* as the shipping companies turned to cruising to make a living. In the battle for Atlantic supremacy, the shipping Goliaths had been comprehensively sunk by the Davids of the airlines.

Not So Far with Fewer People

While the United States corporations battled it out with large airliners, the French gave some thought to producing a smaller jet transport that could operate efficiently over Europe's short-haul routes. Government sponsored trials flown in 1951 with a Nene-powered Sud-Ouest Bretagne led to a design competition won by Sud-Est, which was contracted to build its SE-210. This was proposed as a medium-range, twin-engined, fifty-two-seater, later named

ABOVE *The French Sud SE-210 Caravelle was the first jet airliner produced in continental Europe. It pioneered the rear-mounted engine layout, which led to a quieter passenger compartment. With a total of 279 built, the Caravelle was a most successful design, and the first airliner to make a clear profit for its manufacturer.*
RIGHT *A surprising feature of the Caravelle design was its link with the unfortunate D.H. Comet 1. Both the cockpit layout and the nose section were taken directly from the Comet.*

Caravelle. Apart from the nose section, which was borrowed from the ill-fated Comet, the design broke new ground. For the first time, the engines were mounted one on either side of the fuselage at the tail. This gave the Caravelle the advantage of a clean (and therefore very efficient) wing, and it took the noise of the engines away from the passenger compartment. It also made possible the full span flaps that allowed the Caravelle to offer excellent short field performance. Critics believed that a pure jet airliner could never match the economy of turboprops, but the Caravelle proved them wrong, and its smooth quiet ride made it popular with passengers. Introduced by Air France in 1959, it was soon ordered by many more of the world's major airlines, even managing to penetrate the U.S. market in a small way when United Airlines took delivery of twenty. By the time the 282nd and last Caravelle was delivered to Sterling Airways of Denmark in 1972, the aircraft had been stretched to accommodate as many as 140 passengers and had established itself as Europe's most successful jet airliner. It had also become the model for later designs in other countries.

As Caravelle production wound down, France made one other attempt to build a short-haul airliner. The Dassault Mercure flew in 1972, the result of a joint venture with Aeritalia, CASA and F&W Emmen. It resembled the Boeing 737 but was uncompetitive. Its one claim to fame was that it was the first airliner to feature a head-up display for the pilot. Only ten were built.

Three with Three at the Back

The thought that British European Airways, a state-owned airline, might have to buy a French aircraft to stay competitive led to a proposal in 1956 that British industry should be invited to match BEA's specification for an airliner to carry a 19,000-pound payload 1,000 miles after lifting it from a 6,000-foot runway. Other important requirements were that it should enter service by 1964 and that it should

cruise faster than the Caravelle. The winning design was the de Havilland 121. It followed the Caravelle's lead in placing the engines at the rear of the fuselage, but it added a third engine at the base of the fin, an arrangement that gave rise to the name Trident. Hawker Siddeley absorbed de Havilland in 1960, and the HS 121 Trident first flew in 1962. Good aircraft though it was, the Trident bore the burden of BEA's very specific requirements, and they eventually hampered its prospects for sales in the wider world. Only 100 or so were built, the major users being BEA and, because China was then denied access to the U.S. market, the Civil Aviation Administration of China (CAAC). The Trident did manage to earn a place in aviation history at London's Heathrow Airport on April 1, 1964, by becoming the first airliner to demonstrate an automatic landing by a passenger aircraft on a scheduled service.

At one stage in the late 1950s, Boeing, conscious of developments in Europe and of studies being done at

Douglas and Convair, considered a short-haul jet collaborative venture with both Sud-Aviation and de Havilland, but by 1960 the Seattle-based company decided to go it alone with a "mini-707" design, retaining as many features of the larger aircraft as possible while mounting a cluster of three engines at the rear in a Trident arrangement. The result was the Boeing 727, an aircraft designed to take into account competing requirements from Eastern and United Airlines. Eastern insisted that the 727 should be able to operate from La Guardia's 4,860-foot runway, and United wanted an airliner that could reach either coast with a full load after taking off "hot and high" from Denver in the summer. Boeing's new wing took care of the problem by incorporating leading-edge flaps and slats, together with triple-slotted trailing-edge flaps. When extended, these greatly increased the area and modified the shape of the wing, allowing the 727 to take off and land at lower than the average jet airliner speeds. To

passengers, the disassembling of the wing on final approach sometimes came as a disturbing aerodynamic lesson, the ground below appearing through startlingly wide gaps where a solid wing had been only moments before, leaving the 727 apparently reliant on the mysteries of levitation rather than lift.

Despite achieving its first flight over a year after the Trident, the 727 went into service with Eastern in February 1964, two months ahead of its tri-jet competitor. By then, a demonstration model had completed a world tour and had landed at many airports previously thought to be unacceptable for jets, including La Paz, Bolivia, where the touchdown height was 13,358 feet. Orders for the 727 poured in from Europe, Japan, Australia and Latin America. Its success fueled more orders, and by November 1973, the 1,000th 727, now considerably stretched beyond its original capabilities, rolled off Boeing's line. Production finally ceased in 1984, and the 727 reigned as the most successful airliner of the jet era to that date, 1,832 having been built.

The Soviet Union was late in following the West's development of tri-jet airliners, but in 1968 the Tu-154 (Careless) made its first flight. Aimed at meeting requirements similar to those of the 727, the slightly larger and

The Tu-154 reflected the layout of Western tri-jets, but did not enter service until 1972, eight years after the Boeing 727 and D.H. Trident. It had a higher thrust-to-weight ratio than its Western counterparts and was designed to operate from hard earth or gravel runways. The Tu-154 was flown by Aeroflot and exported to several Soviet client states.

heavier Tu-154 had more powerful engines and was designed to cope with the more rugged conditions experienced at remote Soviet airfields. Although flown only by Tupolev's usual customers, the Tu-154 proved a most successful aircraft, its production continuing through the late 1990s, and a total of at least 1,000 were delivered.

"Bus Stop" Jets

Pressure from the airlines led to the tri-jets being gradually stretched to accept more passengers, but it still seemed that there was room for smaller, more economical jets to operate over short-haul stages not served by the major airlines route systems. Two companies thought so and set out to fill the gap. The British Aircraft Corporation (formed in 1960 by combining Vickers, English Electric and Bristol, with Hunting added later) developed an idea from Hunting Aircraft into the BAC One-Eleven, a rear-engined twin-jet with seating for up to eighty-nine passengers. By the time of its first flight in August 1963, the One-Eleven had attracted orders totaling sixty aircraft from several airlines, including British United and two from the United States — Mohawk and Braniff. BAC had stolen a march on the competition and

seemed set to achieve a major breakthrough in sales, but the loss of the prototype in October 1963 checked the One-Eleven's progress. The problem was one associated with this particular aircraft configuration: low wing, rear-mounted engines, and high T-tail. Pressed in trials beyond the early indications of a stall, the One-Eleven settled into a deep stall from which it was impossible to recover. To guard against a recurrence, systems were developed incorporating not only audible warnings of an approaching stall, but also stick-shakers and pushers that operated automatically. All this took time, and the One-Eleven did not enter service until May 1965, by when the first Douglas DC-9s were in the air.

Like BAC, Douglas had managed to attract orders for its new twin-jet before the first flight in February 1965. Subsequent progress with the ninety-seat DC-9 was rapid, the type entering service with Delta Airlines in December of the same year. In the years that followed, the original DC-9 design formed the basis for a growing family of outstandingly successful airliners, with the well-known Douglas quality of "stretchability" allowing the aircraft to be offered in various sizes and with the customer's choice of engines. Maximum flexibility was gained by the use of rapid-change kits that enabled role changes from passenger to freight carrying in hours. In 1967, Douglas merged with McDonnell Aircraft, but the DC-9 series continued, eventually taking shape as the redesignated MD-80. The ultimate stretch came in 1993, with the MD-90, the proposed Dash 40 version of which was 171 feet long (67 feet longer than the first DC-9) with seats for 180 passengers. The MD-95, introduced in 1995, went back to the 100-seat market and was designed to meet the need for an advanced technology aircraft to replace ageing DC-9s operating on short- to medium-range routes. When Boeing took over McDonnell Douglas in 1997, the aircraft became the Boeing 717, reusing a company designation originally given to USAF KC-135s. Given the 717's advanced avionics and efficient high-bypass Rolls-Royce BR715 engines, Boeing has predicted that it is ideally placed to fill a potential market of some 3,000 airliners in this role. So the DC-9 line continues, much modified and improved, but with its lineage clearly defined and its extended family numbering well over 2,200 and still on the rise. By contrast, the BAC One-Eleven line ended in 1981 after 264 aircraft had been produced.

> *"I've got the greatest job in the world. Northwest sends me to New York ten times a month to have dinner. I've just got to take 187 people with me whenever I go."*
>
> COLIN SOUCY, NORTHWEST AIRLINES PILOT

In the circumstances, with two competing aircraft already well on the way to entering service, it did not seem sensible for Boeing to consider entering the "bus stop" jet market of the 1960s. However, the company thought that advantage could be taken of a design that emphasized commonality with other Boeing airliners and in the process offered six abreast seating rather than the DC-9's five. The resulting Boeing 737 was unflatteringly nicknamed "Fat Albert" and was "all square" — about 100 feet long, 100 feet across, and intended for around 100 passengers. Unlikely contender though it appeared at the time, the 737 proved to be a tribute to Boeing's accurate assessment of the long-term market and of the company's confidence in its ability to build an aircraft with wide international appeal. Indeed, the 737 became the first U.S.-built airliner to attract a non-American launch customer. Lufthansa set the ball rolling, beginning 737 services in April 1968, but by then many other customers were in Boeing's order books. By the end of the century, variants had been built to carry up to 200 passengers, haul freight, fulfill a number of military roles, and satisfy the demands of lofty executives for luxury travel. Three generations of 737s had been redesigned to accommodate state-of-the-art engines and avionics. "Fat Albert" had become the phenomenon of the commercial jet age, with almost 4,000 aircraft being flown by some 330 civil operators and the military of a dozen countries. As the 21st century dawned, 737s had in little over thirty years carried the equivalent of the world population — some six billion people.

Other "Buses"

When the Soviet Union's Tu-134 (Crusty) short-haul airliner first flew in July 1963, it could not be described as another lookalike for a Western design. Although it resembled the BAC and Douglas aircraft (low wing, rear-mounted engines, T-tail) it was developed from the earlier Tu-124 and took to the air a month before the BAC One-Eleven. In terms of passenger/mile costs, engine noise and passenger comfort, the Tu-134 was no match for its Western counterparts, but it had a rugged airframe and could operate into remote rustic airfields. Like other Soviet aircraft of the time, it suffered from relatively poor engine reliability and had a less than desirable safety record, which was at least in part attributable to often being flown over hostile terrain in bad weather with minimal navigation aids. Nor was the standard of aircrew training all that it might have been. Nearly 900 Tu-134s were built and many continued to operate into the 1990s with a number of Russian and former Soviet Union regional carriers.

Another Soviet original was the diminutive Yak-40 (Codling), designed for use on routes where traffic was insufficient to justify using even the forty-seat An-24. Accommodating twenty-four to thirty-two passengers, the Yak-40 was an attractive tri-jet mini-liner that entered service with Aeroflot in September 1968. It was of a size and shape that did not proliferate in the West until many years later. It was reliable and popular in the Soviet bloc. Over 1,000 were made and were flown by the airlines of seventeen countries. In the early 1970s, Yakovlev built on the Yak-40 design to produce the much larger Yak-42, which seats 120 passengers in six-abreast configuration.

Concorde *by Malcolm Root.*

In 1967, the Dutch company Fokker joined the low-wing, rear-engined, T-tail club with its F-28 Fellowship, a sixty-five-seater aimed at the lower end of the DC-9's market. It sold well to smaller airlines and was developed into several versions, gradually stretching to accommodate up to eighty-five passengers. In the mid-1980s, Fokker took the design further to produce the F-100; passenger capacity rose to 122 and the type attracted orders from larger airlines, among them KLM, Swissair and US Air. In spite of the popularity of the F-100 (and its smaller cousin, the F-70), however, Fokker was overcome by the competition in the late

1990s and became part of Stork Aerospace, responsible for manufacturing parts and systems rather than whole aircraft.

Faster, Faster!

As the jet engine began to revolutionize air travel in the post-WWII period, it seemed that there could be no limit to the advances it promised. Airliners would get bigger and safer, and would be able to reach across the globe, linking in hours countries that until then had been weeks apart. The dramatic increase in speed was immediately apparent, and it sparked an appetite for even faster travel. Military aircraft, ignoring economics, showed the way to supersonic flight, and as early as 1954 a group of British aerodynamicists began to study the possibility of building a supersonic airliner. It was no easy task. Overcoming the huge increase of drag as the speed of sound is approached is only the start. There follow a multitude of problems, including the marked rise in surface heat produced by air friction and the need to design a structure that has the ability to maintain supersonic speed over long distances. New alloys and design techniques would be required. In Britain the result of considerable research was the Bristol 223 project, conceived as a four-engined delta capable of carrying 100 passengers from London to New York at Mach 2.

In 1960, Sud Aviation and Dassault in France formed a consortium to develop a Super Caravelle, originally intended to be a Mach 2.2 seventy-six-seater for the transatlantic route. Since the costs of development were going to be high and the

two countries were pointed in the same direction, it seemed only sensible to join forces, and by 1962 the French and British governments had signed an agreement whereby Aérospatiale and BAC would collaborate on the airframe while Rolls-Royce and SNECMA shared development of the Olympus 593 engines. The product of their joint efforts was the Concorde, an elegant delta with a wing leading edge shaped in a gentle S-curve. Plans to have the aircraft in service by 1968 had seriously underestimated the difficulties (aerodynamic, structural and political), and it was not until March 1969 that the first prototype left the ground at Toulouse. The second flew from Filton, near Bristol, a month later. To the surprise of many Western observers, however, another supersonic airliner had beaten them into the air.

Andrei Tupolev was the Soviet designer tasked with ensuring that the West did not claim supersonic airliner travel for themselves alone. Faced by the same challenges as his

The supersonic BAe/Aerospatiale Concorde was a staggering technical achievement, but an economic nightmare. Aeronautical engineers, pilots and passengers who could afford the fare loved it; accountants and those who lived near its takeoff flight paths hated it. Concorde was a brave attempt to define the future of air travel, but it must be considered a magnificent failure.

The first supersonic airliner to fly, on December 31, 1968 (two months before Concorde), was the Tupelov Tu-144, but technical problems troubled it for many years. Limited services were flown within the Soviet Union until the 1980s, but the aircraft was not a success.

British and French counterparts, Tupolev was inevitably driven to similar solutions and his Tu-144 bore superficial resemblance to the Concorde, earning it the nickname of "Concordski" in the Western press. Some evidence of industrial espionage by the Soviets helped to fuel Western speculation that the Tu-144 was a copycat design. Closer examination of the Tu-144 in its final form revealed that it was slightly larger and featured significant differences, among them a double delta wing, retractable foreplanes, and afterburning turbofans mounted close to the fuselage under the center section. Because of the high angle of attack assumed by a delta at low speeds, both aircraft had "droop-snoot" noses that could be lowered to improve visibility on landing.

Political imperatives set by the demands of gaining international prestige for the Soviet Union ensured that the Tu-144 would earn the distinction of being the first supersonic airliner to fly. It did so on the last day of 1968, a little more than two months before the Concorde. Subsequent development was protracted, but a Tu-144 did fly at the 1973 Paris Air Show. Unfortunately it was an appearance made memorable for the wrong reasons. The aircraft broke up in midair during a display, killing the crew and eight people on the ground, besides injuring many more and destroying a number of houses. Later speculation suggested that a contributory cause of the accident had been the presence of a French Mirage flying at the same time as the Tu-144, reportedly to photograph the Soviet aircraft in the air. It was thought that the Tu-144's

pilot had been surprised by the proximity of another machine, and that he took avoiding action which led to the aircraft being overstressed. Whatever the reason, the public disintegration of a proud symbol of Soviet technological achievement effectively destroyed hopes for its success on the international stage. Development continued, and Tu-144s eventually began flying cargo between Moscow and Alma Ata in 1975, followed by passenger services in 1977. A second Tu-144 crash in 1978 led to an enquiry that concluded that the airliner was too costly to operate, and the type was withdrawn from Aeroflot service after just 102 passenger flights. (Gone but not forgotten, the Tu-144 came back to life in the late 1990s when the United States and Russia agreed to restore one for a NASA program studying a future high-speed civil aircraft.)

On the other side of the Atlantic there was some concern in the early 1960s that the United States was being left behind in not facing up to the challenge of the supersonic airliner. In July 1963, shortly after Pan American announced that options had been taken on eight Concordes, President Kennedy called for the United States to develop an SST; Congress eventually agreed that public funds should be used for the project. A design competition involving Boeing, Lockheed and North American followed, but it was not until the end of 1966 that Boeing was chosen to build a prototype. Originally proposed as a swing-wing design, by 1969 the Boeing SST had joined the Concorde and the Tu-144 in adopting a delta plan form, but it was much larger and more ambitious than either. Some 270 feet long, it was intended to carry 250 passengers cruising at Mach 2.7 at 70,000 feet. By 1971, Boeing was well on the way to producing an aircraft. A mockup had been built and the prototype was 15 percent complete. However, economic and environmental arguments against the project had become irresistible. In May 1971, the U.S. Congress accepted the inevitable, withdrawing funding support and halting all work on the Boeing SST.

Meeting Triumph and Disaster

Left with the field to themselves, Aérospatiale and BAC might have hoped that their immensely costly project would at last bring its rewards, but it was not to be. With the oil crisis of the 1970s bringing fears of finite fuel reserves, and more commercially viable alternatives available, those airlines that had taken options on Concorde did not renew them. Spectacular demonstrations of the aircraft's performance (including one in which an Air France Concorde accomplished a round trip between Boston and Paris before a 747 completed a direct flight) drew astonished international applause but did nothing for sales. In 1974, in the absence of further orders, it was agreed that production would be stopped after British Airways and Air France had each received seven aircraft. On January 21, 1976, fourteen years after the Anglo-French agreement was signed, Concorde at last entered commercial service, British Airways flying from London to Bahrein and Air France linking Paris and Buenos Aires. The rich prize of North Atlantic services had to wait until May 1976, after a U.S. government environmental study had opened the way for flights to Washington, D.C.

Until the summer of 2000, British Airways and Air France continued to fly Concordes both on regular scheduled services and on charter flights. The transatlantic service, offering crossings of only three to three and a half hours, was immensely popular with the rich and famous who could afford the exorbitant fare. Those fortunate enough to be able to use Concorde often did so repeatedly and were unstinting in their praise, claiming that the rapidity of the crossing effectively removed the problem of fatigue. For a quarter of a century, Concorde reigned supreme as an aeronautical phenomenon, an aerial high-speed yacht for the rich, admired and desired as unobtainable by most of the traveling public. The achievement of British and French designers and engineers was remarkable and remained unmatched in the 20th century, a collaborative technological triumph that did wonders for Anglo-French prestige. Pilots loved it, too. British Airways' chief of Concorde Flight Operations, Captain Mike Bannister, has said: "Concorde handles so beautifully she's more like a Thoroughbred race horse or a sports car than a truck. All the pilots that fly her take great delight in the physical part of flying the aeroplane." He added: "The first time you do a

> *"'How do you like your coffee, captain — cream & sugar?' We are at 30 west, the half-way point between the European & North American continents, & the stewardess in charge of the forward galley is looking after her aircrew during a pause in serving the passengers' meals. Mach 2. On autopilot, eleven miles high, moving at 23 miles a minute. Nearly twice as high as Mount Everest, faster than a rifle bullet leaving its barrel. The side windows are hot to the touch, from friction of the passing air. Despite the speed we can talk without raising our voices. 'Milk, please, & no sugar.'"*
>
> BRIAN CALVERT, *FLYING CONCORDE*, 1982

take-off in training where you use full power but the aircraft is only about 60 percent of its maximum weight, the acceleration is quite spectacular. You can get from a standing start to airborne at 250 mph in about 20 seconds, and to 3,000 feet in about 35 seconds. For an airliner that is quite remarkable." All that having been said, there is no doubting that Concorde was a commercial disaster. Between them, the British and French taxpayers paid some one and a half billion dollars to put a handful of inefficient aircraft into service for the benefit of very few privileged people.

On July 25, 2000, a wheel of an Air France Concorde, taking off from Charles de Gaulle airport near Paris, struck a loose strip of metal on the runway just before aircraft rotation. (See the fifth volume of *Aviation Century*, Chapter 2, "Malfunctions Miscellaneous.") Large pieces of rubber flew off and struck the underside of the left wing. Fire broke out as fuel gushed from a ruptured fuel tank and the aircraft got airborne trailing flames. Soon afterward, the crew were faced with engine losses and control difficulties that proved impossible to overcome. Less than a minute after the nosewheel burst, the Concorde crashed into a small hotel, killing all 109 people on board plus four more on the ground. All Concordes were grounded pending modifications and the reissuing of Certificates of Airworthiness by the British and French authorities. They returned to service only briefly before their final retirement in October 2003, a little less than twenty-eight years after they began.

Seeing an Elephant Fly

While much energy and oceans of cash were expended in the exotic pursuit of traveling faster than a rifle bullet while drinking champagne, more practical minds believed that the future lay in providing more seats per aircraft at a price the general public could afford. Developments in the aviation world during the 1960s — big turbofans, aerodynamic

The Boeing 747 production line at Everett, Washington State, is acknowledged in the Guinness Book of World Records to be the largest building in the world by volume. It has grown over the years to enclose 472 million cubic feet of space, and its footprint covers 98.3 acres. The 747 is possibly the most complex single machine ever constructed; each 747 is made up of some six million parts.

on his first flight on December 17, 1903.

The origins of the Boeing 747 were rooted in the USAF's need for an outsize cargo aircraft. In 1964, bids on such a machine were requested from Lockheed, Douglas and Boeing. In June 1965, with the lowest bid, Lockheed was declared the winner of the competition to build what became the C-5A. Disappointed, Boeing showed great flexibility, reacting to the growing demand for long-range air travel by adapting the military freighter design and proposing a civil airliner of gargantuan proportions. It was to be capable of accommodating up to 550 passengers, and economic projections showed that it would do so at costs per passenger/mile that were some 30 percent less than the those of the Boeing 707. Juan Trippe of Pan American was impressed and in April 1966 he placed an order for twenty-five of the huge aircraft.

advances, new construction materials and methods, better airports, improved aircraft serviceability, increasing demand for air travel — all suggested that the aircraft and airline industries were ready to take the next big step. It was a step that would see the air transport business revolutionized by aircraft of a size Orville would probably have thought beyond the realms of possibility. When Boeing's Model 747 was revealed to public gaze on September 30, 1968, the aircraft itself was twice as long as the distance Orville had flown

On September 30, 1968, the prototype 747 was rolled out of Boeing's Everett facility. The crowd of workers, reporters, and airline executives waiting outside had heard that Boeing's new airliner was large, but they were unprepared for the massive bulk of the 747. The prototype weighed 710,000 pounds and was 231 feet long. The tail was the height of a six-story building, some of the astonished spectators doubted whether it would ever get off the ground.

BOEING 747

Boeing's 747 became *the* symbol for the airline industry upon its introduction to the traveling public in 1968. Almost forty years later, the venerable original "Jumbo" still soldiers on in the overnight package delivery role. The capacity for 300-plus passengers translates into huge numbers, which make air-cargo flights very practical.

From the beginning, the 747 was designed to serve as an all-cargo transport. The first 747 Freighter could easily carry 100 tons (90,000 kg) across the Atlantic Ocean or across the United States.

A Boeing 747 at the United Parcel Service ramp in Louisville, Kentucky. This is 747-123, registration number N9675, serial number 20390 — the 136th 747 off the production line. It was originally delivered to American Airlines and was the 747 used in the film *Airport 1975*. Its basic American Airlines color scheme was modified to the notional Columbia Airlines colors for filming of exterior sequences.

Given that they were breaking new ground, Boeing's designers and engineers, directed by project chief Joe Sutter, made astonishingly rapid progress. First a new factory, the biggest building in the world, had to be built at Everett, north of Seattle. Production techniques had to be devised and exhaustive testing of every part conducted. When its six million parts came together, the 747 was probably the most complex single machine ever built. The first flight took place on February 9, 1969, with test pilot Jack Waddell at the controls. It was largely uneventful, and the subsequent test program, using five aircraft to accumulate some 1,400 hours in the air, went smoothly enough to allow the FAA to certificate the 747 on December 30, 1969.

Pan Am's transatlantic 747 Jumbo Jet service was launched on January 22, 1970, with a flight from New York to London. Teething troubles with any new type are inevitable, and the 747 was no exception, but not all were faults with the aircraft. The 747's great size and enormous weight affected everything associated with it — ground equipment, taxiways, parking slots, ticketing, catering, baggage handling. During the first two years of 747 operation, the problems of the aircraft and how to cope with it were gradually worked out and its popularity with airlines and their passengers grew. Boeing's order book expanded rapidly, and the 747 became the flagship for airlines worldwide, making intercontinental travel a possibility for more and more people.

As the years went by, Boeing produced 747s in a variety of forms, powered by a range of increasingly powerful engines from Pratt & Whitney, General Electric or Rolls-Royce. The small upper deck behind the cockpit was extended, more fuel was carried, wingtip winglets were added, and freighters and combination passenger/freighters were built. Special short-range, high-passenger-density versions were provided for Japan, and the 747SP (Special Performance) was introduced in 1976, 48 feet shorter and much lighter, to extend the range to almost 8,000 miles with a typical load. One 747 was modified to ferry the Space Shuttle, and two others to serve as "Air Force One," the U.S. President's aircraft. By 1988, the 747-400 was flying with a digital cockpit configured for two-pilot operation, new generation high-bypass turbofans of over 60,000 pounds thrust

each, and a greater fuel load. Maximum takeoff weight had risen to 870,000 pounds, and more than 400 passengers could be carried a distance of 8,400 miles at costs 20 percent lower than earlier 747s. Still in production at the end of the century, Boeing's Jumbo was, after thirty years, still the largest and most popular of the wide-bodied airliners. Well over two billion passengers had traveled in over 1,200 747s built, and in the course of flying 50 million hours the "Jumbo" fleet had covered some 20 billion air miles.

Filling the Gap

Boeing's giant step having doubled airliner passenger-carrying capacity, there was room for an aircraft between the size of the 747 and the 707/DC-8. American Airlines said as much by broadcasting a requirement for a wide-bodied aircraft of 300/350 seat capacity to fly on U.S. domestic routes. Lockheed and Douglas both answered the call with similar designs, large tri-jets with two under-wing engines and a third at the rear, Lockheed's molded into the top of the fuselage and Douglas choosing a less aesthetic mounting in the middle of the fin. American opted for the Douglas DC-10 and ordered twenty-five, reassured that the company's worrying cash-flow and production troubles would be overcome through its 1967 merger with McDonnell. United quickly followed by ordering thirty DC-10s, and then thirty more. Lockheed's problems with the L-1011 TriStar proved more serious. It was designed around Rolls-Royce RB-211 turbofans, engines that promised great things but initially gambled on using new-technology carbon-fiber fan blades. These did not survive foreign-body ingestion tests, and the RB-211 had to be redesigned with titanium blades. This setback slowed down progress on the TriStar, and matters worsened in 1971 when Rolls-Royce was driven to the verge of bankruptcy. A British government-backed rescue of R-R eventually restored the situation, but Lockheed suffered meanwhile, losing both time and prospective orders. Nevertheless, orders for the TriStar came from TWA (44), Eastern (50), and Air Holdings (50). It entered service with Eastern in April 1972, eight months after American launched the DC-10.

> *The Boeing 747 is the commuter train of the global village.*
> H. TENNEKES, *THE SIMPLE SCIENCE OF FLIGHT*, 1996

The Lockheed L-1011 TriStar was the third American wide-body airliner to be launched, and despite having to overcome serious financial and engine development problems, it gained an excellent reputation for reliability, economy of operation, and low noise emissions. The TriStar entered service with Eastern Airlines in 1972 and was subsequently flown by more than two dozen airlines. The last TriStar was delivered in 1984, after 250 had been built. This was only half the number needed for the company to avoid losing money, and the TriStar was the last civil airliner produced by Lockheed.

In the years that followed, both the DC-10 and the TriStar were modified, growing larger and heavier, the DC-10 even sprouting a third main undercarriage leg to bear and spread the extra weight. Designed for U.S. domestic routes, both airliners became international carriers. The DC-10 survived the stigma of several catastrophic accidents to outlast its rival. (See the fifth volume of *Aviation Century,* Chapter 2, "Machines Can Be Fragile.") The 250th and last L-1011 was delivered to Algeria in 1983, but DC-10 production carried on until 1988, by which time 446 had been built. Even then the line was continued by the MD-11, a stretched and much improved aircraft announced in 1986. In all, 177 MD-11s were built, but the line was closed in 1998, after the Boeing takeover of McDonnell Douglas.

Challenging Times

The business of running an airline and making a profit has never been easy, but developments in the 1970s and 1980s made it more challenging than ever. New aircraft, including the incredible, hugely expensive widebodies, came from the manufacturers, demanding substantial investment, and posing the dilemma of which to choose. Older aircraft had to go, both because they were increasingly inefficient and because they could not meet the more restrictive noise abatement requirements at airports. Then the shock of the oil crisis in the 1970s forced operating costs up at a time when airlines were committed to reequipment and could least afford such a punishing additional load. The economic slump of the 1980s made things worse. It was hardly surprising that many formerly healthy airlines found themselves teetering on the brink of extinction. To complicate matters, the U.S. airline industry had to face the prospect of deregulation and try to assess how that might affect commercial operations.

Formed in 1958, the Civil Aeronautics Board (successor to the Civil Aeronautics Authority) told airlines what they could charge for flights, where they could fly and whether they could start or stop flying between two cities. Competition between carriers was almost nonexistent, so airfares were high, consumer choices were limited and passengers on busy routes subsidized the cost of flying half-empty planes to less popular destinations. In the 1970s, operators were actually experimenting with taking seats out of aircraft so that they could add such luxuries as a piano bar because in-flight services and amenities were the only way that airlines could compete. Nevertheless, most major airlines were content with the existing cost-plus fare structure, which gave them the protection of being able to raise prices if their operating costs rose. They argued that deregulation would lead to a loss of revenue if newcomers could start services on their routes, and that would result in them not being able to finance new aircraft. Many airport authorities agreed, afraid they would no longer be able to sell revenue bonds to destitute airlines. Smaller cities feared the loss of major airline service altogether. The financial community was equally nervous, both in its role as financiers to carriers and as investors. The unions feared both pressure on their pay scales and the frightening prospect of non-union airlines. Adding fuel to the fire, almost everybody opposed to deregulation said that airline safety would suffer. These concerns notwithstanding, President Jimmy Carter signed deregulation into law in 1978, convinced that it would lead to more airlines competing for more passengers on more flights to more places at lower fares.

Proponents of U.S. deregulation quote statistics to defend its benefits. By the late 1990s, the average airline ticket was almost 40 percent cheaper than it was in 1978. The overall number of airline departures rose from just over 5 million in 1978 to 8.2 million in 1997, a 63-percent increase in two decades. Air carriers flew roughly 2.5 billion miles in 1978, but logged more than twice that amount in 1997, flying approximately 5.7 billion miles. Airlines served approximately 250 million passengers in 1978 and roughly 600 million in 1997. Before 1978, there was an average of six fatal accidents per year in the United States. After deregulation, the average fell to 3.5 fatal accidents per year. Economists have estimated that consumers save some $19.4 billion per year thanks to the competitive airline marketplace. American cities have been offered much greater air travel access, thanks to the freedom of airlines to provide service when and where demand exists, without having to seek permission from central planners. Airline deregulation, it is claimed, democratized air travel in America, allowing millions of Americans to fly for the first time in their lives. Besides all this, deregulation is also credited with the creation of new airlines, and with generating the concepts of frequent flyer miles and the hub-and-spoke system.

By bringing passengers from multiple origins (the spokes) to a common point (the hub) and placing them on new flights to their ultimate destinations, these systems provide for more frequent flights and more travel options than did the direct "point to point" systems that predominated before deregulation. Thus, instead of having a choice of a few direct flights between their community and a final destination, travelers departing from a small community might now choose from among many flights by several airlines through different hubs to that destination. To the major U.S. carriers, hub-and-spoke operation offers not just convenience, but also control. An airline can focus its routes and maintenance operations on its chosen hub airports at the same time as greatly multiplying the number of cities and people it serves. A good hub-and-spoke operation feeds itself by capturing nearly all of the local market and diverting one-stop traffic from other hubs and airlines.

Critics of deregulation in the United States are not so sure that the quoted statistics are valid. Some studies show that less expensive fares have come from the use of more efficient aircraft, and that ticket prices, adjusted for inflation, were falling at a faster annual rate before 1978. Lower accident rates, too, could be attributed to better equipment and training. In the 1990s, policymakers were besieged with complaints that business fares were up, smaller cities were not receiving the kind of air service they would like, start-up airlines could not compete effectively, in-flight service was in decline, and airport congestion and flight delays were becoming endemic. It was claimed by deregulation opponents that much of the so-called competition fostered by deregulation is a mirage, and that smaller airlines could soon be overwhelmed by the dominant carriers, who weathered temporary price cuts and then raised rates again after outlasting their challengers. In the carnage of the market place, many airlines went out of business or were absorbed by their competitors, among them respected household names such as Eastern, Pan Am, Braniff, Western and National. Deregulation might therefore be said to have created a situation in which ever fewer very large carriers control most of the U.S. market, and thereby the fare structure.

Developments in the European Community led to very similar arrangements between the member countries, which by the mid-1990s were operating a deregulated

> *"Most passengers never notice it's not a new plane, provided the paint is fresh."*
> JAN CARLZSON, CHAIRMAN,
> SCANDINAVIAN AIRWAYS SYSTEM

Ten Minute Turn, by David Schweitzer, depicts a typical scene at a Southwest Airlines hub. Three of Southwest's more than 400 Boeing 737s are in view, together with an assortment of ground equipment, all bearing the airline's distinctive gold, red and orange color scheme. Southwest operates nearly 3,000 daily flights linking fifty-nine cities in the United States.

open-skies policy. Any EC airline is permitted to serve any two points in the Community, and may set whatever fares and schedules it wishes. This freedom of operation has encouraged the formation of many new airlines offering no-frills services at low cost. Since the fall of Communism, there have also been great changes in the air transport systems of the former Soviet Union and its erstwhile allies, where hundreds of new airlines have appeared, and market reforms have had their effect on airlines in China, too.

Rebels with a Cause

A general counsel to the U.S. Civil Aeronautics Board once described the international air transport business as "the most regulated and least competitive industry in the world." In the post-WWII years, it was difficult for any indi-

vidual entrepreneur to break into a system dominated by giant and mostly state-owned airlines. In the mid-1960s, however, a British challenger appeared on the scene prepared to take on the airlines' cartel. Freddie Laker was an ebullient self-made man from a working-class background who had made his way in aviation after starting on the shop floor at Short Brothers. He flew for the Air Transport Auxiliary during the war and had operated a fleet of converted Halifax bombers (Haltons) in the Berlin Airlift. After a spell as chief executive of British United Airways, he founded Laker Airways on February 8, 1966, to operate principally as a charter and ad hoc airline. In 1971, he began a long struggle against the transatlantic status quo, applying for a licence to introduce a low-cost scheduled service between London and New York, "cutting out the traditional

Sir Richard Branson's airline, Virgin Atlantic, began flights to North America on June 22, 1984, flying a single Boeing 747 between London Gatwick and Newark. By 2004, the fleet had increased to twenty-nine 747s and Airbus 340s, with twenty-four more Airbus aircraft on order, including six of the giant 380s. Known for his entrepreneurial flair and flamboyant style, and for his exploits with balloons and high-speed boats, Richard Branson favors eye-catching livery for Virgin's aircraft. The familiar red and silver scheme in 2004 features a pinup girl waving a Union Jack, and aircraft are christened with names such as African Queen, Ruby Tuesday, Indian Princess, California Girl, Atlantic Angel, *and* Queen of the Skies.

costly frills of international air travel." There was to be no reservation system; it would be first come, first served on the day of travel, and meals during flight were to be supplied at extra cost.

It was 1977 before Laker's persistence was rewarded. On September 26 a Laker Airways DC-10 launched the transatlantic "Skytrain" service at a seat price approximately one-third of the normal economy ticket. Suddenly the major airlines had to offer cut-price fares, too. Laker also campaigned for licences to operate up to 630 routes at cheap rates before attacking the major airlines in Europe with a no-frills service between Manchester and Zurich. In 1982, Laker's long political, legal and commercial struggle came to an end when the slump in the airline industry combined with a weakening pound sterling to reduce him to bankruptcy. His ambitions crushed by the international situation and the implacable opposition of his competitors, Laker nevertheless left his mark on the airline business. He attracted huge support for his efforts from the traveling public and from Prime Minister Margaret Thatcher, who said that it was "thanks to Freddie Laker that you can cross the Atlantic for so much less than it would have cost in the 1970s." However, he made bitter enemies of the major airlines' establishment. The Chairman of the Association of European Airlines described Laker Airways as "the most disruptive airline on the North Atlantic," and the boss of

Lufthansa endorsed that sentiment, saying that Laker had "chosen the path of violent disruption." When the dust had settled, a member of the McDonnell Douglas board summed it all up, saying: "Laker has made a unique contribution to the airline passengers of the world, and had a lasting impact on the fare structure."

Undaunted by Laker's fate, in the early 1980s, a flamboyant millionaire from the recorded music business, with no special knowledge of aviation, accepted the challenge of starting an independent airline from scratch. Richard Branson had long been frustrated by what in his opinion was the poor service afforded the customers of large monopolistic airlines. In launching Virgin Atlantic, Mr. Branson designed an airline to please himself, making the assumption that he was representative of the typical airline passenger. Starting with a single 747-200 in 1984, Virgin Atlantic began flying the London – New York route, touting lower prices and better service. It was the first airline to offer more than two meal choices, even in economy, and the first to put seat-back videos in every seat. When not engaged on other aerial adventures, Branson himself flew frequently in his airline's aircraft, often spending the entire flight chatting with passengers, serving drinks, leading games over the public address system and helping the flight crew with even the most menial tasks. (See Chapter 2, "Crossing the Oceans.") In the early days, he regularly appeared at Heathrow Airport to apologize personally to disembarking passengers if a flight was late. In short, he treated his customers as he wished to be treated, an attitude untypical of the airline industry. Virgin Atlantic quickly established itself as an industry favorite, winning numerous awards and expanding its services to include a number of U.S. cities and destinations in Asia and Africa. Confrontations with the major airlines have been frequent, but Richard Branson has survived them all, and Virgin has grown steadily to become the second-largest British long-haul international airline.

Passing Grade

Fred Smith was at Yale University in 1965 when he wrote his now celebrated term paper outlining a possible overnight package delivery service. He argued that existing ways of handling air freight were inefficient and unforgivably slow, taking up valuable space in the holds of airliners engaged principally in getting passengers to destinations rather than packages to theirs. For his efforts he received a "C," a professorial judgment suggesting that his ideas were little more than adequate and

Fred Smith created Federal Express, the world's first overnight delivery network. FedEx operates almost 700 aircraft in serving 215 countries. Chief Executive magazine's panel of CEO judges chose Fred Smith as 2004 CEO of the year for building a $25-billion company that invented an entire industry, transforming other sectors as diverse as manufacturing, retail and transportation, and raising expectations of globalization. Fred Smith has said that he set out "to create a delivery system that operates essentially the way a bank clearinghouse does — put all points on a network and connect them through a central hub. If you take any individual transaction, that seems absurd: it means making at least one extra stop. But if you look at the network as a whole, it's an efficient way to create an enormous number of connections. If, for instance, you want to connect 100 markets with one another and if you do it all with direct point-to-point deliveries, it will take 100 times 99 (9,900) direct deliveries. But if you go through a single clearing system, it will take at most 100 deliveries. So you're looking at a system that is about 100 times as efficient." Fred Smith's ideas were among the most influential in the development of commercial aviation during the last quarter of the 20th century.

that he could do better. Smith was not discouraged and did indeed do better. In the early 1970s he developed his business proposals and in 1973 began operations with his company, Federal Express. At the time, there were no guaranteed overnight package services and the major airlines were doing their best to get rid of cargo carrying, but Smith believed that he could not succeed in taking advantage of the opportunity offered unless the Federal Express system went nationwide from the start. He avoided any possible regulatory difficulties over routes by operating only aircraft capable of lifting 7,500 pounds of cargo or less, which allowed them to fly without restriction from place to place. Dassault Falcon 20s were chosen. He also devised a hub-and-spoke system centered on Memphis, flying packages there from all over the country late at night, then having

them sorted and flown to their destinations early next morning. It took two years to sort out the schedules and attract enough business, but by 1976 it was clear that Fred Smith had fathered a new and profitable industry.

Having shown that his system was feasible, Smith took the next step, lobbying hard with Congress, the Department of Transportation and the Civil Aeronautics Board to obtain an air-cargo operating certificate for large aircraft. The following year, President Carter signed air cargo deregulation into law, and passenger airline deregulation soon followed. FedEx immediately purchased seven Boeing 727s, each with a capacity seven times that of a Falcon. In 1979, FedEx launched its first international service with flights into Canada, and in 1983 it became the first U.S. company to achieve revenues of $1 billion in only ten years without relying on acquisitions or mergers. Operations in Europe and Asia began in 1984, and by 1986 FedEx was able to claim that it was shipping over one million packages per day. As the 21st century dawned, FedEx was operating well over 600 aircraft, including fleets of Airbus A300/310s, Boeing 727s and MD-11s, and Cessna Caravans, and 250 Ayres Loadmasters were on order. The company's network linked over 200 countries and dependencies, and handled more than three million packages on every business day. Fred Smith's grade "C" ideas had borne abundant fruit and had revolutionized the air transport business.

A European Foot in the Door

By the mid-1960s, the big commercial aircraft world outside the Communist bloc was dominated by American manufacturers, and it seemed unlikely that they could be successfully challenged from elsewhere. Even so, the basis of a challenge began to form in 1965 when an Anglo-French group drew up a specification for a mid-sized wide-bodied airliner to meet the requirements of European airlines. In 1967, this evolved into a Memorandum of Understanding between the French, German and British governments giving their support to an aircraft development program. Unfortunately, the British government, alarmed by the costs of Concorde,

> "It was not acceptable in our minds that customers should be willing to take goods that were very valuable to them and just throw them into this big anonymous transportation system and hope they came out on the other end."
>
> FRED SMITH, COMMENTING ON THE FEDEX DEVELOPMENT OF A PACKAGE TRACKING SYSTEM

lost its nerve and withdrew its support in 1969, and when the formal Airbus agreement was established in December 1970, the major partners were France and Germany, with Spain added as a minor player. In Britain, Hawker-Siddeley had the foresight to hang on independently, committing company funds to the project, and in 1979, British Aerospace (which absorbed Hawker-Siddeley in 1977) was able to become a full member of Airbus Industrie. (Aérospatiale controlled 37.9 percent; Deutsche Airbus, 37.9 percent; Bae, 20 percent; and CASA, 4.2 percent.) Without Hawker-Siddeley's commitment, it seems clear that the British aircraft industry would have lost any chance of continuing as a major contributor in the commercial aviation world.

The first product of European collaboration was the Airbus 300B1, a twin-turbofan with 226 seats. First flight was in October 1972 and certification by the various national authorities followed in 1974. Air France launched the type with the flight of an A300B2 carrying 251 passengers from Paris to London on May 22, 1974. To begin with, Airbus Industrie's business was less than brisk, with most major airlines holding back and watching to see if the A300 could prove that it was a reliable and economically rewarding aircraft. Sales picked up in Europe and Asia during the mid-1970s, and then in April 1978 came the break into the U.S. market that Airbus was hoping for. Frank Borman of Eastern Airlines signed for twenty-three A300s at $25 million each. From then on the fortunes of Airbus changed rapidly for the better. By the end of 1979, Airbus had 256 orders from thirty-two customers and eighty-one aircraft in service with fourteen operators.

Now firmly established, the company set itself to expand and create a complete range of airliners, designed with a high degree of commonality. The A310 variant soon followed, and the A320, launched in 1984, was the first all-new design in its category in thirty years. It was also the first commercial aircraft to feature "fly-by-wire" controls and side sticks instead of control wheels. It set the standard for all subsequent Airbus cockpits and for the industry as a whole. When the four-engined A340 entered

The first flight of the Airbus A320 was on February 22, 1987. Designed to compete with the Boeing 737, the Airbus A320 was the first airliner in the world to offer fly-by-wire flight controls. It has an advanced electronic flight deck, with six fully integrated color displays on the instrument panel and sidestick controllers rather than conventional control columns. The A320 is also constructed using a high percentage of composite materials, as compared to earlier designs. Well over a thousand A320s have been delivered.

service in 1993, it was the first entirely new, long-haul aircraft to start commercial operations for more than twenty years. The twin-engined A330 that appeared a year later combined some of the lowest operating costs of any airliner ever designed and was offered in various versions to give operators maximum flexibility over a wide variety of route structures. By the year 2000, Airbus Industrie was recording an annual turnover of $17.2 billion and had accumulated a total of over 4,000 aircraft in their order book. More than one aircraft per working day was being produced, and the Airbus catalogue included multiple variations on seven major types, from a 100-passenger version of the A319 (also available as an executive jet) to a 380-passenger A340 with a range of nearly 10,000 miles. Nonstop flights between London and Perth, Australia, were possible for the first time. The European toehold of the early 1970s had become a major presence on the world's commercial aviation stage.

The Boeing Response

As the Boeing 707 and 727 fleets aged and Airbus loomed as a serious competitor, Boeing was conscious of the need to market new designs. The first of two concurrent projects to appear (out of sequence) was the 767, which first flew in September 1981, followed five months later by the 757. Both were twin-turbofan aircraft, the 757 being a narrow-bodied, single-aisle 230-seater and the 767 a wide-bodied double-aisle aircraft with up to 289 seats. They shared many common parts and systems, including the two-man flight deck, so that it was possible for crews to qualify on both simultaneously, offering operators of both types flexibility in assigning flight crews. Further benefits accrued from similar maintenance procedures, manuals and inspection requirements and reduced spares inventories. Launched by United (767) and Eastern (757), both aircraft proved to be some 30 percent more economical than their predecessors and were immediately successful. They were produced in

Featuring passenger comforts such as "the quietest cabin in the sky," the A340, the largest of the Airbus family of airliners in 2004, is available in several versions. Among them, the A340-200 series typically carries 239 passengers in three classes on flights of up to 8,000 nautical miles, and the A340-300 can take 295 passengers up to 7,300 nautical miles. By the end of 2003, there were 337 A340s in use or ordered by over thirty of the world's airlines. One notable aspect of the proven operating efficiency of the A340 is the capacity of the underfloor holds, which can take up to 60 percent more freight than a Boeing 747, so offering opportunities for generating cargo revenue.

During more than thirty-five years with the Boeing Company, Philip Condit served in many roles. He was an aerodynamics engineer on the Supersonic Transport; Boeing 747 performance lead engineer; manager of 727 marketing; director of program management for the 707/727/737 division; director of 757 engineering; general manager of the 757 division; and vice president of the Renton Division, which built the 707, 727, 737 and 757 airliners. In 1986, Condit was appointed executive vice president of Boeing Commercial Airplane Company and, in 1989, executive vice president and general manager of the New Airplane Division, later the 777 Division. Phil Condit left Boeing in 2004 after serving as chairman and chief executive officer of the world's largest aerospace company.

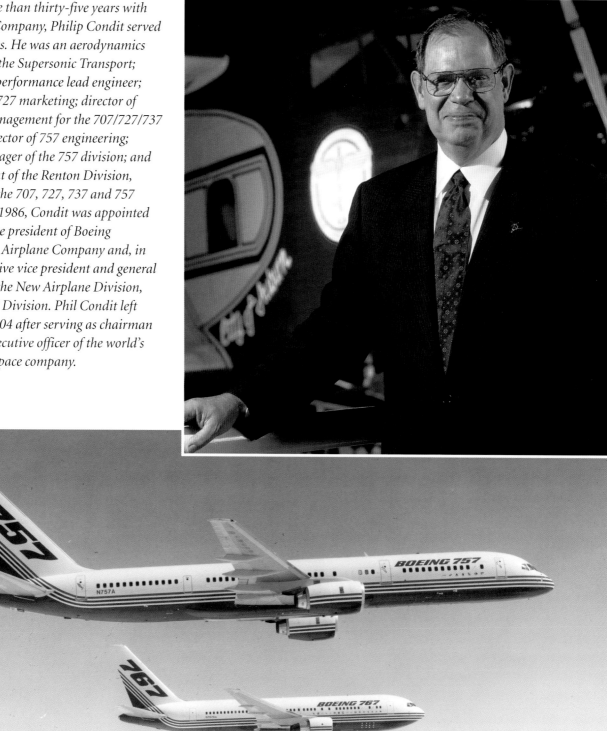

The Boeing 757 and 767 were developed in tandem and entered service within five months of one another, the 767 with United in September 1982 and the 757 with Eastern in January 1983. Both airliners are twin-engined, designed to be fuel efficient, and both have a glass cockpit instrument display. The flight decks of the two are so similar that a pilot cleared to fly one is qualified to fly the other. Designed to replace the tri-jet 727, the 757 has a standard single-aisle configuration in the passenger cabin. The 767 has a larger, two-aisle cabin, which in the 767-300 model has seating for 269 in two classes or 218 in three classes.

many versions, some of which became available for transoceanic operations. This capability was acquired because of the increased power and reliability of jet engines. By the mid-1980s, the regulation requiring long over-water commercial routes to be flown by four-engined aircraft was an anachronism, and it was challenged with the extended-range 767s. Before long, the rule stating that twin-engined aircraft should never be more than ninety minutes from a diversion airfield was relaxed to 180 minutes, and that left few places in the world outside the reach of the new airliners. Operators of Boeing and Airbus twins quickly took advantage of the change, British Airways, United and TWA using them routinely on transoceanic flights.

Even with the introduction of two new types, Boeing found that its traditional customers were looking for a third, bigger than the 767 but smaller than the 747. Stretched versions of the 767 could not be made to satisfy operators' requirements, so Boeing's team went back to the drawing board. The Boeing 777 became an official project in October 1990 and the first flight took place less than four years later, on June 12, 1994. A wide-bodied twin with a maximum of 440 seats, the 777 weighed over 500,000 pounds at takeoff and, like its Airbus 330 competitor, was powered by two enormous turbofans of some 80,000

pounds thrust each. It entered service with United in May 1995, and other early users were British Airways, All Nippon, Malaysia, and Thai International. By the late 1990s, the stretched 777-300 version was capable of carrying up to 400 passengers in a three-class arrangement and flying them from New York to Tokyo in fourteen hours. It was an obvious option for those operators who were looking for an airliner to replace their older model 747s, and it offered at least 30 percent lower seat/mile costs.

Soviets Large and Largest

Ilyushin answered the arrival of wide-bodied airliners in the West with one of his own. Work began on the 350-seat Il-86 (Camber) in 1971, and it flew in 1976. Competent though it was aerodynamically, it was let down by its low-bypass Samara turbofans, and its performance was disappointing, with fuel consumption very high and range well down on target figures. Ilyushin tried again with the Il-96 in the 1980s, shortening the Il-86 fuselage, adding new wings and introducing fly-by-wire controls. After the collapse of the Soviet Union, it became possible to fit Pratt & Whitney engines and Western electronics, improving the type's prospects in the world market.

Development of the twin-engined Tu-204 medium-range airliner started in 1985, when it became clear that a replacement for the Tu-154 would be needed in the Warsaw Pact countries in the 1990s. From the beginning, the Tu-204 looked similar in design and size to the Boeing 757.

TOP *The Antonov An-124 Ruslan was developed both as a strategic military freighter and for use by Aeroflot for the carriage of bulky and oversize cargoes. Features include nose and tail cargo doors to enable simultaneous loading and unloading, a twenty-four-wheel undercarriage allowing operations from rough landing strips, the ability to kneel for easier front loading, and a fly-by-wire control system. The first prototype An-124 flew on December 26, 1982.*
BOTTOM *The An-124's capacious hold makes it useful for a variety of charters. Here it is seen swallowing the 81-foot American yacht Boomerang. In 1993, an An-124 transported a 124-tonne (273,400 pound) powerplant generator and its associated weight-spreading cradle, a total payload weight of 132.4 tonnes (291,940 pounds).*

At the end of powered flight's first century, the world's largest aircraft was the Antonov An-225 Mria (mria being Russian for dream). It was designed to meet the need to transport large items for the Soviet space program. This huge aircraft is 290 feet across the wing and 276 feet long; even the tailplane spans 108 feet. The prototype An-225 first flew on December 21, 1988, and in March 1989, set 106 world and class records in one flight from Kiev, taking off at a weight in excess of 1,100,000 pounds.

Problems with the Perm PS-90A engines slowed the project down and the Tu-204-100 did not enter scheduled service until 1997. After the fall of the Soviet Union, the Tu-204-120 acquired Rolls-Royce RB-511s and this version attracted orders from airlines both in the CIS and the Middle East. In the early 1990s, Tupolev also recognized the need to replace the ageing Tu-134, and that led to the Tu-334, another rear-engined design that was demonstrated during the 1999 Moscow Air and Kosmos Salon.

The Soviet equivalent of the USAF's C-5 was the An-124 Ruslan (NATO Condor), which first flew in 1982. Although primarily a military transport, the Ruslan is used by commercial operators who have found its gigantic size useful in moving awkward outsize loads. (See the fifth volume of *Aviation Century,* Chapter 1, "The Haulers.") The upward-opening nose door and rear loading ramp give access to a cargo hold cleared for lifting a civil payload of 264,000 pounds and carrying it for 2,500 miles. On July 26, 1985, an An-124 set a series of world records in taking a huge payload of 374,000 pounds to 35,000 feet. Despite their great size, An-124s are capable of flying into unimproved sites (such as frozen Siberian tundra) and are operated as a cooperative venture by Russian and Western European cargo airlines through joint business schemes, carrying oil-drilling and earth-moving equipment to places otherwise almost unreachable.

Smaller Fry

At the lower end of the airliner scale are a number of aircraft seating fewer than 100 passengers, although at least one has been stretched to carry more. The Antonov 72 and the later An-74 (Coaler) first made an appearance in the 1970s. They are medium-sized STOL transport aircraft of unusual design, built to operate in the Arctic and other remote regions. Two jet engines are mounted above and ahead of the high wing, making use of their thrust to add lift. Civilian An-74 operators include gas and oil producers.

In the West, an almost equally unusual design was the first commercial aircraft born of British Aerospace after its formation in 1977. The BAe 146 was resuscitated from the shelved HS 146 project of 1972, eventually flying in 1981. It challenged airliner convention by being high-winged and relatively small but four-engined, with an original seating capacity of eighty-four passengers. Four 7,000-pound-thrust Avco-Lycoming turbofans were chosen and their very low decibel readings made the 146 especially valuable for operating into noise-restricted city airports. The launch customer was Dan-Air, and early deliveries followed to Ansett in Australia, and to Air Wisconsin, Pacific Southwest and Air Cal in the United States. Subsequent modifications created a family of small airliners and freighters, including the Avro RJ (Regional Jet) series, which is supplied with more powerful Textron Lycoming LF507 engines and can seat up to 116 passengers. The 146 family has sold steadily year by year since its introduction, and close to 400 of all versions were in service at the end of the century, flown by over 100 operators, ranging from Sabena to Air China, and from Lufthansa to Air Malta.

More recent entrants in the feeder-liner market have included Bombardier of Canada's popular Canadair RJ, a rear-engined twin with a T-tail, which first flew in 1991 and has since been developed into a seventy-seater, used by such operators as Comair and Sky West in the United States, and Lauda Air and Tyrolean Airways in Europe. This was followed in 1995 by the similarly designed Embraer 145 from Brazil, ordered by Continental Express and AMR-Eagle, and in 1998 by the Dornier 328JET, a straightforward modification adding Pratt & Whitney turbofans to Fairchild-Dornier's earlier thirty-three-seat turboprop 328. Plans for the new jet included stretching the fuselage to accommodate up to ninety passengers.

Familiarity and Apathy

The number of airliner types and variations introduced to the flying public in the latter part of the 20th century is vast and bewildering. The situation is made no simpler by the laws of aerodynamics and the marketplace, which tend to drive designers toward similar solutions to problems and thereby into producing aircraft that are similar in both looks and performance. At the same time, air travel has become an everyday affair, and huge numbers of people worldwide from all walks of life have become accustomed to flying. One of the great benefits of the jet revolution has been the dramatic fall in airliner fatal accident rates. Unsettling though every accident is, the general public has come to accept that flying is indeed "the safest way to travel." (In the late 1950s, there were more than forty fatal airline accidents reported worldwide for every million departures. Forty years later the rate was down to less than two. See the fifth volume of *Aviation Century*, Chapter 2.)

The first of the British Aerospace family of quiet regional jet airliners, the BAe 146-100 made its first flight on September 3, 1981. Total production of BAe 146 variants was 394, including 221 BAe 146s, 170 Avro RJs, and three Avro RJXs. BAe ZE701, seen here, is an aircraft flown by 32 (The Royal) Squadron, RAF, which is tasked with providing air transport to members of the Royal Family, government ministers, and senior military commanders.

Since the experience may now be considered almost mundane and airliners thought of as no more than lookalike (and often uncomfortable) aerial buses, it is at least probable that the majority of passengers neither know nor particularly care what type of aircraft they fly in. That is a pity, because, from the An-72 to the Boeing 747, jet airliners are genuine marvels of design and production, the magic carpets of the 20th century and world-shrinkers extraordinary.

The Executives

For the executives of wealthy corporations or those of the rich and famous who can afford the luxury of traveling by air whenever and wherever they wish, without suffering the inconvenience of abiding by airline schedules and routes, business aircraft are an inviting option. Even so, executive aviation took a long time to evolve. It was not until after WWII that aircraft were produced specifically to fill the "executive" niche, although events during that conflict did set the scene for later developments. Managers of companies engaged in essential war work took to borrowing small military transports such as the Beech Expeditor and the Avro Anson when visiting their dispersed factories. The advantages of the practice were made readily apparent, and it seemed logical to continue flying for business reasons once the fighting stopped.

The first British aircraft to appear in executive form was the twin-piston de Havilland Dove 2, a six-seat version of the small airliner, first marketed in 1947. Together with its larger stablemate, the four-engined Heron, it continued in production until the 1960s. Contemporary British types, built in much smaller numbers, were the Percival Prince and the Short Sealand amphibian. In the United States, the prototype high-wing Aero Commander 520 first flew in 1948, and in 1951 gave an impressive demonstration of its

The Hawker Siddeley HS 125 was one of the most successful of the first-generation executive jets. It was originally started a de Havilland project before that company became part of the Hawker Siddeley group. As the D.H.125, it flew for the first time on August 13, 1962. Total sales of HS 125s up to and including the Series 600 reached 358. ABOVE *A Hawker Siddeley 125-400 in JAL markings.* TOP *Completed HS 125s awaiting delivery. Several are in RAF markings, showing that they are examples of the military version known as the Dominie.*

single-engined performance by flying from Oklahoma City to Washington, D.C., with the port propeller removed! Thus proven, the Commander 520 became the forerunner of a very successful line of broadly similar light transports. A USAF version, the U-4B, was used by President Dwight D. Eisenhower from 1956 to 1960 for short trips. It was the smallest *Air Force One,* and the first presidential aircraft to carry the familiar blue-and-white paint scheme. Aero Commanders remained in production successively with Aero, Rockwell and Israel Aircraft Industries for the rest of the century, adapted to take more powerful piston, turboprop and jet powerplants in turn. The limited demand for an executive amphibian was satisfied by the handbuilt Grumman Mallard; it was marketed as a luxury air yacht, and only fifty-nine were built.

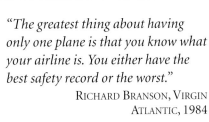

"The greatest thing about having only one plane is that you know what your airline is. You either have the best safety record or the worst."
RICHARD BRANSON, VIRGIN ATLANTIC, 1984

Turbo Execs

When the Turbo Commander flew in the 1960s, a number of other companies jostled to capture a piece of the executive aircraft market with turboprop-powered machines. In the decade that followed, the U.S. "big three" — Beech, Cessna and Piper — became dominant players. Their designs, seating between four and a dozen passengers in considerable comfort, were manufactured by the hundreds. Beech began by building on its success with the piston-powered Twin Bonanza and Queen Air, introducing the first of a series of turboprop designs under the name King Air in 1964. Perennially popular, these versatile machines remained in production in one form or another for the rest of the century, more than 5,000 being produced. Cessna came late to the executive turboprop scene, staying with reliable piston-engined twins such as the 400 series (including the 414 Chancellor and 421 Golden Eagle) and the Titan Ambassador, and then jumping straight to jets before challenging Beech with the Conquest turboprops in 1977. Piper, too, established a line of twin-pistons, notably the PA-31 Navajo, before moving on to the Cheyenne turboprops in the early 1970s. The Cheyenne 400, which entered service in 1984, was capable of cruising above 40,000 feet while carrying eight passengers in great comfort for some 1,500 miles.

Some attempts were made to produce executive turboprops outside the United States, but few met with much success in the face of such strong American competition. In the 1960s DINFIA of Argentina built the IA 50 Guarani II, and at least one of these appeared in executive form for use by the president of Argentina. In Italy, Piaggio designed the gull-winged P.166, powered by two "pusher" turboprops, and Mitsubishi of Japan introduced the Mu-2 utility transport, which was available with executive fittings. Two very successful lines of turboprop light transports were launched in Brazil and Britain during the late 1960s, each of them in various forms. Embraer brought out the Bandeirante and Handley Page (later Scottish Aviation and then British Aerospace) the Jetstream. Although better known in their roles as commuter airliners and military aircraft, both were offered in versions suitable for large corporations.

Arrival of the Jet Set

The business executive aircraft really came into its own when it was fitted with small jet engines. Here was the ultimate symbol of corporate success, a machine that could soar above the common herd of commercial airliners, carrying its well-heeled passengers directly to their chosen destinations at high subsonic speeds in pampered luxury. At first it was thought that jet engines would be too thirsty and jet aircraft too costly to operate for them to be practical propositions for even the richest customers, but the French Morane-Saulnier firm tested the market anyway, edging into the project via work already done on a jet trainer. The MS-760 Paris was no more than a four-seat high-speed communications machine and not very sumptuous, but a number were sold in the United States by Beech and several other companies took note. (When Henry Timken of Canton, Ohio, bought a Morane-Saulnier Paris in 1958, it was the first sale of a jet aircraft to a civilian for business use.) Boosted by a USAF requirement for a VIP transport, Lockheed and North American were the first to produce an executive jet worthy of the name.

Lockheed's efforts, led by designer Kelly Johnson, produced the Jetstar, a sleek ten-seater that established the classic business jet form. When it first flew on September 4,

Raytheon purchased BAe's Corporate Jets Division in 1993, and production of the executive aircraft range was transferred to Wichita, Kansas. Aircraft manufactured in the United States carry the Hawker name, recalling the British company that formed part of BAe. The Hawker Horizon, which first flew in August 2001, is considered a "super mid-size" business jet that seats up to twelve passengers and can fly nonstop across North America in all weather. Aircraft production has become typically an international business, and the Horizon is no exception. The wings, for example, are manufactured by Fuji Heavy Industries in Japan and transported to Raytheon in Wichita for final aircraft assembly.

1957, the Jetstar was powered by two Bristol Siddeley Orpheus engines (4,850 pounds each) mounted at the rear of the fuselage, but by the time it entered service these had been replaced by four Pratt & Whitney JT12A-6s (2,400 pounds thrust each). North American went for something smaller and designed the twin-engined Sabreliner, which first flew in September 1958 and was immediately ordered into quantity production for the USAF as the T-39. By the mid-1960s, two other U.S. manufacturers were in the executive market. Aero introduced the Jet Commander, a practical mid-winged machine that performed and sold well, while Grumman aimed higher with the larger Gulfstream II, the first genuinely transcontinental business jet.

At the same time, on the other side of the Atlantic, de Havilland in Britain and Dassault in France both showed interest in developing small business jets. The D.H.125 began taking shape in 1959, but did not fly until 1962, by when the company had merged with the Hawker Siddeley group, so the aircraft was sold as the HS 125, and later, after a further merger produced British Aerospace, as the BAe 125. Progressively modified, the 125 design was the basis for one of the world's most successful business jet lines. In 1993, an exercise in product rationalization by British Aerospace led the company to sell off its small civilian jet division. By happy coincidence, Raytheon (which had acquired Beech) was looking for a proven jet to partner the already successful King Air turboprop. A deal was agreed, and responsibility for the 125 crossed the Atlantic. Manufacturing initially stayed in the United Kingdom, but

in 1996 the production line moved to Wichita, Kansas, where, in a gesture toward the aircraft's origins, new models such as the 800XP were marketed under the name Hawker. Each aircraft is supplied with a custom-built interior, holding the promise of unashamed luxury in a passenger cabin with stand-up headroom. In-flight access to the baggage compartment is available through a full-width washroom at the rear. The cockpit is equipped with the latest avionics, including flat-panel instrument displays. An unusual feature, praised by Hawker pilots, is the handlebar that replaces the conventional yoke or wheel on each control column. The flagship Hawker Horizon can cruise above 40,000 feet at Mach .84, and has a 3,400-mile range, giving it comfortable transoceanic capability. The 800XP and the Horizon still bear the evidence of their ancestry, but are clearly capable of carrying the Hawker line into the 21st century.

In France, the Dassault company took the wing of its celebrated Mystère fighter and designed a business jet fuselage to mount it on. The result was the Mystère Falcon 20, the forerunner of a perennially successful line. With the Falcon 50 of the 1970s, Dassault offered a larger three-engined variation sometimes called the mini-727, an aircraft that remained in production for two decades and was then reborn, being progressively upgraded with new engines and avionics. Still larger is the Falcon 900 series first introduced in the 1980s, a mini-widebody that in its 900EX version can carry a dozen passengers more than 4,000 miles thanks to a supercritical wing optimized for minimum transonic drag.

Meanwhile, in a relatively short-lived but original venture of the 1960s, HFB in West Germany produced the Hansa, which generally followed the executive jet pattern except for the remarkable fifteen-degree forward sweep of its wings. Most of those built were operated by the Luftwaffe, some as VIP transports.

Little Hot Rods

At least one businessman thought that the 125s and Falcons were too grandiose by far. Bill Lear described them scornfully as the modern equivalent of "royal barges," and set out to produce something more practical. Lear was an unusual genius. He dropped out of high school after six weeks, worked odd jobs, learned to fly and started working on inventions that eventually earned him more than 150 patents, ranging from the first autopilot for a jet aircraft to the eight-track tape player to the first brushless electric motor. He made and lost fortunes four times in his life, and collected several honorary degrees along the way. In the mid-1950s, he became intrigued by the

Swiss FFA P-16 fighter project, and was inspired to establish the Swiss American Aircraft Corporation in 1960 with the aim of manufacturing a relatively simple high-speed executive jet, less costly to buy and operate than any then on the market. A smaller fuselage was at the heart of his design. His argument was that people did not stand up in cars, and they need not do so when traveling by air, so headroom was unnecessary. When it made its appearance in 1963 at the new Lear Jet Industries company facility in Wichita, the Learjet prototype's slim, rakish good looks caught the public imagination like no other. In no time at all, the name Learjet became the term popularly used for executive jets generally, whatever their origins. Highly visible figures from the entertainment world, including Frank Sinatra, were early customers. Golfer Arnold Palmer used a Learjet 36 to put his name into the aviation record books, completing a 20,000 mile round-the-world flight in less than fifty-seven and a half hours during 1976. Bill Lear moved on to other things in 1969, after Gates Rubber acquired a controlling

The design of the Learjet 23 was based on that of a Swiss strike-fighter project, the AFA P-16. The Learjet was a significant technological advance and an aircraft that had a marked effect on the creation of business jet aviation. On October 7, 1963, the prototype Learjet 23, N801L (seen here), made its first flight. This original airplane flew 194 hours before it was destroyed following a test flight from Wichita on June 4, 1964. The aircraft made an emergency belly landing in wheat field after a simulated left engine failure on takeoff. The spoilers had been extended inadvertently.

interest in his company, but the new owners kept the name and continued to develop the aircraft.

Bill Lear's fertile imagination was still in high gear when he left Lear Jet. He began work on another business jet, the Learstar 600, a design that was taken over in 1976 by Canadair and became the Challenger. When it first flew in November 1978, the Challenger brought widebody comfort to executive aviation and was immediately popular on that account. In 1986, Bombardier, a Canadian industrial company, acquired Canadair, and then in 1990 both lines initiated by Bill Lear came together when Gates sold Learjet to Bombardier also. Challenger development has continued and the Learjet family has gone on to retain a solid share of the lighter executive jet market. The Learjet 31 and 45 both possess Learjet's legendary performance, leaping off the ground like fighters and climbing to altitudes as high as 51,000 feet.

The Middle Ground

As each of the companies involved in the struggle for the executive jet market sought to steal a march on the opposition by modifying their aircraft to go faster, further and higher, one latecomer to the field saw an opportunity to slip into the middle ground between the racy swept-wing jets and the utilitarian turboprops. Cessna's Citation, which flew for the first time in September 1969, was a practical straight-wing machine, easy to fly and up to 100 knots slower than its contemporaries. It was an immediate success, surprising those who had thought that a slower business jet would not sell. Cessna reaped the benefits of having seen an unfilled market niche and delivered well over 500 Citation Is and IIs by the end of the 1970s. In time, Cessna recognized that its established customers were ready to move up and the Citation family offered some options,

Cessna became the first of the big three American light aircraft manufacturers (Piper, Beech and Cessna) to develop a jet-powered executive aircraft. The Cessna Citation I prototype (N500CC, seen here) first flew on September 15, 1969. Production of the Citation I ceased in 1985, after a production run of more than 690 aircraft.

The Gulfstream V is the largest of the Gulfstream line of corporate transports, designed to fly intercontinental distances. The first delivery to a customer was on July 1, 1997, and by September the G-V had set thirty-six point-to-point, time-to-climb and altitude records. The most important changes from earlier Gulfstreams are the advanced wing design and new BMW Rolls-Royce BR-710 turbofan engines. The wing is built by Northrop Grumman, and is optimized for high-speed flight. A G-V delivered in September 1997 was the thousandth Gulfstream built.

describing them as "The Sensible Citations." The lighter end of the line grew more powerful, as in the Ultra model, and then, in the Excel, acquired a "stand-up" cabin, and swept the wings a little. There were larger models, too, such as the elegant Sovereign and the Citation X, described with some justification as "the fastest business jet ever built."

Spoiled for Choice

Almost half a century after the marketing of the first executive jet, there is an embarrassment of riches in the flying businessman's marketplace. The aircraft available are increasingly constructed using carbon-fiber materials and are powered by small fan jet engines of dramatically improved efficiency. Their "glass cockpits" carry the most sophisticated avionics suites by Honeywell or Collins, and their passenger cabins exude luxury from their leather seats and exotic wood paneling. Bars, galleys, workstations, communications suites, washrooms and baggage access ensure that executives can work and rest as much as they please in the air, and are able to arrive well groomed at their destination. At the lightest end of the scale, the VisionAire Vantage (takeoff weight 7,500 pounds) and the Citation CJ1 (10,000 pounds) offer moderate performance and cozily snug interiors, but they are relatively cheap and, since they can be operated by a single pilot, have an appeal for those businessmen who prefer to sit in the pilot's seat themselves. The heavy end

The Gulfstream V features state-of-the-art avionics, including a "glass cockpit" of computer screens instead of traditional instruments, and a HUD (Head-Up Display) projecting essential flight information onto the windscreen. The HUD allows the pilot to keep looking forward rather than down at the instrument panel during an approach to landing, particularly in bad weather.

has long since grown beyond the size of the larger Falcons, with aircraft in the mini-airliner class promising the ultimate executive experience. The Gulfstream V and Bombardier's Global Express both have maximum takeoff weights above 90,000 pounds and can travel over 6,000 miles unrefueled, pampering their eight passengers unmercifully in the process. Even they, however, are not at the executive pinnacle. With capacities for opulence limited only by the imagination, the Boeing 737 Business Jet and the Airbus A319 Corporate Jet hold the promise of being the ultimate executive status symbols, and a far cry from Morane-Saulnier's tentative venture of 1954.

POLITICAL AND SOCIAL
EFFECTS OF AVIATION

It was clear from the very beginning of air travel that an airline was a potent symbol of nationhood. A country with an airline could be seen to have taken a firm grip on the 20th century and to be visibly demonstrating that it was capable of using modern technology. Its citizens took pride in the achievements of its aviators and in the machines that carried their flag abroad. In the early days of commercial aviation, airlines such as Pan American, Imperial Airways and Air France were recognized as the national standard bearers of major powers, representing much more than mere means of transport. After WWII, as the colonial empires collapsed and the number of independent states in the United Nations rose from the original fifty-one in 1945 to 189 at the dawn of the 21st century, an airline became an essential part of a new nation's freshly woven fabric, as vital to its status in the world as a flag or a seat alongside the powerful in the U.N.'s General Assembly. Great names such as Pan American and Imperial Airways might be consigned to history, but Air Maldives could be seen with American Airlines at Frankfurt, and Air Mauritius joined British Airways in serving Singapore.

Prestige on the Wing

The breakup of the Soviet Union was quickly followed by the appearance of several new airlines, spawned by Aeroflot and bearing names such as Lithuanian Airlines, Air Armenia, and Air Uzbekistan. The airlines of small but rich states — Kuwait Airways, Qatar Airways, Royal Brunei — were lavishly equipped with the latest Airbus or Boeing aircraft to span the world to the great capital cities, while Air Vanuatu reached out to Australia, and Air Malawi got as far as Kenya and South Africa. From Iceland to Vietnam, and from Argentina to Japan, airliners carry national names abroad, mingling them together in airports worldwide, some perpetuating the image of their home country's well-established prowess, others showing the flag and, at the very least, holding hopes for the future.

Evidence that national pride is closely associated with airline activity is not too hard to find. Wild British enthusiasm over the launching of BOAC's Comet services was matched only by the depth of the despair that followed the airliner's disastrous withdrawal in 1954. (See the fifth volume of *Aviation Century*, Chapter 2, "Machines Can Be Fragile.") American people were understandably proud to see Pan Am leading the world by introducing the first two eras of Boeing dominance with the 707 and 747, and the Soviets have always been keen to show that their technology can hold some surprises for the West, occasionally pulling aircraft such as Aeroflot's Tu-104 and Tu-144 out of their aeronautical magician's hat to seize the headlines in the world's press. British Airways and Air France have between them operated perhaps the ultimate in 20th-century flying prestige symbols, the Concorde. An economic disaster for both countries, Concorde has nevertheless been a success as a technological achievement and as a national flag-waver. Celebrated as the elite transatlantic carriage for the rich and famous, Concorde's unflattering economics were overcome by its glamorous supersonic image and did not discourage its operators from using it as their flagship, Air France proclaiming that they were "Making the sky the best place on Earth," while British Airways modestly announced that "The British simply know how to travel!"

Diplomatic Moves

Former U.S. Secretary of State Henry Kissinger coined the term "shuttle diplomacy" to describe his method of negotiating between countries in dispute by moving rapidly from one to another by air for face-to-face discussions, conveying opposing views and stating U.S. foreign policy while seeking compromise solutions. At the time of the 1973 Arab/Israeli War, Kissinger made multiple visits to Moscow, Tel Aviv and Cairo in the course of bringing about an agreed ceasefire. Subsequently employed by many diplomats and envoys, the method became routine and the accepted way of making high-level personal contact. Madeline Albright repeated the Middle East round during her tenure as Secretary of State, and Alexander Haig performed a prodigious, if unsuccessful, series of "shuttles" in a Boeing 707 during the 1982 Falklands War, flying some 33,000 miles in twelve days between Washington, London and Buenos Aires. Shortly thereafter, the British Foreign Secretary, Francis Pym, had an easier time of it, using Concorde for his dashes across the Atlantic.

In the Victorian era, the Viceroy of India might not expect to get an answer to a question put to the British government until several months had passed. Changes of government and of policy were similarly delayed. Summit

Perhaps the most famous Boeing 707 is USAF 26000. This venerable aircraft, known as Air Force One whenever an American President was on board, carried eight Presidents during its career. This is the airplane that flew President Kennedy to Dallas on November 22, 1963, and later that day, brought President Johnson back to Washington along with Kennedy's casket. The 707s in the Presidential Fleet also were used extensively as aerial shuttle diplomacy became a trademark of American statesmen such as Henry Kissinger, Alexander Haig, James Baker and Madeline Albright. USAF 26000 was retired to the National Museum of the United States Air Force on May 20, 1998.

meetings between heads of state or foreign ministers were almost unknown in the 19th century. Even in the 1930s, traveling beyond their own frontiers was a major event for politicians, and not until Neville Chamberlain's return from his infamous Munich conference with Hitler in 1938 was an aircraft (a Lockheed 14) notably associated with a diplomatic mission. Secret though it was at the time, another notable flight occurred in January 1942, when Churchill crossed the Atlantic in the Boeing 314 flying boat *Berwick* for a meeting with President Roosevelt, taking two days each way with overnight stops in Bermuda. Commercial jet aviation changed all that, making it possible to hold international summit meetings involving heads of state from all over the world, and allowing "shuttle" diplomats to move from country to country in hours rather than days or weeks.

> *"The first rule is — change the rules."*
> FRED SMITH, FEDEX

In the week following the terrorist attacks on New York and Washington in September 2001, British Prime Minister Tony Blair took full advantage of jet aircraft in helping to build an anti-terrorist coalition. After talks with African leaders in the United Kingdom and a telephone conversation with Chinese Premier Jiang Zemin on Tuesday, he had talks in Berlin with Chancellor Gerhard Schroeder on Wednesday, saw President Chirac in Paris on Thursday morning, flew to Washington and New York later on Thursday, and attended the European Union summit meeting in Brussels on Friday. Modern satellite communications may provide instantaneous and secure electronic links, but for politicians, diplomats and businessmen the ability to meet personally remains important. For better or worse, the jet airliner changed the face of politics and business. (See the fifth volume of *Aviation Century*, Chapter 2, "Suicide as an Act of War.")

Mass Migration

Beneficial though its effects on international diplomacy may have been, some of jet travel's other effects have not always been so favorable. The "economic" migration of highly skilled people from one country to another is now accomplished by air more easily than it used to be and is generally welcomed at the receiving end, although the losing nation is not always happy if the migration is evidence of a "brain drain." Quite different effects can follow the introduction of migrant worker populations to solve a labor shortage in the host country, or the catastrophic displacement of huge numbers of refugees after conflict or environmental disaster. Outsize jet transport aircraft have made sizeable movements of people far easier to undertake, but more difficult for the receiving nation's airports to handle. Human migration by air on such a large scale can make things difficult for any nation, but they pale in significance beside the problem of dealing with the rapid global spread of disease.

The vast increase in worldwide air travel in the jet age and the growth of airborne trade in food have facilitated the migration of disease-carrying organisms from one continent to another. Modern air travel makes national borders porous and the distance between nations irrelevant when it comes to infectious diseases. Millions of people every month travel to foreign countries for reasons of business, pleasure, religion and study. To take the experience of the United States as an example, many previously remote areas are now less than a day away by air for American travelers. According to the International Air Travel Association, there were an estimated 78.8 million scheduled passengers between international destinations and the United States in 1993. By the year 2010, this figure is expected to reach 226 million. Frequently, travelers have unknowingly imported diseases that were previously not present in the United States, among them HIV/AIDS. Yellow fever, hepatitis and other often drug resistant viral infections have also been associated with international travel. Tuberculosis, meningitis, cholera, salmonella, influenza and gastroenteritis are among the ailments that can be transmitted to airliner passengers in flight.

Air travel is a particularly potent force for spreading global disease, especially since it is now possible for people to reach the other side of the world in far less time than the incubation period for many ailments. At the same time, adventure tourism is drawing people to fly to ever more remote locations, increasing the chance that microbes will be introduced to vulnerable populations. Outbreaks of the Ebola virus in Zaire caused global alarm as people realized that the disease was only one airliner flight from most of the world's major cities. In October 1999, it was confirmed that at least five people in the New York area died from a new strain of the African West Nile virus. Until then, the rare mosquito-borne disease had never been seen in the

Western hemisphere. As Nobel laureate Joshua Lederberg has said: "No matter how selfish our motives, we can no longer be indifferent to the suffering of others. The microbe that felled one child in a distant continent yesterday can reach yours today, and seed a global pandemic tomorrow."

Spraying and Dumping

The first experiments with aerial crop-dusting were carried out in the early 1920s against the boll weevil, an insect which was destroying American cotton crops. Huff-Daland Dusters developed the technique while based in Louisiana, flying operations in the growing seasons of both the southern United States and Peru. (Huff-Daland moved on to flying passengers from Monroe, Louisiana, forming the Delta Air Service to fly routes between Dallas and Birmingham. This small company was the ancestor of Delta Airlines.) Most of their aircraft were Huff-Daland Petrels, powered by single Liberty engines and able to lift up to 1,500 pounds of calcium arsenate. Success against the boll weevil led them on to other things, such as mosquito control. However, the widespread use of agricultural aircraft did not begin until after WWII, when large numbers of surplus aircraft were adapted for the role.

The first aircraft designed specifically for agricultural use was the Piper Pawnee of 1959, which was an immediate success. Spraying pesticides from very low level calls for a highly maneuverable aircraft, able to lift large chemical loads, either liquid or solid, and distribute them quickly and evenly. It is also important that the machine should be simply constructed, easy to maintain and to disassemble, so that it can be thoroughly cleaned to guard against corrosion. The Pawnee was the forerunner of many specialized agricultural aircraft, including the Cessna Agwagon, Grumman Ag-Cat, and Rockwell Thrush Commander, all of them curiously humped creatures with a loftily placed cockpit from which the pilot views the world. Later developments of these designs by such companies as Air Tractor and the Ayres Corporation were powered by various Pratt & Whitney turboprops and had much improved performance, which enabled them to lift some 500 gallons of liquid pesticide or 4,000 pounds of dry chemical.

By the end of the century, there were about 6,500 aircraft dedicated to agricultural use in the United States, and they accounted for over 65 percent of the chemicals applied to American crops. What was more, over 90 percent of the rice grown in the United States was seeded by air — more than 2.5 million acres per year. One hundred acres per hour can be seeded by one aircraft. The pilots employed in such work were generally very experienced, with an average age of thirty-eight and more than 5,000 flying hours in their logbooks. The story in other parts of the world was very similar. It is claimed by the National Agricultural Aviation Association in the United States that without pesticides the world food

Its chemical tanks for crop dusting refilled at the Flagler Aviation Service in eastern Colorado, a Piper Pawnee prepares for takeoff. These photographs were made in 1971 and illustrate a typical operation of the agricultural aviation services throughout the western USA at that time.

supply would be at least 40 percent smaller than it is, the cost of food generally would be more than 50 percent greater, and the food quality would be noticeably poorer.

More controversial spraying activities are those meant to destroy plants rather than protect them. Questions raised about the morality of using Agent Orange in Vietnam (see the fifth volume of *Aviation Century,* Chapter 1, "On the Trail") were renewed when the "war against drugs" got into its stride and many governments adopted a policy of spray-ing spraying coca and marijuana fields, particularly in South and Central America. In countries such as Belize and Colombia, the operations had a distinctly military character: likely targets were pinpointed by U.S. satellites, and then suspect growing areas were reconnoitered by aircraft equipped with multispectrum cameras that locked on to the infrared signature of the coca leaves. Attack missions usually involved three or more cropdusters flying abreast over wide "spray paths," with gunships high above to cover the mission. Occasionally targeting mistakes were made or an aircraft malfunction forced the spraying pilot to dump his chemical load outside the target area, drawing vocifer-ous complaints from farmers of legitimate crops. However, there is no doubt that large areas of coca were destroyed during operations that were professionally challenging and dangerous. As one pilot described it, "Flying fast at tree-top level and worrying about gunfire — it's not the same as spraying rice, you know!"

Firefighting from the air demands rather larger quanti-ties of liquid than crop-sprayers can deliver, and therefore much more sizeable aircraft. For large forest fires, aerial attack may be the only means of slowing a fire or stopping it from spreading. Both fixed-wing aircraft and helicopters are used, each equipped with a tank that usually carries a mixture of water and a fire-retardant chemical known to be harmless to the environment.

Aerial firefighting operations have become common worldwide, from South America to Indonesia, and from southern France to China, and those conducted in the forests of Canada, the western United States and Russia, where multiple massive fires can rage out of control for weeks, can be on a very large scale. An Ontario Lands and Forests Beaver aircraft made the first recorded fire-bombing attack in Canada in the 1950s, dropping water-filled paper bags on a fire north of Sault Ste. Marie, Ontario. To begin with, aircraft were considered too expen-sive and were used only when all other measures had failed, but forest fire fighters soon found that the key to efficient fire suppression is to hit each potentially dangerous fire while it is still small. It is the aircraft's ability to attack fast, hard and often, in the most difficult terrain, that makes it the firefighter's best initial attack resource.

There are two principal types of firefighting aircraft. "Scoopers" are amphibians or flying boats capable of scooping water on the fly from a lake or river, injecting chemical into the load and dropping it on the fire as a smothering foam. "Scoopers" can attack fires for hours at a time, scooping and dropping their loads as fast as they can shuttle to and from the nearest water. Tankers are land-

The Ilyushin Il-76 is a formidable aerial tanker. For firefighting and ocean oil-spill dispersal, it has a twin-tank system capable of delivering up to 67 tons of liquid at a time, covering an area almost 4,000 feet long by 300 feet wide when dropping from a height of 300 feet at 150 knots. Heat-seeking devices and associated computers help to ensure that the drop is aimed effectively.

The first aircraft ever built specifically for aerial firefighting was the Canadair CL-215, the prototype of which is seen here — appropriately registered as CF-FEU X. (Feu is French for fire.) It first flew in October 1967 and was produced until April 1990. In that time, 125 CL-215s were delivered to Canada, France, Greece, Italy, Spain, Thailand, Venezuela and Yugoslavia. The CL-215 can touch down on a lake and, while still on the move, scoop up some 1,400 gallons of water in about ten seconds.

based planes that carry fire-retardant chemicals to fires from mixing installations at strategically placed airfields. The Canadian authorities operate some 200 fixed-wing firefighting aircraft, including tankers such as the Firecat/Tracker and modified versions of the B-26, and scoopers such as the Canadair CL-215 and the Martin Mars. The Mars, a mighty machine recalling the great days of flying boats, is capable of dumping 7,200 gallons (about 29 tons) of foam-laden water on a fire in one pass.

The Russians, too, have developed aircraft with impressive firefighting capabilities. The Beriev 200 amphibian can take up to 12 tons of water on board during a fourteen-second scoop from a lake. However, the world heavyweight champion is the firefighting version of the Ilyushin 76. Used to disperse oil spills as well as to douse fires, the Il-76 can deliver up to 67 tons of liquid at a time, covering an area almost 4,000 feet long by 300 feet wide when dropping from a height of 300 feet at 150 knots. Heat-seeking devices and associated computers help to ensure that the drop is aimed effectively. Given international concerns about the global environment (a 1999 United Nations report attributed up to 40 percent of carbon dioxide and 38 percent of tropospheric ozone to "biomass burning"), such major firefighting weapons are likely to become increasingly significant.

Care and Protection

In such remote regions as the Australian outback or the heart of rural east Africa, a gunshot wound, meningitis or a heart attack can soon go from emergency to tragedy if not dealt with swiftly. Since its foundation in 1928 the Australian Royal Flying Doctor Service (RFDS) has grown into one of the most respected organizations in the world. Covering an area equivalent in size to Western Europe, it

operates from twenty bases, twenty-four hours a day, 365 days a year. After World War II, RFDS flew D.H.84 Dragons until 1951 when the service reequipped with trimotor D.H.A.3 Drovers. Since then, the aircraft used have included GAF Nomads, Piper Navajos, Beech King Airs and Pilatus PC-XIIs. When an emergency call is received, a doctor, nurse and pilot can be contacted in less than a minute and an aircraft can be airborne in little more than half an hour. Many Australians still live in isolated areas, but with the network of bases across Australia, no one anywhere is more than two hours away from medical help. Reacting to a typical call in the 1990s, an RFDS pilot flying a King Air from Kalgoorlie was told that a cattle station's little used airstrip was "in good condition, but has a few wildflowers on it." There were plenty of wildflowers all right, but nobody had mentioned the cattle. The pilot had to make "one pass downwind to shift the stock," before landing to let the doctor go to work. (The heroics of the RFDS were captured for television in *The Flying Doctor* series of programs, which became popular both in Australia and overseas.)

In East Africa, too, flying doctors respond to crises and give medical aid in areas that would otherwise have few or no medical services. With a control center in Nairobi, Kenya, the doctors are mostly involved in Kenya and Tanzania, but also reach out over a vast area to Somalia, Rwanda, Burundi, Ethiopia, Sudan, Congo, Uganda, Tanzania and Madagascar. Every year the service spends some 2,000 hours in the air and carries out about 600 emergency evacuations, responding to anything from wild animal attacks and traffic accidents to severe cases of infectious disease. A Cessna Citation is used to repatriate seriously sick or injured people to

Europe. For this service and others that link the people of remote areas to the benefits of modern medicine, the Australian example served as the model. As the medical equipment carried by the aircraft grew more sophisticated, so it became possible to provide much more than basic help. Serious illness and injury could be more effectively dealt with, serum could be shipped, and human organs transported. The seed of a system allowing medical aid to travel by air having been planted in Australia in 1928, it flourished and spread until, by the end of the century, air ambulance services had become a flourishing branch of general aviation all over the world, with flying doctors available to answer calls almost anywhere, from the oilfields of the North Sea to South Africa's diamond mines, and from Argentina's pampas to Siberia's Kamchatka Peninsula. In a remarkable extension of the flying doctor idea, airborne hospitals have been developed, with aircraft such as the Orbis DC-10 and the Lockheed TriStar Flying Hospital carrying self-sufficient operating theaters to aid underdeveloped countries.

Once the benefits of using aircraft to bring medical aid to people in remote areas were recognized, flying doctor and ambulance services developed quickly. Looking after the interests of the planet's wildlife took rather longer. Martin and Osa Johnson flew their Sikorsky S-38B and S-39C all over East Africa in the 1930s and their films helped to educate people about animals in the wild, but did little to encourage active conservation measures. Not until the 1950s was a serious aerial conservation effort made,

when Dr. Bernard Grzimek and his son Michael used a zebra-striped Dornier 27 in counting the plains animals in Tanganyika, plotting their main migration routes, and advising on boundaries for the Serengeti National Park. Their valiant efforts came to a tragic end when twenty-eight-year-old Michael was killed in a collision between his small aircraft and a vulture over the rim of the Ngorongoro Crater during the filming of a classic conservation documentary, *Serengeti Shall Not Die*. In later years, as poaching grew into a serious menace to wildlife, aircraft became major tools in the antipoaching war. Regular flights around national parks and game reserves are a most efficient form of patrolling and are a particularly effective deterrent when rangers on the ground act upon aerial reports of poacher incursions. Events in Ghana's Mole National Park were typical.

Poaching gangs there packed up and moved on in a hurry after being caught in the act by pilots of the *Bunny Hugger*, a Zenith STOL CH 701 aircraft. The rugged little two-seater, suitably modified to resist small-arms fire, flew regular antipoaching patrols under some highly irregular conditions in the African bush. The *Bunny Hugger* worked hard. The first takeoff of the day occurred shortly after sunrise and the final landing was usually at sunset. In between, there were hundreds of miles of antipoaching patrol flying to remote corners of the national park. Wildlife populations were monitored, too, with GPS fixes providing precise data on the locations of elephants, buffalos, antelopes and

Christian Moullec and his wife raised lesser white-fronted geese in an endangered species project in Sweden and trained the birds to accept his microlight aircraft as their leader. He then guided them from Sweden over a safe migration route to winter quarters on the Lower Rhine. It is hoped that the birds will pass on the safe route to future generations. Moullec often appears at air shows (here at Duxford, U.K., in 2003) flying with the geese to publicize species conservation. For him, flying with them is a rewarding experience: "They are so skillful in the air and I am so awkward."

baboons. There were also "courtesy calls" to villages well known as poacher havens, just to remind poachers that the risks of getting caught are notably increased with aircraft around. The introduction of light aircraft patrols to South Africa's Kruger National Park has been equally effective. Twelve rhinos were killed in the park in 1994, but not one was lost after the aircraft arrived the following year.

There are other ways in which aircraft influence wildlife conservation. Animals are transported from areas where they are under threat to more remote sites where they can be observed and protected. A family of eight South African elephants was flown to a game park near Luanda, in the first stage of Operation *Noah's Ark*, a project initiated to resettle animals away from the fighting in war-torn

The Bunny Hugger, *a Zenith STOL CH 701 aircraft, on anti-poacher patrol in Ghana's Mole National Park.*

Angola. In Tanzania, a black rhino sanctuary was set up at Mkomazi with four animals flown from Addo National Park in South Africa. A Russian Antonov 124 completed the 2,000-mile journey through the night, so as to minimize turbulence and lessen the rhinos' discomfort. North American wildlife sanctuaries move animals, too. Recalcitrant bears are tranquilized and hauled off to the hills in nets slung under helicopters, and rare whooping cranes are taught to migrate, not by their parents but by an ultralight aircraft. Biologist pilots trained a flock of young whooping cranes to follow an ultralight across seven states from Necedah National Wildlife Refuge in Wisconsin to Chassahowitska National Wildlife Refuge in Florida. In accomplishing that migratory feat, the cranes became the first of their species to have migrated across the skies of eastern North America for more than a century. This whooping crane migration experiment was modeled on the work of Canadian inventor Bill Lishman, who in the 1980s hatched a flock of Canada geese and taught them to follow an ultralight aircraft, a story told in the 1996 feature film *Fly Away Home*.

Service and Sales

Aircraft affect people's daily lives in dozens of supporting roles. In many countries, they are powerful law enforcement tools for police forces, and they are constantly involved in traffic control duties, checking on speeding motorists from the air or reporting on rush-hour traffic flow for local television and radio stations.

Surveys and patrols of all kinds are conducted from aircraft. Besides the human eyeball, an array of airborne sensors can be used to help in producing maps, detecting environmental change, monitoring the condition of forests, estimating land and marine wildlife populations, revealing archaeological sites, locating the Earth's fracture zones, discovering thermally inefficient buildings in cities, checking power lines, uncovering atrocities committed in war, and a host of other significant and rewarding activities.

Aircraft are also useful for spreading the word, whether it be news or advertising. (See the fifth volume of *Aviation Century*, Chapter 2, "Too Close for Comfort.") Helicopters have proved especially useful for covering news events as they happen, holding station overhead while stabilized on-board cameras follow the action and transmit the images to television stations. For displaying the written word, however, fixed-wing aircraft and airships are the preferred vehicles. Blimps, with their vast envelopes, have been used for advertising at sporting events and country fairs from their early days (see Chapter 2), and holiday beaches, offering large, relatively sedentary audiences, have long been favorite patrol lines for small aircraft towing banners that tout products or pass messages.

Not a day passes in which aviators are not affecting the lives of people below them in some way — providing a service, attracting attention, enforcing the law, or in any one of a myriad other roles.

CHAPTER 2

Personal and Private

IN THE BEGINNING, all aviation was "private." The nature of the enterprise at its birth and during its earliest days determined that it would be so. No machines could have fitted the description of private homebuilt aircraft more closely than the Wright biplanes, designed as they were by brothers who were necessarily amateur aircraft builders, and assembled out of items for the most part available at local hardware stores. Except insofar as they were the source of the basic materials, neither big business nor established industry had any part to play in making powered human flight a reality. The machines produced by pioneers such as Curtis, Blériot, Farman, A.V. Roe, Santos-Dumont and the rest were similarly personal achievements. Even after 1908, when the world at last began to recognize that flying might be a practicable activity, the small factories established by the pioneers manufactured aircraft only for those few brave souls who had sufficient money and nerve to gratify their individual appetites for adventure. The rare passengers carried aloft were equally self-indulgent, seeking thrills in the third dimension to exceed those of the fairground and, more important, that others had not known.

As the Blériots, Farmans and Antoinettes became more reliable, and the word about flying spread around the world, there were signs that governments might concern themselves with aviation and that aircraft industries of stature could soon arise, but before WWI the majority of aircraft produced were bought and used for personal pleasure by men of means. The possibility of flying becoming more accessible to a wider public, foreshadowed in the little Demoiselle of Santos-Dumont, was stalled by the outbreak of war in 1914. Even at the personal level, however, there had already been some attempts made to take aircraft beyond the realms of sport and record-breaking and into the everyday world. America's first aerial commuters were Alfred Lawson and Harold McCormick. In 1913, they began using Curtiss flying boats to travel from their waterside homes to their offices. Lawson flew from Raritan Bay, New Jersey, to the New York City waterfront, and McCormick from Evanston, Illinois, to the Chicago Yacht Club. The two men gained some celebrity from their innovation, and helped to spark a wave of speculation that flying for personal convenience rather than mere enjoyment could become common practice in the foreseeable future.

OPPOSITE PAGE
Evening Flight, *by Paul Rendel.*

Between the Wars

In the post-WWI world, the aviation scene was dramatically changed. Aircraft had demonstrated their capabilities and revealed something of their potential between 1914 and 1918. More to the point, there were vast numbers of surplus machines available and plenty of young pilots to fly them. Private ownership of aircraft grew quickly, giving rise to activities such as barnstorming and air taxi services as the new owners sought to keep flying and earn a living at the same time. Those who saw a future for private flying and tried immediately after the war to produce aircraft specifically designed to attract the private owner were generally defeated by the ample supply of cheap ex-military machines. In the United States, the Sperry Messenger and the Loughead S-1 monoplane both failed to sell, admirable designs though they were. In Britain, a rash of new light aircraft appeared in 1919, among them the Sopwith Dove, Blackburn Sidecar, Bristol Babe, and Avro Baby, all of them worthy efforts to promote private flying, but none of them successful.

Other factors limited the postwar rise in the number of people eager to become pilots and in personal plane ownership. Learning to fly was not a simple matter, and it was still expensive. Perhaps more significant, flying was regarded by the general public, with some justification, as a dangerous occupation, and aircraft as frail, untrustworthy creations. The problem for many people was the difficulty they had in seeing pilots as other than reckless daredevils with a casual attitude to safety. Until that barrier could be crossed and the average man and woman could be convinced that flying was not reserved for the intrepid, the growth in aviation's private sector was destined to be slow.

In the mid-1920s, the light plane movement grew rapidly, initially in the United Kingdom and Germany. Private flying in Germany, both of light aircraft and of gliders, was officially encouraged as efforts were made to circumvent the Versailles Treaty's restrictions on military flying. Many pilots of the future Luftwaffe gained their wings in a local flying club. Similar encouragement was offered in Britain, principally through the far-sighted efforts of Sir Sefton Brancker, the Director General of Civil Aviation. He saw that considerable benefits were to be had from making the average person more air-minded, not least because in any future war a nucleus of trained pilots would be invaluable. In 1924, a start was made when he announced a scheme that offered modest subsidies to selected flying clubs. The following year, that money helped to introduce the Moth, an aircraft that became a symbol of flying for pleasure. Francis Chichester described his delight in getting to know his D.H.60G Gipsy Moth: "The day arrives when at last you make two three-point landings in succession. It is the same as being in love; your heart swells with love for your neighbour.... you forget your creditors, the world is at your feet, flying is child's play.... In short, complete happiness is your portion."

Alberto Santos Dumont first flew his little Demoiselle in 1909. His aim was to make an aeroplane cheap and simple enough to popularize flying. Small and quite fast for its day, it was the first practical light aircraft. Santos Dumont offered the plans to the public free of charge and they were published worldwide, enabling aviators of limited means to get into the air at relatively low cost. The Demoiselle was instrumental in promoting the growth of aviation in the early years.

ABOVE *The de Havilland D.H.82 Tiger Moth is one of the most successful light aircraft built. Developed from the earlier D.H.60 Gipsy Moth, it first flew in October 1931. The future of the design was assured by an order from the RAF for Tiger Moths to be used in flying training. The D.H.82 was soon being sold worldwide, and by the time production ceased in 1945, more than 9,000 had been built, over 4,200 of them for the RAF.*
RIGHT *Kondor over Berlin, 1930. In the post-WWI period, gliding was officially encouraged in Germany as a way of easing the Versailles Treaty's restrictions on military flying. Many pilots of the future Luftwaffe gained their basic flying skills in gliders.*

Geoffrey de Havilland's first little two-seat Moth was produced in 1925. The Moth was both light and robust, and it was relatively cheap and easy to fly. It led the way to a worldwide revolution in private flying. Together with its successors, particularly the D.H.82 Tiger Moth, de Havilland's biplane served as the backbone of the private flying movement in half the countries of the world between the wars and continued to be seen as the essence of flying for pure enjoyment for the rest of the century. The writer Roald Dahl learned to fly in a Tiger Moth, and loved the experience: "The Tiger Moth is a thing of great beauty. Everybody who has ever flown a Tiger Moth has fallen in love with it. You could throw one about all over the sky and nothing ever broke. You could glide it upside down hanging in your straps for minutes on end, and although the engine cut out when you did that because the carburettor was also upside down, the motor started at once when you turned her the right way up again. You could spin her vertically downwards for thousands of feet and then all she needed

ABOVE *Over seventy years after its first flight, the Tiger Moth remains a popular light aircraft. The total surviving in various parts of the world approaches 1,000. The aircraft seen here (and on the previous page) is flown by Clive Denny from the Imperial War Museum's airfield at Duxford, near Cambridge, U.K.* BELOW *The de Havilland Moth Club organizes the world's most prestigious Moth Rally at Woburn Abbey, Bedfordshire, during the third weekend of August each year. The first Woburn Rally was staged in 1980, since when it has drawn visitors from around the world, with members flying Moth aircraft from many European countries. Here three beautifully prepared D.H.60 Moths wait their turn to fly.*

was a touch on the rudder-bar, a bit of throttle and the stick pushed forward and out she came in a couple of flips. A Tiger Moth had no vices. She never dropped a wing if you lost flying speed coming in to land, and she would suffer innumerable heavy landings from incompetent beginners without turning a hair."

Pou du Ciel

In time, the Tiger Moth was followed by many other successful British light aircraft designs, notably from the drawing boards of the Miles and Percival companies, that proved themselves both in competition and as personal magic carpets. France, too, had light aircraft successes, but one French enthusiast evolved a machine that proved to be notably less capable than its contemporaries. The Pou du Ciel (literally Sky Louse, but known in English as the Flying Flea) was a genuine attempt by Henri Mignet to bring flying to the masses. He had a passion for aviation but no education in aeronautics, and it was his belief that all aircraft included a serious flaw in their construction. He reasoned rather oddly that "Road vehicles, ships, dirigible balloons — things which go on the land, the sea and in the air — are all stable machines, and do not possess any apparatus for lateral control. Alone among all transport machines the airplane has to

In an attempt to produce a simple aircraft that could be built at home, Henri Mignet designed his Pou du Ciel (Flying Flea) in the early 1930s. The aircraft had two wings one behind the other, no tailplane, no elevators and no ailerons. The rear wing was fixed, while the front one was moved for pitch control. Mignet claimed that anyone who could put a packing-case together could build a Flying Flea and anyone who could drive a car could fly one. The idea attracted considerable attention, and Flying Flea rallies were held to promote the idea (right). In 1935, a young enthusiast, Stephen Appleby, built himself a Flea (G-ADMH) and received a Permit to Fly on July 14. Eleven days later, he flew it and crashed, landing upside down in a field. He was unhurt and the Daily Express *newspaper financed a rebuild, with some design changes. On December 5, 1935, G-ADMH (left) flew across the English Channel.*

be supplied with lateral controls. It is the only one which is unstable and dangerous by reason of its design."

Mignet's solution was to do away with ailerons and rely only on a powerful rudder to induce turns. When it appeared, the tiny wooden Pou proved to be novel in another respect. Its two wings were mounted in tandem, the front one being free to tilt to give control in pitch. With its 25-horsepower motor, it could just about fly, but its performance was marginal and its flying characteristics abominable. Interaction between the wings could induce control reversal and an almost inevitable crash. The problem was that Mignet's persuasive promotion of his Pou in books and magazines convinced hundreds of people that they could build one and learn to fly it by following his instructions. He assured readers that "It is not necessary to have any technical knowledge…if you can nail together a packing case you can construct an aircraft." In the summer of 1935, some 600 Pous were being nailed and glued together by amateurs in sheds and garages all over Britain. As many again were built in France and a considerable number in the United States, too. Flying Flea meetings were held in France and Britain, but thankfully few of the little horrors ever actually flew. Several of those that did killed their pilots, and it was not long before the Pou's "Permit to Fly" was withdrawn. Mignet's laudable

enthusiasm for making aviation generally available was distorted by ignorance and his concept was fatally flawed, but his idea that aircraft could be built at home would return years later in a safer, more organized form.

A Plane in Every Garage

The Pou du Ciel phenomenon was evidence of a growing belief that developments in aviation would lead inevitably to universal ownership of private flying machines. In the United States especially there were frequent predictions that the aircraft would be the "horseless carriage of the future," and that tomorrow's commuters would be able to live in rural tranquility beyond the suburbs created by the automobile. Personal aircraft were envisaged as the primary means of traveling to and from work, shopping, visiting the family, and going on holiday or taking weekend breaks. In short, they would largely take the place of the family car. Where Henry Ford's Model T had gone, so aircraft would follow. Many Americans were actively engaged in the pursuit of this dream. Small towns constructed landing fields, high schools offered courses of flight instruction, designers aimed at producing the "foolproof" light aircraft, and houses were built with planeports as well as garages. The speculators and the dreamers dwelt on the three-dimensional freedom of flying and the sheer pleasure of moving through clear air, and gave little thought to the practical problems of organizing and controlling an airborne population by day or night in all weathers.

Henry Ford himself was influenced by the family plane movement. Ford began building aircraft in 1925, producing the celebrated Trimotor airliner, but in 1926 it was announced that a Ford "flying flivver" was on the way. It proved to be a disappointment, a diminutive machine that eventually killed its pilot, thereby dousing the flame of Ford's enthusiasm and ending the project. Other entrepreneurs persisted, taking the concept of a personal aircraft a stage further by imagining a combined road vehicle and flying machine, a true aerocar. Glenn Curtiss had toyed with such an idea at an early stage of his career, and his Autoplane was unveiled in New York on February 8, 1917. Its appearance was lauded by the press, but U.S. intervention in WWI curtailed its continued development. Frenchman René Tampier introduced his cumbersome Avion-Automobile in October 1921 and then built several more, but the design was not a commercial success. Nor were any of the other proposals floated before WWII — the Caudron Aviocar, the German Aero-Auto, the Pitcairn AC-35.

One of the more ambitious aerocar concepts of the 1930s was the Waterman Arrowbile, which used the engine and parts of a 1937 Studebaker in the construction of a

LEFT AND BELOW RIGHT *On display at the Museum of Flight, Seattle, is an Aerocar Model III, the prototype of which was built by Moulton Taylor in 1949 but not certified for flight until 1956. The Aerocar can be transformed from automobile to aircraft in about fifteen minutes.*
BELOW LEFT *An Aerocar in flight. Moulton Taylor's machine came as close as any to realizing the dream of giving a small car wings. The project ended in the 1970s when, to meet the requirements of automobile legislation in the United States, the Aerocar would have become too heavy and expensive to be practical.*

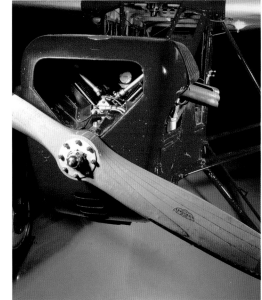

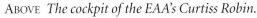
ABOVE *The cockpit of the EAA's Curtiss Robin.*
TOP RIGHT *In Seattle, the Museum of Flight's Curtiss Robin,* The Newsboy, *was purchased in 1929 by the* Daily Gazette *of McCook, Nebraska. It flew 380 miles a day to deliver 5,000 newspapers to forty towns in rural Nebraska. At each town, pilot Steve Tuttle would drop a bundle of newspapers out through a hole in the bottom of the fuselage.*
BOTTOM RIGHT *On display at the EAA's Air Venture Museum in Oshkosh, Wisconsin, is a 1929 Curtiss-Wright Robin B-2. The Robin was of mixed construction with wooden wings and a fuselage made of steel tubing, the whole being fabric-covered. An OX-5 engine initially powered the Robin, but later models fitted the more powerful Wright Whirlwind. The dependable Curtiss Robin became one of the most commercially successful airplanes of the day, with 769 produced from 1928 to 1930. In the summer of 1929, the Curtiss plant in St. Louis was turning out 17 of the popular Robins a week.*

two-seat, three-wheeled car with a detachable wing. It performed quite well, achieving speeds in excess of 100 mph in the air and 45 mph on the ground, but cost of production proved too high. After WWII, the search for the aerocar resumed, with the Consolidated Vultee ConvAircar of 1946 and the AVE Mizar of 1972. Both used conventional automobiles and large detachable wings, and both projects died with their proponents in crashes, the Mizar's Ford Pinto car disintegrating in spectacular fashion after separating from its Cessna Skymaster wing in flight. If any of the combination vehicles could be described as a limited

success, it would have to be the Taylor Aerocar, a compact four-seater with detachable fuselage, wings and tail, all of which folded into a trailer for towing. Its 143-horsepower engine gave it a cruising speed of 135 mph in the air and 60 mph on the road. Seven Aerocars were built and between them were driven hundreds of thousands of miles and flown for thousands of hours. There was talk of Ford wanting to build Aerocars, but the difficulties of ensuring that the vehicles could be operated safely within the regulations controlling travel both on the surface and in the air proved too much to overcome.

WACO, "ASK THE MAN WHO OWNS ONE"

Waco ATO Taperwing, serial number A118, was manufactured in 1929. In August 1934 the aircraft was purchased by Joe Mackey, whose team of flyers was contracted by the Ohio Oil Company (Linco Gasoline and Motor Oil) to perform at air shows, giving aerobatic displays, skywriting and flying signs as the Linco Flying Aces. Mackey replaced the original engine with a more powerful Wright Whirlwind R-975 J6-9, and later replaced the aircraft's fabric skin with aluminum. Invited to take part in the 1936 international airshow near Paris, Mackey performed brilliantly in the Taperwing, gaining the admiration of the crowd and an award of $10,000.

Mackey used his special Waco to earn many other awards for aerobatic excellence, including the coveted Freddie Lund Trophy.

Joe Mackey's Taperwing is now owned by the BF Goodrich Company, which acquired and restored the aircraft to flying condition in 1993. It is flown from Waco Field in Troy, Ohio.

BUILDING A CLASSIC

In the years between the World Wars, Waco (Weaver Aircraft Company) of Troy, Ohio, produced a series of well-designed biplanes, both cabin and open cockpit. In 1983, Classic Aircraft Corporation in Battle Creek, Michigan set out to recreate the classic Waco YMF.

To quote the corporation's founders, "In a world full of computers and high tech, the opportunity to go back in time and experience the most enjoyable era in aviation history is a wonderful vision. This was the era when pilots donned white scarves, goggles and leather flying helmets and introduced the world to the art of flying. It was a time in history when each flight produced memories and stories that would endure a lifetime. The YMF was the culmination of Waco's efforts to produce a gorgeous and rugged biplane with delightful handling qualities."

When production was reestablished in 1986 with the YMF, no company had ever taken a fifty-year-old design and manufactured it under the original FAA type certificate. While maintaining the sanctity of Waco's design, a team of proven professionals modernized the aircraft with over 300 engineering changes, redrew over 1,400 drawings, and built new tooling for production. Each aircraft is hand-built, and more than 5,000 hours of craftsmanship dedicated to the finished product. Improvements such as the use of much stronger steel for the fuselage frame, modern hydraulic toe brakes, and the latest avionics are all quality features one would expect in a new aircraft, now incorporated in a classic.

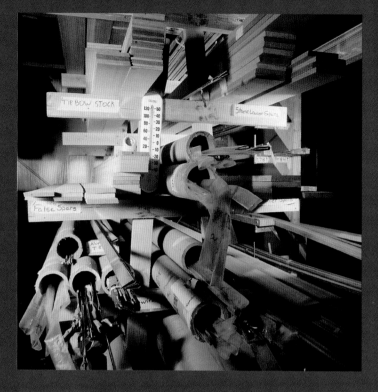

Waco Classic of Battle Creek, Michigan, builds new airplanes the way they used to, by hand. Starting with the original designs from which Wacos were built decades ago, Waco Classic has allowed a few modifications to make the classic biplane more stable at low speeds.

TOP LEFT Carefully selected woods are stored for future use.

TOP RIGHT Hand-forming with a mallet — the aluminum fairings for the vertical stabilizer.

BOTTOM The framework for the fuselage, tubes welded together in a full-size jig.

OPPOSITE, TOP LEFT A Waco craftsman using timeless hand tools to form the wingtip.

OPPOSITE, TOP RIGHT A hand-finished wingtip, as compared to the raw, unfinished wing underneath.

OPPOSITE, BOTTOM LEFT Tacking the delicate wing ribs into place — a background of patterns.

OPPOSITE, BOTTOM RIGHT Attaching the aluminum leading edge with tacks and hand tools.

Aircraft of the Golden Age

The booming U.S. economy of the mid-1920s, and the increasing availability of reliable, lightweight engines such as the Wright Whirlwind radial did much to produce an increase in sales of personal aircraft by 1926, but the event that did more than any other to galvanize American public interest in flying was Lindbergh's Atlantic crossing in 1927. Aircraft manufacturers were suddenly inundated by enquiries from private individuals and the demand for machines soared. Existing firms expanded and new companies formed, some of them poorly organized and destined to founder within months. Among the names to prevail and build successful aircraft during the boom were Waco, Travel Air, Stinson, Swallow, Spartan, Bellanca, Aeronca, Cessna and Taylor. Many of the machines they produced became classics, examples of which survived to fly until the end of the century. At the same time, some small engine firms began to prosper, notably Continental and Lycoming, specialists in four- and six-cylinder "flat" engines, with the cylinders opposed in two rows.

The people who were involved in founding these American companies and building the aircraft were men of

The 1937 Spartan 7W Executive (NC13993) was donated to the EAA's Air Venture Museum by George S. Mennen, of grooming products for men fame. The Executive is a five-place all-metal monoplane with retractable landing gear. It was designed to be fast and comfortable, and had extensive insulation to lower cabin noise levels. Executives set new standards for speed and style when they appeared in the 1930s. The performance would not have disgraced many fighter aircraft of the day. Power was provided by a sleekly cowled, 450-horsepower, nine-cylinder Pratt and Whitney radial. The aircraft's advanced technology was reflected in its high cost — $23,500 in 1937. NC13993 is the second production aircraft of just thirty-four built, and is the only example with a control stick instead of a wheel. It was used extensively for factory flight-testing. When George Mennen flew the aircraft, he sprayed aftershave into the exhaust to advertise his products.

considerable character and flair. One of the first was George "Buck" Weaver, a barnstormer who founded the Weaver Aircraft Company. He died in 1924, but the firm continued to trade using the acronym Waco, developing Weaver's original designs to become manufacturers of a biplane series, including the popular Waco 10 and the classic Taperwing. "Matty" Laird is remembered principally as a designer, but he started by forming the Laird Airplane Company and building the Swallow. The company was remarkable for the men associated with it in the early 1920s — Lloyd Stearman and Walter Beech were among those who began building their careers at Laird's, and Clyde Cessna was an enthusiast for the Swallow. In time, the man who provided the capital for Laird, Jake Moellendick, fell out with all three of his talented airmen. They left what had become the Swallow Airplane Manufacturing Company to go their own ways, but not before it had taken root in Wichita, Kansas, sowing the seeds for a group of factories that together formed the light plane capital of the world. By the late 1920s, the Wichita "big four"

were firmly established around the town — Swallow and Travel Air (formed in 1925 by Stearman, Cessna and Beech), followed later by the independent companies of Stearman and Cessna. In 1932, Walter Beech took the same road and founded his own company, too.

By the mid-1930s, the shape of the light aircraft market had changed. The biggest sellers were Aeronca, Taylor, Piper and Luscombe, all specialists in personal light aircraft, primarily two-seat monoplanes. Those four leading companies were in competition for customers alongside Waco, Stinson, Beech and Cessna, with smaller producers such as Spartan, Monocoupe, Culver and Howard adding variety to the wide selection of models available. This was the era of superb classics such as the Stinson Reliant, Cessna Airmaster, Monocoupe 110 and Beech Staggerwing, but the types built in the most numbers came from the Piper and Aeronca factories. In 1939, Piper was the market leader, with 1,806 Cubs sold during the year. The basic Cub was the first mass-production aircraft ever offered for sale for less than $1,000.

One of Geoffrey de Havilland's delightful Moth family, the D.H.87 Hornet Moth is a development of the smaller D.H.60. Like many of its cousins, it was designed as trainer and touring aircraft, but with an enclosed cabin. The first prototype flew on May 9, 1934, and originally appeared with tapered wings, but these caused problems, especially during a three-point landing, when there was a tendency for the tips to stall. This embarrassed the pilot, at least, and often damaged the aircraft. The problem was solved by fitting wings with square tips. Production of Hornet Moths began in 1935, and 165 were built. This Hornet Moth is owned and flown by Mark Miller.

Successful and long-lasting though the Pipers and Aeroncas were, they were relatively conservative designs. It was left to the smaller manufacturers to try something different and take a peek at what the future might hold. At Erco, designer Fred Weick produced the Ercoupe, a plane intended to be flyable by anyone. Its tricycle landing gear made it easy to taxi, especially since the control yoke was connected to the nosewheel and the Ercoupe could be steered like a car on the ground. There were no rudder pedals because the ailerons and rudder were linked through the yoke to prevent cross-controlling. There was a limit to the amount of up elevator that could be applied, too, and these arrangements made it almost impossible to spin the aircraft. Experienced pilots found its fail-safe design irksome, but it was a pleasant and economical flying club machine. The Luscombe 8 was more of a challenge to fly and was far more significant. It cost $1,900 in 1938 and was introduced with advertising that said "No wood! No nails! No glue!" It was the first all-metal light aircraft and was the forerunner of modern mass production of small private planes.

In Europe, Meanwhile ...

On the other side of the Atlantic the market continued to be dominated by de Havilland's variations on the Moth theme, firmly established as they were both as the heart and soul of light aircraft aviation and, in D.H.82A Tiger Moth form, as primary trainers for the British and Commonwealth air forces. The continental equivalent of the Moth was the very similar Belgian Stampe S.V.4. Impressive aerobatic biplanes also appeared in Germany, where the Bücker Jungman and Jungmeister became popular. Built in smaller numbers were some very attractive monoplanes. In Britain, the Miles Hawk and Percival Gull series were sleek little aircraft offering remarkable performance from relatively low power Gipsy engines, many of them being used to win races and break international records. (See *Aviation Century The Golden Age*, Chapter 2, "Quickest to the Cape," and Chapter 3, "Racing with Restraint.") The French companies of Caudron and Potez produced several neatly designed cabin tourers, and in Czechoslovakia CKD-Praga built the high-wing Air Baby. German designs included the very light Klemm machines with high aspect ratio wings, and two classic cabin monoplanes, the Bücker Bestmann and the Messerschmitt Bf 108 Taifun.

TOP LEFT *The Miles Falcon, seen here bearing the logo of the popular aviation magazine* The Aeroplane, *was the first Miles aircraft with an enclosed cabin. The Falcon was of wooden construction with fabric-covered control surfaces. Flown by H.L. Brook, the prototype Falcon competed in the 1934 MacRobertson England–Australia Air Race, and set a new solo record of seven days, 19 hours, 50 minutes for the return flight. One notable feature was the distinctive raked windscreen, which added about 4 mph to the top speed.*

TOP RIGHT *The Bücker Jungmann (young man) is one of the finest primary aerobatic trainers ever built. It is essentially a simple aircraft, but although light it is very strong, capable of withstanding 12 positive G. Designed with ease of manufacture and maintenance in mind, it has many well thought-out features, including interchangeable upper and lower wings. The Jungmann was first flown in 1934, and was soon in great demand for its admirable handling qualities. Before the outbreak of WWII, it had become a standard Luftwaffe trainer and was being flown in twenty-one countries. It was also built under license in Czechoslovakia, Holland, Spain and Switzerland.*

De Havilland Dragon Rapides,
by Michael Turner.

THE POST-WWII SURGE

With the end of WWII, the prewar dreams of family aircraft were revived and a boom was forecast in the U.S. private aviation industry. It proved to be a self-fulfilling prophecy, at least for a while. In 1946, there was a bustle of activity, with the impressive total of over 31,000 light planes built. The leaders were the established companies of Piper (7,780), Aeronca (7,555) and Cessna (3,959), but the prospects were so attractive that many small firms were encouraged to try their luck and most did sell a few machines. The over-production was serious, however, and a rash of failures and mergers followed a collapse in demand. By 1948, total industry production was down to little more than 7,000. Major companies such as Aeronca and Waco were driven out of manufacturing whole aircraft and relegated to subcontracting and making parts. At this low volume of production it was impossible to keep prices down and the idea of flying as a pursuit for the masses faded.

The "big three" survivors of the postwar mayhem were Cessna, Beech and Piper. Cessna emerged with the all-metal, high-wing 120 and 140 series, and later added the twin-engined 310. Beech introduced the remarkable

V-tailed Bonanza in 1947, and sold 1,229 during the first year, despite its high basic cost of $7,975. The Twin Bonanza matched Cessna's 310. Piper, although still selling machines, came close to failure because of outdated practices, but struggled on to manufacture models such as the PA-18 Super Cub, PA-22 Tri-Pacer, and PA-23 Apache. One new company showing promise in 1948 was Mooney, but by 1950 the names of Erco, Stinson and Waco were missing from the ranks of private plane builders. In 1951, the number of light aircraft produced was down to only 2,302, a discouraging figure that nevertheless presaged a steady improvement in the industry during the 1950s and 1960s.

The further growth of the "big three" was marked by their continually improving products. Piper chose to give its aircraft names associated with Native Americans — Aztec, Comanche, Cherokee, Warrior, Archer, Arrow, Dakota and so on. Beech stayed at the high end of the market with developments of the Bonanza (eventually with a conventional tail), and added the Musketeer and the twin-engined Baron. Cessna rolled on through higher and higher model numbers — 150, 170 (1948 base price $5,400), 172 Skyhawk, 175 Skylark, 180, 182, and 185 Skylane. In May 1972, the success of these machines was confirmed when Cessna became the first manufacturer to exceed a total production of 100,000 aircraft. A newcomer appearing in this period and destined for long production runs was Maule. The M-4 Rocket and its successors were rugged four-seaters that were almost impossible to stall and had excellent short takeoff and landing characteristics. Private pilots with a preference for being flexible about where they touched down could enjoy Lake Aircraft's little LA-4 amphibians, first flown in Colonial

LEFT *A Cessna family portrait. Big brother Cessna 310 watches over a 175 and two 182As in the 1950s. (Swept-back fins began appearing in 1960.) Cessna's dominance of the light and executive aircraft field can be judged from the number of machines of all models built by Cessna factories since the company began — 180,000. As many as half the aircraft flying in the world are Cessnas.*

RIGHT *The Aeronca 7 Champion first flew in 1944 and was a highly popular light aircraft in the immediate post-WWII period, with over 10,000 built. Designated the L-16 by the U.S. Army Air Forces, it was second only to the Piper J-3 in popularity as a trainer. The two seats are in tandem, and the front pilot's seat is positioned high up and well forward, so visibility is excellent and the cockpit seems unusually roomy for a small aircraft.*

The Model 18 Twin Beech, introduced in 1937, became one of general aviation's most versatile and enduring aircraft. With its two 450-horsepower Pratt and Whitney radial engines it cruised in excess of 200 mph carrying eight passengers and a full load of fuel and baggage. The Twin Beech was built in a number of versions for the military — the C-45 Expeditor light transport; the AT-7 navigation trainer; the SNB trainer for bombardiers; the F-2 for aerial reconnaissance and mapping; and the AT-11/SNB-1 Kansan bombing-gunnery trainer.

Skimmer form in 1948 and progressively developed until the end of the century as the only single-engine small amphibian on the market.

The Threat of Litigation

In the 1980s the light aircraft industry went rapidly downhill, and one particularly significant reason for the decline in the United States was the problem of product liability. Companies were taken to court more and more often when aircraft from their factories were involved in accidents. Liability insurance became a necessity, markedly increasing production costs. By the late 1980s, the effects of litigation had helped to almost double the price to the customer of each aircraft built. Independent operation became difficult for even the large companies to sustain. Beech was acquired by Raytheon in 1979, and Cessna was made a subsidiary of General Dynamics in 1985, at the same time suspending single-engine production "until the product liability laws are reformed." In 1992, Cessna changed allegiance again when it was bought by Textron. The strength of Piper's workforce fell from a high of 8,000 to just 45 during the 1980s, and the company declared bankruptcy in July 1991.

> "That this tiny two-seater box of metal managed to rise into the air at all felt unbelievable. Once we broke ground, it seemed as if I were floating on a magic carpet. The lightness and height made me tingle in somewhat the same way I feel aroused before making love. When I took over the controls, I felt as if I were at the center of my universe instead of orbiting someone else's. I felt then, and still believe now, that piloting a small aircraft is about as good as it gets."
>
> BARBARA CUSHMAN ROWELL,
> FLYING SOUTH: A PILOT'S INNER JOURNEY

Build It at Home

One way for private pilots to make the cost of owning aircraft more affordable was to build planes for themselves at home. Soon after WWII, George Bogardus, a leading amateur aircraft builder in the United States, induced the Civil Aviation Authority to relax restrictions on the operation of homebuilt planes, and specific regulations governing the procedures for gaining airworthiness certificates followed in 1951. This was a major incentive to the development of a kitplane industry. The ensuing enthusiasm led to the founding of the Experimental Aviation Association in January 1953. (The term "experimental" was defined by the CAA as including aircraft of original design and construction built for personal use, rather than for business or commercial sale.) Under the leadership of Paul Poborezny, the EAA became the core organization for many different private flying interests, in time embracing not only the homebuilt community but also those whose particular passions were for antique, classic, warbird or aerobatic aircraft.

Apart from the obvious examples of the Wright brothers and other early airmen, people had been building aircraft at home for some time before WWII. The Heath Parasol of 1926 was one of the first to be marketed specifically as a homebuilt machine, and the plans for Pietenpol's Air Camper were published in *Modern Mechanix* magazine in 1932. However, it was not until after the war that the homebuilt movement really became established. The pioneers included Ray Stits, who claimed to have designed and constructed the world's smallest airplane in the Skybaby, and Curtis Pitts, whose single-seat S-1 Special developed into one of the world's most popular aerobatic aircraft. Steve Wittman's W-8 and W-10 Tailwinds were highly regarded two-seat cabin monoplanes.

Until the 1980s the principal construction materials for most homebuilt aircraft were wood and metal, but in the 1980s composite materials (thermoplastics, polycarbonates) offered greater strength while reducing weight. Thereafter the rate of growth in the homebuilt market increased rapidly as the production of the major aircraft manufacturers declined. By 1990 the number of kitplanes sold in the United States exceeded those made in factories by almost two to one. Many of the suppliers' names have become well known in the aeronautical world and their completed kits — such as Richard VanGrunsven's RV series, Skystar Kitfox, Stoddart-Hamilton Glasair, Sequoia Falco (an Italian design), Lancair, Scaled Composites Varieze, Aviat Christen Eagle, and Europa (a British design) — are a common sight in the skies.

OSHKOSH

OPPOSITE A selection of memorabilia from the EAA archives at Oshkosh. Each year the large fly-in generates patches, pennants and awards. Steve Wittman is almost the patron saint of homebuilt aircraft; the model of Bonzo represents one of his more recognizable creations.

OPPOSITE INSET Neal Loving was the only double amputee and the first African American to qualify as a racing pilot. Both legs were lost in a glider accident in 1944. He started the first black flight school in 1946, then got interested in flying racing planes and designed the aircraft that became *Lovings' Love*. This diminutive all-wood aircraft was built in time for the 1951 Goodyear Air Races and was powered by an 85-horsepower Continental engine. It was capable of over 200 mph in level flight, and once reached 266 mph in a diving run. *Loving's Love* is on display at the EAA's Air Venture Museum, Oshkosh, Wisconsin.

TOP RIGHT AND LEFT The Fairchild 24, introduced in 1932, provided more comfort for pilot and passengers. Most aircraft of the day offered an open-cockpit experience, but a brochure for the Fairchild 24 made the point that "Special clothing is not required." Luxuries included cabin heat and roll-down windows. Such amenities made the Fairchild 24 a favorite of the Hollywood crowd, including Robert Taylor, Tyrone Power, Mary Pickford, Jimmy Stewart and Edgar Bergen. The EAA's Fairchild 24H, NC16902, is the deluxe model produced in 1937, which added plush upholstery, wing flaps and improved instrumentation.

BELOW Ray Stits' *Sky Baby* is exhibited at the Experimental Aviation Association's museum in Oshkosh, Wisconsin. Stits designed and built the *Sky Baby* at his home in Riverside, California, to prove that he could build the world's smallest man-carrying airplane. The biplane's wingspan is only 7 feet, 2 inches. To test-fly the tiny aircraft, Stits hired Robert H. Starr, who first flew the *Sky Baby* in April 1952. It was flown at air shows all summer before being retired in November. Starr reported that the *Sky Baby* landed at about 80 mph and could achieve 185 mph flat out.

ANATOMY OF A HOMEBUILT

EAA founder Paul Poberezny designed the Acro-Sport II as a high-performance two-seat aerobatic biplane. Intended for the home-builder, it has no complicated or hard-to-make parts, using welded steel tubing for the airframe, and spruce and plywood wings. The finished airplane is covered with fabric. This example at the EAA Airventure Museum has some of the skin cut away to reveal the simple and durable design.

RIGHT The four-cylinder horizontally opposed engine, seen through the open engine compartment. Beneath the fuselage, the brake line in the open landing-gear fairing.

BELOW A simple and strong basic form works for this classic aircraft: metal tubing is welded into the form, and wooden stringers are used to round out the form. The heavy battery just aft of the cockpit is close to the center of gravity.

OPPOSITE PAGE The wings of the Acro Sport are similar in construction to those of the Waco Classic on page 103. Wing ribs that have the shape of the airfoil in a progression of sizes are tied together by the main spar, a solid piece of wood. All these relatively lightweight elements give the wing great strength.

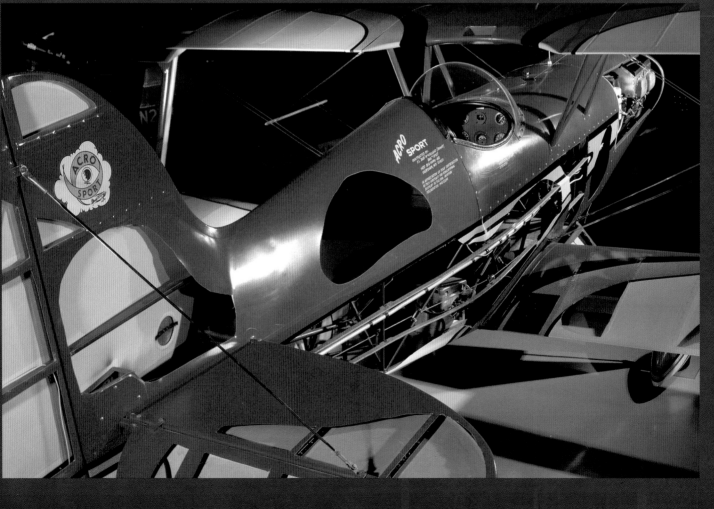

FLYING A CLASSIC

Jerry Kemp of Covington, Ohio, flies airliners for U.S. Airways. When not flying commercially he pilots this immaculately restored and maintained Globe Swift from the grass airstrip next to his home. Jerry flew for the United States Air Force as a fighter pilot and survived a perilous bailout from a stricken F-111 over England in December of 1977 near Scaltback Estate, Newmarket, Suffolk.

The Globe Swift was designed in the early 1940s, and although fewer than 1,500 were built, this gorgeous classic has a dedicated following, with many owner organizations across the United States.

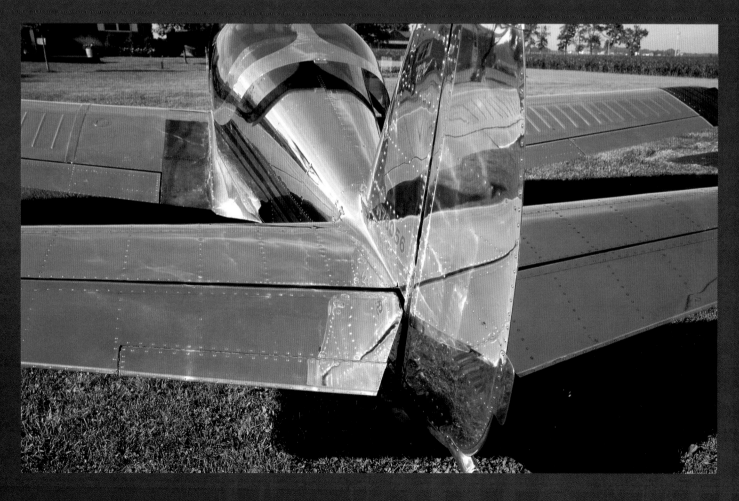

A Kind of Renaissance

Evidence of the striking decline in the private aircraft market brought about by the burden of liability insurance was contained in the U.S. industry's statistics, which showed a reduction of more than 90 percent in the production of single-engined machines between 1980 and the early 1990s. Some relief came in 1994 when the General Aviation Revitalization Act came into effect in the United States, establishing an eighteen-year statute of repose against makers of general aviation aircraft and parts. (The term "general aviation" covers aircraft other than those employed in military and major commercial operations — private and business use, plus those used for medical, agricultural, survey purposes, et cetera.) Almost immediately, Piper returned to

private aircraft manufacturing, reorganized under the name New Piper Aircraft Inc. Cessna announced its return, too, and by the late 1990s the company's popular high-wing single-engine models were back in production. The Cessna 172 Skyhawk was among those that reappeared, suitably updated but still recognizable as the descendant of the original 172 manufactured almost fifty years before. It is one of the most successful aircraft designs ever conceived; over 37,000 individuals of the Skyhawk family had been built by the end of the century. This extraordinary achievement reflects the dominance of both Cessna and the United States in the field of general aviation. Some 80 percent of the world's general aviation aircraft are in the United States, and Cessna has built a total of more than 180,000 aircraft of

LEFT *Wittman Regional Airport in Oshkosh is the home of the Experimental Aircraft Association's Air Venture, the world's largest annual aviation gathering. As many as 15,000 aircraft in a bewildering variety of sizes and shapes are parked along the flight line. There are warbirds, homebuilts, antiques, ultralights and experimentals; front-line military and general aviation aircraft fly in from all over the world. More than 500 educational forums, seminars and workshops are offered throughout the event and over 700 exhibitors show off their aeronautical products. Daily air shows showcase the talents of the world's top aerobatics performers. During the week, at least three-quarters of a million people come to enjoy the show. Those who fly in arrive prepared; they unpack their gear and camp among the serried ranks of aircraft.*

BELOW *Among the regulars at the annual EAA gathering at Oshkosh are the Maules. The Maule M-7 series of STOL (short takeoff and landing) aircraft is descended from the original Maule design of the late 1950s. The basic form has remained the same as improvements have been made in engines, avionics, landing gear and high-lift devices. The Maule is rugged, simple and reliable; there is no region in the world where it cannot operate, whether on wheels, floats or skis.*

TOP *Paul H. Poberezny is one of the most recognized men in aviation. He has received literally hundreds of awards and for his contributions to the world of flight, and is celebrated for founding the Experimental Aircraft Association in 1953. In 1999 he was inducted to the National Aviation Hall of Fame in Dayton, Ohio, and is a recipient of the National Business Aviation Association's Award for Meritorious Service to Aviation (2001) and the Wright Memorial Award Trophy (2002). Paul Poberezny has logged more than 30,000 hours in nearly 400 different types of aircraft, including some 170 planes built by amateurs, and has designed and built over a dozen aircraft himself.*

BOTTOM *Cessna has taken an evolutionary approach to building aircraft. If something works on one airframe, the company improves it on later models. This makes them simple to manufacture and maintain, while each machine retains docile flying qualities. The popular Cessna 182 began as a tricycle-undercarriage development of the Cessna 180. It first flew in 1956 and from 1957 was known as the Skylane. The 182 was produced in several forms, including the retractable landing gear (RG) version of the late 1970s. Well over 20,000 Skylanes have been built. Seen here is the 182 RG often flown by photographer Dan Patterson from Crossroads Aero Club, Dayton.*

all models. It has been estimated that perhaps half of the aircraft being flown worldwide are from a Cessna factory.

As the 20th century drew to a close, and it seemed probable that the renaissance of private aviation was assured, it was generally recognized that it was time for the industry to come up with some new ideas. The basic models in production by the major manufacturers in the 1990s did not appear to have changed significantly in decades. However, a new generation of designs on the drawing boards offered considerable promise for the future. The respected kitplane company Lancair proposed moving into production with the Columbia, a four-seat, low-wing monoplane built from advanced composites and shaped by computer. The Cirrus SR20 is similarly advanced in construction and includes some remarkable safety features. A built-in parachute system is capable of supporting the whole aircraft and lowering it to the ground in the ultimate emergency, and this is combined with energy absorbing seats to cushion impact. The Austro-Canadian Diamond Aircraft Industries produces the DA-40 Star, an elegant

four-seater with high-aspect-ratio wings, and Toyota Motors has engaged in serious research into a four-place, piston-powered light aircraft made of composite materials and equipped with modern avionics. The price of all this innovation does not come cheap. When introduced, the Cirrus SR20 started at $188,000 or so, and even Toyota did not aim to enter the market asking less for its proposed light aircraft than the basic Cessna 172, or about $125,000, hardly the fulfillment of the hope for an "airplane in every garage."

Alongside the new designs, a number of old ones serve again in modern guise. Aviat Aircraft of Wyoming led the way in this category with the reborn Globe Swift of 1945, naming the new version the Millennium Swift and almost doubling its cruising speed. Aviat also planned to recreate the 1933 Clipwing Monocoupe 110 Special. Renaissance Aircraft in Maryland favored the return of the Luscombe 8, and the Taiwanese Tong Lung Metal Products based in West Virginia set itself to build modernized copies of Grumman four-seaters from the 1970s, the Cheetah and the Tiger. In Wisconsin, American Champion carried on the tradition that began with Aeronca and passed through Champion and Bellanca, producing modified versions of such classic tail-draggers as the Citabria series. All of these aircraft, the old designs and the new, have incorporated equipment that makes them markedly superior to their light aircraft ancestors. Their structural and safety features are much improved, and their cockpits carry the latest avionics, available in multifunction displays featuring such things as moving maps, trip/fuel planning, vertical navigation, wind calculation, auto zoom, extended track, nearest airports and navigation aids, and interface capability to luxuries such as a stormscope and a ground proximity warning system. The engines that power the aircraft are improved, too, but more often than not they bear familiar, if modified, names: Textron Lycoming and Teledyne Continental.

Alternatives Elsewhere

Although the world of personal aviation was dominated by American companies, manufacturers in other countries designed and built competing light aircraft, many of which enjoyed series production. French firms were particularly prominent, with Robin, Socata, DynAero and Jodel leading the way. Italy's SIAI-Marchetti produced the lively SF.260, a fast, fully aerobatic three-seater often described as the airman's Ferrari, and in Switzerland, FFA (under agreement with SIAI) developed the AS-202 Bravo flying club aircraft. From Germany came Valentin's Taifun, the Grob 115/120, and Gyroflug's remarkable little Speed Canards. Ganzavia of Hungary tried a change of style with a small staggerwing biplane, the GAK-22 Dino, and in Czechoslovakia Zlin produced superb aerobatic and touring aircraft, such as the 143L and the 242. In the United Kingdom, the Slingsby Firefly was designed to meet the needs of both civil and military flying training. South American builders followed traditional lines with Argentina's Aero Boero 115, a Cessna 172 lookalike, and Brazil's CTA Paulistinha. In Japan, Fuji produced the Aero Subaru.

(Left) Lancair in Redmond, Oregon, has played a key role in defining the character of the kit plane industry, a market segment that now outsells the production market fleet by more than three to one. The Lancair family covers the range of private pilot aircraft, including the two-seat aerobatic Lancair Legacy (seen here), the 330-mph Lancair IV, and the turbine-engined, pressurized Lancair IV-P, capable of speeds up to 370 mph. Lancairs are owned and operated in thirty-four countries on five continents.
(Right) A powered paraglider is the smallest, simplest powered aircraft in the world, and the easiest to learn to fly. The sport of paragliding uses a flexible wing like a parachute, so if the engine fails, the parachute allows a gentle descent and a stand-up landing. The owner of a paraglider does not need an expensive hangar or a special pilot license and can haul it around in a car or truck. Most notably, paragliding does not incur the same level of costs as conventional aircraft ownership.

TOP *The Saab MFI-15 Safari was developed in the 1970s as a primary trainer and military utility aircraft. The production variant, of which 150 were built, was powered by a 200-horsepower Lycoming engine. Most Safaris were sold for private use, but a number were sold to the air forces of Sierra Leone, Pakistan, Denmark, Norway and Zambia. An earlier version of the Safari, the MFI-9, was flown by a Swedish aristocrat, Count Carl Gustav von Rosen, on relief flights in Nigeria during the Biafran war. (Count von Rosen's aunt Karin was married to Hermann Göring.)*

TOP LEFT *The name of Czechoslovakian aircraft manufacturer Zlin has been associated with excellence in aerobatic aircraft since the firm was founded in 1934. Ladislav Bezáák flew a Zlin 226T Trener to win the 1960 World Championships at Bratislava, Czechoslovakia, in 1960. This example can be seen at the Muzeum Lotnictwa Polskiego (Polish Aviation Museum) in Krakow, Poland.*

BOTTOM LEFT *Cirrus began in 1984 as a kit airplane design and manufacturing company, but it moved into the 21st century as the world's second-largest manufacturer of single-engine, piston-powered aircraft, and the Cirrus SR22 became the industry's best-selling model. By the end of 2003, more than 1,000 new aircraft had been sold. Cirrus aircraft are built to take advantage of composite construction and advanced aerodynamics, and they incorporate flat-panel, multi-function display technology and state-of-the-art safety measures, including a final level of safety known as the Cirrus Airframe Parachute System (CAPS). In the ultimate emergency, a large parachute can be deployed to lower the aircraft to the ground. The SR22 seen here, with a Cessna in the background, was photographed at Commander Aero Incorporated, a major servicing facility near Dayton, Ohio.*

The third Wright glider in flight from the Kill Devil Hills, North Carolina, in 1902. The sheds built by the Wrights to protect themselves and their aircraft from the sometimes severe weather on the Outer Banks can be seen in the background.

FLOATING ON AIR

The history of manned unpowered flight may be longer than is generally recognized. In 1922, Jane's *All the World's Aircraft* commented that there was reason to believe that "the first experimental gliders were built in a period of remote antiquity." Records claim successful glider flights in Bengal during the 9th century, by Aztecs in the 14th century, and by Danti, a mathematician from Perugia, about 1490. It is usually accepted that the first man in recent times to construct a flyable glider was Sir George Cayley. In 1853, his reluctant coachman was launched across an English valley in a craft described by the *Mechanics' Magazine* of the time as a "governable parachute." By the end of the 19th century, several pioneers had built frail gliders and managed to make short flights from hills or platforms. The most celebrated of these, including Octave Chanute (and his pilot A.M. Herring), the German Otto Lilienthal and the Scot Percy Pilcher, conducted their trials during the 1890s. Lilienthal made some 2,500 successful glides between 1893

and 1896, mostly in rigid monoplane hang gliders in which he achieved control by shifting his weight. Lilienthal and Pilcher eventually paid the ultimate price, both men being killed in crashes after losing control of their creations. Their work encouraged others, however, the Wrights in particular being strongly influenced by Lilienthal's experiments.

As the 20th century dawned, the Wright brothers began their glider experiments near Kitty Hawk, on North Carolina's Outer Banks. Three gliders were built, in 1900, 1901 and 1902. All were flown successfully and several hundred flights were made, some exceeding 600 feet. In the process, both Wilbur and Orville became adept glider pilots, learning the art of controlling their biplanes in the strong Kitty Hawk winds. (See *Aviation Century The Early Years.*) In Europe, Ernest Archdeacon, Gabriel Voisin, Captain Ferdinand Ferber and Samuel Cody were among the earliest of those who experimented with gliding flight, unfortunately without grasping the real significance of the Wright's system of control and therefore with only moderate success.

A remarkable American contemporary was John Montgomery of California. He claimed to have made successful gliding flights as early as 1883, when he was twenty-five years old: "There was a little run and a jump and I found myself launched in the air. I proceeded against the wind, gliding downhill for a distance of six hundred feet. In the experience I was able to direct my course at will."

Montgomery returned to flight-testing models at the turn of the century and in 1903 he built a full-size tandem-wing glider that he named *Santa Clara*. On March 16, 1905, this craft was carried aloft by a hot-air balloon and performed the first aerial glider launch when it was released at 800 feet. Flown by John Maloney, it landed in an apple orchard. There was no serious injury to either the pilot or the glider, so a second flight was made, this time from 3,000 feet. John Maloney's description was ecstatic — if a little premature in its conclusions: "For a few minutes I simply poised in the air and then flew around in different directions, circling, darting back and forth, up and down, as easily as an eagle could have done it. I was up in the air for eighteen minutes and never had the least difficulty in gliding. I don't believe there is a single improvement that could be made in the machine. It is perfect. The problem of aerial navigation is solved."

Alas for Montgomery and Maloney, the euphoria of their success was shattered four months later when Maloney failed to realize that the glider had been damaged by a dangling balloon cable. Soon after release, the right rear wing folded and the glider tumbled to the ground. Maloney died a few hours later. Montgomery persisted with his experiments, and in 1911 he produced the

Evergreen, a monoplane glider controlled by wing-warping. Over fifty flights were conducted with this machine, but on October 31, it stalled just after takeoff, struck the ground right wingtip first and turned over. The glider was hardly damaged, but Montgomery hit his head on the end of a bolt and was killed.

ABOVE *A smiling Herr Hentzen in his glider* Vampyr *at the Wasserkuppe in the Rhön Mountains of Germany. In August 1922, he made several record-breaking flights in this glider, one lasting 3 hours, 6 minutes.*

BELOW *In the 1920s, gliding experiments were conducted in Germany with a number of tailless gliders, not always successfully. On August 19, 1921, the tailless glider designed by Friedrich Wenk and piloted by Wilhelm Leusch climbed to over 1,000 feet before the wing collapsed and the glider crashed, killing the pilot. Wenk's work nevertheless influenced Alexander Lippisch, who produced over fifty tailless designs, including the rocket-powered Messerschmitt 163 in WWII.*

Largely overtaken by the thrills of powered flight and set aside during WWI, gliding was neglected until the 1920s. It then developed as a major sport in Germany, where it was encouraged as one way of circumventing the restrictions of the Versailles Treaty. (See *Aviation Century The Golden Age.*) The principal German gliding center was established at the Wasserkuppe mountain after Oskar Ursinus, the editor of *Flugsport* magazine, promoted a gliding rally there in 1920. Usually, gliders were towed off by winch or motor vehicle, but as early as 1920 Anthony Fokker built a glider modeled on his D.VIII fighter and experimented with towing it behind one of his biplanes. Gottlob Espenlaub demonstrated its possibilities more fully in 1927.

Only three gliders flew during the first Wasserkuppe meeting, but twenty were registered for the 1921 rally, when Arthur Martens established a distance world record of 8.9 kilometers and Friedrich Harth stayed airborne for 21 minutes. The next year, fifty-three gliders appeared and the endurance record was raised to more than three hours. For the most part, the glider pilots used air rising from the slopes of the Wasserkuppe to extend their flights, but in 1926 Max Kegel was caught by the updraft of a thunderstorm and landed almost 55 kilometers from his starting point, describing his

involuntary ascent as being "like a piece of paper pulled up a chimney." By 1929 the possibilities of thermal updrafts in thunderstorms were recognized, and Robert Kronfeld entered a cloud that lifted him to almost 10,000 feet and carried his Wien glider 143 kilometers from the Wasserkuppe. Soon after, the standing wave phenomenon was discovered in the lee of hills and many more glider pilots began achieving heights in excess of 5,000 feet.

The American record of 9 minutes, 45 seconds, for motorless flight, set by Orville Wright at Kitty Hawk on October 24, 1911, was not surpassed until August 18, 1929, when Ralph Barnaby stayed airborne for 15 minutes, 6 seconds. Subsequent progress in the United States was rapid. Two months later, William Hawley Bowlus became the first American to soar for more than one hour. On April 29, 1930, John C. Barstow flew for 15 hours, 13 minutes, exceeding the world soaring record. The record was broken again in December 1931 by William Cocke, who kept his Nighthawk glider aloft for 21 hours, 34 minutes.

In the mid-1930s, German glider pilots soared to the first altitude gain of 3,000 meters and the first 500-kilometer flight. The outright altitude record, however, went to the Soviet pilot Fydoroff; in 1937 he was towed to 28,050 feet before soaring to 39,946 feet. By then, the art of soaring was well developed and sailplanes had become sophisticated, elegant designs, most with long, high-aspect-ratio wings and pencil-thin fuselages. The gull-winged German Minimoa, constructed of wood and fabric, had a best glide ratio of 1:26. (In still air it descended 1 foot for every 26 flown at its best glide speed of 53 mph). The Horten brothers' designs were the most distinctive, pure flying wings of great span and incredibly narrow chord, prodigious slender parabolas. The German emphasis on gliding during the 1920s had brought them notable benefits — much valuable aerodynamic work had been done on drag reduction, and gliding clubs had proliferated, providing a solid foundation for the growing Luftwaffe.

The Polish team competing at the Wasserkuppe in 1937 flew the graceful gull-winged PWS 101.

The Schempp Hirth Minimoa (foreground) was first flown in 1935 and soon became the world's leading high-performance glider. Between 1935 and 1939, 110 were built. Minimoas achieved several world records, including the altitude record of 21,939 feet in 1938. The Meise Olympia (rear) won the contest to be the standard type used in soaring competition at the 1940 Olympic Games. WWII intervened but the design was widely produced in Germany and elsewhere.

Powerless Transports

While the sport of gliding languished during WWII, large transport gliders were involved in campaigns on every front. They were used by both sides and featured in the invasion of Belgium, the assault on Crete, the D-Day invasion, the attack on the bridge at Arnhem, and the insertion of the Chindits behind the Japanese lines in Burma. (See *Aviation Century World War II*.) Once again, the Germans produced the most extreme design. The Messerschmitt 361 Gigant was conceived for use during a possible invasion of Britain after the Soviet Union had been overcome. It was enormous, capable of accommodating 200 soldiers. Towing the beast off the ground was hazardous and was often conducted by three Bf 110s in formation. Later, a special Heinkel towplane was devised by joining two He 111s together, adding another engine at the join. Known as the Zwilling, this five-engined monstrosity was surprisingly successful as a tug, handling the huge Gigant without difficulty. The combination's significant contribution was to evacuate of thousands of wounded from the Kuban bridgehead in 1943.

Postwar Gliding Achievements

After the war, the influence of the prewar German club gliders was still apparent. The British Olympia sailplane was based on the Meise design, and other countries developed versions of the Grunau Baby and the Focke-Wulf Weihe. In 1957, Germany pioneered the use of glass fiber construction with the Phönix, a sailplane that could achieve a glide ratio of 1:40. By 1964, that figure had been improved to 1:44 with another German design, the glass fiber D-36 Circe, which boasted a T-tail, flaps, spoilers, and a retractable landing wheel. This was followed by the remarkable but unwieldy two-seat SB-10, which had a wingspan of 85 feet and an astonishing glide ratio of 1:50. In 1975, the Germans went further and produced the FS-29 with telescopic wings; in an attempt to get the best of both long and short span configurations, its wings could be stretched from 43 feet to 63 feet.

As the sport of gliding increased in worldwide popularity, competitions to challenge the proficiency of pilots grew more common. Complex glider aerobatic displays became regular events at air shows and the gliding performance envelope was continually stretched. Manufacturers Schleicher, Scheibe, Schempp-Hirth and Schweizer led the way. By the end of the century, James Payne of California held the Open Class record for the highest speed over a closed circuit, averaging 135 mph in a Schempp-Hirth Discus around a 100-kilometer course in 1997. However, the Open Class records for distance and altitude were of longer standing: Hans Werner Grosse of Germany traveled 908 miles from Lubeck to Biarritz in 1972, and Robert Harris reached 49,009 feet over California in 1986.

On December 12, 2002, flying from Omarama, New Zealand, Terry Delore and Steve Fossett set a new gliding world speed record for a flight of 1,000 kilometers out and back. Defying difficult wind and cloud conditions, they flew at an average speed of 166.46 km/h, breaking the record of

152.74 km/h set by Walter Binder in South Africa in 1999. Flying a Schleicher ASH-25 high-performance sailplane, this was Delore and Fossett's third attempt at the record. A month earlier, the same team smashed the 500-kilometer triangle record in 2 hours and 44 minutes, setting a new glider world record of 185.63 km/h (115 mph).

The next year, flying in the Andes, Fossett and Delore set further gliding records. On December 13, 2003, they succeeded in flying the first ever 1,500-kilometer triangle. Their aircraft was an ASH 25 carbon-composite sailplane, capable of a 60-1 glide ratio. Steve Fossett described the flight: "We started at 5:45 A.M. from Bariloche International Airport and initially flew south in the mountain wave to the first corner of the triangle. Then it got more difficult. We climbed to 30,500 feet (9,296 m) before beginning the long downwind glide to the second corner. We then had to find thermals to fly back upwind to the third corner." Along with improving the mark for the longest triangle (previously 1,400.19 kilometers set by Klaus Holighaus in January 1993) by over 100 kilometers, Fossett and Delore's 13-hour flight established three new world records: the longest triangle on a pre-declared course (1,502.6 km) the longest free triangle (1,509.7 km) and the speed record for a 1,500-kilometer triangle (119.11 km/h).

The following year, Fossett and Delore went for distance, flying their ASH 25M high-performance sailplane between the Argentine cities of El Calafate in Patagonia and San Juan, a straight-line world record of 2,187 kilometers (1,358 miles). The flight took 15 hours, 42 minutes, and covered almost two-thirds of the length of Argentina.

BACK TO FIRST PRINCIPLES

The first successful gliders, flown by men such as Lilienthal and Pilcher, were hang gliders, contraptions in which the pilot hung below the wing and operated both as the control system (by shifting his weight) and the undercarriage. The concept began to enjoy a comeback in 1948, when Francis and Gertrude Rogallo achieved the first successful flight of their flexible wing, made from Gertrude's kitchen curtains

"I am alive. Up here with the song of the engine and the air whispering on my face as the sunlight and shadows play upon the banking, wheeling wings, I am completely, vibrantly alive. With the stick in my right hand, the throttle in my left, and the rudder beneath my feet, I can savor that essence from which life is made."

STEPHEN COONTS, FLY! A COLORADO SUNRISE, A STEARMAN, AND A VISION

and developed from research conducted in their home-made wind tunnel. The Rogallo wing had no rigid members but assumed an airfoil shape when in the air.

The Rogallos developed the aerodynamic principles of the flexwing, but it was an Australian, John Dickenson, who went on to pioneer the design of a flexwing hang glider so that it could be enjoyed by a wider public. By May 1963 he had a half-size model in which he could be towed. The maiden flight of the full-size version was made in September 1963. The first of Dickenson's hang gliders had wooden leading edges, aluminum cross-booms, iron A-frames and wings of blue plastic sheeting. The total cost of materials was just $24! By 1964 all flight and construction problems had been overcome, and Dickenson's production Ski Wing was made of aluminum over a mild steel A-frame; the part-battened sails were nylon and the rigging was wire cable. It was designed for easy disassembly and cartop transport. Adventurous water skiers started towing them behind their boats to use as kites. In 1968, an Australian engineer, Bill Moyes, invented a triangular trapeze from which to suspend his weight under the Rogallo wing. The next year, at the 1969 World Water Ski Championships in Copenhagen, Moyes put on a kite demonstration and amazed the crowd by unhooking himself from the towline and successfully gliding down to alight on the water. The practical hang glider was unveiled to the world.

Most hang glider flights are relatively short, but they can establish impressive figures. In the United States on September 5, 1999, Peter DeBellis coaxed his Moyes Xlite up to 17,100 feet at Mammoth Mountain, and on August 8, 2000, Mark Bolt stayed airborne with his Aeros Stealth over Texas for 4 hours and 45 minutes while traveling 116 miles. In July 1994, Larry Tudor flew his weight-shift hang glider a distance of 307 miles, and in July 2000, David Sharp managed 312 miles using a hang glider with movable controls. Lilienthal, exhilarated by his 19th-century airborne forays of several hundred feet, would be suitably amazed at what the hang glider was able to accomplish a hundred years later.

Francis and Gertrude Rogallo invented the technology that made it possible for millions of people around the world to fly inexpensively. Working for NASA in the 1940s, Francis Rogallo conceived the idea that flexible wings provided more stability than fixed surfaces. He aimed at providing minimum supporting area with maximum lift, and worked toward the total elimination of rigid spars. Before the end of 1948, Rogallo had produced the first flexible-wing kite. A patent was granted in 1951. In acknowledgment of Gertrude's contribution to the project, she holds the patent on the Flexi-Kite. It was Gertrude who cut and sewed the fabric for the experimental wings. The wings were tested in a homemade wind tunnel. In 2003, Dan Patterson photographed the Rogallos in their home. Francis holds the first successful Rogallo wing, made from Gertrude's kitchen curtains.

Lighter than Light

The first Rogallo wings to leave the ground under power did so in 1961, flown by NASA test pilot Lou Everett during a series of investigations into methods of recovering Saturn Rocket first stages. It was soon realized that such powered hang gliders offered people the prospect of flying for pure enjoyment, and at a cost far below that of more conventional light aircraft. Numerous and varied designs, using both Rogallo-type flexwings and fixed wings, were developed by in the 1960s and 1970s as the sport began to take root. Powered by engines as small as those from chainsaws and often weighing little more than 100 pounds, these machines became known as ultralights, or in some parts of the world as microlights. Among the early aircraft produced were Herman Kolb's Kolb Flyer and Bob Hovey's Whing Ding. Frenchman Michel Colomban unveiled his Cri Cri, a remarkable little twin that could achieve 125 mph powered by two chainsaw engines. In Australia, Ron

Wheeler produced his Scout in 1974. The world's first commercially available fixed-wing ultralight, it had a conventional tail and was a machine of which Santos Dumont would have been proud.

By the 1980s, development in the ultralight world was explosive. Ultralight aviators in Australia, the United States, Britain and France led the way, with most Europeans concentrating on powered Rogallos, and Australians and Americans favoring aircraft with control surfaces. A succession of innovative designs revolutionized the sport and made it immeasurably safer. In October 1979, Roland Magallon began marketing what became known as the "trike," a machine with a tricycle undercarriage and a pusher propeller. The design put the thrust line in the right position to aid stability and made it possible to use a large-diameter propeller for additional performance.

As the sport matured, so major achievements began to be recorded. Starting in 1986 and on into 1987, Eve Jackson flew her CFM Shadow from London to Sydney, an adventurous 12,500-mile flight during which she was shot at, arrested, suffered endless agonies of red tape, and overcame an engine failure. The achievement led to her being awarded the Royal Aeronautical Society's Gold Medal, the first microlight pilot to be so honored. The South Atlantic was crossed by Frenchman Guy Delage flying a flexwing in 1992, an astonishing feat that involved staying awake for

twenty-six hours. Russian progress in the microlight field was evidenced in 1993 when four aircraft braved the Bering Strait to fly from Asia to North America. In many ways even more remarkable was the use of microlights by two Canadians to act as formation leader for a flock of young Canadian geese, guiding them through their first migration from Ontario to Virginia. By the mid-1990s, it seemed that microlights were capable of accomplishing almost anything, and long-distance flights crossing considerable stretches of water and difficult terrain (Scotland to Scandinavia; England to Jordan) were being undertaken to raise funds for charities. Flights were also made from London to South Africa, India, and China. London to Sydney was flown by Colin Bodill in just forty-nine days.

Perhaps the ultimate long-distance epic was begun in 1998, when Brian Milton and Keith Reynolds set out from Brooklands, England, in an attempt to fly their Quantum 912 round the world in 80 days. Reynolds left the endeavor halfway through, but Milton struggled on alone and completed the circumnavigation in 117 days, having endured numerous bureaucratic encounters, a buzzing by a Syrian Mig-21, and a crossing of the Greenland ice cap at 12,000 feet. Even this achievement was surpassed in 2000, when Colin Bodill became the first microlight pilot to fly round the world solo, traveling 22,173 miles and touching down in twenty-nine countries during a journey of 99 days.

As the century ended, world records in the various microlight classes were held by pilots from Germany, Britain, Belgium, the United States, Australia, and France. In Group 1 (weight-shift trikes), Patricia Taillebresse of France had flown 504 miles in a straight line without landing, and her countryman, Serge Zin, had climbed to 31,890 feet. Richard Meredith-Hardy of Britain had recorded a speed of 79.54 mph. Group 2 (rigid wings with aerodynamic controls) had seen Bernard d'Otreppe of Belgium cover 849 miles, and Eric Winton of Australia reach 30,000 feet. Frenchman Serge Ferrari had achieved the fastest outright speed with 105 mph.

Pedal Pushing

The earliest dreams of human flight had imagined that it could be accomplished on the strength of mankind's muscles alone. By the 1950s, the development of efficient propellers and strong lightweight materials suggested that the dreams might be made reality. In 1955, British industrialist Henry Kremer offered a prize of £5,000 sterling to the first person successful in flying a human-powered aircraft over a figure-of-eight course set around two pylons half a mile apart. Several attempts were made during the 1960s by English university students, but although their designs managed to fly as far as 2,000 feet, they proved unable to make the required 180-degree turns.

In 1973, Kremer raised the prize money to £50,000. This attracted the attention of American Paul MacCready, who set out to create an original design solely for the purpose of winning the prize. The result was the *Gossamer*

Condor, constructed from aluminum tubes, Mylar plastic, and steel bracing wire, with wing leading edges of corrugated cardboard and Styrofoam. Ninety-six feet across the wing, it weighed only 70 pounds. Bicycle technology was used to turn its 12-foot propeller. On August 23, 1977, piloted by champion cyclist Bryan Allen, the *Gossamer Condor* took off from Shafter Airport, California, and covered the figure-of-eight course in just under 7½ minutes, averaging a little over 10 mph. Kremer promptly issued another challenge — £100,000 for the first human-powered aircraft to fly across the English Channel. MacCready responded with the *Gossamer Albatross*, an improved version of the *Condor*. On June 12, 1979, Allen again provided the power, flying the *Albatross* some 10 feet above the waves while crossing from Folkestone to Cap Gris Nez. Battling the resistance of a slight headwind, Allen pedaled for 2 hours and 50 minutes in completing a 35-mile journey. (In the 1980s, MacCready went on to design a series of solar-powered propeller-driven aircraft [*Pathfinder, Centurion, Helios*] that could fly at altitudes from 50,000 feet to 100,000 feet, and could be used as cheap satellite substitutes. *Helios*, a 247-foot flying wing, was designed to stay airborne for six months or more.)

Since Bryan Allen's feats of stamina, there have been several other epic performances in human-powered aircraft. In January 1987, the *Michelob Light Eagle*, designed by students at the Massachusetts Institute of Technology, covered 36½ miles in 2 hours and 13 minutes at Edwards AFB, California, flown by Glenn Tremml, a twenty-six-year-old triathlete. His teammate Lois McCallin used the same aircraft to establish female records of 9.6 miles and 37½ minutes. Encouraged by their success, the MIT team prepared for their ultimate challenge — bringing the Daedalus myth to life. Building and testing the *Daedalus 88* aircraft took 15,000 hours and cost $1 million. Five cycling champions were selected and put through rigorous training and endurance tests. Early on the morning of April 23, 1988, Kanellos Kanellopoulos took off from Heraklion, Crete, and set off for the island of Santorini, 74 miles away. Three hours and 54 minutes later, as he approached a beach on Santorini, a gust of wind over-stressed the aircraft and snapped off its tail. The *Daedalus* plunged into the sea only 30 feet from shore. It seemed that the spirit of Icarus still haunted the straits. Kanellopoulos ignored the omen and swam the last few yards to claim his world human-power flight records — the longest flight of 74 miles and the longest airborne time of 3 hours and 54 minutes.

Sailplanes on exhibit at the Polish National Aviation Museum, in Krakow, Poland. The gliders are (from the back) SZD-18 CZAJKA (Tchaya – Pewitt), SZD-15 SROKA (Magpie), and SZD-10 CZAPLA (Tchapla – Heron).

SILENT FLIGHT

The Caesar Creek Soaring Club located near Waynesville, Ohio, is one of the largest and oldest soaring clubs in the United States. In October of 2000, club member Randy Wright took photographer Dan Patterson for a flight in the Grob G-103 Twin Astir. Dr. Richard Garrison provided an air-to-air camera platform with his Super Cub. Dick Garrison's grandfather, Orlando Garrison, was a machinist in Dayton in 1903 and was contracted by the Wright brothers' mechanician, Charlie Taylor, to cut the gears for the first three 1903 Wright aeroplane motors (see *Aviation Century The Early Years*), which powered the first flight on December 17, 1903.

OPPOSITE LEFT A sailplane approaches the field for a landing as another club member secures the tow rope to the nose of a Schweizer 2-33.

OPPOSITE RIGHT The club's Piper Pawnee towplane ahead of the Grob sailplane.

OPPOSITE BOTTOM Over the runway of the Caesar Creek Soaring Club, a Schweizer 2-33 circles inside a thermal, looking for lift. The art of soaring requires very close attention to the conditions, which will allow the pilot to detect the rising air currents of a thermal. A thermal is a rising column of air, sometimes given away by circling turkey vultures, a common sight in Ohio.

ABOVE Final approach to landing for this Grob G-103 Twin Astir.

BELOW The spoiler along the top of the wing of an LETL-23 Super Blanik sailplane. At times, pilots need to "spoil" the lift on their draft to slow down or descend. These useful tools are often deployed on final approach to landing, to get the sailplane over the runway.

Top Sailplanes display a fairly simple instrument panel. On top of the panel is a "whiskey" compass. Just beyond that and outside the cockpit is an aviation instrument that hails from the very earliest days of manned flight, a piece of string. Across the top of the panel is, at left, an airspeed indicator, and center, the vertical speed indicator, which tells the sailplane pilot if he or she has found the rising air, here showing a neutral reading. Below that is the altimeter.

Bottom Circling inside a thermal.

Opposite Top Randy Wright, a website designer from Fort Thomas, Kentucky, devotedly pilots both sailplanes and powered aircraft. Always ready with a smile, even when he's just talking about flying, Randy often refers to himself as that "other Wright brother."

Opposite Bottom The club's Grob G-103 Twin Astir soaring over southwestern Ohio, autumn trees and farmlands.

ENTHUSIASTS

Top Floyd McGowin, Chapman, Alabama, and his spectacular Cessna 185 at the grass strip near his home. Floyd, who has flown all of his life, is a longtime supporter of the National Museum of Naval Aviation and of the Gathering of Eagles at Maxwell Air Force Base.

Bottom Ralph Charles of Somerset, Ohio. Ralph's life spanned three centuries and all of powered flight's history. He was born on November 22, 1899—more than four years before the Wright brothers' epic flight at Kitty Hawk—and by age nineteen was working as a welder with Orville Wright at Dayton Wright Field. During his life, Ralph saw Lincoln Beachy fly at local fairs and flew the space shuttle simulator at the Johnson Space Center in Houston, Texas. Ralph flew Ford Trimotors for TWA and was a test pilot for Curtiss-Wright during World War II. After the war his wife told him that it was her or the airplanes, so he quit flying for fifty years. After his wife died in 1995, Ralph renewed his medical certificate and began flying again. Until his death in the spring of 2003, he was the oldest active pilot in the United States.

FIXED BASE OPERATOR
COMMANDER – AERO

Commander-Aero, Inc., of Dayton, Ohio, is a fixed base operator and a certified FAA repair facility, offering a large hangar, on-staff repair and avionics technicians, and a sheet-metal shop, as well as a pilots' lounge and fuel sales. The ubiquitous fixed base operators – the FBO – are part of the fabric that holds together the corporate and general aviation communities. Many of these companies are not located at the large airports, which are dominated by airline operations. However, they provide a myriad of important services to the aviation population, including everything from courtesy cars to hot coffee and restrooms. They can be counted on for the last-ditch option, when everything else is closed — the FBO meal of a can of soda and some peanut butter crackers from a vending machine.

ONLY IN AMERICA
A PARADE OF PLANES

On the Fourth of July the town of New Carlisle, Ohio, has a procession of airplanes for its parade to celebrate American Independence. Organized by motion picture storyboard artist J. Todd Anderson and the "Flying Angels" from nearby Barnhart Memorial Airfield, this annual event showcases the Ohio fascination with flight. These photos were made during their 2001 parade.

ABOVE Robert Signon provided equally rare transportation from the Packard Museum in Dayton, Ohio.

RIGHT Complete with color guard and reproduction Wright gliders, the parade winds through the town. The brick building in the background was once a bank, and on June 10, 1933, was robbed by John Dillinger.

OPPOSITE A variety of tractors and vehicles provide the towing for the parade through the residential neighborhoods of New Carlisle.

WOMEN AVIATORS

ABOVE Women Aviation International President and founder Peggy Chabrian at her airstrip, "Morning Star" in Ohio. A longtime aviation enthusiast and professional aviation educator, Dr. Chabrian is a 2,000-hour commercial/instrument multi-engine pilot and flight instructor who has been flying for over fifteen years.

Dr. Chabrian has held several top positions in aviation education including Academic Dean and Associate Vice President of Parks College; Dean of Academic Support for Embry-Riddle Aeronautical University's Prescott, Arizona campus; Director of the Center of Excellence for Aviation/Space Education at ERAU's Daytona Beach campus; and Department Chair of the aviation department at Georgia State University in Atlanta, Georgia.

TOP Aviation pioneer Evelyn "Bobbi" Trout (right), in 1929 the first woman to perform air-to-air refueling, and Dr. Terri I. von Thaden, granddaughter of Louise Thaden, who competed against "Bobbi" Trout in winning the first Women's Transcontinental Air Derby, also in 1929. Dr. von Thaden researches aviation human factors at the University of Illinois, Urbana-Champaign.

BOTTOM Jeanie R. Carter flies as Command Pilot for the Commonwealth of Virginia in King Air and Citation aircraft. She is also Virginia's Safety Program Administrator for General Aviation. Jeanie is a single mother and comes from a family of aviators. Her father flew H-19 helicopters in Korea, and then DC-3s, DC-4s and Viscounts for Capital Airlines.

TOP LEFT Caro Bosca of Springfield, Ohio, flew with the WASPs (Women Airforce Service Pilots) during WWII and has served as president of the postwar WASP organization. WASPs ferried all types of military aircraft around the United States, so releasing male pilots for combat duties.

TOP RIGHT Women pilots of the United States Customs Service, photographed at the Women in Aviation International Convention in 2002: Jeanie Blankenship, Corpus Christi, Texas; Kimberly Elsholz, Miami, Florida; Melanie Dziadulewicz, Washington, DC; Laura Goldsberry, Tucson, Arizona. They patrol the borders of the United States, flying a variety of fixed- and rotary-wing aircraft.

CENTER RIGHT Connie Bowlin is a remarkably accomplished aviator. In 1978, she became the fourth woman hired by Delta Airlines as a pilot. In 1990, she moved to the captain's seat in the McDonnell Douglas DC-9, and since then, has captained the Boeing 757 and 767. Connie has amassed over 14,000 hours in some seventy types, including the B-17 Flying Fortress, P-47 Thunderbolt, P-51 Mustang and T-6 Texan.

BOTTOM RIGHT Wally Funk (left) has been flying professionally since 1957 and has logged over 16,800 hours as a pilot. In 1961 she was one of only thirteen women to qualify as a candidate for the Mercury astronaut program, and in 1974 she became the first female Air Safety Investigator with the National Transportation Safety Board. Susan Maule (right) comes from the family that manufactures STOL aircraft and is a captain for U.S. Airways. She is also celebrated as a writer of poetry about flight.

PRECISE AND MINATURE FLIGHT

The Academy of Model Aeronautics has over 17,000 members from all walks of life. At their museum in Muncie, Indiana, the flying models on show include some made over 100 years ago. (Opposite) Recreated in the center of the museum is a typical hobby shop from an earlier age, with representative model aircraft and a jumble of accessories. BELOW LEFT The display in the window of the hobby shop tempts even the casual modeler to go inside to see what other wonders are on offer.
BELOW RIGHT Some of the flying models on show at the AMA Museum. In the foreground is a meticulously prepared Curtiss P-6E Hawk representing hundreds of hours of careful work by a dedicated modeler. Among the models in the background are a magnificent B-17, Al Williams' Gulfhawk, and a Spitfire inverted in a victory roll, all of them exact small-scale replicas of classic aircraft.

ABOVE Jerry Brinkman of Dayton, Ohio, winner of the duration aloft (nonprofessional) category of the First International Paper Airplane Competition sponsored by Scientific American magazine. The competition's four categories (aerobatics, distance, duration aloft, and origami) were decided at the New York Hall of Science in February 1967.

The Zeppelin Company's Hindenburg *was the largest airship ever built, 803 feet long and 135 feet in diameter. In 1936, the* Hindenburg *completed ten successful return flights carrying a total of 1,002 passengers between Frankfurt and Lakehurst, New Jersey, and was so popular that customers were turned away. For the* Hindenburg's *luxury, a passenger paid $720 for a round trip, which was $200 more than the cost of crossing by sea on the* Queen Mary. *In this photograph, the* Hindenburg *is moored near the vast airship hangars at Lakehurst in 1936.*

CHAPTER 3

Lighter than Air

ALTHOUGH REAL PROGRESS in the aerodynamics of heavier-than-air flight was not achieved until the 19th century, human beings had by then become accustomed to the fact that they could defy gravity and float above the Earth. In 1783, the first of aviation's many pairs of cooperating brothers, Étienne and Joseph Montgolfier, successfully demonstrated hot-air balloons, or "aerostatic machines," in France. Prudently, the Montgolfiers (like the creators of the first space vehicles two centuries later) chose not to test their aerostats themselves. The first aeronauts were a sheep, a rooster and a duck. These creatures having survived an eight-minute flight, the first men to travel by air were Pilatre de Rozier and the Marquis d'Arlandes, who stoked a fire of straw to keep their Montgolfier aloft as they flew across Paris in the course of a twenty-five-minute flight on November 21, 1783. (De Rozier proved also to be the first aviation fatality. In June 1785, he attempted to cross the English Channel in a balloon combining both hot air and hydrogen as lifting agents. It appeared that flames from the open fire ignited escaping gas.) Only ten days later, Professor J.A.C. Charles also rose from Paris in a balloon, this time one filled with hydrogen. On December 1, he was in the air for over two hours and at one stage reached a height estimated at some 9,000 feet.

Fascinations and Fears

Within a very short time, ballooning became a popular craze. In spite of the unpredictable nature of balloons, which could travel only in directions chosen for them by the winds, the attraction of reaching for the clouds was such that the intrepid and wealthy rushed to experience the new adventure. Fresh achievements crowded upon one another and, just over a year after the Montgolfier success, a balloon carrying Jean-Pierre Blanchard and an American doctor, John Jeffries, left Dover and crossed the English Channel. English strategists were alarmed, seeing a threat to the island nation's security in a device that could ignore the water barrier of the English Channel and fly over the ships of the Royal Navy.

Such fears were not entirely without foundation. There are engravings depicting a Napoleonic balloon-borne invasion of England, and there are sketches of kites bearing English soldiers ready to meet an aerial threat. These ideas may have been premature and fanciful, but they anticipated a need for Britain's air defense that would prove to be very real in the 20th century. They were not, however, by any means the first speculations on the possible use of the air for military purposes. Benjamin Franklin was an eyewitness of Professor Charles' first ascent, and he was impressed by the thought that it would be difficult to defend against an aerial

armada of balloons carrying armed men. (See *Aviation Century The Early Years*, Chapter 1, "Creeds Martial and Messianic.")

The French Army was already using tethered balloons for reconnaissance of the battlefield by 1794, but in many ways it was a surprise that it had taken Western soldiers so long to take advantage of the high ground of the air. Airborne military development, after all, had been predicted for a very long time. Man-carrying kites had been used for reconnaissance in the Far East for centuries, and in 1670 a Jesuit priest named Francesco de Lana suggested that a warring airship could be borne aloft by large evacuated copper balls. He made no attempt to construct such a vessel because, he said: "God would not suffer such an invention to take effect, by reason of the civil disturbance

On November 21, 1783, Pilatre de Rozier and the Marquis d'Arlandes became the first humans to fly. They were airborne beneath a balloon designed by the Montgolfier brothers that was made of a colorful cotton envelope lined with paper. Lift was provided by hot air rising from an open fire. It was sufficient to allow the aeronauts to fly above Paris for 25 minutes and cover a distance of 9 kilometers.

it would cause to the government of men." Francesco de Lana was ahead of his time, and it was almost two hundred years before his similar ideas were expressed and took shape. With the United States at war with Mexico in 1846, John Wise proposed that a tethered balloon should be flown over the fortress of Vera Cruz to drop bombs on the defenders. The U.S. War Department did not pursue the idea, but only three years later a city actually was attacked from the air when the Austrians used unmanned balloons to drop bombs on Venice. Exaggerated expectations of reducing the city to rubble were not met, but that would not be the last time in aerial warfare that prediction would exceed capability.

The value of balloons for reconnaissance was apparent to American soldiers, and, in September 1861, the Balloon Corps of the Army of the Potomac was formed. This small precursor of American air power started with just two balloons under the command of Chief Aeronaut Thaddeus Lowe. His reports from the battle of Fair Oaks at the end of May 1862 suggest that his corps was a valuable addition to the army. More than once he saw enemy movements, undetected on the ground, that posed threats to Union forces. Following one report of Confederate troops massing, General McLellan hurriedly brought up reserves on his army's left, and Lowe says: "Had not our forces been concentrated, it is very evident that our left ... would have been driven back and in consequence the whole army routed."

Despite the fact that similarly useful information about the enemy was obtained on many occasions, the balloon unit was disbanded in 1863. It was not until 1892 that a balloon section was reformed as part of the Signal Corps of the U.S. Army. Even then, it was a minor affair, with only one balloon. Nevertheless, it was sent to Cuba during the Spanish-American War, and was flown under fire to spy out the land before the famous charge of the Rough Riders up San Juan Hill.

Dirigibles

The quality lacking in a balloon was "dirigibility" — the capacity to be directed. Without it, lighter-than-air machines had to be tethered or remain at the mercy of the winds. The problem was understood from the start and, in 1784, one far-sighted French officer produced a design for a dirigible airship. Lieutenant (later General) Meusnier proposed a cigar-shaped balloon 260 feet long carrying a car powered by three propellers. In the absence of a suitable power source, his proposal was dropped, but the idea was sound and, as practical power plants began to appear, it was put into practice. The French again led the way with Henri Giffard, who in 1852 managed to steer his steam-driven airship to a point some 16 miles southwest of Paris. During the second half of the 19th century, he was followed by a number of others, primarily Frenchmen, who built airships powered inadequately either by steam or electricity. Then, in 1885, events in Germany opened the door to practical manned flight. Karl Benz and Gottlieb Daimler, building on the work of Nikolaus Otto, constructed the first gasoline-fueled engines with a reasonable power-to-weight ratio. They did their work for the benefit of surface transport, but engines based on their designs soon became the first choice for the aviation world.

France remained at the center of airship development for a while, principally as a result of the efforts of the Lebaudy brothers and the showmanship of the Brazilian Alberto Santos-Dumont, who, in the early 1900s, flew his "little runabouts" all over Paris. Santos-Dumont airship No. 1 made its first trial run from the zoological gardens in Paris on September 18, 1898, but it ran foul of a tree soon after leaving the ground. It did a little better on its next attempt, but neither No. 1 nor its immediate successors were notable performers. Even so, they captivated Santos-Dumont: "I cannot describe the delight, the wonder and intoxication of this free diagonal movement onward and upward, or onward and downward, combined at will with brusque changes of direction horizontally when the airship answers to a touch of the rudder."

It was Santos-Dumont's No. 6 that won him international renown. In 1900, the industrialist Henri Deutsch de la Meurthe offered a 100,000-franc prize for the first person to leave St. Cloud by air and return to the starting point within thirty minutes, having rounded the Eiffel Tower (7 miles away) in the process. Santos-Dumont succeeded in October 1901, flying No. 6 over the stipulated course in just under the half hour. (It says something about the character — and wealth — of Santos-Dumont that he took none of the prize money, which had grown to 125,000 francs, for himself: 75,000 francs went to the poor of Paris, and 50,000 francs to those who worked on his aeronautical projects.) His achievement helped to encourage other French aeronauts who were building dirigible airships, notably the Lebaudy brothers, Paul and Pierre. With ample spare funds available from their sugar refining business, they employed the engineer Henri Julliot to construct a lighter-than-air craft, which was completed in 1902. It was a semi-rigid airship, 187 feet long, formally named *Lebaudy I* but more usually known as *La Jaune* because of its protective coating of yellow paint. It proved to be a successful design and was the precursor of a series of workmanlike Lebaudy-Julliot airships used in France, Russia and Britain.

In 1903, Alberto Santos-Dumont often flew his airship No. 9, Baladeuse, *to travel between Neuilly St. James and St. Cloud in Paris, dropping in on unsuspecting friends or landing outside a café for a drink.* Baladeuse *was powered by a motor of only 3 horsepower and was not very quick, but it gave Santos-Dumont considerable freedom of movement within the city. His confidence in the airship was demonstrated when he allowed Aida de Acosta, an American debutante he had met, to use it to become the first woman to fly solo.*

German Giants

Even more significant airship developments were taking place in Germany, on the shores of the Bodensee. The guiding genius was Count Ferdinand von Zeppelin, for whom vastness seemed to be a guiding principle. From the outset, he emphasized rigid construction, a method in which the structure incorporates an internal framework, so allowing greater size and therefore increased lifting capability. His airships were more than 400 feet long, dwarfing efforts elsewhere, and Luftschiff Zeppelin 1 (LZ 1) made its maiden flight on the evening of July 2, 1900. Emerging from its floating hangar on the Bodensee, LZ 1 was towed into the air from its raft by a small tugboat and then the monster's two 15-horsepower engines were started. This first aerial venture was not an unqualified success. The tiny engines struggled with the task of propelling LZ 1's enormous bulk and Count Zeppelin did his best to trim the creature into level flight by winding a 220-pound weight backward and forward along a cable slung underneath its belly.

Unfortunately, first the winding mechanism jammed with the airship's nose down, and then one of the engines failed. Zeppelin accepted the inevitable and settled the LZ 1 onto the lake from which it had risen only eighteen minutes before. Suitably repaired, LZ 1 flew twice more, confirming as it did so that its control response was poor and its power inadequate. Worse still, it became clear that it was structurally weak. These hard lessons having been learned, the Count had his first airship dismantled early in 1901.

With some encouragement from Kaiser Wilhelm and patriotic support from the German people, Count Zeppelin endured a long series of disasters and financial crises as he fought his way toward a practical large airship. He believed that such craft could become powerful instruments of war, and he was determined that Germany should lead the airship's military development. Not many senior German Army officers shared Zeppelin's enthusiasm, and his case was not helped when LZ 2 was wrecked in 1906 because both engines failed on only its second flight. It survived the crash landing but was battered to pieces on the ground by strong winds. LZ 3 was far more controllable and reliable, and was eventually accepted by the German Army as a training airship, but LZ 4 was forced down by another engine failure during a trip along the Rhine valley in 1908. At Echterdingen, near Stuttgart, a squall blew the airship into some trees, ripping open a hydrogen gas cell. Ignited by sparks of static electricity, the gas exploded, consuming the LZ 4 in a tower of flame. The Count, now devoid of funds, began to think his airship dreams were over, but by this time his exploits had made him something of a national celebrity, and his airships showed promise of becoming symbols of national might. The future British prime minister, David Lloyd George, was in Stuttgart at the time of the LZ 4's destruction, and he recorded his astonishment at the reaction of the German people: "Disappointment was a totally inadequate word for the agony of grief and dismay which swept over the massed Germans who witnessed the

The shape of things to come. In the early days of manned flight, British Army officers were not always sure that taking to the air was a good thing. Nor were many of them convinced that any machine could be as useful or reliable as a horse. In 1913, the British Army airship Delta *made a cavalry horse put its ears back.*

catastrophe. The crowd swung into the chanting of 'Deutschland über Alles' with a fanatic fervour of patriotism." That patriotism produced a flood of contributions from Germans at home and abroad, bringing in six and a quarter million marks and ensuring the future of Count Zeppelin's airships.

It was not the end of the Count's problems, however. LZ 5 was reasonably satisfactory and was bought by the government, but the Army considered it too slow and were not altogether sorry when, in 1910, it suffered the same fate as LZ 4. The Army's continued reluctance to support airship development forced Zeppelin to consider widening his market. Although he had always thought of his airships as weapons, in 1909 he cooperated in the forming of the Deutsche Luftschiffahrts Aktien Gesellschaft (the German Airship Transport Company) to promote air travel between German cities. DELAG, as it was known, began operations in June 1910 with LZ 7, the *Deutschland*. The problems commonly associated with airship operations surfaced quickly. On June 28, the *Deutschland*, on only its seventh flight with passengers, lost an engine and was caught by bad weather. Heavy from rain and unable to make headway against a strong wind, the airship crashed into the trees of the Teutoburger Forest and was destroyed. LZ 6 was brought into service as an interim replacement, but by September it was gone too, burned to ashes in a hangar fire. LZ 8, *Deutschland II*, which was ready by March 1911, managed a few flights before being irreparably damaged when strong winds tore it away from its ground-handling party and blew it against the unforgiving walls of its hangar. It might have been thought that commercial lighter-than-air operations would not survive, DELAG having lost all three of its airships in less than a year, but the Count was determined and the German people remained tolerant. Incredibly, no lives had been lost in any of the accidents, and at such an early stage in the history of manned flight, airships still seemed to offer the best option for the future of long-range air travel.

The commander of LZ 8 at the time of its unfortunate demise was Hugo Eckener, a man of considerable practical capability in both technical and business matters.

> "A new era of transportation is coming nearer, in which the airship will have a place as a conveyance of peace as well as an instrument of war."
>
> JUNIUS B. WOOD,
> *NATIONAL GEOGRAPHIC*, JANUARY 1925

Appointed DELAG's flight director, he improved personnel training, set up a weather-forecasting network, and had docking rails installed beside the hangars to hold airships steady when they were outside and exposed to the wind. Daimler engines had proved unreliable, so the Maybach Company was contracted to provide the power for future airships. These measures, and Count Zeppelin's persistence, led to DELAG's first real success, the 459-foot-long LZ 10 *Schwaben*. Powered by three 150-horsepower Maybachs, it had a twenty-seat cabin and could cruise at 44 mph. In the summer of 1912, the LZ 10 also met a fiery end in a storm, but not before it had made 218 flights and carried 4,354 passengers. It did so in some style, its passengers seated at small tables near the windows being served with paté and champagne as they admired the passing world below. (The flights of the *Schwaben* were the first in which a steward provided a meal service to passengers.) The *Schwaben* flew all over Germany, demonstrating the promise of airship travel, and thereafter three more airships went into service before World War I — LZ 11 *Viktoria Luise*, LZ 13 *Hansa* and LZ 17 *Sachsen*. These massive vehicles never managed to establish DELAG's original intention of a scheduled service between the major German cities. They were made available for sightseeing and air experience flights in various parts of Germany, and in their four years of peacetime operation they carried over 34,000 people. Remarkably, in view of the early airship accident record, they accomplished this without recording a single fatality.

Less Rigid Germans

Count Zeppelin was not the only German building airships before WWI. August von Parseval, a German Army officer who invented the kite balloon (*Drachenballon*) in 1897, constructed his first airship, PL 1, in 1906. Like all the others he produced, it was non-rigid, a characteristic that made it possible to collapse it into a relatively small package for easy transportation. This advantage of mobility led to several of von Parseval's airships being bought by the armed forces not only of Germany, but also Russia, Italy, Japan and Britain. In 1910, it was a Parseval airship that introduced the idea of the aerial billboard, so effectively used in later years by Goodyear and others. PL 6 made a number of night flights over Berlin during which searchlights projected advertisements for Stallwerck chocolates onto white screens hung along the sides of the airship's envelope.

Smaller Fry

By comparison with the extraordinary achievements in Germany, progress in airship design elsewhere before WWI was not nearly so impressive. In France, Lebaudy-Julliot semi-rigid craft continued to be built, notably the *République* class, 215 feet long and capable of cruising at 31 mph. Other French firms producing airships were the Astra and Clément-Bayard companies. By the time war broke out in 1914, the French Army, primarily in response to developments in Germany, had acquired some twenty semi-rigid airships of various designs, but only two, both built by Clément-Bayard, were considered to be of any military value. One of these, the *Dupuy de Lôme*, was promptly identified as a Zeppelin by a French antiaircraft battery, which demonstrated its proficiency by shooting down the supposed intruder near Reims.

The only British airship pioneer worthy of the name is E.T. Willows, who built his first small airship in 1905 at the age of nineteen, and produced five before WWI, one of which went to the navy and another to the army. Willows No. 3 succeeded in crossing the English Channel in November 1910. Other British lighter-than-air achievements were less commendable. A 120-foot-long sausage-shaped semi-rigid airship appeared in 1907 and was given the inappropriate name of *Nulli Secundus* by its Army owners. Powered by one 50-horsepower engine, it was flat out at 16 mph, and it had neither stabilizers nor adequate control surfaces, so flying it in any sort of breeze was unwise. In October 1907, its commander, Colonel Capper, induced the celebrated aeronaut

Samuel Cody to join him in venturing across London with this dangerous machine. Traveling downwind, they succeeded in reaching and circling St. Paul's Cathedral and Buckingham Palace, but could make no headway in their efforts to return to their starting point. They put the airship down reasonably successfully near London's Crystal Palace, but *Nulli Secundus* was badly damaged by exposure to the elements overnight and never flew again. A similar but larger craft, *Nulli Secundus II*, was built in 1908, but it was an equally poor design and did not last long. However, the Army did use one of its brief flights to carry some naval personnel aloft to stimulate their interest in airships. The effort evidently bore fruit. From 1909 onward, the Royal Navy took formal responsibility for operating large airships. The Admiralty had already made a proposal for the acquisition of a large rigid airship in 1908. Since it was to be on the bulky scale of the German Zeppelins, its eventual name of *Mayfly* seems to be evidence of naval humor. The Vickers submarine yard was given the job of constructing the monster, learning how as it went along. Arguments over design and specifications were endless, changes were frequent, and the work went very slowly. At last, on May 24, 1911, it emerged from its waterborne chrysalis of a shed, pulled into the open by tugs. Flying proved beyond the capabilities of the overweight *Mayfly*, however, so it was taken back inside. Several months later, a much lighter airship emerged once more, but the wind gave it a buffeting which was too much for its weakened structure. There were loud noises of rending metal as the *Mayfly* broke its back and collapsed into a watery grave, never having gained the freedom of the air, even for a moment.

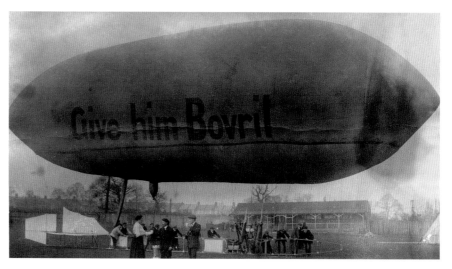

It did not take long for someone to see the advantages of using the skin of an airship to spread the word. In 1913, the blunt message on the side of this gasbag advertised Bovril, a thick, salty beef extract.

LEFT *Domestic animals soon got use to flying machines. Holstein-Friesian cows graze quietly in an English field, ignoring the chubby blimp passing by above.* RIGHT *In 1915, men of the Royal Navy dash forward to gather in an SS airship, which is being driven by a crew occupying the wingless fuselage of a B.E.2c.*

In the United States, a newspaperman named Walter Wellman had gained something of a reputation as an explorer, albeit not a very successful one. In the 1890s, he had twice tried to reach the North Pole, first being shipwrecked off Spitzbergen and then being denied on his second attempt when his dogsleds were confronted by impassable ice formations. News of the advances made in airship design by Lebaudy-Julliot inspired him to start planning to make a third attempt by air. By 1907, his French-built airship *America* was assembled and ready at Spitzbergen. Bad weather delayed his start until September, but even then he did not get far, being forced to land among Spitzbergen's rugged mountains. Two years later, he was off again, only to come down at sea and be rescued by the Norwegian Arctic ship *Fram*. This time, the *America* was severely damaged while under tow and had to be rebuilt. Wellman's enthusiasm, undimmed by all these mishaps, now turned him to the idea of crossing the Atlantic. Encouraged by the generous sponsorship of three newspapers — the *New York Times*, the *Chicago Record-Herald*, and London's *Daily Telegraph* — he had the *America* extensively modified. The 228-foot-long airship was powered by two engines (a British E.N.V. of 80 horsepower and a French 75-horsepower Lorraine-Dietrich) driving four propellers. On October 15, 1910, Wellman and his crew (plus a cat) lifted off from Atlantic City, New Jersey, and set off to the east. Hopes were high, but the airship was overloaded, the engines inadequate and unreliable, and the winds unhelpful. After almost seventy-two hours in the air, *America* gave up the unequal struggle and splashed into the cold waters of the Atlantic near the British steamer *Trent*. The aeronauts had managed to travel 1,000 erratic miles from New Jersey, but had reached a point only 400 miles off the U.S. coast before coming to grief. Walter Wellman lived for another quarter century but never again climbed aboard any type of aircraft.

The first practical airship to fly in the United States was built in 1904 by Thomas Scott Baldwin. It was 52 feet long and powered by a five-horsepower Curtiss engine. Its name, *California Arrow,* smacked of wishful thinking, but it gave successful exhibition flights at the St. Louis World's Fair. In 1908, the U.S. Army Signal Corps ordered its first airship from Baldwin. Designated Dirigible No. 1, it was acquired mainly for evaluation purposes. It was a cylindrical semi-rigid dirigible capable of carrying a crew of two at a maximum speed of less than 20 mph. Frank Lahm, Thomas Selfridge and Benjamin Foulois all learned to fly it, but their lack of enthusiasm for the airship as a military vehicle is evident from the fact that Dirigible No. 1 remained in service for just three years and was the U.S. Army's only dirigible.

German Lighter-than-Air War

Although the DELAG Zeppelins had completed their pre-war operations without anyone being killed, the same was not true of their military counterparts. Casualties were heavy when the Naval airships L 1 and L 2 both crashed in the autumn of 1913. Their loss meant that the Germans, for all their much vaunted and feared capacity to launch the Zeppelins against their enemies in an orgy of destruction, began the war by using their remaining great airships tentatively, sending them no further than the front lines or on naval reconnaissance sorties. Cautious though they intended to be, the German Army lost four Zeppelins in quick succession when, late in August 1914, they were launched on raids against French targets in broad daylight. Not until they had been replaced was the German Army able to turn its attention to raiding Britain. (See *Aviation Century The Early Years,* Chapter 2, "The Zeppelins.")

In 1915, the Army joined the Navy in an airship bombing offensive against Britain, but by 1917, the Army high command had lost confidence in airships for strategic bombing and was shifting the emphasis to large aircraft such as the Gothas. No further airships were constructed for the Army after the beginning of 1917, and the last air attack by an Army Zeppelin was made by LZ 107 on February 16 of that year against Boulogne. Since clouds obscured the ground over the French coastal towns during that final raid, an observer car was used — a small gondola lowered from the parent airship. In this way, the attacker could remain above cloud while being guided by telephone from a crewman who cruised along like bait on a fishing line perhaps as

far as 3,000 feet below. One observer described riding in the "sub-cloud car" as like being "in a bucket, down a well." This terrifying duty often demanded considerable qualities of endurance besides raw courage. On the Boulogne raid, the unfortunate observer was condemned to spend seven cold and lonely hours of the return flight in his car when the winch used for hauling him back up jammed. His only solace was the chance to smoke his cigarettes, a relaxation forbidden to those in the main gondola, close to the hydrogen-filled envelope of the parent ship.

Thirty-five Zeppelins were operated by the German Army at one time or another during WWI. Sixteen of them were lost in action (either shot down or wrecked on landing after being damaged), one was carried away by a storm, while four more were wrecked and three severely damaged in forced landings in German-controlled territory. Between them, on all fronts, they were involved in 282 bombing and reconnaissance missions, and, despite the accidents and losses, only thirty-six crew members died. The Zeppelins remaining when the Army ceased airship operations in 1917 were either broken up or transferred to the Navy.

The driving force behind the use of Zeppelins for strategic bombing was Commander Peter Strasser. He was appointed Chief of the Naval Airship Division in 1913, after his predecessor was killed in the crash of Zeppelin L 2. Under his leadership, the Naval Airship Division expanded and began its assault on Britain in January 1915, when bombs fell on the coastal towns of Great Yarmouth and King's Lynn. Although the material damage inflicted by the attack was slight, the effect on civilian morale was significant. People were alarmed to discover that the long-feared Zeppelin threat was real. As foretold, they were indeed being attacked in their own homes, far from the military confrontation in the trenches. The thought of bombs falling from the sky, unannounced and indiscriminate, was frightening, and the sense of menace was heightened if a Zeppelin raid was witnessed. To those on the ground, the great airships seemed inexorable as they floated over their potential victims, unloading their deadly cargo at leisure and killing at random. They brought the horrors of war to the civilian's front door.

Besides their strategic bombing role, the German Navy's Zeppelins had contributions to make to the war at sea, both by attacking enemy shipping and as maritime reconnaissance vehicles. Admiral Scheer, the commander-in-chief of the German North Sea Fleet, considered them vital to his operations, and his British opponent, Admiral Jellicoe, was wary of their attentions. During the naval Battle of Jutland in 1916, Scheer believed he had been well served by his airships, and a British Admiralty after-action report agreed, commenting that: "It is no small achievement for Zeppelins to have saved the [German] High Seas Fleet at the Battle of Jutland." In fact, both sides had been misled and tended to overrate the capabilities of the Zeppelins. Their achievements at Jutland were more imagined than real. Of the nine airships launched during the battle, only two contributed anything at all. L 24 transmitted reports on the morning of June 1, 1916, which proved to be entirely erroneous, and although L 11 did somewhat better with a series of reports on the British warships seen, its navigation was at fault, so the positions given were misplaced by at least 25 miles. However, if the work done by the Zeppelins at Jutland was subsequently shown to have been inconsequential, there is no doubting their negative impact some two months later.

On August 18, 1916, Admiral Scheer ventured to sea again with a fleet which included eighteen battleships and two battlecruisers, and came closer to annihilation than he knew at the time. At one point on August 19, he was steaming on a northerly heading, unknowingly toward Jellicoe's far superior force (twenty-nine battleships and six battlecruisers), when he received a report from Zeppelin L 13 that some thirty British ships, battleships and cruisers among them, were to his south. Assuming that these were from a force commanded by Admiral Beatty and inferior to his own, Scheer turned toward them and away from Jellicoe, then merely an hour distant. L 13's report was inaccurate, no contact was made, and a disappointed Scheer eventually turned for home, unaware that a possibly disastrous battle had been averted because he had reacted to an airship observer's false information.

As the war progressed and the defenses facing the German airmen grew more formidable, so the performance of the Zeppelins had to improve. L 30, the first of a series nicknamed "Super-Zeppelins," 640 feet long and more streamlined than its predecessors, appeared in 1916. Powered by six 240-horsepower Maybach engines, it had a maximum speed of 64 mph and could reach over 17,000 feet. Even larger was the L 59, later known as the African airship because of a remarkable voyage undertaken in November 1917. After three years of resisting the assault of his enemies, the commander of the German forces in East Africa, General von Lettow-Vorbeck, was in dire need of

The Royal Navy's NS 6 floating above the National Gallery on the north side of London's Trafalgar Square. The message reflects the public mood following the German bombing campaign against Britain in WWI, conducted first with Zeppelins and later with heavy bombers.

Zeppelin LZ 1, by Michael Turner. Count Zeppelin's LZ 1 was the world's first rigid dirigible. It rose into the air for the first time from a raft on Lake Constance, near Friedrichshafen, on July 2, 1900.

outside help. On the morning of November 3, L 59 left Staaken, near Berlin, carrying weapons, ammunition, spares and medical supplies, and set course for Jamboli, Bulgaria, the nearest Central Powers base to Africa. From there, the airship eventually left for Mahenge in German East Africa (Tanganyika) on November 21. After crossing the Mediterranean and the Libyan desert, L 59 had reached a point some 125 miles west of Khartoum when a message was received recalling the airship because von Lettow-Vorbeck's forces had surrendered to the British. Much depressed by the news, the L 59's crew turned back, returning to Jamboli after covering 4,400 miles and spending an unbroken ninety-five hours in the air. Unavailing though it was, the performance was recognized by airmen everywhere as a remarkable achievement. It was unfortunate for the Germans that the information that brought it about was incorrect. As L 59 turned back, General von Lettow-Vorbeck was still fighting.

The last of the "Super-Zeppelins" was L 70, nearly 700 feet long and powered by seven 260-horsepower super-charged Maybach engines. Its maximum speed was over 80 mph and its operational ceiling was 23,000 feet. It was built to carry four tons of bombs and to fly high above defenses. On August 5, 1918, with the end of hostilities only three months away, L 70, with Captain Peter Strasser on board, was one of five Zeppelins that launched the final airship raid of the war against Britain. As they approached the English coast, they were intercepted by a D.H.4 flown by Major Egbert Cadbury and Captain Robert Leckie. Explosive shells from the D.H. 4's machine guns found their mark and L 70 burst into flame, plunging thousands of feet into the sea. The remaining airships jettisoned their bombs and turned for home. Peter Strasser was dead, and without his determined leadership, the Zeppelin offensive against Britain came to a halt. It had been a costly and materially ineffective campaign. By the time WWI ended, 115 Zeppelin airships had been built for the German Navy and Army. (Twenty-two other large military airships were built in Germany by the Schütte-Lanz company. Most had wooden frames and were generally poor performers compared to the Zeppelins.) Twenty-two became obsolete and were retired; thirty-six were either shot down or wrecked after being severely damaged in action; eight were destroyed by bombing; seven were forced to land in enemy or neutral territory; twenty-six were lost in accidents; crews destroyed seven rather than surrender them at the end of the war; and nine were handed over to the Allies as part of the Armistice arrangements. More than 380 airship crewmen lost their lives.

British and Italian Airships at War

The Royal Navy made some attempt to emulate German developments by ordering several rigid airships during WWI. Known as the 23 and 23X class, they were over 500 feet long and powered by four Rolls-Royce Eagle engines. None of them was able to come close to matching the capabilities of the Zeppelins, however, and they contributed very little to the war at sea. Far more practical were the small,

non-rigid craft acquired for maritime patrol duties. Simply designed and quick to construct, the SS (Sea Scout) class first appeared in 1915 and saw use in various improved forms throughout the war. About 150 were built, and a few of these were transferred to France, Italy and the United States. The story is that one of the SS class gave rise to the word most commonly used to refer to a non-rigid airship. During an inspection tour in 1915, Commander A.D. Cunningham, the commanding officer of a British air station, is said to have flicked the fabric envelope of the SS 12 with a finger and then to have imitated the sound, saying "blimp." Non-rigids have been "blimps" ever since.

The best of the naval blimps used by the British in WWI were those of the NS (North Sea) class, which entered service in February 1917. They were 262 feet long and were powered by two 260-horsepower Fiat A.12 engines. They cruised at about 40 mph and could maintain patrols of at least 24 hours. In 1919, NS 11 remained in the air for nearly 102 hours, covering some 3,000 miles in the process. Just six months later, NS 11 was a rare casualty when it was struck by lightning and lost with all hands while searching for mines in the North Sea.

The Vickers airship R 23 was completed for the Royal Navy in 1917. Its performance was disappointingly inferior to that of contemporary German Zeppelins. Although some patrols were completed over the North Sea, R 23 was used principally as a training and trials airship. For one trial, a two-pounder gun was fired from a platform on top, and for another a Sopwith Camel was suspended beneath the envelope by specially prepared slings. After the aircraft was released, the pilot (Lieutenant Keys) started the engine and flew round the airship before landing safely.

The ZMC-2 at the right of this group was built by the Metalclad Airship Corporation (formerly the Aircraft Development Corporation) in Detroit, Michigan. It was the only metal-clad airship built. (In the designation, MC stood for metal clad and the figure 2 indicated the gas capacity, which was 200,000 cubic feet.) ZMC-2 was delivered to the U.S. Navy in September 1929, and was used for trials and on several humanitarian missions. Although quite hard to control in rough weather, it remained in service for twelve years and logging over 2,200 hours in the air.

The Italian Army and Navy both made extensive use of semi-rigid airships during WWI. They were of four types — P for Piccolo (small); M for Medium; V for Velore (fast); and G for Grande (large). Besides their reconnaissance and patrol duties, they were used to drop almost half a million pounds of bombs on such targets as docks, railway junctions and marshaling yards, and the Austro-Hungarian naval base at Pola on the Adriatic.

Postwar Rigids

Rigid airship developments outside Germany were influenced by examination of Zeppelins either shot down or captured in the course of WWI. The British R 33 and R 34 were notably successful airships, having benefited from studies of the German L 33, shot down over Essex in 1916, and the L 49, which was forced to land in France the following year. The R 33 survived until being dismantled in

1928, and the R 34 guaranteed its place in aviation history by completing the first double crossing of the Atlantic in 1919. (See *Aviation Century The Golden Age*, Chapter 2, "A Ship of the Air.") The R 36, based on Zeppelin L 48, was the first of the British naval airships to be converted for civilian use. Intended to carry passengers and freight between the United Kingdom and Egypt, it first got airborne in April 1921, having been given accommodation for fifty passengers, with such luxuries as wicker chairs in the spacious saloon, a galley, toilets, and cabins with sleeping berths. None of the R 36's promise was fulfilled, however, and its limited career was dogged by accidents, including its near loss after the collapse of two fins in flight. The last British airship conceived during the WWI era was the R 80, designed by Barnes Wallis of Vickers, which was handed over to the Royal Air Force in 1921. It flew only a total of seventy-five hours before being broken up in 1924, but before that happened it had a part to play in the postwar development of American interest in large airship operation.

In 1921, a detachment of U.S. Navy airshipmen arrived in the United Kingdom to gain experience in large airship operation before taking delivery of the British-built R 38 (U.S. designation ZR-2). Experience was gained in the R 32, 33, 34 and 80 before the R 38 began its trials on June 23, 1921. The new airship was the largest then in existence. Based on a Zeppelin design, but with an extra bay inserted in the middle, it was 699 feet long and powered by six 350-horsepower engines. From the outset, the American crewmen were not too keen about the way the R 38 handled, one of them writing that "The damn gas bag is a lousy lemon." On its third flight, control became difficult and girders near the tail buckled when the airship was given a speed test, but repairs were made and U.S. colors were painted on the fin in preparation for the acceptance flight on August 23. Now flying as the ZR-2, the airship remained aloft for thirty-four hours, and was over the Humber River conducting the last of its trials, involving the rapid application of full rudder

control, when a number of girders failed. The ZR-2 cracked open amidships and exploded, falling into the river in pieces. Forty-four of the forty-nine men aboard were killed. The shock of the disaster came close to ending U.S. enthusiasm for large airships, but Admiral Moffett, the U.S. Navy's Chief of Aeronautics, insisted that the program should continue, saying: "We will carry on and build and operate as many big rigid dirigibles as necessary so these brave men shall not have given their lives in vain." Given the number of "brave men" (including Moffett himself) who were yet to die in rigid airships, it might be argued that those who were killed in the ZR-2 would not have "given their lives in vain" if the United States had taken the hint and chosen to stop large airship operations from that moment on.

Majestic Misadventures

The imposing size of airships, their stately progress, their apparent solidity — these things tended to create a false sense of security both in those who traveled in them and those who merely admired them from afar. In spite of mounting evidence between the wars that all was not as it

seemed, the belief in airships as a safe and desirable way to move about the globe took a long time to wither. The list of lighter-than-air disasters grew steadily longer as the years went by. Considering that the total number of big airships operating in the world was never very large, their accident record was not encouraging. A few months after the ZR-2 crash, in February 1922, the U.S. Army's *Roma*, a 410-foot-long Italian-built semi-rigid, snapped a control cable and was committed to what would

The U.S. Navy emphasized the economy of its blimps, pointing out that patrols were carried out by small crews of only two or three men. The numbers needed to catch ropes and control the blimp on the ground was not often mentioned.

On display at the National Museum of Naval Aviation at Pensacola, Florida, is the nose cone of a U.S. Navy ZPG-2 airship, at 324 feet long, one of the largest blimps ever built. The ZPG-2 became operational in the 1950s and was intended for antisubmarine warfare patrols lasting two or three days. In 1957, ZPG-2 Snowbird *flew nonstop across the Atlantic from Massachusetts to Portugal, the Canary and Cape Verde Islands, then back via Puerto Rico to land at Key West, Florida. The flight set airship world records for distance (9,448 miles) and endurance (264.2 hours).*

have been a fairly rough forced landing at Langley Field, Virginia. On its approach, the *Roma* hit high-tension wires, rupturing the gas bag and igniting the hydrogen. Thirty-three men died in the holocaust. In December 1923, the French *Dixmude* (formerly Zeppelin L 72, acquired from Germany as part of war reparations) disappeared during storms over the Mediterranean. The only clue to its loss was a report that a bright light had flared for a few seconds off the Sicilian coast on the night of December 23. It was later found that the commander of the *Dixmude* had not been happy with his airship. Among his written comments was the remark that "in design the *Dixmude* is defective. She ought to be the last dirigible constructed on these lines."

The *Dixmude* experience ended French large airship ambitions, but the United States was not discouraged. The first homemade American dirigible was the U.S. Navy's ZR-1, the 680-foot-long *Shenandoah*. Based on Zeppelin L 49, it first flew in September 1923 and remained in service for just two eventful years. Mooring masts were developed and plans were made to place them all over the United States and on ships so that the *Shenandoah* would have plenty of permanent roosts. A supply of helium was procured at great expense to give the airship its lift, so avoiding the dangers of operating with hydrogen. (Most of the world's supply of helium, a safe inert gas, is found in Texas. Between the wars, it was particularly rare and could be obtained only from the United States. In the 1920s, there was not even enough available to fill both American airships at once. When *Los Angeles* was cruising, *Shenandoah* was grounded.)

In the course of its service, the *Shenandoah* completed thirty-seven trips, including a double crossing of the American continent. Severe storms were encountered and survived on several occasions, including one fierce gale that ripped the airship from its Lakehurst mooring mast and swept it away with only a skeleton crew in control. Professor C.P. Burgess of the Bureau of Aeronautics, who was on board for the wild ride that followed, was suitably impressed: "Can you imagine a liner with two compartments caved in, a hole in her bow, half the steering gear torn away, bucking a gale of 75 mph and returning to port?"

> *"Anyone who wants to can leave the car."*
> LIEUTENANT COMMANDER ZACHARY LANSDOWNE, COMMANDER OF THE *SHENANDOAH*, MOMENTS BEFORE THE CONTROL CAR TORE LOOSE OVER OHIO, SEPTEMBER 3, 1925

Admiral Moffett was ecstatic, saying: "The *Shenandoah* has demonstrated that she is the best and strongest rigid in the world." The admiral's statement may have been true, but if so, it proved to be a prophetic testament to the general fragility of large airships when confronted by extreme natural forces. On September 3, 1925, the *Shenandoah* ran into a squall line and out of luck over Ohio. The storm first pushed the airship to more than 6,000 feet, well above its safe pressure height, bursting several gas bags in the process. Severe turbulence was encountered during the ensuing descent, and the *Shenandoah* was subjected to savage stresses that eventually caused the structure to break up, the control and engine gondolas ripping loose and the main body of the airship being torn into three parts. Astonishingly, the separate sections behaved somewhat like free balloons. Fourteen men in the gondolas died, but twenty-nine more survived the disaster, clinging to the remnants of their airship as they floated to earth.

American public confidence in airships was shaken by the *Shenandoah*'s loss, but it was gradually restored by the consistent performance of the *Los Angeles*. Built by the Zeppelin works at Friedrichshafen for the U.S. Navy as part of war reparations, the new rigid was designated LZ 126 by the Germans and became ZR-3 when delivered to the United States by Dr. Hugo Eckener in October 1924. (In the course of the negotiations leading to the construction of the LZ 126, the Goodyear Company acquired the Zeppelin patents, formed the Goodyear-Zeppelin Corporation, and became established as the leading U.S. manufacturer of lighter-than-air craft.) The huge dirigible's arrival in New York generated remarkable public enthusiasm and was seen as an event of international significance. Eckener and his men got a ticker tape welcome and were fêted everywhere. President Coolidge reflected the view of the American people when he said in a message to Dr. Eckener that "the friendly relations between Germany and America are reaffirmed ... this great airship has so happily introduced the first direct air connection between the two nations." In a euphoric tribute, one reporter gave the LZ 126 credit for much more, writing that "Germany has rehabilitated herself in the eyes of the world."

A PERSONAL ALBUM OF AIRSHIPS

These photographs of the *Hindenburg* and *Graf Zeppelin* were made by U.S. Navy Chief Petty Officer George Martin Pickering. Stationed at the Lakehurst airship base in the 1930s, he was assigned the duty of recording the activities surrounding the airship hangar and facilities. Petty Officer Pickering's grandson, Jim Clark, of Beavercreek, Ohio, has kept this unique album that documents the arrivals and departures of these great airships. Lakehurst saw great aerial dirigibles that came in from across the Atlantic as well as the U.S. Navy's own large rigid airships and blimps, used for coastal patrol.

Naval Air Station Lakehurst was established by the purchase of 1,700 acres in 1919 by the Acting Secretary of the Navy, Franklin D. Roosevelt, for "use as a dirigible field." Hangar Number One was completed and the station commissioned in the summer of 1921. NAS Lakehurst became the U.S. Navy's center of airship operations on the east coast of the United States, and remained so until 1964 when the Navy discontinued airship operations.

This facility is now known as the Naval Air Engineering Station (NAES), Lakehurst, New Jersey. Recent developments, however, have seen a rebirth of lighter-than-air operations, and the base is being used for the testing of unmanned airships and the use of airships for homeland security and coastal patrols in drug interdiction efforts.

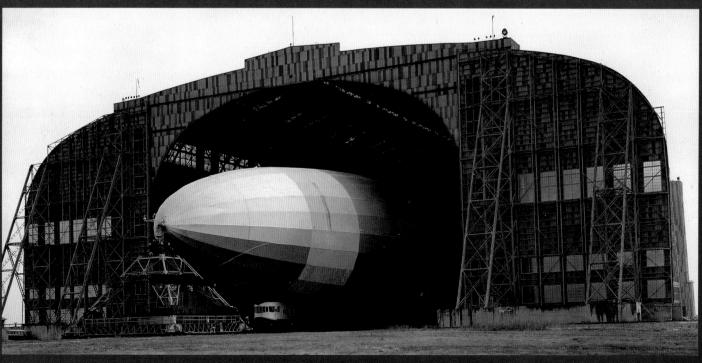

Hangar Number One has an open floor space of over 200,000 square feet. At times the airship hangar could house two of the Navy's huge airships. It was also capable of handling the German Zeppelins when they stopped at Lakehurst, although the Navy was apparently reluctant to house the hydrogen-filled German airships. The events of May 6, 1937, and the destruction of the Hindenberg proved their fears correct.

Hangar Number One remains standing today and was designated a National Landmark in 1968.

The *Los Angeles* pioneered several airship techniques for the U.S. Navy. In 1927, a landing was made on the stern of the aircraft carrier *Saratoga*, and on July 3, 1929, Lieutenant "Jake" Gorton successfully engaged a trapeze fitted to the airship's ample belly with a hook fitted above the top wing of his Vought UO-1 biplane, making the *Los Angeles* an aircraft carrier in its own right. (This was not the first time "hooking-on" experiments had been done. By 1918, Germany, Britain and the United States had all carried out trials. Zeppelin L 35 had launched an Albatros D.III; the R-23, a Camel; and a U.S. Navy blimp had dropped a Curtiss JN-4.) Another unique procedure was devised by the big dirigible itself in 1927, but, to the relief of the crew, was performed only once. The *Los Angeles* was moored to its 158-foot Lakehurst mast, swinging gently in a light northwesterly breeze. A cold contrary current swept in from the sea, taking the airship from the rear and raising its stern. Needing to weathercock into wind, the great dirigible chose not to swing round sideways, but to continue upward, eventually becoming vertical above the mast, making a temporary tower more than 800 feet high. There it pirouetted gracefully and descended on the other side, coming to rest in its normal horizontal position to leeward of the mast. Neither the crew on board nor those watching could do anything about this extraordinary performance. The crewmen inside the airship slid into the nose along with other loose objects, such as tools and spare parts, some of which crashed through the outer skin. Remarkably, there were no serious injuries and the damage was slight. On this and other occasions, the *Los Angeles* earned a reputation as a lucky ship, and it went on to serve until being laid up during the Depression in 1932. Although it was not broken up until 1940, the *Los Angeles* did not fly again. In all, it completed 331 flights and logged 4,398 hours in the air.

Unfortunately, the almost trouble-free life of the *Los Angeles* was anything but typical of U.S. rigid airships. Two other huge dirigibles built by Goodyear-Zeppelin for the U.S. Navy, ZRS-4 and ZRS-5, were welcomed into service in the early 1930s, but both were destined for

> *"Suddenly the entire bottom of the bag dropped out. We could look up into the whole bare inside of the balloon…. It was a pretty sight, quite round and tight and symmetrical — but a bit too tight for safety!"*
> CAPTAIN ALBERT W. STEVENS, U.S. ARMY AIR CORPS, BEFORE ABANDONING THE *Explorer* GONDOLA, JULY 1934

violent ends. ZRS-4, the *Akron*, was 785 feet long and had a volume of six and a half million cubic feet. The enormous helium capacity gave the airship the ability to lift 403,000 pounds, of which 160,000 pounds could be payload. Eight 560-horsepower Maybachs, buried inside the structure, could drive the monster forward at nearly 90 mph. Three passageways ran down the length of the airship and were connected by crossways. In addition, the *Akron* had been designed from the outset as an aircraft carrier. Five small fighters could be accommodated in hangars inside the vast hull.

Impressive though it was, the *Akron* attracted controversy and was thought of as being jinxed. In January 1932, it was torn away from a ship's mooring mast, and the next month the lower fin was crushed when a gust of wind slammed the airship to the ground as it prepared to pick up a party of congressmen. In May, excess buoyancy induced by rising temperatures caused difficulties in landing at San Diego. After the men of the ground party had gripped the trail ropes lowered from the airship, the landing was aborted and the *Akron* shot upward, carrying three men still hanging on to the ropes. Two fell off and were killed, but the third, a young sailor named Bill Cowart, clung to his rope in a ninety-minute ordeal some 2,000 feet above the Pacific before a system was devised for hauling him to safety. Finally, in April 1933, the brief turbulent career of the *Akron* was brought to a close during its fifty-ninth flight. The airship got airborne from Lakehurst in thick fog and darkness carrying seventy-six men. Among them were five survivors of the *Shenandoah* crash and the Navy's Chief of Aeronautics, Admiral Moffett. Shortly after climbing away, flashes of lightning were seen and the *Akron* turned east over the Atlantic in an attempt to run before the storms. It was to no avail. Overtaken by a violent squall, the *Akron* was driven down into the sea. There was almost no survival equipment on board. Only three men, picked up by the German tanker *Phoebus*, survived the crash and the icy water. Admiral Moffett went down with his ship, a victim of his enthusiasm for the big rigid dirigibles.

ZEPPELIN SUITE

Six etchings from a folio of ten in *The Zeppelin Book* by Brian Cohen (1999). TOP LEFT *Zeppelin and Eiffel Tower.* TOP RIGHT *Zeppelin and Pyramids.* CENTRE LEFT *Zeppelin Interior.* CENTRE RIGHT *Zeppelin, River and Rainbow.* BOTTOM LEFT *Zeppelin and Biplane.* BOTTOM RIGHT *Zeppelin and Searchlights.*

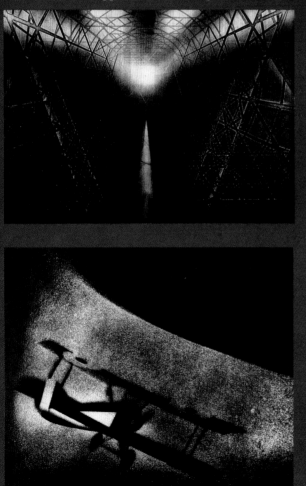

One of the three survivors of the *Akron* was Commander Herbert Wiley, who in May 1934 was given command of the very similar ZRS-5, the *Macon*. In the months that followed, he earned a reputation for making the most of his airship's capabilities and those of its scout aircraft in naval maneuvers, and in February 1935 the *Macon* was an important part of exercises held off the Californian coast. Shaken by gusts while returning from a scouting mission in worsening weather, the airship's structure began to fail. The upper fin tore away and the rearmost gas cells deflated, making the airship excessively tail heavy. A large amount of ballast was dumped in a desperate attempt to level the *Macon,* but it quickly became evident

that control had been lost. The *Macon* struck the ocean tail-down late in the afternoon of February 12. There any similarity with the crash of the *Akron* ceased. The men were well prepared and had both life jackets and rafts. Of the eighty-one serving on board the *Macon,* seventy-nine were rescued. However, the two who died were not the only casualties. The loss of the *Macon* finally killed American interest in operating big rigid dirigibles.

Ordeal on the Ice

Italian adventures with large airships in the 1920s were led by Umberto Nobile. In 1926, he had been the commander of the *Norge* when it carried the Norwegian explorer Roald

Poleward — the Third Attempt, *by Don Connolly. On May 11, 1926, the Italian airship* Norge, *captained by Umberto Nobile and carrying a team led by Norwegian explorer Roald Amundsen, left Spitzbergen to fly over the North Pole to Alaska. The Ford Trimotor* Josephine Ford, *flown by Floyd Bennett and Richard Byrd, got airborne soon afterward and for a while escorted the airship, circling round it as it cruised slowly northward.*

Amundsen over the North Pole. (See *Aviation Century The Golden Age*, Chapter 2, "To the Top of the World.") Relations between the two men had soured afterward as each sought to belittle the contributions of the other. Amundsen declared that Nobile had been no more than a paid chauffeur; Nobile responded, with some justification, that Amundsen had been a mere passenger on "a pleasure trip." Inspired by what he had seen in the Arctic and angered by the denigration of his role, Nobile began planning a second aerial expedition with a new semi-rigid airship, the *Italia*. Scientific research was to be its principal object.

The *Italia* rose from its base at King's Bay, Spitzbergen, on May 23, 1928, and turned north. In the early hours of the next morning, hustled along by a rising tailwind, the airship reached the North Pole. With conscious ceremony, Nobile dropped the Italian flag, the gonfalon of the City of Milan, a medal of the Virgin of the Fire, and a large oak cross presented by Pope Pius XI. Concerned about the headwinds and deteriorating weather that threatened to confront them on a return flight to Spitzbergen, Nobile had to consider whether it might be better to continue to Alaska, as he had done in the *Norge*. However, the Swedish meteorologist Dr. Malmgren believed that the storms would pass and felt that it would be better to go back to base, from where further scientific studies could be undertaken. Nobile bowed to his advice, a decision he would forever regret. As it headed south on May 25, the *Italia* battled increasingly strong headwinds, its groundspeed reduced at times to little more than walking pace. Storms pounded the airship and ice accumulated on its outer shell. Eventually it proved impossible to stop the *Italia* from losing height, and it crashed on to the Arctic ice. The impact was so great that the control gondola was torn off. The airship, relieved of the gondola's weight, rose rapidly and was swept away by the wind. Neither the *Italia* nor the six people still on board were ever seen again.

Of the ten people in the *Italia*'s control gondola, one soon died and the others had all been injured to some extent. Nobile himself had broken his right arm and leg.

> *"Heavier-than-air apparatus did not appeal to me .... even if a successful landing is managed, the resumption of flight is problematical, owing to the continuous movements in the formation of ice .... with a dirigible there is the possibility of slowing down and even coming to a full stop in the air ..."*
>
> GENERAL UMBERTO NOBILE,
> COMMENTING ON HIS PREFERENCE
> FOR AIRSHIPS ON POLAR FLIGHTS,
> *NATIONAL GEOGRAPHIC*, AUGUST 1927

The position of the survivors was desperate, but they had a tent, provisions for about forty-five days, and an emergency radio. Transmissions were made at regular intervals, but there was no response. The crew of the support ship in King's Bay, convinced that the *Italia* had been lost and that its men were all dead, were not listening. Discouraged by the continuing silence, Dr. Malmgren and two others left the main party and set out for help on May 30. On June 6 the radio told the remaining survivors that an alert Russian farmer near Archangel had heard their SOS three days before. Rescue efforts were launched by seven countries, but it was not until June 20 that an Italian flying boat found the *Italia*'s tent. (Roald Amundsen, dismissing old animosities, left Tromsö in a French flying boat to lead a rescue mission. The aircraft disappeared over the Barents Sea and no trace of it or the crew was ever found.) Supplies were dropped, and on June 23 a Swedish ski-equipped Fokker C.V, flown by Lieutenant Einar Lundborg, managed to land on the ice. Lundborg could take only one passenger, and he had strict orders to pick up Nobile first. Much against his wishes, Nobile allowed himself to be flown out. Lundborg soon returned to pick up others, but this time wrecked his aircraft. The Swedes managed to get another aircraft to the site on July 6 to collect Lundborg, but it was then decided that conditions were too dangerous to attempt further landings. The only hope now was a Soviet icebreaker, the *Krassin*, which had been slowly plowing its way toward the survivors since leaving port on June 20.

The *Krassin* reached the five remaining men from the *Italia* on July 12. They had been on the ice for seven weeks. Shortly before picking them up, the *Krassin* rescued two of those who had tried to walk out. They reported that Dr. Malmgren was dead. It seemed that the expedition's ordeal was at last over, but for Nobile himself that was far from true. On his return to Italy, Nobile discovered that Mussolini's Fascist government and the Italian press intended to hold him to account. An official inquiry found him responsible for the *Italia*'s loss, abandoning his men on the ice, and dishonoring his country. To escape the disgrace, Nobile first emigrated to the Soviet Union, where he designed small airships, and then moved to the United States in 1939. After the fall of Mussolini, he returned to Italy and, in time, his name was cleared. Any ideas there may have been for building other large Italian airships, however, were long since gone, doomed from the moment the *Italia* drifted away over the Arctic ice.

The Last R

The British, too, had their airship problems. After the R 38 (ZR-2) disaster, airship development work in Britain was suspended, but interest was revived in 1924 by a proposal for an airship service aimed at linking the principal countries of the British Empire. Two airships were to be built, one (R 100) by private enterprise and the other (R 101) as a state sponsored venture, supported by the Labour government. The Cabinet Committee set up to examine the scheme recommended that "The Air Ministry at Cardington shall build an airship of a certain size, load-carrying capacity and speed, and Vickers Ltd. shall build another one to the same contract specification. By this ingenious device we shall find out which is the better principle — capitalism or state enterprise." As a result of this extraordinary competitive arrangement they were soon generally referred to as the "Capitalist Airship" and the "Socialist Airship."

The R 100 design team was led by Barnes Wallis and included Neville Shute Norway, who later dropped his last name and became a celebrated writer. In his autobiography, Neville Shute had some harsh things to say about the "Socialist Airship" team. He had not been associated with dirigibles before, so on taking up his appointment he read as much as he could about the technicalities of airship construction. To his astonishment he found that the people who had built the ill-fated R 38 had done no aerodynamic calculations beforehand. A senior member of Vickers confirmed the truth of that, and, as Shute recalled, "he pointed out that no one had been sacked over it, nor even suffered censure. Indeed, the same team of men had been entrusted with the construction of the R 101." Some of his staff, Shute wrote, thought that many of the R 101 team "ought to be in gaol for manslaughter."

It took some five years before the two British airships were ready to fly. The R 101 flew first, on October 14, 1929. It was quickly apparent that the airship was underpowered

and overweight, capable of lifting only 35 tons of useful load rather than the planned-for 60 tons. The R 100 began its trials in December and completed them without undue difficulty, and although it was too heavy also, it noticeably outperformed its rival, lifting 54 tons of payload and demonstrating a top speed of 81 mph, some 10 mph faster than the R 101. The "Socialist Airship" also had control and structural problems that it was never to be given time to overcome.

The ultimate test for both airships was to be a proving flight over an imperial route. The R 100 was to fly to Canada and the R 101 to India. By the summer of 1930, the R 100 was ready to go, but its competitor was still in trouble. In a desperate effort to get more lift, the R 101 was cut in half and an extra bay inserted to hold more gas bags. As one problem was tackled, others appeared — the gas bags chafed on girders and leaked through the resulting holes, the outer covering became brittle on contact with glue and was liable to split, and test flights revealed some longitudinal instability. It was suggested by the R 101 team that the proving flights should be delayed until 1931, but the privately funded R 100 could not afford to wait and set off for Canada on July 29, 1930. A successful round-trip, with visits to Montreal, Ottawa and Toronto, was completed on August 16, when the R 100 was taken into its Cardington hangar for examination and overhaul. The westbound crossing to Montreal had taken almost seventy-nine hours, with the return some twenty-two hours faster. Throughout the flight, the R 100 had proved itself sturdy, stable and comfortable. Neville Shute was on board and was content, writing in his diary: "This has not been a bad trip. We have done what we set out to do when we left England more or less on the time scheduled, and at this stage of airship development I think that constitutes a good performance."

Pride and political pressure now became factors in the British airship saga. The R 101 team felt pressed to emulate the R 100's success, and the Secretary of State for Air, Lord Thomson, who had ambitions to becoming the next Viceroy of India, announced that he would be flying to India on the R 101. He demanded that the trip should be completed in time for him to attend the Imperial Conference to be held in London during October 1930. Technical difficulties did not seem to bother him. Hearing of the problems being worked on, he wrote: "So long as

Journeys in a Zeppelin were undertaken in considerable comfort. As one passenger wrote, "Even the person with taut nerves may know a relaxation, a serenity and calm like none other in the field of travel." The lounge of the Graf Zeppelin *was spacious and tastefully decorated, and at meal times would be transformed with white tablecloths, crystal glasses, silver cutlery and flowers. See page 157 for an exterior view.*

R-101 is ready to go to India by the last week in September this further delay in getting her altered may pass. I must insist on the programme for the Indian flight being adhered to, as I have made my plans accordingly." Faced with such intransigence, the R 101 team did their best, but they were not able to get the airship ready to fly until October 1. A hasty test flight, completed in calm conditions, could not include a full speed trial because one engine's oil cooler failed. Although a thorough trial had not been carried out, a certificate of airworthiness was issued, and the R 101, with its distinguished passenger and several of the airship's designers on board, left for India on the evening of October 4. By the time the English Channel was reached, the weather had deteriorated and progress was being hampered by a strong headwind accompanied by low cloud and heavy rain. At 2 A.M. on October 5, after flying for seven and a half hours, the R 101 was only 220 miles from Cardington, approaching the French town of Beauvais at about 1,000 feet. At that point, the massive airship entered a steep dive and hit the ground, bursting into flame and being completely consumed in seconds. Of the fifty-four people on board, only six survived. Lord Thomson's ambition had proved fatal, not only to himself and forty-seven others, but to the British airship program as well. The R 100 was never allowed to fly again and all plans for further rigid airship development in Britain were abandoned.

The Greatest Zeppelin

With the departure of France, Italy and Britain from the large airship business, only the United States and Germany remained, and the Zeppelins sailed serenely on well after the *Akron* and *Macon* were gone. When the post-WWI restrictions on German airship building were removed by the international agreements reached at the Locarno Conference in 1925, Dr. Hugo Eckener decided to build a new Zeppelin to demonstrate that the airship was superior to other forms of transport for long-distance travel. Contributions from the German people helped to finance the project, which came to fruition in 1928 as airship L 127, the *Graf Zeppelin*. The *Graf* was 776 feet long and capable of lifting a 33,000-pound payload; it was powered by five 580-horsepower Maybachs. These gave the airship a cruising speed of 68 mph, which could be maintained for a range of well over 7,000 miles. The passenger accommodation was luxurious — a carpeted lounge with armchairs and a baby grand piano, a dining saloon, sleeping cabins, toilets and washrooms.

Without doubt, the *Graf Zeppelin* was the most successful rigid dirigible ever built. In 1928/29, it completed over fifty long-range flights, including a Mediterranean cruise and a double crossing of the Atlantic. On August 1, 1929, the *Graf* arrived at Lakehurst, New Jersey, where it picked up the newspaperman William Randolph Hearst, who was a sponsor for a round-the-world trip. It then flew to its home base at Friedrichshafen before setting out on its circumnavigation, crossing Siberia on the way to Tokyo. After stops at Los Angeles and New York, the *Graf* returned to Friedrichshafen, having averaged 1,000 miles per day for just over twenty-one days. Every year thereafter, successful flights followed one after another, among them cruises to the Mediterranean and the Arctic, a rendezvous with the Soviet icebreaker *Malygin* off Franz Josef's Land, and a regular mail and passenger service across the South Atlantic. By the time of its formal retirement in 1937, the *Graf Zeppelin* had completed 590 flights totaling 17,178 hours in the air, and had carried some 16,000 passengers in covering over a million miles.

Götterdämmerung

The blazing wreck of the R 101 in 1930 did not deter the Germans from going ahead with their airship program, but it did suggest to Dr. Eckener that it might be better for a new design to be drawn up with helium in mind for the lifting agent rather than hydrogen. Since helium is a slightly less buoyant gas, it was apparent that, for the new airship to be more capable than the *Graf*, it would need to be much larger. Work on the LZ 129 began in 1931, and the finished product emerged in 1936 as the *Hindenburg*, the largest airship ever completed. It was 803 feet long and had a volume of more than seven million cubic feet. However, Dr. Eckener's plan to use helium became a victim of international politics. With Hitler and the Nazis in power, the U.S. government refused to allow the export of the rare gas to Germany, so the *Hindenburg* had to be filled with the more dangerous hydrogen. This had the effect of producing more lift and removed any inhibitions about the *Hindenburg* being sumptuously furnished. Besides the space for a crew of twenty-five and the usual control car beneath the nose, there were two main decks, eventually modified to hold thirty-four passenger cabins. There were promenade decks, a large dining room, a reading room, and even a smoking room equipped with an airlock door. The baggage holds could take thirteen tons of freight. At takeoff, the *Hindenburg* weighed over half a million pounds.

During 1936/37, the *Hindenburg* completed a series of ocean crossings of both the North and South Atlantic. It was invariably fully booked and drew considerable praise from its passengers for its quiet comfort and great stability. On May 4, 1937, commanded by Captain Max Pruss, the *Hindenburg* left Frankfurt on the first of eighteen flights to North America planned for that season. It was carrying a

> *"Add a new, thrilling experience to your holiday!"*
> PUBLICITY SLOGAN FOR THE *HINDENBURG*, 1937

crew of sixty-one and thirty-six passengers. Local thunderstorms delayed the arrival at Lakehurst until the evening of May 6, but there were none nearby when Max Pruss brought his airship over the field and approached the mooring mast. (Note that up to this moment, although the airship story had been plagued by disaster, no passenger had ever died in a commercial airship.) The landing ropes were dropped to the ground crew and the *Hindenburg*'s propellers were reversed, slowing the airship to a crawl some 75 feet above the ground. There was no reason to think that the mooring would be anything but routine. Suddenly a tongue of flame shot out of the hull just ahead of the tail. In seconds the *Hindenburg* was a raging inferno. The tail, now devoid of lift, crashed to the ground and the rest of the huge structure followed as the fire rushed forward, engulfing every part of the airship. It seemed impossible for anyone to live through such a holocaust, but there were many miraculous escapes. Captain Max Pruss was one of those who jumped from the control car as it hit the ground and ran to safety as white-hot girders fell about them. Once clear of the fire, Pruss gave his rings and his wallet to someone in the crowd, and then ran back to help his passengers. He made several trips into the wreckage before being restrained and led, severely burned, to an ambulance. When a count was taken, it was found that twenty-three passengers and thirty-nine crewmen had survived.

The *Hindenburg*'s loss was never satisfactorily explained. There were many theories, including the ignition of leaking gas by static electricity or St. Elmo's fire. Some believed it could even have been sabotage. With no conclusive proof, however, the only sure thing was that the root cause was the use of hydrogen. Whatever the truth of the matter, the day of large rigid dirigibles made in the Zeppelin image was over. The *Graf Zeppelin* was immediately retired, and it was clear that the newly finished *Graf Zeppelin II* had no future as a passenger vessel. Although many airshipmen greatly regretted the decisions, the end of the commercial airship era was already at hand for other reasons. The tremendous advances in aeronautics made during the 1930s made it inevitable that heavier-than-air machines would soon displace the huge, expensive, lumbering creatures fathered by

Count Zeppelin. They had brought the comfort of luxury liners to air travel, but they were slow, cumbersome, and often at the mercy of the weather. In the end, uncertainty over their safety destroyed the public's confidence in them as a means of transport. Even so, the great *Grafs* were not quite finished. In 1939, several reconnaissance sorties were flown along Britain's east coast by large airships in an attempt to monitor transmissions from the curious new aerials then beginning to appear. The Luftwaffe does not seem to have been very successful in interpreting what they learned, however, as the events of the Battle of Britain were to show.

Smaller but Safer

The Goodyear Company was already involved with lighter-than-air craft before it began the construction of the ill-fated rigid dirigibles *Akron* and *Macon*. Non-rigids were supplied to the U.S. Navy during WWI, and in 1925 the first commercial blimp was built and named *Pilgrim*. It was just 110 feet long and could carry only the pilot plus two passengers in a gondola attached directly to the envelope. Powered by one 60-horsepower radial engine, it cruised at 37 mph. Helium was used as the lifting agent, as it has been for all subsequent Goodyear blimps. Between 1928 and 1932, *Pilgrim* was followed by a series of larger blimps, most of which could carry six passengers. The flagship was *Defender*, which held 178,000 cubic feet of helium and carried a ten-passenger gondola. It was with these blimps of

the interwar years that Goodyear began its tradition of promotional tours, using the airships both to demonstrate the capabilities of lighter-than-air craft and as aerial advertising billboards. By the time the United States entered WWII, the Goodyear blimps had built up an enviable safety record, having carried some 400,000 people without loss or injury. Once war had been declared, the blimps of this series were acquired by the U.S. Navy for use as training airships.

During WWII, Goodyear built over 200 blimps of the G, K, and M classes for operations with the U.S. Navy, mostly for maritime patrol duties. They proved to be remarkably effective. Not a single ship was sunk in a convoy with an airship escort, and only one blimp was lost to enemy action. The determined captain of K-74 took on the surfaced submarine U-134 and had his blimp's envelope so riddled by machine-gun fire that it settled on the sea. However, merchant ships in the area had been spared the U-boat's attentions and U-134 was later sunk on its way back to Germany. The K class blimps were 252 feet long and carried a crew of twelve. In 1944, six of the Ks were ordered to Port Lyautey in French Morocco for patrol duties along the Atlantic coast. They became the first non-rigid airships to cross the Atlantic when they flew from Massachusetts to Morocco via Newfoundland and the Azores in fifty-eight hours.

After WWII, arguments were made for retaining the U.S. Navy's airship service, and a few advanced blimps of the N class were introduced in the 1950s. The last four of these were much larger than previous non-rigids, over 400 feet long and with a volume of more than one and a half million cubic feet. They carried a crew of twenty-one and were equipped for airborne early-warning duties, with

ABOVE *Goodyear* Europa *cruising over a gathering of Tiger Moths at the annual international de Havilland Moth Rally in the grounds of Woburn Abbey, near Milton Keynes, U.K.* RIGHT *Goodyear Type GZ20A* Europa *was built in the United Kingdom and operated throughout Europe from its base in Italy from 1972 to 1986.*

massive radar antennae contained within their envelopes. In 1957, an N class airship demonstrated its remarkable range, circling the North Atlantic and staying airborne for just over eleven days. These were the last blimps built for the U.S. Navy. By 1960, it had already been decided that no further orders would be placed, and the decision to stop using blimps was hastened by a fatal accident. The envelope of an N class blimp collapsed during an Atlantic patrol and it crashed into the sea with the loss of the crew. Operations by non-rigid airships were formally suspended by the U.S. Navy on June 28, 1961.

Blimp Revival

For a while, it seemed that the non-rigid airship would follow its larger cousins into history. By the early 1960s only one Goodyear blimp, *Mayflower*, remained. Then the company decided to revive the program of publicity tours that had been successful in the past. A second airship, *Columbia*, started flying in 1968, and a much larger third, *America*, joined in during 1969. *Europa*, built in the United Kingdom, began operations in Europe in 1972. The envelopes of these blimps are made of polyester fiber and they carry "Super Skytacular" electronic displays comprised of almost 4,000 colored lights. The computer-controlled displays produce complex animated images capable of being read easily when the blimp is at an altitude of 1,000 feet.

The Goodyear revival helped to spark interest in airships elsewhere and a number of other organizations entered the field of both blimp and rigid airship production. By the 1990s, it seemed that the advantages of the airship were once more being recognized and that modern technologies existed that could ameliorate, if not eliminate, the disadvantages. In the United States, the companies involved included Global Skyship Industries and the American Blimp Corporation, whose *Lightships* were in use all over the world. A Canadian company, 21st Century Airships, was flying its amazing spherical blimps, one in the shape of an enormous baseball. A later version called the *Voyage of Dreams*, 75 feet in diameter and powered by four engines, was intended to carry twelve passengers on sightseeing trips in a glass-bottomed cabin. In the United Kingdom, Airship Technologies was working on its *Skycat* series of freight-carrying airships, aiming eventually to build an immense vehicle capable of lifting a 1,000-ton payload. CargoLifter in Germany was similarly engaged, planning to fly its 260-meter-long CL160 freighter with a 160-ton payload by 2005. The international investment in non-rigid airships was readily apparent; although the efforts of rigid airship designers were not so obvious, they were still considerable. In the Netherlands, the Rigid Airship Design company was promoting its classically shaped *Holland Navigator*, and LTAS in Las Vegas was constructing airships with lenticular shells. Perhaps the most remarkable twist to the story was that Zeppelin had revived their lighter-than-air tradition and had begun building airships at Friedrichshafen again. Their LZ NO7 was a mere shadow of the *Hindenburg*—246 feet long and with a 4,000-pound payload — but it was a hint of greater things to come. All of these projects were promising, but they seem almost insignificant when compared to an astonishing scheme proposed by a team from the Illinois Institute of Technology. Their monstrous AeroCarrier is a circular design, a mile and a half across, supposed to be capable of lifting 35,000 tons of cargo or 3,500 passengers.

Many of these developments were made practicable by the use of advanced technologies. Composite materials made for lighter, stronger structures, and reliable turboprop engines could be used to provide excellent power-to-weight ratios. This power, together with careful aerodynamic design, meant that airships could attain higher speeds and were less liable to be affected by the vagaries of the weather than they had been. Big, slow-turning propellers ensured quiet operation with minimum vibration, and could be tilted to direct thrust as desired, making precise control of an airship a simple matter. Inert helium gas, now plentiful, provided a safe lifting agent. Modern control cabins, with satellite navigation systems, reliable communications, and radar offering collision avoidance and severe weather warning, promised a high degree of flight safety.

Manufacturers promoted these advantages of modern airship design and pointed out that airships did not need huge airfields for their operation. It was claimed that the airships of the 21st century would be the safest flying machines ever built and that they could fill a vast array of roles, both military and civil, more effectively and cheaply than their heavier-than-air equivalents — including maritime and border patrol, anti-smuggling and intelligence-gathering operations, law enforcement, disaster relief, environmental patrol, scientific research, passenger-carrying for tourism or sightseeing, freight delivery, advertising and sales promotion, and television coverage. Count Zeppelin's shattered dreams for his ships of the air were at last taking new shape and becoming realities, full of capabilities he could never have imagined.

LEFT *The* Skyship 600 *was originally designed by Airship Industries in the U.K. in the early 1980s. Airship Management Services in Connecticut has operated the Fuji Skyship 600, the world's largest passenger airship, in Asia, Australia, Europe and the United States since the 1980s. It has been seen over many major sporting events, such as the Super Bowl and the U.S. Open tennis tournament.*

ABOVE *In 1990, Richard Branson formed Virgin Lightships, to manage advertising airships that could be illuminated internally at night. The first production* Lightship, *the A-60, was manufactured by American Blimp at Hillsboro, Oregon. The A-60 was upgraded in 1991 to A-60+ to increase the lifting capability of the airship. American Blimp Lightships have advertised companies worldwide, including Blockbuster Video, Mazda, Sanyo and Metropolitan Life, the last featuring the comic-strip character Snoopy.*

ABOVE *In the wicker basket, Howard Steele lights the propane burner, heating the air in the balloon.* BELOW *Balloon crews wear work gloves to protect their hands.* RIGHT TOP *Ocean Fantasy casts its shadow across the green fields of Michigan.* RIGHT BOTTOM *Howard Steele, balloonist, electrician, father.*

At the Whim of the Winds

Throughout the first half of the 20th century, there were always adventurers who were prepared to entrust themselves to a basket hung beneath a gas-filled balloon, to be borne aloft and carried wherever the wind directed. After the Montgolfier period at the end of the 18th century, hot-air balloons had largely fallen into disfavor. The drawbacks of using fire to provide lift had quickly become apparent. To produce a reasonable amount of lift, the balloon had to be enormous, up to three times the volume of a hydrogen balloon. Sparks from the open fire made the whole project dangerous and the fuels used created foul-smelling smoke. Using gas instead was a relatively expensive business, however, limiting the practice of the art to a favored few. Rivalry among these fortunate enthusiasts was evident from an early stage, and this grew into an international competition of stature in 1906 with the introduction of the Gordon Bennett Cup for balloon racing. In fact, it was never strictly a race, the winner being the balloon that covered the greatest distance nonstop. Each country was allowed to enter up to three of its best balloon teams, with two pilots to a team, and all of the balloons had to be of a similar design and use the same lifting gas.

The first Gordon Bennett "race" set off from Paris watched by 200,000 spectators and was won by the U.S. Army's Frank Lahm, who came to earth in Yorkshire, some 400 miles to the north. Since the winner's country had the honor of staging the subsequent event, the second race in 1907 started from St. Louis, where there were 300,000 spectators. By 1909, the competition had become so popular that 400,000 spectators were at the starting point and special memorabilia items were being flown in the balloons. From the contest's earliest years, there were often remarkable performances. In 1908, the Swiss winners set a world endurance record for small gas sport balloons of 73 hours aloft, an achievement that remained unmatched until 1995, when a German team finally set a new record of 92

Howard Steele's hot-air balloon, Ocean Fantasy, *from the inside looking out as the colorful fabric envelope fills with air from the gasoline-powered fan at the opening.*

hours. Some of the distances recorded were astonishing. In 1910, an American team covered 729 miles. Two years later, French competitors flew 100 miles further, recording a distance for the Gordon Bennett that was not reached again until 1993, when an Austrian balloon was wafted 1,133 miles from Albuquerque, New Mexico, to Campbellsport, Wisconsin. (In a 1914 private venture, a German crew led by Hans Berliner flew 3,053 kilometers [1,897 miles] from Bitterfeld to the Urals. It was the first balloon flight over 3,000 kilometers and was a record that stood until 1978.)

The competition for the Gordon Bennett Cup was held regularly from 1906 to 1938, apart from the WWI years and 1931. In that time the successful balloon crews came from six nations. The most successful teams were those from the United States, who won the Cup ten times. The Belgians claimed it seven times, the Poles four, the Germans and the

Swiss twice each, and the French once. With the coming of WWII, the competition was set aside and was not revived until 1983, after which it regained its former popularity and was held in every year but one (1998) before the end of the century. In the modern period, the formerly dominant Americans could manage only one win, the most successful nation being Austria with seven, all of them led by pilot Josef Starkbaum.

In general, the Gordon Bennett contests were splendid examples of thoroughly enjoyable international competition, but in 1995 the event was marred by an incident of needless savagery. That year the event started with the balloons lifting off in Switzerland on Saturday, September 9. By Wednesday morning, four teams were still in the air. Then the magic of the contest was shattered by an AP wire story from Minsk, Belarus, which said that a balloon had been shot down by a Belarussian military helicopter near the Polish border. The shooting happened on Tuesday, September 12, but the Belarus government waited twenty-four hours to inform the U.S. Embassy that the two pilots, who were carrying American passports, had been killed. Alan Fraenckel, fifty-five, and John Stuart-Jervis, sixty-eight, representing the Virgin Islands, had been shot down after crossing into Belarus airspace from Poland and, according to an official statement from Belarus, failing to respond to radio calls and warning shots. Their balloon was said to have been near the Osovtsy military base and an adjoining missile base. Both pilots died from injuries suffered when their deflated balloon fell to the forest floor near Beryoza, about 60 miles from the Polish border. Although the Belarus authorities admitted receiving information about the race in May, they maintained that proper flight plans had not been filed at the time of the event.

The Fédération Aéronautique Internationale refuted the Belarus government statement in a press release: "The race organizers had obtained clearance from the Belarussian authorities for the Gordon Bennett balloon race competitors to enter the air space of Belarus. Specific flight plans had been filed, in accordance with standard International Civil Aviation Organization procedures, for each balloon intending to enter Belarus air space. The competition organizers in Switzerland spoke on the telephone with Minsk air traffic control on the morning of Tuesday, 12 September at 11 A.M., Belarus time. Minsk gave position reports for the participating balloons, without indicating anything was amiss. The Minsk authorities were therefore clearly aware of the origins of the balloons in Belarus airspace."

Shocked though they were by this appalling flashback to the attitudes of the Cold War, the FAI issued a strong statement of their intention to continue the Gordon Bennett series: "We are concerned that this incident will damage international relations. This is the exact opposite of what the sport of ballooning and FAI seek to achieve, which is to bring together the peoples of the world…. We are therefore determined not to let this incident affect future Coupe Gordon Bennett races and other air sport events. We intend to continue conducting races across international borders, whilst respecting the legal requirements of each sovereign state regarding airspace penetration."

At a Higher Level

From their inception, it was recognized that gas balloons offered a means of satisfying human curiosity about the upper atmosphere. As early as 1862, the British balloonists Coxwell and Glaisher rose to almost 30,000 feet in an open wicker basket, nearly dying from cold and lack of oxygen as they did so. In 1901, a German meteorologist, Arthur Berson, reached 35,000 feet while breathing oxygen. The U.S. Army's Captain Hawthorn Gray used both oxygen and a heated suit in climbing to 42,470 feet in 1927. When he tried again later that year, he reported being at 44,300 feet, but then his radio messages ceased. The balloon's gondola was later found hanging from a tree with Gray

"The best way of travel, however, if you aren't in any hurry at all, if you don't care where you are going, if you don't like to use your legs, if you don't want to be annoyed at all by any choice of directions, is in a balloon. In a balloon, you can decide only when to start, and usually when to stop. The rest is left entirely to nature."

WILLIAM PENE DU BOIS,
THE TWENTY-ONE BALLOONS

Hot-air balloons from the Barry King Invitational race, an event that gathers balloon enthusiasts who launch from a field near Metamora, Michigan. They fly in the late summer skies over the gently rolling countryside. After the race they return to the launching field to share stories and enjoy a cookout.

One of the Metamora balloons shares the sky with a flight of geese.

inside it, dead from the effects of flying at extreme altitude.

Auguste and Jean Piccard, twin brothers, were born in Basle, Switzerland, on January 28, 1884. Auguste became a physicist, and Jean an organic chemist and aeronautical engineer. In collaboration, they worked to unlock the secrets of the stratosphere, in the process advancing the art of ballooning and developing the means for human beings to endure at high altitudes. Auguste was convinced that a pressurized cabin was needed for survival in the stratosphere. In 1930, he devised a spherical aluminum gondola for that purpose, equipped with a system for reusing its own air supply. His first attempt to fly this unique creation led to him being written off as an eccentric. He and his assistant appeared padded with pillows and wearing wicker basket-like helmets. To complete the farce, the balloon refused to leave the ground. However, on May 27, 1931, equipped with a balloon of greater capacity, Auguste and

his assistant, Paul Kipfer, ascended from Augsburg, Germany, and reached a record altitude of 15,785 meters (51,775 feet). Later, on August 18, 1932, he made a second record-breaking ascent to 16,700 meters (54,789 feet).

Following his brother's high-altitude flights, Jean Piccard and his wife, Jeanette, flew a balloon from Dearborn, Michigan, on October 23, 1934, and reached 17,672 meters (57,979 feet). During this flight, they tested a liquid oxygen system. Jean went on to develop a liquid oxygen converter for use in balloons and high-flying aircraft. In 1936, he launched the first plastic film balloon, and the next year made the first manned ascent using multiple balloons. He was also instrumental in the design of polyethylene balloons that eventually made possible manned flights to altitudes in excess of 30,480 meters (100,000 feet).

In the remaining years before WWII, the effort to probe ever higher into the stratosphere became a competition between the Soviet Union and the United States. The altitude record went back and forth, but in January 1934, the Soviets seemed to have made a huge advance when their balloon *Ossoaviakhim*, carrying three men, reached 22,000 meters (72,178 feet). Unfortunately the pressurized capsule separated from the balloon during the descent and the crew plummeted to their deaths. It was November 11, 1935, before an American crew climbed higher, using a balloon made of rubberized fabric and having a capacity of 3.7 million cubic feet. Albert Stevens and Orvil Anderson boarded the *Explorer II* capsule, equipped with dozens of instruments for scientific research, at the "Stratobowl," near Rapid City, South Dakota, and rose to 22,066 meters (72,395 feet). It was a record that would stand for over twenty years.

After WWII, the United States revived high-altitude balloon research flights with the aim of paving the way for the forthcoming space program. In November 1956, Lewis and Ross at last raised the high-altitude bar by reaching 23,100 meters (75,787 feet). The next year, Major David Simons, a USAF doctor, took a pressurized capsule to 101,000 feet and stayed there for almost two days. Then in 1961, Commander Malcolm Ross and Lieutenant Commander Victor Prather of the U.S. Navy climbed to 34,688 meters (113,739.9 feet) in a polyethylene balloon named *Lee Lewis Memorial*. They came down in the Gulf of Mexico, where Prather's pressure suit filled with water and he drowned. It was a sad ending to a memorable achievement. The balloon altitude record set by Ross and Prather still stood at the century's close and seemed unlikely to be broken.

Notwithstanding his countrymen's considerable accomplishments, Captain Joe Kittinger, USAF, might claim to have had the most remarkable career in (and out of) high-altitude balloons. During the first flight of the *Manhigh* pro-

The lead balloon heads off into the late August sky, with the wind.

gram in 1957, he reached 96,000 feet, and in 1959 he pioneered high-altitude parachuting when he left the gondola of *Excelsior I* at 76,400 feet. It was a jump that could have proved fatal. A failure of the stabilizing chute put him into a spin so fast that he became unconscious, and was saved by a barometric device that opened his main parachute automatically at 11,000 feet. Undeterred by the experience, he repeated the performance a month later in *Excelsior II*, this time without difficulty. On August 16, 1960, *Excelsior III* took him to 102,800 feet, where he stepped out of the open gondola. His free-fall descent of 84,700 feet lasted more than four and a half minutes, during which he recorded a Mach number of 0.93 as a free-falling body. Slowed by the atmosphere to less than 200 mph before his parachute opened at 18,000 feet, he reached the ground 13 minutes and 45 seconds after leaving the gondola.

Crossing the Oceans

The development of advanced technology balloons, capable of reaching and maintaining high altitudes, led some aerial adventurers to revive the long dormant dream of a lighter-than-air crossing of the Atlantic. Surprisingly, the first attempt, made in 1958, was from east to west, with the starting point in the Canary Islands. Common sense suggested a boat-shaped gondola, which was just as well, since the balloon dumped its crew of four into the ocean after covering 1,450 miles. They sailed the gondola boat into Barbados some days later. In the next twenty years, a number of west-to-east attempts were made, but all of them failed, some with the loss of the crew. Finally, in August 1978, Maxie Anderson, Ben Abruzzo and Larry Newman left Maine in *Double Eagle II*. A little over 137 hours later, they touched down 60 miles from Paris, having covered 3,106 miles and set records for both time and distance in a gas balloon. They were not records that would endure. Among those to exceed them was Joe Kittinger, who accomplished the first solo balloon crossing of the Atlantic in 1984, traveling 3,544 miles from Caribou, Maine, to land his *Rosie O'Grady* at Cairo Montenotte, Italy.

The Pacific posed a somewhat greater challenge, but was conquered in 1981. *Double Eagle V*, piloted by Ben Abruzzo, Larry Newman, Ron Clark and Rocky Aoki of Japan, launched from Nagashimi, Japan, on November 10, and landed 84 hours, 31 minutes later in Mendocino National Forest, California, setting a new distance record of 5,768 miles.

The ocean trails having been blazed by gas balloons, it remained to be seen whether their hot-air counterparts could follow. Starting in 1987, they did. In June of that year, Per Lindstrand and Richard Branson inflated what was then the largest balloon ever made. Their *Virgin Atlantic*, named after Branson's airline, had a capacity of 2.3 million cubic feet and carried an enclosed gondola lavishly equipped with modern navigation gear and safety devices. After launching from New England their ocean crossing was trouble-free until they neared Northern Ireland, when bad weather and battery failure combined to make things difficult. An attempted touchdown near Limavady in deteriorating visibility went badly wrong when strong downdrafts increased the balloon's rate of descent. With the burners on full to counter the fall, they impacted heavily in a field before soaring upward again. Now out over the Irish Sea and being blown into low cloud with the prospect of the Scottish mountains ahead, Lindstrand decided to ditch. They let down onto the sea and tried to detonate the explosive bolts that were meant to separate the balloon from the gondola. Nothing happened, since the faulty batteries failed to fire the bolts. Lindstrand elected to jump overboard rather than risk the balloon lifting off again, but Branson did not follow. Now relieved of Lindstrand's weight, the balloon rose and disappeared into the clouds, carrying Branson and all the safety equipment with it. The *Virgin Atlantic* climbed to 5,000 feet before beginning another descent, finally touching down gently on the sea before reaching the Scottish coast. Both of the intrepid balloonists were rescued, Lindstrand by helicopter and Branson by a Royal Navy frigate, and lived to fly again. Their epic adventure with the *Virgin Atlantic* had led them to unexpected hazards, but they had achieved their goal — the Atlantic had been crossed by hot-air balloon.

His spirits undampened by his dunking in the Irish Sea, Per Lindstrand did not take long to set another record for hot-air balloons. In June 1988, he induced one to climb to an astonishing 65,000 feet. Then in 1991, he rejoined Richard Branson in Japan to challenge the Pacific in a new balloon, the *Virgin Pacific Flyer*. Once again, their flight was not an easy one. Ascending into the jet stream, they made rapid if turbulent progress, at times registering ground speeds of well over 200 mph. However, the extremely low temperatures caused droplets of fuel to freeze into crystals round the burner jets. At one point, a mass of these crystals fell burning into the gondola, starting a fire. All traces of the blaze were eventually extinguished by taking the balloon even higher into more rarified air. This consumed fuel they could ill afford, and put them into winds which carried them far to the north of their planned track to California. After some forty-six hours, they brought the balloon down on a frozen lake in Arctic Canada, having covered 4,767 miles and added the Pacific to their conquests.

Rozier Returns

The death of Pilatre de Rozier in 1785 had clearly demonstrated the folly of combining an open fire with an inflammable gas such as hydrogen to provide a balloon's lift. However, in the second half of the 20th century, helium became more easily obtainable, suggesting that the Rozier principle might be worth further examination. The idea places a helium envelope at the upper part of the balloon with a hot-air envelope beneath. During the day, the warmth provided by the sun allows the helium to expand and provide most of the lift, so cutting down on the need to use burners and thus saving fuel. As the balloon cools after sunset, the burners add hot air, replacing any lost lift and warming the helium, keeping it expanded. Another advantage is that a Rozier balloon can be much smaller than its hot-air counterpart.

With the return of the Rozier principle, long-range flights became more feasible, and the race was on to see who would be the first to circle the Earth in a balloon. The most persistent competitor was the American Stephen Fossett. He had no doubts about the advantages of the Rozier design: "It was the invention of the Rozier balloon in the early '80s by Donald Cameron that makes it possible to stay up long enough to go around the world, which hot air or gas balloons can't really do. A hot air balloon requires a great deal of fuel to keep it aloft, and a gas balloon, which usually uses helium, has the problem that the helium cools at night when the sun is not on it, and you have to throw ballast overboard to keep it from going to the surface. The next day, when the balloon warms as the sun comes up again, it actually starts to fly too high, and you have to valve out helium. Practically speaking you can't make a gas balloon big enough to do that cycle for more than about five days, and an around-the-world flight could take up to three weeks. The Rozier is basically a gas balloon, but instead of ballast we carry fuel and a hot air burner to warm the helium at night, which is much more efficient than carrying ballast."

Fossett's long-range navigation career began in February 1995, when he piloted his Cameron-built Rozier from Seoul, South Korea, as far as Saskatchewan, to record the first solo balloon crossing of the Pacific and post an absolute world distance record of 8,748 kilometers (5,436 miles). Early the next year he launched from South Dakota but came down soon after when his balloon's outer envelope started shredding. In 1997, his *Solo Spirit* got him from St. Louis to India (10,421 miles), where he landed low on fuel; then in 1998 he made it from Missouri to Krasnodar, Russia (5,836 miles), before being forced down by technical problems. The following August he tried again from Argentina, this time traveling in the southern hemisphere, but his Rozier ruptured during a thunderstorm, and he ditched in the Coral Sea (14,319 miles). In the process of these various attempts he had become the first to cross the South Atlantic and the Indian Ocean, and he had flown across the Atlantic four times.

Richard Branson was keen to add a round-the-world success to his Atlantic and Pacific achievements. He began his campaign in January 1997 from Marrakech, Morocco, with the bravely named *Global Challenger*, but equipment

> *What a treat to stroll through the veils of twilight, to float across the sky like a slowly forming thought. Flying an airplane, one usually travels the shortest distance between two points. Balloonists can dawdle, lollygag, cast their fate to the wind and become part of the ebb and flow of nature, part of the sky itself, held aloft like any bird, leaf or spore. In that silent realm, far from the mischief and toil of society, all one hears is the urgent breathing of the wind and, now and then, an inspiring gasp of hot air.*
> DIANE ACKERMAN, "TRAVELING LIGHT," *THE NEW YORK TIMES*, JANUARY 11, 1997

problems brought the flight to an end after only 400 miles. By the end of the year he was ready to try again, but an accident during the balloon inflation process tore the envelope from its moorings and sent it off by itself into Algeria. In December 1998, Branson began his third attempt, this time with both Per Lindstrand and the now balloonless Fossett on board. Success appeared to be within their grasp, but in seeking winds that would allow them to avoid both Iraq and China they used too much fuel and were forced down into the Pacific after 19,962 kilometers (12,476 miles).

Among the other round-the-world contenders were the *J Renee*, flown solo by Kevin Uliassi, which wound up in a field in Indiana on New Year's Eve 1997 when the base of the balloon burst. The *Global Hilton*, piloted by Dick Rutan and Dave Melton, took off on January 9, 1998, but soon thereafter the helium cell ruptured and they were forced to take to their parachutes. British pilots Colin Prescot and Andy Elson launched their balloon *Cable and Wireless* on February 17, 1999, from a golf course in the South of Spain, and landed in the ocean 50 miles off the coast of Japan on March 7. The remaining challenger was a balloon made by Cameron Balloons of Bristol, England, and sponsored by the Breitling Swiss watch company. For a while, it seemed that it, too, was being dogged by ill fortune. Captained by the Swiss Bertrand Piccard, a member of the pioneering balloon family, the *Breitling Orbiter* ditched six hours into its 1997 attempt when a tiny clip came loose on a fuel line and the gondola flooded with kerosene fumes. In January 1998, Piccard and copilots Wim Vertsraeten and Andy Elson took *Breitling Orbiter 2* from Switzerland as far as Myanmar (Burma) but had to come down when the Chinese refused the balloon permission to enter their airspace.

As determined and persistent as their competitors, the Breitling team started again on March 1, 1999, with *Breitling III*. Bertrand Piccard, accompanied this time by Briton Brian Jones, left from the Alpine village of Chateau d'Oex and moved initially southward to find favorable winds over North Africa. Their route then took them over Egypt, India, Bangladesh, southern China, Mexico, and the Caribbean. Finally, on March 20, they crossed the latitude of their outbound track over Mauritania to become the first balloonists to circle the Earth. In no hurry to end their epic journey, they stayed in the air for another day before coming down in Egypt's western desert, nearly twenty days after launching. Their technology, the weather and international politics had all behaved benignly to give them their achievement. Besides completing a global circuit in 370 hours, 24 minutes, they had set other world records, including total distance flown 40,814 kilometers (25,361 miles), and duration of flight 477 hours, 47 minutes.

From June 19 to July 4, 2002, Steve Fossett became the first man to fly a balloon round the world solo, in the process gaining the absolute world balloon speed record and the 24-hour balloon distance record.

Balloons for Everyone

Until the 1960s, ballooning was generally thought of only as a fringe sport, a pastime for the rich, or as a research tool, useful for those with unlimited funds. That all began to change in the 1950s when Ed Yost moved to Sioux Falls, South Dakota, and formed Raven Industries. One of Raven's first projects was a commission from the U.S. Navy's Office of Naval Research (ONR) to create an aircraft that would carry one man and enough fuel to fly for three hours, take a load to 10,000 feet, and be reusable. The system was to be of small size and weight and have a fast launching system that required minimum manpower. Reaching back to the 18th century to the Montgolfiers, Yost developed the concept of a modern hot-air balloon, and in October 1955 conducted a successful moored test flight. The envelope was plastic film, and heat was provided by plumber's pots burning kerosene. On October 22, 1960, Yost made the first free flight of a modern hot-air balloon from Bruning, Nebraska. By then he was using nylon for the envelope, and had created a propane heater. The gross weight of the balloon, including Yost and fuel, was 404 pounds. He was in the air for 25 minutes and landed 3 miles from his takeoff point.

The next flight was on November 12, 1960, from the Stratobowl in South Dakota. Yost had increased the burner power, reinforced the envelope to add handling lines, and increased the size of the deflation port at the top from 9 to 13 feet. The inflation took 6 minutes, and he lifted off with a gross weight of 465 pounds. He ascended at 300 feet per minute to 9,000 feet, then initiated a descent at 600 feet per minute that he successfully slowed with the new burner as he neared the surface. He landed after a flight of one hour, 50 minutes, having covered 39 miles and proved the hot-air balloon was a viable concept, both cheap and reliable.

In a report in October 1961, Ed Yost summed up the advantages of the hot-air balloon: "By the application of modern materials, design techniques and instrumentation, an aerostat which had been known for more than 175 years was resurrected and shown to have substantial value in modern research and operations. The low cost, simplicity of operation, and logistic advantage which hot air balloons provide, when compared with light-gas balloons, are most impressive. Within the altitude limits where hot air balloons may be used, these modern Montgolfier systems may become an important tool for atmospheric and low-level lifting and transport tasks."

Yost recognized that there was more to it than that. Raven Industries sold their first sport balloon in November 1961, and the new leisure activity of hot-air ballooning was born. Soon after, Don Piccard (son of Jean Piccard) joined Yost to manage the company's sport balloon program. Don Piccard, following his family's tradtion, was already a major figure in American ballooning. In 1947, while attending the University of Minnesota, he had procured a WWII Japanese *FO-GO* balloon. Made from paper and silk, *FO-GO*s had been used by the Japanese to send incendiary bombs across the Pacific. Piccard added a small basket to the balloon and, with the aid of a volunteer ground crew, he made a two-hour solo flight from downtown Minneapolis. That qualified him to become the first

Breitling Orbiter III lifts off from the Swiss village of Chateau d'Oex on March 1, 1999. Designed and built by Cameron Balloons, of Bristol, England, Breitling Orbiter III stood 180 feet tall when fully inflated. It combined the advantages of hot air and helium technologies. The envelope was of a nylon fabric welded to a membrane and covered with a protective skin coated with aluminum. The gondola was a weave of Kevlar and carbon fiber material.

Bertrand Piccard (left) and Bryan Jones guided Breitling Orbiter III *round the world to a landing in the Egyptian desert on March 21, 1999. The flight lasted 19 days, 21 hours and 47 minutes and covered 25,361 miles. Their route took them over Egypt, India, Bangladesh, southern China, the Pacific, Mexico, the Caribbean, and Mauritania. During the flight, the balloon climbed to a maximum altitude of 37,313 feet, and reached ground speeds as high as 185 mph.*

CAA licensed balloon pilot after WWII and the only active licensed pilot in the United States at that time. In 1948, Don Piccard founded the Balloon Club of America, which later grew to become the Balloon Federation of America. Having joined forces with Ed Yost, he organized the first hot-air balloon meet, attracting three balloons to the St. Paul Winter Carnival in 1962. The following year he was Clerk of Course for the first U.S. National Hot Air Balloon Championship held in Kalamazoo, Michigan, after which he and Yost went to Europe and became the first to cross the English Channel in a hot-air balloon since the 18th century. In 1964, Piccard formed a separate company and went on to design his own balloons, introducing many new features to make ballooning safer and more accessible to people generally.

The efforts of Yost and Piccard made it possible for the sport of ballooning to become popular and pointed the way for those besides themselves who would go on to develop balloons as sightseeing vehicles, tourist attractions, commercial billboards, or simply as a means by which people could enjoy the thrilling sensation of free flight. In 1972, an International Balloon Fiesta was staged in Albuquerque, New Mexico. It attracted thirteen hot-air balloons. The next year, representatives of thirteen countries traveled to New Mexico and took part in the first World Hot Air Balloon Championships. Since then the Fiesta has become an annual event, the largest balloon gathering in the world. By the year 2000, it was expected that close to a thousand balloons would wish to take part, and arrangements had to be made for over a million spectators to enjoy at first hand the nine-day extravaganza of color and excitement, a huge celebration of the world's oldest aviation sport. The eye-catching special events of the Fiesta, including mass ascensions, a "night magic glow," and a special shapes rodeo, have made it one of the world's most photographed spectacles, a fact recognized by Kodak when they became the principal sponsor in 1992. Thanks to the use of computer software to ease the problem of accurate measuring and cutting of balloon material, the special shapes can be almost anything that can be imagined. Those flown have included a Taj Mahal, cartoon characters, a beer mug, bottles of wine, a steam locomotive, the head of Uncle Sam, Noah's Ark complete with animals, and an endless variety of corporate advertising symbols.

> *"I am going to have a cup of tea, like any good Englishman."*
> BRIAN JONES, AFTER FLYING ROUND THE WORLD IN THE *BREITLING ORBITER III* BALLOON IN 1999

The Fiesta has been instrumental in changing the character of ballooning, each year showing new pilots and owners from some thirty countries what a thrilling and safe experience ballooning can be. Coverage is given by the media of more than fifty nations, with live satellite broadcasts to Japan and television documentaries prepared by Britain, Germany, the Netherlands and France.

While the Albuquerque Fiesta is ballooning's great spectacular, there are now many meets and festivals all over the world, bringing balloons of all shapes and sizes together at fairs, county shows and specialist events. The competitive elements of these gatherings often include contests for the highest altitude reached, the greatest distance flown, or the longest time spent in the air. There might also be various tests of pilot skill in maintaining a specific altitude, making a controlled descent, or following a predetermined flight profile. The commonest race is the "hare and hounds," in which an official balloon leads the way and the other balloonists follow, attempting to land or drop a marker as close as they can to wherever the hare comes down or places his own marker. There are many variations, sometimes involving touching the balloon basket on the surface of a lake, or carrying a passenger who has to disembark with a bicycle and race back to the launch site. Inevitably, more dramatic activities have been added as time has gone by. Parachutists using steerable parachutes are induced to step out of baskets at altitudes high enough for the balloon to overtake them in the descent. The idea then is for the parachutist to aim for a safety net hanging beneath the basket and, once ensnared, to climb back aboard. Other thrill-seekers abseil or bungee-jump from balloons, or even walk a tightrope (actually a metal bar) between two balloon baskets. Balloons can also be used to lift hang gliders to altitude before releasing them to sail away on silent wings. The spread of the sport as a result of so much public exposure has been dramatic. In the early 1970s there were fewer than fifty privately owned hot-air balloons in the United States, with less than half that number in the United Kingdom and only a handful elsewhere. At the end of the century, there were some 20,000 licensed balloon pilots in the world, and hundreds of ballooning clubs. It seemed clear that the ability to fly in relative silence and largely at the whim of nature, looking down on the world and its concerns with some detachment for a while, held a special appeal for the human spirit.

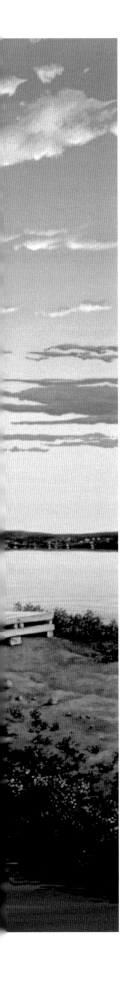

CHAPTER 4

The Wings Rotate

Aᴌᴛʜᴏᴜɢʜ ᴛʜᴇ sᴇᴇᴅs of maple trees provide readily observed evolutionary evidence of flight accomplished by rotating aerofoils, and the helicopter has become a commonplace of daily life, most people still find something disturbingly unnatural about rotary-wing flight. (In the 1860s, the French Viscount Gustave de Ponton d'Amécourt, who was researching rotary-wing flight, joined two Greek words — heliko [spiral] and pteron [wing] — to form the new term "helicopters.") The human mind can accept the logic of fixed wings, a concept reassuringly confirmed by the soaring flight of many birds. Aircraft with rotating wings, on the other hand, can give the impression of having no visible means of support. Developed during the 20th century despite intimidating difficulties, they have become creatures of unnerving complexity, surmounted by noisy, whirling masses of machinery that seem hell-bent on flying apart in an orgy of centrifugal disintegration.

Even in its simplest form, rotary-wing flight is aerodynamically complicated, apparently offering the least promising prospects for anyone wrestling with the basic problem of how to fly. Nevertheless, the idea has a very long history. The best-known early design for a helicopter is the clockwork-driven helix contained in one of Leonardo da Vinci's notebooks from the 1480s, but there is plenty of evidence of rotating wings well before that. The Chinese had flying toys that used the principle perhaps two thousand years ago, and by the 14th century they had reached Europe. There is a Flemish illustration from about 1320 that shows a four-bladed rotor toy apparently modeled on the sails of a windmill.

In 1784, two Frenchmen, Launoy and Bienvenu, successfully demonstrated a rotating wing model at a meeting of the French Academy of Sciences, and Sir George Cayley (the "Father of Aerial Navigation") designed several rotary-wing machines in the 1800s. In 1842, W.H. Phillips actually flew a small one that burned a combination of charcoal, saltpeter and gypsum, rotating the "wings" by blowing the resulting gas from the tips. More flying models appeared during the second half of the 19th century, notably those designed in France by the Vicomte d'Amécourt and Alphonse Pénaud. All sorts of power sources were employed in attempts to find the most efficient (twisted rubber, gunpowder, compressed air and a gas turbine among them), but the Italian Enrico Forlanini was more successful than most when he used a small steam engine. However, none of these commendable efforts came close to producing a machine that could be flown while carrying a man. That remained possible only through a flight of the imagination. In 1887, a translation of a Jules Verne novel appeared under the English title *Clipper of the Clouds*. It featured the *Albatross*, a ship of the air carried vertically

Peacefully, by *Hélène Croft. A Bell 206 of Great Slave Helicopters of Yellowknife, Northwest Territories, Canada, rests beside Lac de Gras, close to the Arctic Circle. Award-winning artist Hélène Croft lives in Fort Smith, NWT. Her paintings vividly depict the landscape, wildlife and people of northern Canada. Aviation is an essential part of life in the far north and is her favorite subject.*

fixed-wing flight. Nevertheless, in 1907, two Frenchmen built machines that managed to make the first tentative hops toward a helicopter future. In Douai, Louis Breguet, after considerable research and much testing of aerofoils, constructed a vast spider's web of a machine he called a gyroplane. It had the engine and the pilot set at the center of four radiating arms, each of which had a 26-foot-diameter rotor at its outer end. Each rotor consisted of eight blades, arranged in four biplane sets, making thirty-two blades in all. When it was assembled in the yard of Breguet's workshop, this contraption's prospects did not look too promising, especially since, with its pilot, it weighed over 1,000 pounds and the powerplant was capable of producing no more than 40 horsepower. The pilot, a diminutive young engineer named Volumard, was chosen principally because he tipped the scale at only 110 pounds. On September 29, 1907, Volumard took his seat surrounded by four men strategically placed at points on each arm, all standing ready to restrain the beast, a necessary precaution since it lacked flight controls of any kind. To Breguet's delight, when Volumard opened up the engine, his gyroplane rose some two feet and hovered for about a minute, its stability assured by the exertions of its four anxious wardens. Since it could not be controlled, it could not be claimed that Breguet had created a true helicopter, but he had at least built a rotary-winged machine that, for the first time, had succeeded in lifting both itself and a man clear of the ground.

aloft by multi-bladed fans mounted horizontally on top of a forest of thirty-seven masts. Large propellers at the bow and stern thrust the imaginary vessel round the world in only eight days, a time not approached in the real world until the heroics of Wiley Post over forty years later. Until the advent of the 20th century, Jules Verne's *Albatross* was the best that could be done.

Lift Off!

Colorful fictional fantasies notwithstanding, the helicopter idea generally attracted relatively little public interest in the period before WWI. The problems associated with it were too daunting and, in any case, the concept was overshadowed by all the excitement surrounding the dawning of

Not too far away, in the Norman town of Lisieux, lived Paul Cornu. Like the Wright brothers, he was in the bicycle business. In 1907, he was hard at work on his ideas for vertical flight, and was building a helicopter based on a model he had flown the year before. The wheels and framework of his completed machine owed a great deal to his background in bicycle engineering. Unlike Breguet's gyroplane, it relied on just two 20-foot rotors, each consisting of only two broad blades made of steel tubing covered with rubber-proofed silk and mounted fore and aft of the pilot on long outriggers. Large controllable paddles that extended to front and rear were intended to use downwash from the rotors to provide stability. With Cornu himself on board, the whole machine's weight was less than half that of Breguet's. On November 13, 1907, Cornu started his 24-horsepower Antoinette engine and coaxed his helicopter into the air. It hovered just above the ground, so becoming the first true helicopter, since it did so without external assistance or tethering. During a second try later in the day, Cornu's brother did attempt to steady the rising machine and, somewhat to his surprise, was lifted off the ground, too.

Both Breguet and Cornu persisted with their experiments for a while without making significant progress, and eventually both turned to more rewarding fields of endeavor. For Breguet, however, the helicopter challenge was merely postponed. Having made his name during WWI and thereafter by manufacturing fixed-wing aircraft, he came back to flying beneath rotating wings in the 1930s. There were other rotary-wing experimenters in the early 1900s, but none of them could claim even the small successes of the French for their often bizarre ideas. George Clout, A.E. Hunt, James Scott and Wilbur Kimball were among those who constructed large (in Hunt's case, enormous) meandering piles of machinery that produced more than their fair share of downwash and vibration without lifting an inch. Experiments took place in Russia, too, which were almost equally disheartening, but in that country at least they were the opening chapters of a very different story.

Igor Sikorsky was a brilliant aircraft designer. His most successful early machines were fixed-wing, but he was fascinated by the idea of rotary flight and began work on helicopters as early as 1910. Although his efforts were at first disappointing, he persevered and his VS-300 eventually flew in 1940. All modern single-rotor helicopters are descended from that machine.

Igor Sikorsky had been attracted to aeronautics while still a child and had always dreamed of building flying machines. Helicopters in particular fascinated him. After training as an engineer in Paris and then at Kiev's Polytechnic Institute, he set about making his dream a reality. By 1909 he was back in Paris, at that time the heart of the aeronautical world, to see for himself the progress being made in aviation. He examined the aircraft of the day and discussed his ideas with leading pioneers, among them Ferdinand Ferber, who advised him not to waste his time on the insuperable problems of vertical flight. Sikorsky, however, was not to be so easily dissuaded. In 1909 he returned to Kiev and began building his first helicopter. It took shape as a skeletal wooden framework surmounted by twin rotors geared to turn in opposite directions. Power came from a 25-horsepower motorcycle engine. The finished article, cursed as it was by massive vibration and incapable of lifting even itself, was not a success. Sikorsky later commented that: "This machine was a failure to the extent that it could not fly. In other respects it was a very important and necessary stepping stone."

Having learned a great deal from testing his first machine, Sikorsky moved on to design a second helicopter. He retained the twin-rotor design, but took care to limit the machine's weight. When completed, Sikorsky No. 2 was a fragile-looking creature towering to three times its builder's

height and weighing 400 pounds. To his disappointment, No. 2 proved no more capable of leaving the ground than had No. 1, even though its behavior under power was less alarming. At this stage of his research, Sikorsky began to appreciate that he had neither the basic knowledge of rotary flight nor the materials necessary for him to achieve success. He could see that he needed to develop a more powerful engine mounted in a lighter, stronger structure. Then there was the question of control once the machine was in the air, a subject he had not even begun to understand. Faced with these temporarily intractable problems, and by the fact that he was spending too much of his family's money, Sikorsky set his helicopter vision aside for the time being and turned to designing fixed-wing aircraft. By 1913, his *Russkyi Vitiaz* (or *Bolshoi Baltisky*), the world's first four-engined aircraft and a wonder of the age, was in the air. However, Sikorsky's passion for rotating wings was not spent. Decades later and half a world away from Kiev, he would start to dream once more of leaving the ground by going straight up.

> *Rare is the man of vision whose dreams become reality. Rarer still is one whose vision brings a better life to others while fulfilling his own. Such a man was Igor I. Sikorsky, aeronautical pioneer, father of the helicopter, inventor and philosopher.*
>
> INSCRIPTION ON THE HEADSTONE OF IGOR SIKORSKY'S GRAVE IN SAINT JOHN'S RUSSIAN ORTHODOX CEMETERY, STRATFORD, CONNECTICUT

Seeking Control

G.A. Crocco, an Italian, had first suggested the principle of cyclic pitch control in 1906, and it was tested by the Dane Jacob Ellehammer in a rotary-wing machine that managed to raise itself and its pilot a few inches off the ground during a demonstration near Copenhagen in 1912. WWI then intervened with its heavy emphasis on fixed-wing biplanes, and helicopter research became a luxury necessarily neglected until the end of hostilities. Even so, some experiments were carried out by the Austro-Hungarians, who believed that a hovering machine would be useful for reconnaissance. Their Zurovec PKZ 2, fitted with three 100-horsepower engines, did manage to reach an altitude of more than 100 feet, but could not be effectively controlled and was eventually wrecked. By the 1920s, lighter and more powerful engines were more widely available and several attempts were made to solve the vexed problem of control. Among the most prominent helicopter builders of the time were Etienne Oehmichen and the Argentine

Marquis de Pescara in France, while the United States saw machines produced by Henry Berliner and George de Bothezat. Of these, the most complex and ambitious was that built for the U.S. Army by the Russian-born de Bothezat. Completed in December 1922, it was an immense cruciform creation, 65 feet across and weighing 3,600 pounds. Its single 180-horsepower Le Rhône engine drove four six-bladed fans, each of which had a diameter of 26 feet. It did fly, but not for very long and not very high. Having spent some $200,000 on the project, the U.S. Army thought better of it and ordered de Bothezat's monster scrapped in 1924.

While de Bothezat's efforts did little to advance understanding of vertical flight problems, the work of the Marquis de Pescara certainly did. He developed a method of changing the pitch of the rotor blades in succession at a selected point in their rotation. This "cyclic pitch control," first touched on by Crocco and Ellehammer before WWI, gave a pilot the ability to produce additional thrust where he wished in the rotor disc, so allowing the helicopter to be tilted in the direction required. The capacity of the machine to fly forward, backward or sideways was thus made more than a theoretical possibility. The Marquis also developed the concept of autorotation, relieving the general anxiety felt about engine failure in helicopters. He correctly believed that the upward rush of air through the rotor disc of a falling helicopter would enable the whirling blades to provide both "gliding" lift and stored energy. As the inevitable contact with the surface approached in an engine-off forced landing, it was necessary only to time an increase in the rotor's pitch so that a soft landing would be assured.

Spanish Windmill

The difficulties of making the single direct leap to vertical flight were proving immense, but one man thought it might be possible to succeed at an intermediate level. In Spain, Juan de la Cierva realized that most of the helicopter's complex problems resulted from powering the rotor blades. Taking the example of simple rotary toys, he believed that sufficient lift could be gained from rotating wings merely by ensuring that the aircraft they supported kept moving, driven forward either by the influence of gravity (as in de Pescara's theoretical forced landing) or by the thrust of a conventionally positioned propeller. The beauty of such a solution was that, with unpowered rotor blades, the hazards of torque, in which blades turning one way forced the fuselage in the other, would be avoided. However, a major problem remained. Unequal lift, produced by the rotor's blades as they retreated and advanced, threatened to capsize the aircraft every time it tried to get off the ground.

In the early 1920s, de la Cierva built and tested several "autogyros" without finding a solution to the phenomenon of unequal lift. Once again, it was a model that suggested the answer. He noticed that a model fitted with rattan blades seemed to fly perfectly, and it dawned on him that it was because the rattan was flexible, allowing an advancing blade to ride up as its airspeed and lift increased, so changing its angle of attack and thereby reducing lift. The opposite was happening on the retreating side of the rotor. The result was balanced flight. To reproduce the effect on his full-size autogyro he connected the blades to the rotor hub with angled hinges, so making it possible for them to move freely up and down within certain limits. On January 9, 1923, de la Cierva's C.4

autogyro, with a Spanish Army pilot in the cockpit, flew smoothly through its initial tests. The door to rotary-winged flight at last stood ready to open.

Two years of fine tuning followed, and by the summer of 1925 de la Cierva had some customers identified. Frank Courtney, a de Havilland test pilot, was hired to fly the autogyro in Britain, and his demonstrations so impressed Air Ministry officials that they awarded de la Cierva a production contract. The first hurdle having been cleared, suddenly the Spanish inventor was internationally acclaimed. Courtney performed in front of royalty and put the autogyro through its paces before admiring crowds in France, Belgium and Italy. The first hint that all might not be well came in Germany in September 1926. The blades began to show some deformation at the root. Courtney suggested that it might be necessary to fit an additional set of hinges that would allow the blades some freedom of movement horizontally as well as vertically, but de la Cierva demurred. New blades were fitted and the demonstrations continued. Some months later, Courtney's idea was seen to have been eminently sensible. He was flying at 1,000 feet over southern England when the autogyro started to groan and shake. He lowered the nose and looked for a place to land, but at 200 feet the vibration increased alarmingly as one rotor blade broke away. Another snapped off just before the autogyro struck the ground. The impact was severe, but Courtney survived, suffering a concussion and broken ribs. When he emerged from hospital, he announced that he would

The Cierva C.30A was built under license in the United Kingdom by Avro as the Rota. Twelve were supplied to the RAF in 1934/35. Rotas served with the School of Army Cooperation and with 529 Squadron until 1945.

no longer be flying autogyros. Even the assurance that additional hinges would be fitted to the blades could not change his mind. Courtney was content to return to fixed-wing aviation.

With the addition of the new hinges, rotary-winged flight came of age. By the late 1920s, Cierva autogyros were being used all over the world. Manufacturing licences were issued to companies in Japan, Germany, France and the Soviet Union, and de la Cierva moved his main base to the United Kingdom. In the United States, the Pitcairn and Kellett companies built eighty Cierva autogyros between them. They were used by the Forest Service to combat fires and by newspapers to rush reporters to cover breaking stories. Harold Pitcairn was sure that he held the rights to the Model T of the air and he offered the PA-18 sports model for sale at $5,000. The advertising stressed safety and convenience, enticing customers with such copy as: "The open areas surrounding almost any country club offer room for the owner of the Pitcairn Autogyro to fly direct to his golf game." The advantages of being able to fly as fast as 100 mph or as slowly as 20 mph were certainly considerable, but flying an autogyro was not as easy as it was made to appear and there was still a lot of development work to do. A clutch was introduced to connect the engine to the rotor so that the blades could be wound up to a suitable speed before takeoff, and, more significantly, a system was devised that allowed the pitch of all the blades to be altered from the cockpit at the same time. This collective pitch control, which gave pilot the ability to regulate lift, thrust and rotor speed, was the last major step toward the true helicopter.

There were some other minor developments of the autogyro. Pitcairn introduced the "roadable" model, with folding blades and steerable front wheels, which caused some excitement by appearing on a few city streets. However, the autogyro's shortcomings were now becoming evident. Vertical takeoff and landing were dependent on a strong headwind, and hovering flight could not be achieved in still air. Load-carrying capacity was limited, and that restricted the possible number of passengers and the range. As its market appeal

> *"Professor Focke and his technicians standing below grew ever smaller as I continued to rise straight up, 50 metres, 75 metres, 100 metres. Then I gently began to throttle back and the speed of ascent dwindled till I was hovering motionless in midair. This was intoxicating! I thought of the lark, so light and small of wing, hovering over the summer fields. Now man had wrested from him his lovely secret."*
> HANNA REITSCH, GERMAN TEST PILOT, DESCRIBING HER FIRST HELICOPTER FLIGHT

lessened, the voice of the autogyro's principal champion fell silent. In December 1936, Juan de la Cierva was killed in the crash of a Dutch airliner at Croydon Airport near London. With his passing, autogyro development stagnated, but because of his work, the helicopter was ready for takeoff.

Power to the Rotor

In the early 1930s, a number of designers turned their attention to the challenge of producing a true helicopter, an aircraft capable of taking off and landing vertically, hovering, and flying not only forward but backward and sideways as well. Prominent among them was Louis Breguet, returning to the charge after two decades of building successful fixed-wing aircraft. Now more aware of the difficulties to be overcome, he gave his new venture the name Gyroplane-Laboratoire, so emphasizing its research function. It was ready for testing in November 1933, but the first attempt at flight was disastrous. As soon as power was applied to its twin rotors, the machine rolled quickly onto its right side, smashing its blades. Breguet persevered, however, and the rebuilt aircraft was wheeled out again on June 26, 1935. This time it flew. The design had been refined by making it possible to tilt the rotors and change the pitch of the blades. Even so, control was marginal and, according to test pilot Maurice Claisse, the machine vibrated "like a bag of walnuts." By November 1936, Claisse had coaxed the G-L into climbing up to 500 feet and staying in the air for over an hour, but it was still a long way from being a practical helicopter. Work on it continued until 1939 without significant progress being made, and at that point Breguet was, for the second time, diverted by the onset of a war.

More obviously successful efforts were made in Germany by two designers new to vertical flight. Heinrich Focke had been a founder of the Focke-Wulf firm in the 1920s and the name had become established as the maker of a variety of aircraft, ranging from small passenger monoplanes to the less conventional twin-engined F-19 canard. In 1933, Focke had acquired a licence to build autogyros and

The twin-rotor Focke-Achgelis Fa 61 first flew in 1936 and was the first fully controllable helicopter. It was designed around the fuselage and engine of a Focke-Wulf Fw 44 Stieglitz basic trainer, with the tailplane moved to the top of the fin. The propeller was cut down to serve purely as an engine cooling fan. D-EKRA was the second prototype. Before WWI the Fa 61 set helicopter world records for altitude (11,243 feet); endurance (one hour, 21 minutes); and distance (143 miles).

had begun manufacturing Cierva C.30s. He became intrigued by the problems of adding power to the rotor blades and was soon devoting most of his time to helicopter design. By 1936 he had completed a series of wind tunnel and flight tests on a twin-rotor aircraft he designated the Fw 61, and the following year he left his original company to found Focke-Achgelis with the aerobatic pilot Gerd Achgelis. The Fw 61 was based on the fuselage and engine of an Fw 44 Stieglitz trainer but with the propeller reduced in size so that it functioned as not much more than an engine cooling fan. It was by far the best helicopter design of its day and at one time it held all of the rotary flight records, including a climb to over 11,000 feet and the first successful autorotation ever performed. The Fw 61 remained little more than an interesting phenomenon, however, until test pilot Hanna Reitsch began to demonstrate the machine. Charles Lindbergh was one of those who saw her fly, and later said that the Fw 61 was one of the most remarkable aeronautical developments he had ever seen. In February 1938, Hanna Reitsch showed off the Fw 61 to astonished audiences under the roof of Berlin's huge Deutschlandhalle arena, hovering and changing direction at will while inside the building. Impressed by both the performance and the propaganda value of a German technological triumph, the Nazi regime awarded Focke-Achgelis a contract to develop and produce helicopters. The Fa 223 was the result. It was a much larger and more advanced machine

than its predecessor, capable of carrying four passengers inside and a further eight in seats along the sides. It could fly at over 100 mph and lift external loads of a ton, but it was complex and needed considerable development work. Although it reached the production stage, only nine flew before the end of WWII. In the meantime, Focke's pride of place in German rotary-winged flight was quietly usurped.

Anton Flettner had been experimenting with helicopters since the early 1930s. His first efforts were undistinguished, and in 1933 he decided to start again by building the simpler autogyro. His Fl 184 leant heavily on the Cierva designs and had a full cyclic control, allowing the pilot to tilt the rotor in any direction he wished. Once his autogyro had been proved a success, Flettner took the next step and added power to the rotor. Indeed, he used two rotors, but avoided the inconvenience of Focke's wide outrigger design by mounting them close together, intermeshing the blades and driving them through a common gearbox. With its development financed by the German Navy, Flettner's Fl 265 first flew in May 1939, and an improved version, the Fl 282 Kolibri, was flying by the following year. Tests showed that it could operate from a cruiser's gun turret in heavy seas and that it held obvious promise as a naval reconnaissance aircraft, especially in the antisubmarine role. German sailors were suitably impressed, and a production order was issued for the Kolibri, thus giving it a claim to being one of the earliest helicopters to go beyond the development stage and be accepted as a practical machine. Twenty-four were built.

RUSSIAN CONCEPTION, AMERICAN BIRTH

Effective though the advances in rotary flight were in Germany, they did not have the last word in establishing a standard basic helicopter design. That took shape in the United States and was brought about primarily by Igor Sikorsky. He arrived in America via Paris in 1919, having chosen to leave Russia after the Bolshevik Revolution. In the 1920s, he persevered through difficult times to become a respected builder of fixed-wing aircraft, notably large flying boats, in Connecticut. However, his passion for vertical flight still burned, and in 1931 he applied for a patent on a machine that relied on a single overhead rotor and had a small vertical rotor mounted at the rear. The effects of the worldwide depression and his commitment to flying boats kept Sikorsky from pursuing rotary-wing research with the vigor he would have wished. However, by 1939 the demand for large flying boats was diminishing and Sikorsky was faced with the threat of having his factory shut down by his parent company, United Aircraft. To save his business, Sikorsky convinced UA's management that he should be allowed to change direction and concentrate his efforts on designing and producing a helicopter. Always assiduous in studying the work of others, he had kept in touch with developments elsewhere and had been to Europe to see both the Fw 61 and Breguet's G-L fly. He was now sure that practical helicopters

could be produced, but nothing he had seen or read revised his opinion that his patented layout was the form to be preferred. Nevertheless, he recognized that he was faced with a considerable challenge. As he later put it: "It was a chance to design a new type of flying machine without really knowing how to design it; then to build it without really knowing how to build it; and then the chance to climb into the pilot's seat and try to test fly it, without ever having flown a helicopter before."

In September 1939, two weeks after German forces burst across the Polish frontier, Sikorsky brought his VS-300 into the open and climbed into the pilot's seat. He believed that he should "take the blame for occasional flight trouble if I am to accept any of the credit for success later." No more than a simple skeleton of flimsy-looking tubing surrounding a 75-horsepower engine, with the pilot precariously seated under the downdraft from its single overhead rotor, the VS-300 was not an encouraging sight. Prudently, the creature was tethered to a tray of heavy weights to ensure that it could not get too far from the ground. During that first test session, Sikorsky did no more than lift his helicopter inches off the ground a few times, but by November the machine was flying several feet up for minutes at a stretch. In a careful process of trial and error, Sikorsky built up his experience and took the machine through a number of redesigns. For a while, two additional small horizontal rotors were mounted on outriggers to improve the aircraft's controllability. By December 1940, the VS-300, its tubing now modestly clothed in fabric skin, was sufficiently well-behaved for a U.S. Army test pilot to fly it and recommend that funds should be set aside for

In 1937 Anton Flettner began to design the first helicopter to use inter-meshing contra-rotating synchronized rotors. The following year the German Navy gave Flettner an order for six single-seat helicopters, powered by a seven-cylinder air-cooled engine and fitted with an inertia damping system to reduce the shake of the control stick. Flettner's Fl 265 first flew in May 1939, and its success led to the development of the Fl 282, which was flown by the German Navy operationally from 1942.

At the Berlin Motor Show in 1938, the Fa 61 caused a sensation when it was demonstrated by test pilot Hanna Reitsch inside the Deutschlandhalle stadium in Berlin. She performed in front of packed crowds every night for three weeks, demonstrating that the helicopter could lift off vertically, hover, fly sideways and rotate through 360 degrees.

Sikorsky to develop a military helicopter. The specification issued stated that the desired machine, designated XR-4, should be a closed-cabin two-seater.

The VS-300 continued to operate as the Sikorsky test and development vehicle during 1941. In its final form, the VS-300 employed full cyclic pitch control and had reverted to a single tail rotor. (Cyclic pitch control was reinstated once it was realized that the main rotor was in fact a giant gyroscope. Control inputs were therefore precessed through 90 degrees in taking effect. The solution was simply to offset the controls by that amount so that the aircraft would not roll when the pilot wanted it to pitch.) With this arrangement the machine had become responsive and docile, and the XR-4 was therefore fitted with the same systems. On January 14, 1942, the boxy new helicopter was wheeled out of its hangar and test pilot Les Morris carried out several brief hovering flights. By May, it was ready for delivery to the U.S. Army and was flown in stages from Bridgeport, Connecticut, to Dayton, Ohio, for its acceptance trials. Orville Wright was among those on hand at Wright Field to congratulate Sikorsky on his achievement.

At the end of 1942, the Army was satisfied with its helicopter trials and placed a production order for the R-4. In all, 130 R-4s were built and used principally as training helicopters by the USAAF, the U.S. Navy, the U.S. Coast Guard, and by the RAF as the Hoverfly. There were occasions, however, when the little helicopter's special charac-

teristics showed its operational value. In January 1944, a U.S. Coast Guard YR-4 rushed blood plasma from New York City direct to Sandy Hook hospital to help victims of an explosion aboard the destroyer USS *Turner,* cutting the delivery time from hours to minutes and saving several lives. Then, in April of that year, Lieutenant Carter Harmon, USAAF, was sent to fly a YR-4 in support of British forces fighting behind Japanese lines in Burma. Limited though its lifting capacity was, especially in the tropical heat, the YR-4 nevertheless rescued a number of wounded soldiers, one at a time, from jungle where fixed-wing aircraft could not land. Battlefield rescue was a role with which helicopters would become increasingly associated, particularly in post-WWII conflicts.

American Rotary Proliferation

Once the secrets of controlled rotary-winged flight had been unlocked, progress was rapid, with more and more manufacturers in the industrial countries introducing new types every year. In the United States in particular, the profusion of helicopter ideas was dramatic; over seventy projects were being actively pursued by 1950. Few of these survived to see the light of day, but it was clear that the enthusiasm for vertical flight was considerable. Sikorsky capitalized on his leading position in the industry by introducing the R-5 and R-6 helicopters. Initially ordered off the drawing board to operate from the decks of ships in the antisubmarine role, the R-5 was the world's first helicopter produced specifically to fill a military requirement. As such, it was the vanguard of a "whirlybird" boom that would

The Cierva W.11 Air Horse was under development in 1951 when Saunders Roe acquired the company. A single engine drove three rotors mounted on outriggers, each at the tip of a triangle. All three turned in the same direction, but their plane of rotation was sufficiently tilted to compensate for torque. The project was shelved in 1953.

bring about profound changes in many aspects of military operations during the second half of the 20th century.

Powered by a 450-horsepower Pratt & Whitney engine, the R-5 was developed for the civil market as the widely used four-seat S-51, first produced in 1946. Marked improvement though it was from its predecessors, the S-51 was still very limited in performance. Its hovering ceiling while assisted by ground effect was only 5,000 feet and, under ideal conditions at sea level, it could lift a maximum load of fuel, baggage, passengers and extraneous equipment totaling no more than 1,250 pounds. These figures were quickly left behind as helicopter technology made rapid advances. At Bridgeport in the late 1940s and the 1950s, hundreds of Sikorsky machines came off the production lines, including large helicopters such as the S-55, S-56 and S-58. The S-56 had a main rotor 72 feet across powered by two P&W R-2800 radials of 2,100-horsepower each and could routinely lift a useful load of 10,000 pounds. Constructed to meet a U.S. Marine Corps requirement for an assault helicopter, it was big enough to take vehicles inside, and its winch could carry an external load of one ton. In 1956, the S-56

set a helicopter speed record of 162.7 mph and lifted 11,050 pounds to over 12,000 feet. Its legendary stablemate, the S-58, became the world's large helicopter workhorse; eventually nearly 1,900 of them were built and saw service all over the world. When they first flew in the early 1950s, it was hard to believe that Sikorsky had such powerful monsters in the air only a decade after the emergence of his fragile-looking R-4.

Impressive though Sikorsky's creations were, they were far from being the only helicopters on the U.S. market by the 1950s. Among the great names to emerge in the burgeoning field of rotary flight were Bell, Piasecki, Hiller, Kaman and Hughes. Bell's first helicopter, designed by Arthur Young, flew for the first time in June 1943. Two years later it had developed into the Bell 47, a diminutive machine most often seen with its two seats enclosed in a bubble of plexiglass, giving it the appearance of a bulbous-eyed insect. In March 1946, the Bell 47 became the first helicopter to be licenced for commercial use by the Civil Aviation Authority, and it went on to prove itself one of the most versatile "choppers" ever built, evolving into models used for air taxi and executive transport services, movie-making, forest patrol, newspaper work, power and pipeline inspection, and for geological survey. All of the armed services adopted it for a variety of military roles. It was built under licence by Agusta of Italy and Westland of the United Kingdom, and was exported all over the world. In 1947, the Bell 47 became the first helicopter licenced for crop-dusting and immediately recorded a spectacular success in Argentina, where a major plague of locusts threatened the crops. Bell 47s were used to spray tens of thousands of acres, curbing the locusts and saving crops worth millions of dollars. Versatile as it was, the Bell 47 was continually improved and remained in production for more than a quarter of a century.

In 1948, serious competition for Bell in the light helicopter field arrived in the shape of the little Hiller 360. Starting from scratch in California, thousands of miles away from the influence of Sikorsky and Bell, Stanley Hiller approached rotary-winged flight in a distinctive way and produced an original helicopter different in basic concept from those of his rivals. He also could claim that he did so as a private venture, without any kind of military sponsorship. From the outset, his first full-size machine, the XH-44 Hiller-copter, had two rigid contra-rotating two-bladed coaxial rotors and therefore no need for a tail rotor. The

XH-44 was ready for tethered testing early in 1944. Operating on a shoestring budget, Hiller could not afford to hire a test pilot, so, having learned how to build a helicopter by trial and error, he had to learn how to fly it that way too. He carried out the machine's first free flight on July 4, 1944, and gave a number of demonstrations thereafter, not always without incident. His first attempt at an autorotation landing uncovered the fact that coaxial helicopters suffered from control reversal when the power was removed from the rotors. With the machine spinning wildly and headed for disaster, Hiller was quick enough to try applying rudder into the spin. The rotation stopped and a shaken pilot managed a fairly normal landing. On another occasion, Hiller landed on the company rooftop, which was flat but had a slight incline. Having touched down, he got out, leaving the rotors turning. Looking back, he saw that the two ground handlers could not stop the helicopter rolling down the slope. He jumped back into the cockpit and applied power as the machine dropped off the edge of the three-story building. Once again, he got control just in time and landed with a much-increased pulse rate on the normal ground-level helipad.

Among the novel helicopters developed at the Hiller plant in an attempt to find a niche in the market was the

The Sikorsky R-4 first flew in January 1942. Although its performance was limited, it became the world's first mass-production helicopter and went into service with the US Navy in 1943. A YR-4, equipped with pontoons, made the first helicopter deck landing on the aircraft carrier Bunker Hill *on May 6, 1943. An Army YR-4B performed the first rescue behind enemy lines in Burma on April 25/26, 1944. Taxed to the limit, the YR-4B took four trips over two days to rescue four casualties.*

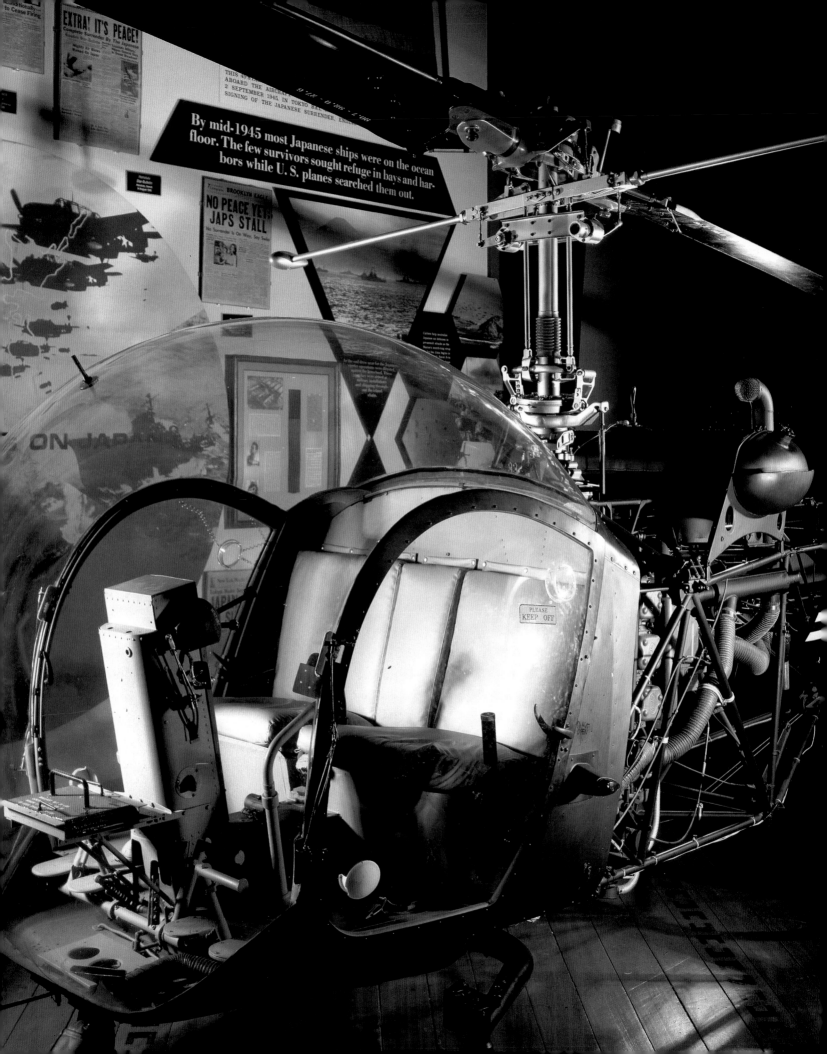

OPPOSITE PAGE *The first Bell 47 was flying in 1945 and it soon became established as the classic image of the helicopter. The goldfish-bowl canopy and open framework of the Bell 47D were instantly recognizable and could be sketched by any schoolchild. They starred in countless Hollywood movies, including* Air America, Crocodile Dundee, It's a Mad, Mad, Mad, Mad World, The Manchurian Candidate, *James Bond epics such as* Thunderball *and* You Only Live Twice, *and most memorably in the television series* M*A*S*H. *Well over 4,000 Bell 47s were built before production ceased in 1974. This example (along with several other Bell 47s) is on display at the American Helicopter Museum, West Chester, Pennsylvania.*
RIGHT *In 1941, Larry Bell hired an enthusiastic, freelance engineer named Arthur Young. Young's innovative rotor design was a major factor in the success of Bell helicopters. A stabilizer bar was introduced on the rotor mast perpendicular to the rotor blades. This counterbalance system caused the rotor to teeter when the airframe of the helicopter moved in response to turbulence or control inputs, and it dampened further oscillation, allowing an unprecedented level of stability.*

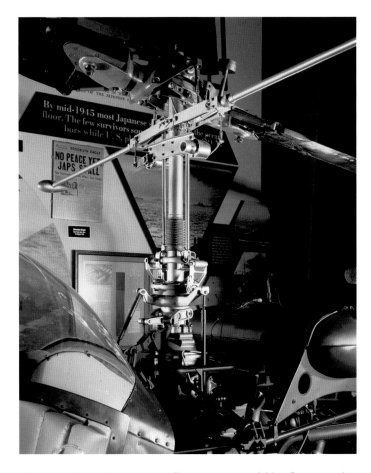

UH-4 Commuter, so called because it was specifically intended for personal use. Immediately after WWII, most Americans still clung to the hope that aviation would progress in the same direction as the automobile, with flying machines appearing in the garage of every home. This vision carried with it an image of unprecedented personal freedom that was wonderfully liberating to people whose world had been dominated by war and depression for the best part of two decades. At a more mundane level, it was naively believed that traffic congestion on the roads could be overcome if people leapt up and over the problem. Appealing though the excellent Commuter was, however, it was not long before the dream of personal helicopters was overtaken by reality and Hiller was forced to abandon the project to concentrate his efforts on more commercial machines.

One problem that bedeviled Hiller's experimental helicopters at this stage was that of being uncomfortably unstable in the hover. Several crashes were attributable to instability. After test pilot Frank Peterson had walked away from the wreckage of one such accident, a solution was suggested. Aerofoil paddles were introduced at right angles to the rotor blades and connected directly to the pilot's cyclic control. The resulting change in handling characteristics was dramatic. Once Hiller's J-5 test-bed machine had been fitted with the "Rotormatic" system, it could be flown in the hover hands off. To demonstrate his confidence in the new system, Hiller even allowed a press photographer who had never flown any kind of aircraft to hover the J-5 solo after only a few minutes of ground instruction. Adding the paddles to coaxial rotors, however, proved too complicated, so the decision was taken to proceed with a more conventional design for production. Hiller machines then had the single main rotor balanced by a tail rotor already made familiar by Sikorsky and Bell.

The Hiller 360 (later UH-12), a three-seat light helicopter, received its CAA certificate in October 1948. Its maker promoted its qualities with vigor, even going so far as to stage a photographic session over San Francisco Bay in which he and a copilot, prudently equipped with parachutes, climbed out of their seats and spent some time clinging to the fuselage aft of the cockpit while the helicopter cruised steadily on. When it came onto the market, the Hiller 360 was offered to dealers at only $16,000 and to private buyers at $19,995, which was half the cost of a Bell 47 at the time. Bell soon dropped their price to $23,500 to stay in contention.

More than anything else, however, it was a highly publicized rescue that boosted Hiller's sales efforts. In August 1949, a twelve-year-old boy suffered a fractured skull in falling from a horse in the remote High Sierra of Yosemite National Park. Neither military helicopters nor a stripped-down Bell 47 proved capable of reaching him. A standard Hiller 360 was taken from the production line and trucked to Yosemite, where it was reassembled on site and then flown to where the boy lay at over 8,000 feet. The rescue was accomplished without difficulty and given wide press coverage. Such a direct comparison of the Hiller and Bell products had an immediate effect on sales, and the Hiller 360 went on to record the longest production life of any helicopter, and orders were still being taken for improved models half a century after the type's first appearance.

The fourth major American manufacturer of rotary-winged aircraft was actually the second to build and fly a successful helicopter in the United States. Frank Piasecki gained valuable experience in rotary-wing design while working for the Platt-Lepage company, which had been awarded a U.S. Army contract in 1940 to develop a

The Kaman H-43 Huskie had a distinctive twin-rotor configuration. It first flew in 1956 and was used primarily for firefighting and rescue duties. It has the distinction of being the first helicopter to go through its service life with no aircraft attributable loss of life or accidents.

helicopter based on the proven twin-rotor configuration of Germany's Fa 61. (Designated XR-1, the Platt-LePage helicopter never exhibited satisfactory handling and the Army canceled the project in April 1945.) By 1943, Piasecki had formed his own engineering group and was flight-testing his first flyable helicopter, the PV-2. A notable showman who dressed with style in homburg, bowtie and spats, he demonstrated his machine with flair to a large crowd at Washington's National Airport, and then completed a newsreel sequence that took advantage of the American belief in personal vehicles. It was called "An Air Flivver in Every Garage," and it showed Piasecki taking his helicopter out of his suburban garage and flying off for a round of golf, refueling at the pumps of a local gas station on the way.

Having gained the publicity he sought, Piasecki turned to the military and set out to convince a reluctant U.S. Navy that they needed a large helicopter. Helped by Congressional criticism of the Navy for not pursuing rotary-wing development, Piasecki got his contract on January 1, 1944. It laid down a requirement for the world's first transport helicopter. Just over a year later, the XHRP-X emerged, a banana-shaped twin-rotor aircraft almost 50 feet long powered by a 450-horsepower engine, designed to be flown by two pilots and to carry ten passengers. Initially flight-tested as an

The Hiller 360 appeared in 1948, when its designer, Stanley Hiller, was just twenty-two years old. It came to prominence in the summer of 1949 when it made the first U.S. transcontinental commercial helicopter flight. The tiny HJ-1 Hornet was unveiled by Hiller in February 1951. It was designed to be a small artillery spotter and used ramjet engines to power the rotor blades at the tips. The Hornet went through 45 gallons of fuel in about 25 minutes, and it was extremely noisy. It was known as "a machine for changing fuel into noise." Only seventeen were built.

Delivered to the Navy in early 1949, the Piasecki HUP-3 Retriever could carry two crew and five passengers. It was used primarily for air-sea rescue, liaison, replenishment, and plane guard duties, all of which it performed admirably during the Korean War. The Retriever seen here is on display at the National Museum of Naval Aviation at Pensacola, Florida.

open-framework skeleton, it was known to Piasecki's work force as the "Dogship." Experience with this helicopter led in the years that followed to a series of similarly shaped twin-rotor machines that established Piasecki as the world's premier builder of large transport helicopters. By late 1947, the XHJP-1 had claimed the world helicopter speed record at 131 mph, and had shown that it could climb vertically at 1,500 feet per minute. In one set of tests involving the application of increasing G-forces, pilot Jim Ryan pulled back on the cyclic control and found himself unable to stop the nose rising to the vertical. Seemingly committed, he elected to continue in the same direction and so completed what was probably the first helicopter loop ever executed.

The capabilities of large helicopters were clearly demonstrated to the public at a number of air shows in 1948. During New York City's golden jubilee celebrations, a Piasecki HRP-1 staged a rescue of six sailors sitting on the ground in a yellow life raft. The rescuer hovered overhead, dropping down a chain ladder that the men then mounted, all six of them being suspended under the clattering

"banana" at once. Later that year, at Cleveland's National Air Races, the HRP-1 flew with an underslung 37 mm anti-tank gun while carrying its crew and ammunition inside. It was not long before U.S. Marine Corps HRP-1s were demonstrating aerial assault tactics that would change the nature of the battlefield. Other HRP-1s developed hunter-killer techniques in antisubmarine warfare and became the first aircraft to engage in minesweeping. The big Piaseckis had shown that their twin-rotor form was here to stay.

Early European Rotaries

Outside the United States, post-WWII rotorcraft research was led by Britain, France and the Soviet Union. In Britain, the Cierva Company began to move from autogyros to helicopters with the W.9, a two-seat machine that used a ducted air jet in place of a tail rotor. It first flew in 1947, and was one of several Cierva rotary-wing projects, including the W.11, a large triple-rotor helicopter known as the Air Horse. By the early 1950s, Cierva had been taken over by Saunders-Roe and that company then continued development of both

The prototype Hiller Rotorcycle first flew on January 10, 1957. It was a one man, foldable, observation and self-rescue helicopter. A design requirement was that it could be dropped by parachute to a downed pilot. Without tools, the helicopter could then be rapidly assembled to carry the pilot across enemy lines to safety. Twelve Rotorcycles were built but did not enter service.

the Air Horse and a light helicopter called the Skeeter. The Bristol Aeroplane Company produced the Sycamore, a four-seat general-purpose machine, and the Belvedere, a large twin-rotor helicopter that first flew in 1952 and was comparable with the big Piasecki "banana." Westland entered the rotary-winged field in 1947 by acquiring the licence to build the Sikorsky S-51 (Westland Dragonfly). Licences for the S-55 (Whirlwind) and S-58 (Wessex) followed during the 1950s, and Westland expanded their rotary-wing capacity at the end of the decade by taking over the helicopter interests of the Bristol, Fairey and Saunders-Roe companies.

In France by 1950 there were several experimental rotorcraft flying, including a twin-coaxial-rotor helicopter by pioneer Louis Breguet. The Sud-Est and Sud-Ouest companies began working separately on helicopter designs. Sud-Ouest had acquired members of the wartime Austrian design team that had successfully flown a jet-rotor machine, in which the blades were driven round by small jets at the tips. The result was the So 1221 Djinn, which was the only jet-rotor helicopter to reach the production stage. Sud-Est, on the other hand, concentrated on more conventional forms. In 1957 the two companies merged into Sud-Aviation and produced the Se 3130 Alouette, which became one of the most successful light helicopters ever built. (Other members of the Austrian team joined Fairey in the United Kingdom. They went on

to produce the short-lived Gyrodyne, a stub-winged aircraft with a jet rotor and an offset conventional propeller in place of a tail rotor. It took off as a helicopter, but in normal forward flight, power was removed from the rotor, which then supplied lift through autorotation as the wing-mounted engine provided the thrust.)

Rotorcraft development in the Soviet Union proceeded slowly at first, although Boris Yurev, Ivan Bratukhin and others had been working on rotating winged flight since the years between the World Wars. On Soviet Aviation Day in 1946, the Bratukhin Omega was unveiled to public view. First flown in 1941, it was a twin-engined helicopter with two rotors widely separated to each side. In the same period, Nicolai Kamov, who had been responsible in 1929 for the *Red Engineer*, the first Soviet helicopter to leave the ground, was building and testing light helicopters. These included the Ka-17, a twin-rotor machine that was little more than a flying motorcycle. Kamov later went on to greater things, becoming a major supplier of naval and agricultural helicopters. The manufacturer who grew to have the largest influence on the Soviet helicopter world, however, was Mikhail Mil. His Mi-1 (NATO Hare) first flew in 1950 and entered military service the next year. It was followed in 1952 by the more capable Mi-4 (NATO Hound), which was modified in 1955 to claim several world records, including taking a 4,400-pound payload to 20,000 feet and capturing the 500-kilometer closed-circuit speed record at 187 km/h (116 mph). The Mi-4 quickly became a Soviet workhorse and was built in many versions. The military types were used for a variety of roles over land and sea, and those built for civilian purposes served to carry passengers for Aeroflot and were employed as crop-sprayers, firefighters and ambulances. As the helicopters of Mil and Kamov spread to all parts of the Soviet Union, they began to have profound effects both on the conduct of military operations and on the way of life in remote areas of Siberia and the Arctic.

"CHOPPERS" IN KOREA

When the Korean War began in June 1950, U.S. forces were ill-prepared for their intervention under the United Nations banner. In no area of operations was that more apparent than in the provision of close air support to troops on the battlefield. The problem was that the U.S. Army had very few aircraft of its own. The USAF had become an independent service in 1947 and, following the guidelines of a 1942 roles and missions agreement, had assumed responsibility for almost all air operations involving the Army, leaving the soldiers flying only unarmed aircraft weighing less than 5,000 pounds and used principally for liaison duties. The problem was that, in the post-WWII period, the USAF felt that it had more important concerns than cooperating with the Army. The limited funds available were expended primarily on building an air force equipped with jet fighters and strategic bombers. Helicopters came well down the list of the USAF's priorities,

although a number were acquired to fill rescue and VIP transport roles.

USAF rescue "choppers" adopted the motto "That Others May Live," and before the end of the Korean War they had evacuated nearly 8,600 wounded from the front lines. They were also responsible for recovering almost 1,000 UN personnel from enemy-held territory and for some dramatic rescue operations, notably one in which F-86 pilot Captain Joseph McConnell was pulled from the Yellow Sea by a 3rd Air Rescue Group H-19 (Sikorsky S.55). McConnell went on to become the top American ace of the war, claiming sixteen MiG-15s destroyed. Another F-86 pilot, Major "Dee" Harper of the 18th Fighter Bomber Wing, was shot down over North Korea on June 28, 1953. As he listened to the voices of enemy soldiers searching for him nearby, he heard the distinctive slapping sound of a helicopter's rotor. Soon afterward, "the most beautiful bird I ever saw popped over the crest of the hill. It was an H-19 scrambled from Chodo."

To army commanders, even in the 1940s, the advantages of the helicopter were immediately obvious. The heretical thought occurred that, in many ways, it might even come to replace the horse in a soldier's affections. Helicopters, it appeared, should be able to reach any part of the battlefield quickly, no matter what the terrain, and seemed to offer the capability to fill any number of roles — reconnaissance, rescue, artillery spotting, liaison, wire-laying, and rapid resupply among them. Accordingly, in line with the agreement limiting them to aircraft of less

In 1945, Piasecki built the first tandem-rotor helicopter for the U.S. Navy. The HRP-1 Rescuer was nicknamed the "Flying Banana" because of its curved shape. In May 1949, eight Marine HRP-1s gave a demonstration to President Truman and members of his cabinet at Quantico, Virginia, that changed military tactics. Eight HRP-1s showed how quickly they could move forty two fully equipped troops, weapons, and supplies from a simulated carrier deck to a landing zone.

The H-21 Shawnee was the fourth in a line of tandem rotor helicopters designed by Piasecki.

RIGHT *Large vertical stabilizers were fitted either side of the rear rotor and the single piston-engine of 1,150 horsepower (later uprated to 1,425 horsepower) was positioned further forward in the upswept rear fuselage. The H-21 seen here is on display at the American Helicopter Museum in West Chester, Pennsylvania.*

BELOW *The front rotor of the Shawnee sits above the cockpit, connected to the engine in the rear fuselage by a long drive-shaft. Relatively underpowered, the H-21 was not very fast, and its shafts, cables and fuel lines were unprotected. In Vietnam it was found to be vulnerable to small-arms fire, and one CH-21 was said to have been downed by a Viet Cong spear.*

than 5,000 pounds, the post-WWII U.S. Army began to evaluate light helicopters, but there were far too few of them when the Korean fighting started. USAF and Marine Corps helicopters were pressed into service to perform the first evacuations of wounded soldiers in July 1950, but by the beginning of 1951, the Army was using litter-equipped Bell H-13s and Hiller H-23s to carry casualties from the front to Mobile Army Surgical Hospital (MASH) units. In the course of the war, these choppers cut the fatality rate of the wounded by half compared to WWII, with pilots often administering plasma in flight from a bottle hung beside them in the cockpit.

After the war, the importance of rapid casualty evacuation was emphasized by Lieutenant William Brake, a chopper pilot with some 545 missions to his credit: "Most evacuation trips took about thirty minutes from the time the men were hit until they were in the hospital. The same trip by ambulance would sometimes take four hours, which could mean the difference between life and death." (Lieutenant Brake was being conservative. Motor vehicle ambulances often drove over rough roads for many more hours than four to reach a hospital.) By 1952, the irrationality of the limitations imposed on the Army was readily apparent and the restrictions were being ignored. Larger transport helicopters were on the way, although even these were still prohibited from carrying armaments.

Initially skeptical about the value of helicopters, the U.S. Navy had begun its rotary flight program only under pressure from Congress and gentle prodding from the U.S. Coast Guard. In fact, the Coast Guard was given the responsibility for running the program to introduce U.S. maritime helicopters and, in the process, did some valuable development work. As the work progressed, some difficult rescues were accomplished from the ocean and from ice-covered landscape, and a Coast Guard mechanic (Sergei Sikorsky, son of Igor) perfected the cable hoist that became a standard feature of helicopter rescue missions. Once helicopters had been acquired and their usefulness demonstrated, the Navy relented. The advantages of having aircraft with vertical flight capability at sea were soon evident. Submarines could

> *"I never liked riding in helicopters because there's a fair probability that the bottom part will get going around as fast as the top part."*
> LIEUTENANT COLONEL JOHN WITTENBORN, USAF

be scouted for, downed aircrew could be plucked from the water, mail could be delivered and personnel transferred between ships — all duties that had previously been done typically and more laboriously by the fleet's destroyers.

During the Korean War, the Navy was quick to develop techniques to make the most of their new aircraft. An extract from a Presidential Unit Citation indicates the variety of roles covered: "This resourceful and intrepid squadron [HU-1] spotted and directed naval gunfire in actual combat; spotted and destroyed enemy mines; effected the rescue of 429 persons, many of which rescues were carried out over hostile territory in the face of enemy fire; transported personnel and prodigious amounts of mail and material at sea; relieved destroyers of daylight plane guard duties; and maintained ninety five per cent availability for assigned missions."

The U.S. Marines did not receive their first helicopters until 1948, but the Corps flew the first helicopter missions of the Korean War and was the service that introduced the S-55 into war operations. Late into rotary-winged flight though they had been, the Marines were quick to see the value of large transport helicopters as vehicles for carrying troops into combat, thereby gaining the flexibility of air-launched assault and avoiding many of the hazards associated with vulnerable surface craft in WWII. The doctrine of air-launched assault (or vertical envelopment) was developed in USMC exercises and demonstrations held during the late 1940s, and its principles were carefully noted by other services, notably the U.S. and French Armies for the immediate future, but soon thereafter by armed forces worldwide. The performance of USMC helicopters in Korea was such that they were soon recognized as being essential to the operational and logistical effectiveness of the Corps. By late 1951, battalion strength lifts were being tackled, whisking Marine units and their equipment over the rugged Korean terrain to their places at the front. If Marines had one regret, it was that their helicopters were still unarmed and so unable to intervene directly in the land battle, although they were frequently in a position to do so. The convictions of both Marine and Army observers on this subject would eventually bear fruit, but not during the Korean War.

LEFT *Jimmy Viner flew the first Sikorsky helicopter, the VS-300, and in 1947 he became the first pilot to log 1,000 helicopter hours. Viner's other achievements include first flights of the S-51, the S-55 and the S-58; the first helicopter mail service in New York City; the first pilot to operate a helicopter plane guard from an aircraft carrier in 1947; and a helicopter world speed record of 115 mph in 1946.* BELOW *On November 29, 1945, a Sikorsky R-5 flown by Jimmy Viner completes the first helicopter hoist rescues in aviation history. Two crewmen were pulled from a grounded oil barge during a storm in Long Island.*

Commercial Realities

In the 1940s, the prospects for civil helicopters seemed bright, whether for commercial or private use. Several attempts were made by department stores in the United States to promote the convenience of helicopters both for delivering goods to customers or for bringing the customers to the stores. By the early 1950s, however, the enthusiasm for such personal services diminished considerably as the true costs of vertical flight became apparent. Euphoric predictions of a ubiquitous future for the helicopter were tempered by the realization that the use of such complex and expensive machinery could only be justified when its special capabilities gave it a clear advantage over more conventional aircraft. Generally speaking, fixed wings promised better performance at lower cost, so it was necessary to show that a helicopter either could do a job that other forms of transport could not or could do it more easily and quickly.

The agricultural world offered the most obvious market for commercial helicopters. Vast areas of crops could be dusted or sprayed very effectively, not least because of the rotor's downwash. Even in a light helicopter such as the Bell 47 or the Hiller 360, the flow of air through the rotor reached almost two million cubic feet per minute and its swirling motion ensured that all plant surfaces were given comprehensive coverage. It was also found that helicopters could prevent crop damage due to frost or excessive rainfall, their downwash

stirring up low-lying cold air or producing the effect of an outsize blowdryer. Other commercial users were those who saw that the ability to take off and land vertically or to hover in one place could yield particular benefits — aerial photography, filmmaking, news reporting, power-line patrolling, and providing services to very remote or otherwise inaccessible places were among the activities for which helicopters were well suited. These were not, however, undertakings that demanded large numbers of machines.

Proposals to use helicopters for such things as mail delivery or for regularly scheduled short-haul airline services were plentiful in the late 1940s. It seemed sensible to assume that valuable time could be saved if surface traffic problems were avoided by whirling mailbags from sorting centers to post offices and passengers to and from airports or ships, and that the demand for such services would more than meet the cost. Almost invariably, the premise behind scheduled helicopter services proved to be false. Some U.S. operators (Los Angeles Airways, New York Airways, and San Francisco and Oakland Airlines, for example) were able to achieve temporary success during the decades of the 1950s, '60s and '70s with the help of substantial subsidies, but all eventually had to face the fact that helicopters are not economically competitive when fixed-wing alternatives are feasible. The same was found to be true in other countries. Airlines in Britain and Belgium were early into the commercial operation of helicopters, and there is no denying that both British European Airways and Sabena provided admirable rotary-wing services for many years, but they were never profitable. Similarly in such widely spaced parts of the world as Australia, Canada and the Soviet Union, passenger helicopter services were established, but if they managed to continue it was because they had some overriding value to the community, not because their costs could be covered by their customers.

That helicopters cannot be successfully operated interchangeably with fixed-wing aircraft was a hard lesson to learn. Disillusionment was dearly bought, but with it came the realization that "whirlybirds" have their particular place in civil aviation and that there are circumstances in which they are indispensable. Helicopter development turned in the direction of adapting to meet a wide variety of specialized tasks, although overall rotary-wing progress was generally led by the requirements of the military, where operational essentials took pride of place over questions of economics.

AIRBORNE CAVALRY

Questions about how to make the most of rotary-wing capabilities in combat zones remained largely unresolved after the Korean War. It fell to the French to point the way to the future for military helicopters. In the course of limited use during their ill-fated operations in what was then French Indo-China, they had become convinced that helicopters could offer many supporting benefits to soldiers on the battlefield. In particular, the advantages of employing them for rescue missions, often deep into enemy territory, had been more than adequately demonstrated, notably by a courageous young woman, Capitaine Valérie André, who combined the skills of a helicopter pilot with those of a parachutist and physician. (Valérie André flew 485 helicopter combat missions in Southeast Asia and Algeria. She was awarded the Croix de Guerre in 1952, and in 1976 became the first French woman to reach the rank of general.)

Madame General Valérie André became a noted neuro-surgeon and the first woman to reach flag rank in the French military. She is a recipient of her nation's highest award, the Grand Officier de la Légion d'Honneur. In 1949, she volunteered to serve in Indochina and was first assigned to a hospital at My Tho, a small city in the Mekong River delta. In May 1950, her unit received two Hiller 360 helicopters and she was checked out on the type. She points out that " the limited power of the engine was a handicap in those tropical conditions, This meant that the missions had to be carried out without an escorting nurse or doctor, just the pilot." She completed 129 missions, many of them under enemy fire, and evacuated 165 wounded soldiers. She even parachuted into a remote outpost in Laos to provide medical aid to soldiers. From 1959 to 1962, she served as chief doctor of a helicopter squadron and flew 356 missions during the war in Algeria.

BELOW *The Sikorsky H-5 Dragonfly (originally R-5) was one of the earliest genuinely practical helicopters. The example exhibited at the National Museum of the USAF, Dayton, Ohio, is a YH-5A, one of twenty-six ordered in 1944. During the Korean War, H-5s were called upon repeatedly to rescue pilots shot down behind enemy lines and to evacuate wounded personnel from front-line areas.*

RIGHT *The arrangement of the cockpit in the YH-5A is not ideal from the pilot's point of view. The crew of two sit in tandem, with the observer ahead in the clear bubble of the nose, and the pilot behind, with restricted visibility. Looking in through the door on the starboard side, the pilot appears sealed off behind the instrument panel placed between him and the observer.*

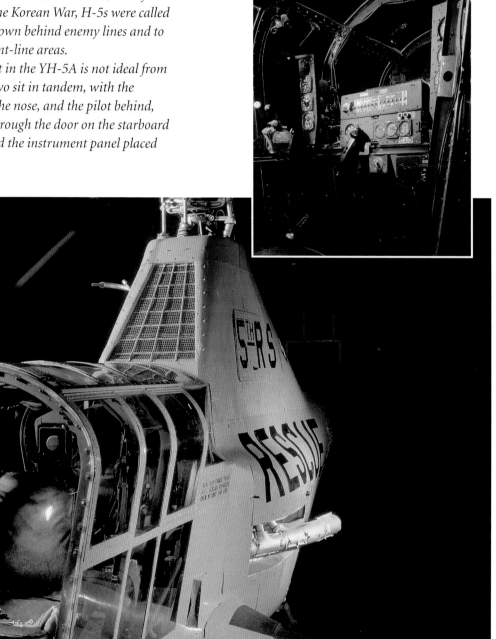

Algerian Lessons

When an escalation of guerrilla warfare occurred in Algeria in the mid-1950s, the reaction of the French government to the crisis included placing sizeable orders with helicopter manufacturers in the United States and France. Within three years, hundreds of light helicopters were being operated by French forces in Algeria, together with more than a hundred each of Sikorsky H-34s (S-55s) and Vertol H-21s. (The H-21 was the Piasecki Workhorse. The company name was changed to Vertol after Frank Piasecki left in 1955.) As the helicopter buildup increased, so did the temperature of the heated debate in France over which service should have control of aircraft tasked with close support of ground operations. Final resolution of the argument was set aside with a compromise. It was ruled that the army should have control in the east of Algeria, while the air force would be the authority in the west.

Generally speaking, the French experience indicated that army units needed to control their own helicopters. In western areas of Algeria, where requests for helicopter support from local ground commanders had to pass through the communications centers of two services, the response was much slower and less precise than was the case in the east. For troops in contact with the opposing force, the resulting delays and occasional blunders were unacceptable. The French duly gave their soldiers what they wanted, and the armed forces of other countries took note. In the United States, the lessons of Algeria were sufficient to persuade the Pentagon that the U.S. Army should have control of the helicopters it needed, and also of a cer-

The final USAF version of Kaman's twin-rotor helicopter was the HH-43F, which was used extensively on firefighting and rescue duties. A Huskie on rescue alert could be airborne in about one minute. It carried two firefighters and a fire-suppression kit slung below. It often reached a crash site before ground vehicles arrived. Foam from the kit plus the powerful downwash from the rotors were used to open a path to trapped crash victims.

tain number of other specialized support aircraft. Measures were taken to arm battlefield helicopters, and to ensure the provision of features aimed at making them both more survivable and effective, such as armored protection for the crews and loading doors on either side of the fuselage. Just as important was finding a way to supply more engine power to lift heavier payloads and improve overall performance. Higher top speeds, quicker acceleration and greater maneuverability were significant factors when it came to reducing combat losses. The problem of inadequate power was something that had always dogged helicopter development, but in the 1950s the solution was already coming to hand.

Turbo Power

Kaman helicopters were flown experimentally with Boeing gas turbine engines during the early 1950s, but the big breakthrough in making full use of the new technology for rotary flight finally came in France. The SE.3130 Alouette II light helicopter first flew in March 1955. It was powered by a very small 360-horsepower Turbomeca Artouste engine that ran at a speed of 35,000 rpm and was geared down to turn the main rotor via a shaft at 350 rpm. The improvement in performance was immediately apparent, and on June 13, 1958, an Alouette II gave a dramatic demonstration of its turbine-driven capabilities when it climbed to

10,000 feet in eleven minutes and went on to over 36,000 feet, figures that were unimaginable with a piston engine. Being first in the field of production of turboshaft helicopters, the Alouette II was able to take advantage of its head start and became internationally popular. It was manufactured until 1975, more than 1,300 of them seeing service in various forms with forty-six countries. Later developments in the series were even more successful — the Alouette III was used by seventy-four countries — and they continued to set records. In 1969, an Aérospatiale SA 315B Lama achieved a landing and takeoff in the Himalayas at 24,600 feet while carrying a crew of two, and in 1972 a Lama was flown to 40,820 feet.

Almost everything about the turboshaft engine gave it an advantage over its piston-powered counterpart. It was simpler, lighter and more reliable, and it used less expensive fuel. The problem of vibration was much reduced, and the engine's small size made it possible to mount it close to the rotor head, so eliminating the need for a long, heavy transmission system and making more payload space available. Most significantly, the vast increase in power-to-weight ratio opened the door to higher speeds and greater lifting capacity. The introduction of the turboshaft engine in the 1950s freed helicopter designers from their chains and they soon made the most of their new opportunities. In the United States, their efforts were necessarily driven forward by the suddenly escalating needs of the armed forces.

THE HELICOPTER WAR

It was American involvement in Southeast Asia that brought helicopters to the front rank as an instrument of war and thereby greatly accelerated their development. Before the Vietnam War was over, U.S. manufacturers were producing helicopters with a range of capabilities that may have surpassed the expectations of even the most visionary advocates of rotary-winged flight.

In the early 1960s, when U.S. personnel were ostensibly in Vietnam only as instructors or advisers, their helicopters were still piston-powered and ill-suited to the job at hand. The first helicopter combat assault operation, mounted on December 23, 1961, was carried out by Piasecki H-21 Shawnees. Flown by U.S. Army crews, they carried 1,000 paratroopers of the Army of the Republic of Vietnam (ARVN) into battle against a Viet Cong stronghold. It was a small beginning, but it showed that even the lumbering Shawnees could be effective at getting an assault force where it needed to go — quickly. Helicopters freed soldiers from using roads and ensured that the enemy never knew when they might be attacked, nor from which direction. The priceless element of surprise was preserved and the risk of ambush avoided. The piston-engined Shawnee, however, was very vulnerable to small-arms fire and sorely underpowered. Vietnam's steamy heat exacerbated the lack of power and made it impossible to lift the extra weight that adequate armor or weaponry would have imposed. It was clear from the outset that more capable helicopters would be needed, and in the spring of 1962, units began arriving equipped with a machine that, more than any other single piece of hardware, would come to symbolize the Vietnam conflict for those Americans who fought there.

The Aérospatiale SA 318 Alouette II was the first turboshaft-powered helicopter in the world to go into large-scale production, in 1956. It quickly showed its superiority over piston-powered helicopters, with a much faster cruising speed and remarkable high-altitude capability.

Westland Belvedere, *by Michael Turner. A Westland (original Bristol) Belvedere of 26 Squadron, based in Aden in 1964, lifts a 105 mm howitzer into position for J Battery of the Royal Artillery during operations in the Radfan of Southern Arabia.*

U for Ubiquitous

The Bell HU-1 (Helicopter Utility 1, later changed to UH-1) Iroquois was acquired by the U.S. Army as a general-purpose helicopter. In its basic HU-1B form, powered by a 960-horsepower Lycoming T53 turboshaft, it could carry the pilot and typical loads of eight soldiers or two litters and a medic, or 3,000 pounds of freight. Its maximum speed was 138 mph and it had a range of 230 miles. The official name of Iroquois was hardly ever used, soldiers preferring to adapt the aircraft's original designation, forming the nickname "Huey." The first Hueys to reach Vietnam were assigned to medical evacuation (medevac) duties, but their crews soon found that they were in a conflict markedly different from

that fought in Korea. This was a war effectively without front lines, with the enemy liable to appear on every side and with no MASH units safely placed in friendly areas close to the fighting. Medevac helicopters, marked with red crosses and operating under the call sign "Dustoff," always flew under threat and had to carry the wounded back to base hospitals, usually many miles away. Far from offering any guarantee of safe passage, the red cross symbol was largely ignored by both sides. Helicopters in all their forms attracted enemy fire, and Dustoff pilots often carried ammunition to hard-pressed soldiers before picking up the wounded.

Helicopter operations in Vietnam, frequently undertaken in the face of heavy fire and necessarily low and slow,

returned to the United States, the Novosels between them had rescued over 8,000 men.)

The Huey was a remarkably flexible design, and it was modified in various ways to meet the operational requirements of all the services. Although it was originally shipped to Vietnam for unarmed medevac duties, it was not long before armament

demanded a high degree of courage from their crews. Several Medals of Honor were awarded for helicopter exploits, none more thoroughly deserved than that given to CWO Michael Novosel for his actions on October 2, 1969, when he was in the air for eleven hours during the day and repeatedly returned to an area under intense enemy fire to rescue wounded. His Huey was hit many times and so severely shot up in the process that it had to be written off. A B-29 pilot in WWII and a lieutenant colonel in the Air Force Reserve, Novosel had been unable to get back to active duty until he took the unusual step for an air force officer of enlisting in the U.S. Army. When he reached Vietnam, he was forty-two and the oldest helicopter pilot to enter combat. In two Dustoff tours, he flew over 2,000 combat hours, and brought 5,589 wounded soldiers back to safety. Well might he say, in his autobiography *Dustoff*: "I heard the cries of the wounded and endured the loss of friends. Yet I have survived and I don't know why." (Mike Novosel was eventually joined in Vietnam by his son, also a Dustoff pilot. In one period of a week, each had the experience of rescuing the other after their helicopters had been forced down. By the time they

was added, and the basic design was continually upgraded to accept more power and offer greater lifting capacity. By the early 1970s, Bell was manufacturing single- and twin-engined variations on the Huey theme and making up to 1,400 horsepower available. The most numerous types were the UH-1D and H, which had enlarged cabins, allowing the carriage of twelve troops or six litters and a medic, or 4,000 pounds of freight. An underslung load of 5,000 pounds could be lifted. Nearly 7,000 UH-1Ds and Hs were built. Other versions included those produced to meet the specialized requirements of assault and close support, battlefield targeting, antisubmarine warfare, search and rescue, electronic countermeasures, psychological warfare, and aircrew training. Armament ran the gamut, with Hueys carrying such widely differing weaponry as 0.3-inch machine guns, 2.75-inch unguided rockets, wire-guided antitank missiles, and homing torpedoes. The narrow-bodied AH-1 Cobra attack helicopter had tandem seating for a crew of two, with the gunner in front of and below the pilot. Crew protection was afforded by armor placed around the cockpit and engine, and by an

LEFT *The ubiquitous "Huey." The Bell UH-1 Iroquois was developed from the Bell Model 204. The initial designation was HU-1 (helicopter utility), which led to its nickname. The Huey went into triservice production in 1962 and began arriving in Vietnam in 1963. More than 5,000 served in Southeast Asia, used for medical evacuation, command and control, air assault, and as gun ships. More than 9,000 Hueys were produced and were operated by more than forty countries.*

armored windscreen. A chin turret held a 7.62 mm Minigun and a 40 mm grenade launcher, while stub-wing hard points typically could carry fifty-two rockets in four pods. Huey mission equipment varied to meet the tasks, but grew to include such things as powerful rescue winches, automatic stabilization, all-weather instrumentation, search radar, dunking sonar, low-light television, and searchlights.

It is arguable that the ubiquitous Huey, in all its forms, became the most significant aircraft of the Vietnam War. More of them were operated in combat than any other type, fixed or rotary wing, and the scale of their contribution may be judged from the losses they suffered. Between 1962 and 1973, the U.S. forces lost 1,293 UH-1s and 180 AH-1s in combat. Of these, the U.S. Army accounted for 1,211 and 173 respectively.

It is an unfortunate fact that the figures for operational (noncombat) losses of UH-1s are even greater: 1,418 were written off in accidents, 1,380 of them by the U.S. Army. The total number of U.S. helicopter losses in Southeast Asia (all types and all causes) was 4,869, of which 2,587 were in combat.

Development of the Huey family did not stop with the end of the Vietnam War. The U.S. Army alone retains well over 2,000 of the breed as the 21st century begins, and they have acquired such improvements as composite rotor blades, infrared suppression, radar warning receivers,

ABOVE *The Sikorsky S-56 was designed as a large assault helicopter for the U.S. Marine Corps, but almost 60 percent of those built went to the U.S. Army as the H-37 Mojave. First flown in 1953, the S-56 was Sikorsky's first twin-engined helicopter and the first production helicopter with retractable undercarriage. Later versions could lift 11,000 pounds of cargo, loaded through clamshell nose doors. Seen beneath the Mojave is a Sikorsky S-55, which was the first transport helicopter to be cleared for commercial operation. Starting in 1949, Sikorsky manufactured a total of 1,281 S-55s over a period of ten years.*

ABOVE *The cockpit of the Alabama National Guard Huey. The instruments are sensibly arranged, and the cockpit is spacious, with lots of glass to give excellent all-round visibility.*

The distinctive shape of the Huey, and the unmistakable sound of its two-bladed rotor, came to be irrevocably identified with the war in South-East Asia. They were everywhere — delivering troops and supplies, providing fire support to infantry, and, above all, evacuating wounded soldiers. Tough, versatile and reliable, Hueys were essential to the U.S. military in Vietnam. Dan Patterson photographed this one at the Patton Museum of Cavalry and Armor, Fort Knox, Kentucky.

chaff/flare dispensers, better communications and avionics, crash-resistant fuel systems, and more efficient engines. By the time it is retired, Bell's remarkable design will have given over half a century of service.

Lesser and Greater

Capable and flexible though they were, the Hueys were not ideally suited for every combat situation. As the Vietnam War intensified, more specialized helicopters appeared. The smallest were the "Loaches," so called because of their formal description — Light Observation and Command Helicopters. The little Hughes OH-6 Cayuse and the Bell OH-58 Kiowa were in this class, replacing the earlier piston-engined Hiller OH-23 Raven and Bell OH-13 Sioux. They operated mainly in the forward reconnaissance role, engaged in the dangerous occupation of scouting at low level for enemy positions and marking likely targets for accompanying gunships. Despite its remarkable speed and agility, the more numerous Cayuse suffered harsh treatment from the opposing ground forces, a total of 658 being lost in combat, 635 of them to small arms or AAA fire. One Loach pilot was shot down no fewer than fourteen times.

At the other end of the scale were the heavy lifters, machines used for transporting large numbers of troops, moving significant quantities of freight, recovering crashed aircraft, or carrying out long-range rescue missions. In the early days of the Vietnam War, the aircraft tasked with such duties were the Sikorsky CH-37 Mojave and the Kaman HH-43 Huskie. Both were replaced when more capable aircraft appeared, although the Huskie soldiered on in the limited role of USAF base rescue for the rest of the conflict. Really heavy lifting became the province of the CH-54 Tarhe, a massive sky-crane, while the principal transports were the U.S. Army's CH-47 Chinook, and the USMC's CH-46 Sea Knight and CH-53 Sea Stallion. The CH-53 was a descendant of the Sikorsky S-61, which entered the USN in 1961 as the SH-3 Sea King, employed in the antisubmarine role. This powerful twin-turbine amphibious helicopter was subsequently developed to meet many other requirements, among the most important of which were search and rescue. The twin-rotor Chinook has proved itself a classic battlefield workhorse, invaluable in Vietnam and in subsequent conflicts for moving soldiers, vehicles, stores and artillery.

> *"The thing is, helicopters are different from planes. An airplane by its nature wants to fly, and if not interfered with too strongly by unusual events or by a deliberately incompetent pilot, it will fly. A helicopter does not want to fly. It is maintained in the air by a variety of forces and controls working in opposition to each other, and if there is any disturbance in this delicate balance the helicopter stops flying; immediately and disastrously. There is no such thing as a gliding helicopter. This is why being a helicopter pilot is so different from being an airplane pilot, and why in generality, airplane pilots are open, clear-eyed, buoyant extroverts and helicopter pilots are brooding introspective anticipators of trouble. They know if something bad has not happened it is about to."*
>
> HARRY REASONER, 1971

"That Others Might Live"

During the war in Southeast Asia, the crews of the USAF's Aerospace Rescue and Recovery Service (ARRS) lived up to their motto. They routinely risked their own skins for anyone downed in enemy territory. It grew to be generally understood by all aircrew that, if they were shot down, search and rescue teams would make every effort to get them out, regardless of the location or the risk. Such a policy did wonders for the morale of crew members being asked to face one of the most effective air defense systems in the world. Unfortunately, once the opposition recognized what was happening, it also meant that any downed flier was used by the enemy as a lure around which they could gather a flak trap. Rescue missions therefore tended to increase in danger as time went by. Before it was all over, three Medals of Honor were earned in the course of USAF rescue operations, two by helicopter pilots (Captain Gerald Young and Lieutenant James Fleming) and one by the pilot of an escorting A-1H (Lieutenant Colonel William Jones III).

The first Sikorsky HH-3Es, large, well-armored helicopters with a range of over 600 miles, arrived in Vietnam in 1965. Fitted with a refueling probe, they could reach anywhere in Southeast Asia. (On June 1, 1967, two HH-3Es flew 4,167 miles across the Atlantic nonstop from New York to the Paris air show. They were refueled nine times

(later on, A-37Bs or A-7Ds could be included), and top cover by F-4s. Additional help in the shape of gunships might be added. The "Jolly Green" carried a para-rescue jumper, trained as a scuba diver and medic, who was ready to jump or be winched down to the assistance of grounded aircrew. The helicopter's winch had 240 feet of cable ending in a heavy jungle penetrator, so that rescues could be accomplished through the jungle canopy.

The crowning glory for the helicopter crews should have been a daring rescue of POWs from a camp outside Hanoi on November 21, 1971. The raid was well planned and brilliantly executed. One HH-3E full of U.S. Rangers deliberately crash-landed inside the prison compound while five CH-53Cs waited outside. Sadly, the cupboard was bare. The prisoners had been moved to another site some time before. Out-of-date intelligence had led the rescuers to a rare failure. However, in this attempt and in more conventional rescues, it was clear that the rescue teams were dedicated to their task. An example of their determination not to abandon aircrew to their fate was the rescue of Lieutenant Colonel Iceal Hambleton, the sole survivor from an EB-66 shot down on April 2, 1972. Hambleton avoided capture by the enemy for twelve days under an umbrella of A-1Es, OV-10s and an assortment of jet fighters and helicopters. Before he was recovered, concern for Hambleton's safety had led to the further loss of an OV-10, an HH-53 and a Huey, but there was never any consideration of giving up the effort as long as he was free.

on the way by HC-130P tankers.) Before long, the jungle camouflage of the HH-3E had gained it the nickname "Jolly Green Giant." Two years later, the even more capable HH-53C "Super Jolly Green" made its debut and proved to be one of the great successes of the war. Nearly twice as large as the HH-3E, the HH-53C was also faster, more heavily armored, and formidably armed with three 7.62 mm Miniguns. Powered by two General Electric T-64 turboshafts of 3,925 horsepower each, the "Super Jolly" had a maximum speed of 170 knots and could lift a useful load of 13,000 pounds. With this impressive machine at its core, an ARRS mission into enemy territory was conducted by a rescue package of aircraft. By 1969, the mission commander was usually flying in an HC-130P equipped as a tanker and carrying an aerial tracker system for locating downed airmen. Escort was provided by A1E/H "Sandies"

From almost any point of view, the creative innovation demanded by the rescue challenge and the massive effort expended were well worth it. No service was more respected, and perhaps none more rewarding. By the end of the war, the ARRS had recovered 4,170 men. It was not done without cost. In the process, forty-five rescue aircraft were lost and seventy-one rescuers gave their lives.

Painful Withdrawal

In 1975, helicopters featured in Operation Frequent Wind, the final withdrawal of Americans and many of their South Vietnamese colleagues from Vietnam. Conducted in the challenging atmosphere of city-wide panic as North Vietnamese troops entered Saigon, it was the largest helicopter evacuation ever carried out. For eighteen hours, beginning on April 29, a fleet of big USMC and USAF helicopters, helped by some Air America UH-1s, shuttled back and forth from Saigon to the USN aircraft carriers waiting offshore. A number of sites throughout the city were used, including the U.S. Embassy, where CH-53s operated from the compound and CH-46s flew from the roof. There were agonizing scenes as crowds of people, growing more desperate as the North Vietnamese closed in, tried to rush the helicopters and had to be beaten back by marines.

Every one of the flights into Saigon on that last panic-filled day was a nail-biting experience, and the helicopter crews were always relieved when they had a full load and could pull away back to the ship. Even then there could be hazards, as at least one HH-53 crew found out. They had just packed ninety-seven men, women and children into the cabin and were on their way out over the eastern suburbs of Saigon when a flight mechanic spotted an SA-7 missile streaking toward them. Reacting quickly, he fired a flare pistol out of the door and was gratified to see that the SAM went for the flare,

Helicopters are noisy machines, and much of the noise comes from the tail rotor. Rotors resent being dragged through the air sideways. This four-bladed tail rotor, essential to the S-58's controllability, is mounted on the left side of the machine at Pensacola.

missing the aircraft by no more than 60 feet. When it was all over, more than 1,000 Americans and nearly 6,000 Vietnamese had been lifted to safety, some 2,000 of them from the U.S. Embassy. Only helicopters could have done it.

New Sword, Brave Savior

Having gone to Vietnam with their theoretical potential denied by their inadequate performance, helicopters emerged from the conflict transformed into powerful instruments of war. Initially unarmed, underpowered, marginally reliable machines with limited capabilities for search and rescue or minor movements of troops and supplies, they had become wonderfully flexible creatures, exerting their influence over every aspect of the war. Day or night and in all weathers, they could reach deep into enemy territory to conduct rescues or clandestine operations, observe

The Boeing Chinook is used primarily for trooping and for load carrying, either internal or underslung, and can carry up to 54 troops or 10 tonnes of freight. The spacious hold can take twenty-four stretchers. Chinooks have been invaluable in supporting United Nations operations. Here a Chinook of the British Joint Helicopter Support Unit assists the UNHCR in providing relief to refugees in the Banja Luka area of the former Republic of Yugoslavia.

and mark targets, thrust the maximum number of troops into combat in the minimum possible time wherever and whenever they were needed, act as aerial tanks and deliver awesome firepower against the enemy, lift artillery or armored vehicles, do the duty of airborne trucks, transport wounded, conduct psychological warfare, sink ships, and even act as fleet minesweepers. Often, because of their ability to hover and to move backward and sideways as well as forward, they were the only vehicles that could intervene in a particular place. In just about every operation, commanders of both sides needed to consider how helicopters might be involved. More than any other aircraft, they had changed the field of battle.

Convergent Evolution

While the demands of the Vietnam War had driven U.S. manufacturers to expand the capabilities of their rotary-wing products dramatically, their counterparts in the eastern hemisphere had been far from idle. The Soviet Union,

with its fondness for gigantism, was soon into production with outsize machines. Announced in 1957, the Mi-6 (Hook) was then the world's largest helicopter. Powered by two 5,500-horsepower turboshafts, the Hook had a single rotor 115 feet across and could take an internal load of more than 13 tons. By 1961, this monster had spawned the Mi-10 (Harke), which was basically the same airframe with the fuselage cut away below cockpit level and fitted with stilt-like, wide-straddling quadricycle landing gear to produce a gawky flying crane. In this configuration, it could lift a loading platform and freight with a combined weight of over 16 tons. Even more startling was the huge Mi-12 (Homer). Conceived as a heavy lifter that could accommodate such large items as ICBM bodies and haul outsize loads in remote regions of the Soviet Union, the Homer made use of two intermeshing rotor systems mounted side by side at the end of inversely tapered wings, which gave a span across the rotors of 220 feet. With four Soloviev turboshafts producing a total of 26,000 horsepower, a normal payload of 33 tons could be accepted by using a short takeoff technique rather than a vertical liftoff. On August 6, 1969, in a convincing demonstration of Homer's strength, pilot Vasily Kolochenko lifted a payload of 88,636 pounds to over 7,000 feet, taking off at almost a quarter of a million pounds gross weight, a figure never approached by any other helicopter. Impressive though it was, however, the Homer did not progress beyond the prototype stage. Nor did all of its weight-lifting records survive. By the 1980s, the Mil factory had produced the Mi-26 (Halo), which was the first helicopter in the world to operate successfully with an eight-bladed rotor. In February 1982, under the impulse of two Lotarev turboshafts of 11,240 horsepower each, the Halo set a number of payload-to-height records, including taking 44,400 pounds to over 15,000 feet. With a cargo hold similar to that of a C-130 Hercules, the Halo functions as a major transport both in military operations and in the exploitation of resources found in remote swamp and tundra areas of Siberia.

Back in 1952, the Soviet designer Nikolai Kamov produced his coaxial twin-rotor machines, the Ka-15 (Hen) and Ka-18 (Hog). They introduced the only series of helicopters ever consistently successful using that rotor system. In the 1960s, the Ka-25 (Hormone) appeared and became the principal helicopter for the Soviet Navy. Its coaxial design removed the need for a tail rotor and allowed the aircraft to be made much shorter than its contemporaries, which was an advantage for shipboard handling. The Hormone, in its various forms, was equipped for rescue and antisubmarine warfare, and for providing targeting data and midcourse correction to guided missiles launched from ships. The more powerful successors to the Hormone, the Ka-27/29/31 (Helix), became operational in the early 1980s, adding infantry assault and AEW duties to their list of capabilities. Kamov retained the coaxial form in designing the world's first single-seat close-support helicopter, the Ka-50 (Hokum). Fast and very agile, the Hokum was intended to take on targets from very low down, using armament that includes a 30 mm cannon, unguided rockets and laser-guided missiles. The pilot's hopes for survival rely on the Hokum's spritely performance, cockpit armor capable of withstanding hits by 20 mm rounds, comprehensive defensive measures, and an ejection seat fired in conjunction with explosively detached rotor blades.

At the medium helicopter level, Mil developed a few basic designs out of which numerous variations grew. The Mi-8 (Hip) appeared in public for the first time at the 1961 Soviet Aviation Day display. In production as a single-rotor, twin-turboshaft machine, the Hip and its successors — Mi-9/17, and the boat-hulled Mi-14 (Haze) ASW helicopter — have served much the same general utility purpose for the Soviet Union and Russia as has the Huey for the United States: civil passenger/freight transport and military jack-of-all-trades. Over 10,000 were built and were operated by thirty-nine countries, making the series among the most successful helicopters ever designed. Another Mil machine, the Mi-24 (Hind), began its operational service in the early 1970s as an assault transport helicopter (Hind-A), armed with an assortment of weapons intended to clear a path through opposing defences and keep the heads down of any enemy troops found in the landing zone. Heavily modified, it became, in stages, the Hind D, E and F. None of them had the slim silhouette ideal for gunships, but they were formidable armored machines carrying a chin-mounted four-barreled Gatling machine gun or a 20 mm cannon pack, plus a choice of rocket/gun pods, antitank or air-to-air missiles, bombs or mines on stub-wing pylons. Designed to meet the challenge of confronting NATO forces in Europe, the Hips and Hinds got their combat blooding in the 1980s during the Soviet Union's intervention in Afghanistan.

> *"Real planes use only a single stick to fly. This is why bulldozers and helicopters — in that order — need two."*
>
> PAUL SLATTERY

Military Choppers Beyond Vietnam

As the capabilities of helicopters became more widely understood in the wider world, they became the essential tools for confrontations on every continent. As early as 1950, British forces used the Dragonfly (S-51) in the communist insurgency in Malaya, and by the mid-1950s they were operating Sycamores in a search-and-destroy campaign against EOKA terrorists in Cyprus. In the 1960s, RAF Belvederes from Aden gave invaluable support to army operations in the southern Arabian Peninsula. Helicopters of every kind have played their parts in numerous African conflicts from Morocco and Sierra Leone to Angola and the Horn of Africa. They have been heavily involved in the war against the Tamil Tigers in Sri Lanka, and have seen action throughout Central and South America. Of crucial importance in the various Arab-Israeli conflicts, they proved equally so in wars between Iran and Iraq, and India and Pakistan. In more recent years, helicopters have become increasingly significant in the war against drugs waged in Latin America.

Gunships and Guerrillas

As the Americans had found in Vietnam, so the Soviets discovered that rotary-wing capability was indispensable for their operations in Afghanistan. Helicopters enabled Soviet forces to respond rapidly to attacks by Mujahideen guerrillas, no matter how rugged the terrain. Hips and Hinds became flying APCs and tanks, escorting convoys, conducting defensive patrols, and mounting offensive sweeps. Potent instruments though they were, they did not have things all their own way. The Afghan guerrillas fought back with handheld Stinger and Blowpipe ground-to-air missiles and were very successful in bringing down Soviet machines. As the war dragged on, Soviet airmen learned quickly, developing tactics and seeking better equipment to make themselves more effective. As early as May 1980, Mi-24s were seen operating with rearward-firing machine guns to counter guerrillas who were letting helicopters pass by their positions before opening fire. Bulletproof windscreens, armored protection, radar warning receivers, infrared jammers and decoy flare dispensers helped to improve the survival rate, but helicopter losses remained significant until the Soviet withdrawal from Afghanistan in 1986. Like their American counterparts in Vietnam, the Soviets found that operating in an undeveloped country without front lines against determined guerrilla forces was a costly business. In both conflicts, the firepower and mobility brought to the battlefield by helicopters made them major force multipliers, allowing ground forces to be far more effective than they otherwise could have been. Given the eventually disastrous results of their interventions for both major powers, it is arguable that it was the powerful presence of remarkably capable helicopters which made it possible for them to prolong their respective agonies.

Falklands Epic

In the immediate post-Vietnam period, British combat experience was gained during the Falklands War of 1982, another conflict in which helicopters proved invaluable. Sea Kings landed intelligence-gathering patrols behind enemy lines and flew antisubmarine patrols lasting as long as ten hours. A Wasp struck an Argentine submarine with a missile, forcing it to beach. Scouts and Gazelles kept their eyes on the enemy, took ammunition forward and evacuated wounded. Wessex and Sea King transports made it possible for troops to maintain their advance over mountain and peat bog. However, if one helicopter stood out from the crowd, it was the single Chinook operated by the RAF that performed prodigious feats.

On May 25, 1982, an Exocet missile fired from a Super Etendard struck the British container ship *Atlantic Conveyor*. The ship later sank, taking with it a significant portion of the task force's helicopter strength — six Wessex,

The Mil Mi-4 (Hound) assault transport helicopter, powered by a Shvetsov ASh-82V radial engine, first flew in 1952. It has since become the most widely built of all Soviet helicopters. More than 3000 Mi-4s were built for service with the Warsaw Pact and for civil operations with Aeroflot. Others were supplied to China, India and Cuba. The Mi-4S is used for agricultural operations, fitted with a dust hopper or a tank holding pesticide or firefighting chemical. They have also been used extensively in the Polar regions on ice patrol and geological survey.

The Mil Mi-26 (Halo) is a giant among helicopters. Powered by two 11,400-shaft-horsepower Lotarev engines, it is the first helicopter to use an eight bladed rotor, the blades of which are 105 feet across. Even the five-bladed tail rotor spans 25 feet. The Mi-26 can lift a payload of 44,000 pounds, accommodate over 100 troops, and cruise at 180 mph.

a Lynx and three Chinooks. Fortunately, one Chinook had flown off earlier in the day. However, the equipment and spares thought necessary to keep it serviceable in the field had gone down with the ship. Since the Chinook represented a significant percentage of the total helicopter force's lifting capacity, there was no option but to fly it until it would fly no more. To the surprise of its pilot, Squadron Leader Dick Langworthy, it kept going despite the difficult conditions, lifting 10 tons of ammunition forward each trip and coming back packed with Argentine prisoners, sixty at a time. As he later said: "That aeroplane went on day after day with bits going unserviceable; but the engines kept going, the rotors kept turning, and she continued to do the job."

The ruggedness of the Chinook was never more dramatically demonstrated than during a night mission to deliver twenty-two troops and three 105 mm guns to the side of Mount Kent. On the return trip, keeping low because of enemy fire, Langworthy flew into a heavy snow shower. Blinded, his night vision goggles rendered useless by the snow, he felt the helicopter shudder. The nose was well up, but the rear end had struck the surface of a creek. As the flat-bottomed Chinook planed across the water, it threw spray into the engine intakes, making them start to run down and causing the hydraulic power controls to

revert to manual. Understandably alarmed, the copilot jettisoned his door before helping Langworthy to heave on the collective control. The big machine, now moving much more slowly, lurched clear of the water. The spray stopped, the engines picked up, and the Chinook was flying again. Landing at Port San Carlos after what he described as the Chinook's "water-skiing trials," Langworthy found that the aircraft had suffered little more than a few dents. Increasingly battered and lacking proper maintenance, it put up with its deficiencies and kept going until the end of the war.

American Lessons Learned

Having acquired experience the hard way in the heat of Southeast Asian battles, the American military believed they knew the sort of helicopters needed to meet the demands of future conflict. It was realized that the basics of rotary-winged flight were now so well understood that revolutionary advances were unlikely. It was more a matter of refining what was already there. Improvements would come from machines that were essentially arranged as before, but made more efficient aerodynamically and mechanically, and equipped with more advanced avionics and weaponry.

The principle of holding on to and upgrading a good airframe was exemplified in the retention of the proven Huey design. Nevertheless, Huey replacements were needed, and they came in the form of the Sikorsky S-70 Hawk series. The first production model of the UH-60A Black Hawk, an assault transport version for the U.S. Army, was flown in 1978. The U.S. Navy has the Sea Hawk and the

The Boeing Chinook is a tandem-rotored, twin-engined medium-lift helicopter. It has a crew of four and is capable of lifting a variety of heavy loads of up to 10 tons, or carrying forty-five fully equipped troops. However, during the Gulf War, a single Chinook is known to have carried 110 Iraqi prisoners. The Chinook HC-2 operated by the RAF (seen here) is equipped with infrared jammers, missile approach warning indicators, chaff and flare dispensers, a long-range fuel system and machine-gun mountings.

USAF uses the Pave Hawk. Conventional in appearance, the Hawks have many advanced operational features. The fuselage is constructed to withstand a 40-foot-per-second vertical impact, and the rotor blades can survive hits from 23 mm cannon shells. Powered by two General Electric T700 turboshafts, its maximum speed can exceed 180 knots. The Hawks were compactly built so that one could be carried by a C-130, or as many as six by a C-5. A bewildering array of equipment can be fitted according to role, ranging from pylons on which to hang missiles, gunpods, mine-dispensers, extra fuel tanks, and so on, to the complex avionics to support missions as diverse as infantry assault, command and control, all-weather search and rescue, clandestine operations, electronic countermeasures, and anti-submarine warfare. Other versions of the Hawk are built in the United Kingdom, Japan, and Australia.

Bigger and Better

During the 1980s, Sikorsky continued to develop its Stallion family of large helicopters — the "Jolly Greens" of Vietnam. Impressive though the series already was, it nevertheless took a major step forward with the S-80 (H-53E) Super Stallion. The difference was made by the addition of a third 4,380-horsepower engine, raising the available muscle to more than 13,000 horsepower — a far cry from the 25 horsepower with which Igor Sikorsky began in 1909. A new drive train and a bigger rotor with seven blades were fitted to absorb the extra power. The fuselage was lengthened by 6 feet compared to earlier H-53s, and the tail rotor enlarged. Systems included infrared exhaust suppression, Omega navigation, ground-proximity warning, a freight handling system, missile warning, chaff/flare dispensers, fuel tank nitrogen, and a night vision system. AIM-9 Sidewinders could be added for self-defence. Among variants produced were the MH-53J Pave Low for special operations, and the MH-53E Sea Dragon for mine countermeasures. The Pave Low is equipped with FLIR (forward-looking infrared), terrain-following radar, GPS (global positioning system), and secure communications. The Sea Dragon carries a mine-sweeping hydrofoil, towed sonar, and mine neutralizing equipment.

At Sea

In the early 1960s, the U.S. Navy began taking delivery of the Kaman H-2 Sea Sprite series of helicopters, which became standard equipment aboard frigates. By the 1970s, all Sea Sprites were being either built or modified to meet the requirements of the LAMPS (Light Airborne Multi-Purpose System) program, ensuring that they can perform in the ASW (antisubmarine warfare), ASST (antiship surveillance and targeting), SAR (search and rescue) and utility transport roles. When fitted with the necessary gear, they can also defend against antiship missiles. Over the years, the Sea Sprite has been continually updated, becoming in the process a most capable and reliable twin-engined, all-weather helicopter carrying a complex set of modern avionics and defensive systems. The U.S. Navy intends to keep the type in service well into the 21st century.

Diminutive Destroyers

In the light helicopter field, the U.S. Army persisted with variants of the Bell OH-58 Kiowa and the Hughes OH-6 Cayuse (developed as the McDonnell Douglas 500/530 series Defender after 1984). Pound for pound, the tiny Cayuse has shown itself to be one of the most effective aircraft ever built. Weighing only 3,000 pounds at takeoff and with a main rotor diameter of just 26 feet, it is nevertheless a most capable machine, packed with modern avionics and able to carry a wide range of powerful weapons, from TOW missiles to unguided rockets and machine gun pods. One variant, the NOTAR, which comes in both military and civil versions, flies with "NO TAil Rotor," relying instead on air diverted from the engine through a slot in the tail boom. Built under licence in Italy and Japan, the MD Defender is operated by the armed forces of twenty-six countries. In the early 1960s, Bell's proposal for a lightweight helicopter lost out to the Cayuse, but in 1981 the Bell OH-58D Kiowa Warrior was named the winner of the U.S. Army's AHIP (Army Helicopter Improvement Program) competition. The Kiowa Warrior features a ball-shaped mast-mounted sight above the main rotor that contains television and infrared optics, together with a laser designator and automatic target tracking. Among the armament options available are Hellfire air-to-surface and Stinger air-to-air missiles. Variants are built under licence in Italy and Australia, and operated by the armed forces of forty-five countries.

Battlefield Attack

The U.S. Army had begun to think seriously about a specialized attack helicopter in the early stages of the U.S. involvement in Vietnam. By 1965, the Lockheed AH-56 Cheyenne program was underway, aiming to produce an advanced helicopter capable carrying a wide range of weapons and of flying at speeds up to 220 knots. To achieve the high speed, Lockheed proposed a slender design with substantial wings and a pusher propeller behind the tail rotor. Once speed was increased after a vertical takeoff, the wings took care of the lift and power was transferred from the main rotor to the propeller. The program was canceled

The Sikorsky S-61L/N Sea King is one of the most widely used airliner and oil-rig-support helicopters built. The S-61L flew for the first time in 1961. When production ended in 1979, 116 S61L/Ns had been delivered. British International uses S-61s in operating the longest-running scheduled helicopter service in the world from Penzance, Cornwall, U.K., to the Isles of Scilly, and also to service oil rigs in the North Sea.

potent machine. Powered by two 1,900-horsepower turboshafts, it has a maximum level speed of 160 knots and a service ceiling of 21,000 feet. Out of ground effect, it can hover up to 11,500 feet. Gross weights can reach over 21,000 pounds. In its AH-64D form, the Apache is fitted with the Longbow fire-control system for rapid target area search, automatic detection and classification of targets, and all-weather fire-and-forget engagement using Hellfire missiles. Lightweight air-to-air missiles are carried for self-protection and a 30 mm chain gun is mounted in a turret under the nose. Mission visionics comprise three systems: TADS (Target Acquisition and Designation Sight), mounted beneath the nose; PNVS (Pilot Night Vision System) above the nose; and IHADDS (Integrated Helmet and Display Sighting System), attached to the helmets of both crew members. TADS consists of a low-light television, an optical telescope, a FLIR, and a laser rangefinder, target designator and spot tracker. PNVS uses a FLIR system to enable the pilot to fly at very low level in

in 1972, a victim of development difficulties, rising costs, and the Army's conclusion that such high speeds were not really necessary. A new AAH (Advanced Attack Helicopter) competition opened in 1973 and was won by the Hughes AH-64 Apache.

First flight of the prototype AH-64 took place in September 1975, but the first production aircraft were not delivered until January 1984, the same month that Hughes became a subsidiary of McDonnell Douglas. Smaller and lighter than the Cheyenne, the Apache is nonetheless a most

The HH-52 Sea Guardian was ordered in 1962 as a replacement for the HH-34. Coast Guard squadrons operated the HH-52 as a search-and rescue-helicopter. It was fully amphibious, with the main wheels retracting into pontoons located forward on both sides of the fuselage. The helicopter also employed a folding platform along the side of the fuselage and a winch above the door, both of which facilitated helicopter rescue. HH-52A 1355 was acquired by the National Naval Aviation Museum, Pensacola, from the U.S. Coast Guard in 1987.

The cockpit of HH-52 1355. The HH-52 was a variant of the civilian Sikorsky S-62, which was the first turbine-powered helicopter to be granted a type approval certificate by the U.S. Federal Aviation Agency, and the first cleared for commercial passenger carrying. In 1963 the U.S. Coast Guard took delivery of the first of ninety-nine HH-52s, so becoming the largest single user of the type. HH-52s have the distinction of having rescued more people than any other helicopter in the world.

BELOW *The Boeing (formerly McDonnell Douglas) AH-64D Apache is fitted with the Longbow millimeter wave fire control radar and can carry armaments as necessary to suit a particular mission. In the close support role it carries sixteen Hellfire missiles on four four-rail launchers and four air-to-air missiles. The AH-64D Apache is equipped with the Target Acquisition Designation Sight (TADS) and the Pilot Night Vision Sensor (PNVS) developed by Lockheed Martin. The turret-mounted TADS provides direct view optics, television and three fields of view forward-looking infrared (FLIR) to carry out search, detection and recognition. PNVS has a FLIR in a rotating turret on the nose above the TADS. The image from the PNVS is seen in the eyepiece of the Honeywell Integrated Helmet and Display Sighting System (IHADSS) worn by the pilot and copilot/gunner.*

complete darkness. Through a monocle placed in front of the crew member's right eye, IHADDS transmits visual information directly from either TADS or PNVS. Selection of either slaves it to the IHADDS, so that it will follow the movements of a crew member's head. The selected system therefore looks in the same direction as the crew member, and weapons can be aimed merely by looking at the target.

American Interventions

The United States has a long history of intervening when affairs get out of hand in the Caribbean and Central America. There were three such interventions during the last two decades of the 20th century, as U.S. forces became involved in Grenada (1983), Panama (1989) and Haiti (1994). Helicopters were heavily engaged in all three. CH-46Es and CH-53As put marines ashore in Grenada, and the landings were covered by AH-1T Cobras. In Panama, the most celebrated helicopter among many was the UH-60A that was used to fly a chastened Manuel Noriega away to captivity. For the Haiti intervention, in a joint operation, U.S. Army helicopters were moved within range aboard the carrier USS *Dwight D. Eisenhower*. UH-60s then ferried troops ashore under cover from AH-1s.

All of these were successful operations, but success could not always be guaranteed. In April 1980, Operation Eagle Claw was launched in an attempt to free hostages being held by Islamic militants in the U.S. Embassy in Tehran. Eight RH-53Ds were flown off the carrier USS *Nimitz* steaming off the Iranian coast close to the mouth of the Persian Gulf. Their destination was Desert One, a remote airstrip some 300 miles from Teheran. They did not have an easy passage. No. 6 landed in the desert after a blade malfunction and No. 5 returned to the carrier with a major instrument failure. The remaining six had to fight their way through a huge sandstorm and arrived at Desert One at intervals up to two and a half hours late. The refueling aircraft, EC-130H Hercules tankers from Masirah, had arrived on time, soon after 18:00 hours GMT. RH-43D No. 2 was now found to have unserviceable hydraulics and could not be repaired. Since the minimum number of helicopters required for the rescue to work was six, the operation was aborted and the five serviceable RH-43Ds began refueling for the return flight to the carrier. No. 3 finished taking on fuel and lifted off to make way for No. 4, but moved forward in the process, the main rotor blades striking the rear of the Hercules. Explosions and fire followed the destruction of the two aircraft, and ammunition began cooking off. All the remaining helicopters were damaged in the maelstrom and had to be abandoned. The surviving Hercules took off for Masirah, carrying many burned and wounded and leaving eight dead behind. The superior technology embodied in the RH-43Ds had not been sufficient to overcome a combination of human error and unexpected mechanical failure in an operation that began in audacity and ended in disaster.

Vindication in the Gulf

Well over 500 Coalition helicopters were committed to the war against Iraq in 1991, and they were involved in every phase of the conflict from the beginning. They were the first Coalition aircraft into action when Operation Desert Storm broke in the early hours of January 17. U.S. Army AH-64 Apaches, led by two USAF MH-53J Pave Lows, crossed into Iraq to destroy two key radar sites, opening a gap in the Iraqi air defenses through which the initial waves of strike aircraft could make their way undetected to Baghdad. The Pave Lows, from the USAF's Special Operations Wing, used their sophisticated navigation equipment to ensure the success of that initial attack. Together with the Wing's MH-60 Pave Hawks, the Pave Lows undertook many penetration missions, inserting and extracting special forces troops and seeking out mobile Scud launchers. They also conducted search and rescue, recovering aircrew downed in enemy territory, one of whom was Lieutenant Devon Jones, the pilot of an F-14A shot down about 150 miles inside Iraq by an SA-2 missile on the morning of January 21. Understandably relieved at being rescued after spending some eight hours on the ground expecting to become a POW, Jones said: "I had never seen such a beautiful sight as that big, brown American H-53…. I jumped in and off we went, 140 miles to go at 140 knots at 20 feet. Pretty impressive machine!"

The principal attack helicopter in support of the land battle was the AH-64 Apache, which operated in pairs well ahead of Coalition armor, clearing corridors through the defenses with fire and maneuver attacks and bringing up replacement pairs in a constant stream, so that the enemy was kept under fire and the momentum of the advance was maintained. In the words of Lieutenant Colonel William Bryan of the 229th Aviation Regiment, the Apache was an outstanding machine: "There was no other platform in the Gulf that could fly so low, or could engage such an array of targets with pinpoint accuracy, whatever the weather or the time of day or night." U.S. Marine Corps AH-1W Cobras also played their part, notably when they repulsed an attempted Iraqi counterattack outside Kuwait City on the first day of the war. One marine described the action as "a slaughter. They were taking out tanks and BTRs all over the area — the Iraqi counterattack got nowhere." Cobras and Apaches were also prominent in the destruction of Iraqi forces during the "turkey shoot" of the retreat along the Basra road in the closing hours of the war.

On February 24, 1991, the day the Coalition forces launched their ground assault against the Iraqis, the sky was black with helicopters, many of them carrying troops both for the feint on the coast to the east and for the "left hook" far to the west. USMC CH-46Es and U.S. Army CH-47Ds did much of the heavy lifting. Together with CH-53s and UH-60s, they bore the brunt of the largest helicopter operation in history, including taking 2,000 air assault troops and their equipment 50 miles into Iraq to run round the end of Iraqi defenses. Once the Coalition advance was off and running, the big choppers were in the air continually, reinforcing and resupplying the force with trucks, artillery, ammunition and fuel, and maintaining the momentum of the fast-moving attack.

On their sectors of the front, French Gazelles destroyed Iraqi armor and Pumas ferried troops into battle. Helicopters of all three British services saw action. RAF Chinooks carried special forces deep into enemy territory, engaged in continuous logistics support (including carrying unserviceable Pumas and Sea Kings back for maintenance), and lifted some 3,000 Iraqi prisoners of war to the rear. Missile-armed Lynx units were involved over both land and sea. The most heavily armed naval helicopter in the theater, the Royal Navy's Lynx was used to great effect, destroying

In 1992, Aérospatiale and MBB formed Eurocopter to produce a battlefield helicopter for the French and German armed forces. The first prototype of the Tiger flew in April 1991, but the helicopter's first major public appearance was in the 1995 James Bond film Goldeneye. *Serial production began in March 2002 and delivery in September 2003. The Tiger will be flown by the military of Germany (80), France (80), Spain (24), and Australia (22).*

fifteen ships of the small Iraqi navy with its Sea Skua missiles. The Lynx was also a prominent element in the blockade of Iraqi ports, often taking boarding parties to search suspicious vessels.

In 1991, Iraq was defeated in just six weeks of the air campaign followed by 100 hours of ground war. Undeniably, it would have taken far longer without the contributions of Coalition helicopters.

Helicopters proved to be equally valuable during the campaign in Afghanistan and in the second assault on Iraq in 2003. However, lessons learned by the Soviets in Afghanistan remained valid. In the postwar phase of both

campaigns it became clear that helicopters were vulnerable to guerilla activity and to the wear and tear of prolonged intensive operations away from main bases. The U.S. Army lost more than sixty helicopters in Iraq and Afghanistan to accidents and hostile fire in two years. The challenging conditions highlighted the need for caution in flying helicopter operations over territory harboring insurgents, and the importance of equipment such as flares and ground-surveillance radar that could help to guard helicopters against shoulder-fired missiles. Invaluable weapons of war though they are, military helicopters are flown relatively slowly and at low level. By the very nature of its operational profiles, a technologically advanced and very costly machine and its highly trained crew can quickly be destroyed by a single tribesman using a relatively cheap and simple weapon.

What Next?

It was intended that the next generation of attack helicopters would be represented by the Boeing Sikorsky RAH-66 Comanche. (RAH stands for Reconnaissance and Attack Helicopter.) This very advanced stealth technology machine first flew in January 1996, and production was originally planned for 2006. A suite of passive sensors provided a target identification range twice that of current systems, and computers analyzed battlefield information both for the crew and for transmission to other friendly forces. Armaments included a Gatling gun, and a variety of missiles carried internally in weapons bays on each side of the fuselage. Two identical cockpits, stepped in tandem, had flat-screen liquid-crystal displays with digital moving maps. The cockpits were sealed and given positive pressure to protect against chemical/biological warfare. Designed to ensure a high degree of survivability and of system redundancy, the Comanche promised to be a formidable addition to the U.S. Army's front line. However, after devoting twenty-one years and almost $7 billion to the project, the U.S. Army decided in 2004 that the Comanche was a luxury they could live without. For the time being, the 21st century's combat helicopter was set aside and the U.S. Army turned instead to investing more heavily in unmanned aircraft. Much of the remaining Comanche development money is likely to be spent on buying nearly 800 additional Black Hawk and other helicopters and on modernizing 1,400 helicopters already in the fleet.

European Progress

By the early 1970s, helicopter design and manufacturing in Europe was led by four major companies: Aérospatiale (France), Agusta (Italy), MBB (Germany), and Westland (U.K.). Early U.S. leadership in the rotorcraft field had been evident from the way in which much of the European industry had become established. Agusta and Westland, for example, had profited by building hundreds of machines such as Sikorsky S-55/58/61s and Bell 47/204s under licence, and Sud-Aviation (later Aérospatiale) had employed a Sikorsky design team when introducing its heavy-lift helicopter, the SA 321 Super Frelon, which first flew in December 1962. Powered by three Turboméca turboshafts, the prototype SA 321 proved very fast, reaching a closed-circuit speed of 218 mph. It was offered in both civil and military versions, seeing use as a thirty-seven-seat airliner, utility transport, and maritime patrol aircraft. In its naval role, the Super Frelon could be armed with homing torpedoes and Exocet anti-ship missiles. Export SA 321s were supplied to eight countries, including such varied customers as Iraq, China, Zaire, South Africa, Israel and Libya. Aérospatiale continued its independent light helicopter success with the Gazelle (a modernized Alouette), Ecureuil and Dauphin, the latter a fast twin-turbine ten-seater that could cover the 200 miles from Paris to London in one hour.

Long associated with the production of Bell helicopters in Italy, Agusta began in the late 1960s working on independent rotorcraft designs. The A 109 Hirundo, a useful general-purpose machine, and the A 129 Mangusta, an attack helicopter for the Italian Army, have been the result. The Mangusta, the first tandem-seat attack helicopter designed in Europe, first flew in 1983 and entered service in 1990. It is small, fast and agile, and offers full day/night antitank capability, besides being suitable for the battlefield surveillance and antishipping roles. In the United Kingdom, most of Westland's work was initially concerned

with the production of modified Sikorsky machines, but development of an original Saunders-Roe design led to a successful turboshaft-powered light military helicopter, known as the Scout, which first flew in 1958. A naval version named the Wasp was intended primarily for operations from small platforms on the quarterdecks of frigates. It was provided with folding rotor blades and tail that, together with a four-wheel swiveling undercarriage, simplified handling and storage in the limited space available aboard small ships. Lively and adaptable, examples of the Scout/Wasp saw service not only with the British forces, but also in various roles with the forces of eight other countries.

The Eurocopter Gazelle light helicopter was produced as part of an Anglo-French venture between Aérospatiale and Westland in 1968. Its missions include reconnaissance, forward air controller, communications relay, casualty evacuation, antitank, antihelicopter, training, and utility transport. The Gazelle is still one of the most maneuverable and fastest helicopters ever built (maximum speed 190 mph).

Collaborative Agreements

The increasing cost and complexity of helicopters forced European companies to examine ways of spreading the development load. They tackled the problem in two ways — first by ensuring that each design was made as versatile as possible, offering customers multirole capabilities, and second by entering into collaborative arrangements. In 1967, Aérospatiale and Westland began talks that led to an Anglo-French agreement for the development of three tactical helicopters. The French were to have design leadership for two — the Aérospatiale SA 330 Puma and SA 341 Gazelle — while responsibility for the third — the Westland WG.13 Lynx — rested with the British. All three became successful, and were ordered in quantity not only by their national forces but also by the military of other nations worldwide.

Among the other agreements reached in later years, Germany's MBB GmbH developed the BK 117, a popular choice for air ambulance duties, with Kawasaki in Japan,

and went on to form Eurocopter with Aérospatiale to develop the Tigre antitank helicopter. In 1980, Westland joined Agusta to create EHI Ltd., initially to investigate the joint development of an antisubmarine helicopter for their respective navies. Studies showed that the proposed naval machine could meet the requirements of both civil and other military roles so the decision was made to proceed with a basic design that could give rise to three principal variants. The result was the EH 101, a medium-sized helicopter with extraordinary flexibility of operation. Among its original features is an Active Vibration Control System, an arrangement of torque struts between the airframe and the rotor gearbox that, together with the use of carbon-glass rotor blades filled with honeycombed foam, eases much of the tiring noise and vibration usually associated with helicopter flight. In the EH 101, advanced systems and materials have been combined to produce a helicopter that monitors its own maintenance needs and can be flown for long periods by a single pilot.

North Sea Oil Rig, *by Michael Turner. The artist has painted a typical scene in the oil fields of the North Sea — gray clouds, gray sea, oil rigs flaring gas, and roughnecks hustling to board a Bell 212 of Bristow Helicopters for two weeks ashore at the end of their two-week work period. Bristow has been at the forefront of operations in the challenging environment of the North Sea since 1965.*

CIVIL OPERATIONS

The single most important factor in the development of the rotorcraft industry has always been the military interest. Design teams have been kept together and have gained experience principally because of programs funded to meet military requirements. Helicopters developed for the armed forces and proven by them operationally have eased the way for the production of new designs or of variants modified to satisfy the needs of the civil market. An indication of the early relationship between the military and civil markets is given by the fact that, up to 1960, sales of helicopters in the United States totaled approximately $2.5 billion, of which commercial machines accounted for no more than 20 percent. Still today, the demands of the military are the force that gives impetus to the rotorcraft industry, and the military heritage of most helicopters used in commercial operations is betrayed by their appearance.

The problem for commercial operators is that helicopters do just one thing supremely well: they take off and land vertically. Once in the air, they are an inefficient method of moving from place to place. Their special capability allows them to exploit certain niches in aviation, but they do so at a price. In terms of passengers or pounds of freight per mile, helicopters are among the most expensive means of transport yet devised — within the atmosphere, at least. Nevertheless, there are times when only a helicopter will do, and the rotorcraft industry has been adept at creating an appropriate tool to meet every need.

From the very beginning, the helicopter's most dramatic public role was that of rescue, and so it remains. The sight of a hovering aircraft lowering a rescue hoist to the victims of catastrophe has become a familiar but riveting image on televison screens. Thousands of survivors from the ravages of typhoon, earthquake, flood and fire have been lifted to safety by the one machine capable of bringing help. Those seriously injured in road accidents have been whisked away over impenetrable traffic to medical care with lifesaving swiftness. Mountaineers overtaken by avalanche and seamen in foundering ships have heard the distinctive slap of whirling blades and been plucked from imminent disaster. Food and medicine have been delivered to sick and starving people in places accessible only to aircraft capable of vertical flight. Relief has come under thrashing blades to those suffering deprivation in the aftermath of upheavals in Bosnia, Kosovo, East Timor and elsewhere.

Television has brought these dramas into the living room, putting the helicopter at center stage in unforgettable scenes — people being lifted from the balconies of the Las Vegas MGM Hotel to escape a raging fire in 1980; a helicopter dragging a skid in the icy water of Washington's wintry Potomac River to recover a survivor of the Air Florida crash in December 1982. Helicopter pilots have often risked their lives to save others, flying their machines into impossible situations. In May 1996, in the highest helicopter rescue ever accomplished, Madan Khatri Chhetri of the Royal Nepalese Army went to the aid of climbers stranded by a fierce storm on the upper slopes of Mount Everest. Twice he took his Eurocopter Ecureuil to a height almost 3,000 feet above its supposed ceiling to pick men off the mountain who were close to death. Asked why he took the risks, he said: "If I can save one more life, my inner soul will be happier."

At a less dramatic level, helicopters are the indispensable tools of the oil industry, ferrying workers and supplies to and from oil rigs and super tankers out at sea. Foresters, geologists and the like who need to reach remote places in jungle, desert or tundra take it for granted that rotary wings can get them there. Corporate executives, too, see helicopters as an essential part of doing business, aerial taxis that save time and are therefore worth the money. In countless other ways, helicopters prove their value, and it is sometimes hard to imagine how a job was done before such flexible and powerful machines existed. Lifting spires and capstones to the top of tall buildings, fighting brush fires, spraying crops, herding cattle, patrolling powerlines, policing national wildlife parks, monitoring traffic, taking fishermen or skiers to out-of-the-way places — helicopters have woven their way into the fabric of everyday life.

The Long Way Round

Occasionally, a rotary-wing enthusiast will do something just for the thrill of it, because, as the mountaineers say, "It was there." On September 1, 1982, Ross Perot Jr. and Jay Coburn left Dallas in the Bell 206L-1 *Spirit of Texas* and set off to become the first to fly a helicopter round the world. Twenty-nine days, three hours and eight minutes later, they landed back at their starting point having covered 24,754 miles during 246.5 hours in the air. The epic flight was completed in

The Boeing V-22 Osprey is a joint-service, multi-mission tilt-rotor aircraft. It operates as a helicopter to take off and land vertically. The nacelles rotate forward once airborne, and the V-22 becomes a turboprop aircraft. It can fly nearly twice as fast, three times as far and more than 10,000 feet higher than the helicopters it is intended to replace. Bedeviled by technical difficulties, cost overruns, and political opposition, the revolutionary Osprey has survived the challenges of its protracted development and is to become operational in 2006, seventeen years after its first flight.

LEFT The Osprey is powered by two Rolls-Royce T406 turboshafts that deliver 6,150 shaft horsepower each. They drive three-bladed proprotors 38 feet in diameter. The blades and wings can be folded for hangar storage aboard ship. This Osprey can be seen at the American Helicopter Museum, West Chester, Pennsylvania.

twenty-nine stages, one of which ended in the vast reaches of the Pacific with a landing on the container ship *President McKinley*. Australian Dick Smith left Fort Worth, Texas, in a similar Bell model a month before Perot and Coburn. Smith, however, took his time, reaching Australia in October 1982 but not setting off again until May 1983. On July 22, 1983, he landed at Fort Worth, so completing the first solo round the world helicopter flight. In his meandering, he had covered 35,298 miles in 320 flying hours.

At a Personal Level

The dream of an aircraft in every garage may have been abandoned as impractical after WWII, but the idea of affordable personal flying machines never went away. Fixed-wing enthusiasts developed microlights, but there were other ways of satisfying the need. There are several lightweight alternatives among the rotorcraft, ranging from traditional open-frame autogyros to small versions of the all-enclosed helicopter. In between there are variations on partially enclosed designs.

Tiny autogyros caught the public imagination after James Bond flew one armed with an assortment of sophisticated weapons in the 1967 movie *You Only Live Twice*, shooting down four pursuing helicopters in the service of the Queen. It was an autogyro named *Little Nellie*, and it was actually flown by Ken Wallis, the designer. Flying machines powered by engines of 60 or 90 horsepower, Wallis held all but one of the autogyro world records by the turn of the century, including a time to 3,000 meters of 7 minutes, 20 seconds, set in 1998 when he was eighty-one years old. His remarkable little aircraft have been popular vehicles for sport and recreation, but they have also been used for coastal and marine ecology, archeological investigations, detection of leaks in water pipes, air photography and remote sensing, police searches, military reconnaissance and the search for the Loch Ness monster. Wallis has been at the forefront of modern autogyro development, but there have been plenty of designers eager to follow his lead, and there are now dozens of models on the market, available to private owners keen to try their hands at emulating James Bond.

For those who prefer true helicopters, a large number of home-build kits were developed. Fully enclosed two-seat machines came from builders such as Helisport of Turin, Italy, and Rotorway International of Arizona.

Helisport's Angel Kompress and Rotorway's Exec 162F are sleek creations capable of 120 mph or more. Hillberg of California offered a remarkable single-seater, the Rotormouse, which claimed a top speed of 160 mph. Enthusiasts for the wind-in-the-face experience could go to Maryland for Vortech's Skylark or to Canada for Innovator Technology's Mosquito, in either of which the pilot is exposed to the weather in a way that the Wrights or Glenn Curtiss would have understood. Even more extreme are strap-ons such as the GENH-4 ultralight from Masumi Yanagisawa of Japan, a machine that weighs only 155 pounds and is worn rather than climbed into. Less physically challenging but still sporty are partially enclosed helicopters such as those offered by American Sports Copter of Newport News, Virginia.

Perhaps the ultimate in personal flying machines is the rocket belt. In 1953, Bell Aerospace's Wendell Moore conceived of a one-man device consisting of two small jet nozzles and fuel tanks, plus sundry lines, valves, gauges and controls. In the 1960s he was funded by the U.S. Army to develop his idea as the Small Rocket Lifting Device (SLRD), to improve the mobility of the individual soldier. In its basic form the SLRD was nothing more than a backpack. The tanks contained nitrogen and hydrogen peroxide. Nitrogen pressure forced the hydrogen peroxide into a catalyst chamber where it was broken down to provide the thrust. Later models included a "pogo-stick" and a chair. For many of the early flights the pilots wore a full body suit as protection against being burned.

Once the prototype SLRD was built, Moore made the first test flights indoors on a safety tether. During one of the flights a cable snapped, and he fell, injuring his knee. A young engineer at Bell, Harold Graham, took over as test pilot and on April 20, 1961, made the first outdoor tether-free flight, shooting forward 112 feet. Once they were made public, the flights attracted a good deal of public attention and the SLRD was demonstrated all over the world. Various versions appeared in television series and commercials, at the Paris Air Show and the Carnival in Rio, and at the opening of the 1984 Olympics. One even provided James Bond with some much needed mobility at a critical point of the movie *Thunderball*. Spectacular though the device was, it was able to carry fuel for only twenty seconds or so, and was therefore of little practical use.

CAREFLIGHT

The use of helicopters in Korea and Vietnam proved the value of emergency medical services that could literally pluck the injured out of the danger zone and fly them to early trauma care for stabilization or more dramatic life-saving efforts. The smaller helicopters of those conflicts, which were limited to transporting the wounded to assistance, have given way to much larger and more powerful systems that actually bring medical care directly to those who need it. These images of CareFlight represent similar efforts and operations around the world.

Since 1983, Miami Valley Hospital of Dayton, Ohio, has been providing round-the-clock advanced life support and skilled nursing care to seriously ill and injured patients within a 150-mile radius. The vital service has expanded in size since its beginnings and is a familiar sight in the region, now flying three helicopters, two 365N2 Dauphin helicopters and, the newest in the fleet in 2005, a 365N3 Dauphin. The twin-engine gas-turbine-powered helicopter flies with a crew of three, a command pilot and two flight nurses.

ABOVE *CareFlight Number One* lifts off from the rooftop facility at Miami Valley Hospital.
CENTER TOP CareFlight crew answers the call.
CENTER MIDDLE Newest member of the CareFlight fleet, Dauphin N3.
CENTER BOTTOM Compared to the cockpit of the UH-1 Huey on page 208, the N3 cockpit features some of the latest avionics, including electronic instrumentation.

LEFT AND ABOVE Flight nurses Liz Denlinger and Matt McCarty secure a patient to the stretcher. Once the injured is secure, the flight crew can access the emergency health care systems they have flown to the patient. These systems include oxygen, cardiac care defibrillators, orthopedic supports, and sophisticated pharmaceuticals. CareFlight and others like it are airborne intensive care units. Usually CareFlight crews accept a patient from a paramedic crew that served as first response to the incident. The patient's vital information is analyzed and the next appropriate actions are taken.

ABOVE Approaching the Helipad, the shadow of *CareFlight Number One.*
RIGHT The flight crew is met by emergency staff and the injured is wheeled into the hospital and further emergency care.

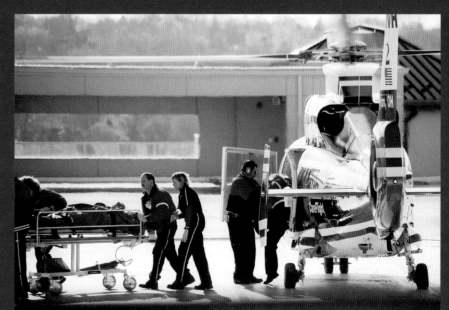

As the 20th century ended, the helicopter industry could be proud of its achievements. The problems that had baffled pioneers such as Igor Sikorsky and Louis Breguet in the early days had been solved and helicopters had evolved into practical and reliable flying machines. They had become quieter and suffered less from vibration; safety had improved and they could fly by day and night in all weathers. Continued research into ideas such as X-wings and the advancing blade concept offered new prospects, and refinements of details such as blades and bearings promised further improvements, but only in degree. Most of the basic development work has been done, and helicopters are likely both to retain their familiar shape and to perform in much the same way for the foreseeable future. If there is to be a revolutionary change in rotary-winged flight, it will probably come in a less familiar form, perhaps with rotors a-tilt.

TILT ROTORS

In the 1930s, a number of designers pursued the idea of a winged aircraft with propellers big enough to serve as horizontal rotors for vertical takeoff, but which could be rotated to an upright position once in flight to provide forward thrust. The 1937 Baynes Heliplane was a British design which never flew, but which bears a striking resemblance to Bell's successful tilt-rotors of half a century later. Equally impressive was the design for the German Focke-Achgelis Fa 269 pusher tilt-rotor of WWII. In the United States, LePage suggested a tilt-rotor based on the design of his XR-1 helicopter. Neither the German nor the American designs reached the construction stage, not least because the power of the engines then available could not have coped with the weights of the proposed machines. LePage's ideas, however, bore fruit. In 1945, Robert Lichten, one of LePage's engineers, formed Transcendental Aircraft with Mario Guerierri and began working on the development of a tilt-rotor aircraft designated Model 1-G. Lichten later left Transcendental and went to Bell, where he headed that company's tilt-rotor program, but Guerierri persisted with the 1-G which achieved free flight in July 1954. During the following year the aircraft flew more than one hundred times, but was then destroyed when it crashed into the Delaware River. Transcendental went on to build a Model 2, which was flown successfully in 1956 but had by then been overtaken by the work being done at Bell.

The Bell XV-3 hovered for the first time in August 1955. It was powered by a single 450-horsepower Pratt & Whitney radial driving two 23-foot rotors mounted on long stalky shafts at the wingtips. After a crash wrecked the first machine, a second XV-3 was flown with shorter driving shafts and it successfully converted from vertical to horizontal flight in December 1958. Seven years of testing with the XV-3 yielded a mass of valuable information and established a foundation for Bell's later work on tilt-rotors.

In 1962, the USAF ordered five prototypes and a static test airframe from the team of Chance Vought (later LTV), Hiller and Ryan. The aircraft designation was XC-142A, and it was intended primarily for carrying troops from assault ships or airfields into unprepared areas in all weathers. The resulting design was a tubby transport with a wingspan of 68 feet. Powered by four GE T-64 3,000-horsepower turboprops driving four-bladed propellers of 15 feet, 6 inches diameter, it could take thirty-two fully equipped troops or four tons of freight. To control movement in pitch during the hover, a small tail rotor was fitted behind the fin. Hovering roll control was accomplished by varying propeller pitch, and yaw by means of the ailerons operating in the propeller slipstream. The test program validated the concept and was carried out with commendable speed. The XC-142A's first conventional flight was made on September 29, 1964, and hovering was achieved three months later. Only two weeks after that, on January 11, 1965, full conversions were carried out from the hover to horizontal flight and back again. Before the program was terminated, the XC-142As between them had flown at speeds up to 400 mph forward and 35 mph backward, climbed to 25,000 feet, and operated from the aircraft carrier USS *Bennington.*

In July 1973, Bell Helicopter Textron was awarded a NASA/Army contract to develop a tilt-wing technology demonstrator. The result was the XV-15A, an attractive aircraft weighing some 13,000 pounds and powered by two 1,550-horsepower Avco Lycoming LTC1K turboshafts driving 25-foot rotors. The first free hovering flight was carried out on May 3, 1977, and progress toward a full conversion to forward flight was approached cautiously thereafter. A meticulously planned program took the aircraft through a series of tests and then the conversion sequence in stages. The first partial wing rotation, from 90 to 85 degrees, took place on May 5, 1979. Finally, on July 24, 1979, a full conversion was

The Chance Vought/Hiller/Ryan (later LTV) XC-142A was probably an aeronautical step too far for the 1960s, but it was an extraordinary achievement. Conceived as a VTOL (vertical take-off and landing) transport, it first flew in September 1964, and within the following five months had achieved both hovering and transitional flight. During testing, the XC-142A was flown forwards at 400 mph, backwards at 35 mph, and sideways at 60 mph. It flew over 1,000 miles nonstop and lifted payloads of four tons. The complexity of the design was challenging; the transmission, for example, was linked so that one engine alone could turn all four propellers and the tail rotor. Accidents and rising costs brought the program to an end in 1967. Five XC-142As were built; one survives and is in the collection of the National Museum of the USAF, Dayton, Ohio.

achieved, with the wings rotated through 90 degrees and the rotors acting as propellers to provide forward thrust. After that, the development program proceeded more quickly, and the predicted level flight cruise speed of 300 knots was recorded in June 1980. Pilots who flew the XV-15A reported that it was no more difficult to fly in the hover than a normal helicopter, and that the conversion to forward flight was a simple process. All were impressed by the quality of the aircraft's handling and by the smoothness of the ride.

To take the tilt-rotor concept a step closer to an operational VSTOL aircraft, Bell joined with Boeing in 1982 to embark on a program to produce the V-22 Osprey. It was a process bedeviled by both technical and political problems. First flight of the prototype took place at Arlington, Texas, on March 19, 1989, but it was another decade before the first production model made it into the air. However, through the persistence of the companies and the determination of the U.S. Marine Corps, the Osprey made progress toward front-line service. It was planned

principally as an assault transport for the USMC, to replace the ageing CH-46 and CH-53, but was also proposed for the special operations and search-and-rescue roles of other services. Powered by two Allison T406 turboprops of 6,150 horsepower each driving impressive proprotors 38 feet across, the Osprey can carry twenty-four fully equipped troops at speeds up to 300 knots. Enormous though it is when in flying trim — almost 84 feet across the blade tips — the Osprey folds its blades and rotates its wing to come down to a width of less than 19 feet for storage aboard ship. Constructed largely of composite materials and making use of the most modern avionics and systems, the Osprey opens the door on a concept for the 21st century. When the technical problems are eventually solved, the unique capabilities offered by the tilt-rotor — hovering like a helicopter and flying at the speeds of a turboprop aircraft — promise greater operational flexibility for the military, and civil developments could provide the ideal short-haul intercity airliner.

CHAPTER 5

At the Frontier

Research and development endeavor has been at the core of aeronautical progress from the beginning. Before a new aircraft takes wing, designers and constructors may spend years on the painstaking work of conceiving, drawing, building, shaping and modifying the machine to ensure that it will function as efficiently as possible. Flight-testing, a frequently hazardous and invariably challenging activity for the pilots involved, has always been an essential part of the process. As the 20th century advanced, and the fund of knowledge about aerodynamics and aircraft structures grew, the role of the test pilot began to change. In the early days, pilots knew that in testing a new aircraft they would be exploring the unknown, depending largely on trial and error to establish the machine's characteristics and achieve improvement. With experience and the evolution of sensible testing techniques, the element of pure exploration diminished and the test pilot became more of an analyst, a technician trained to evaluate every aspect of an aircraft's performance with care and precision. Work done with wind tunnels and later with simulators and computers steadily reduced the nervous uncertainty with which a first flight was approached. Even so, the day still comes when a test pilot must go to full power and commit the machine to its natural element for the first time, and that is always a moment of truth, when pulses quicken and mouths go dry. The calculations have been made, the designers seem satisfied, the preliminaries are over, the aircraft trembles with life — but will it really fly?

The pioneers of powered flight designed and built their machines, and then learned how to fly them, in the process testing their aircraft and revealing some of flight's mysteries. The Wright brothers, with their meticulously scientific yet practical methods, were the first successful test pilots of powered aircraft, setting a standard for flight-testing that few other pioneers could match. Wilbur was explicit about the need to gain airborne experience, saying: "If you really wish to learn you must mount a machine and become acquainted with its tricks by actual trial." (See *Aviation*

OPPOSITE *Early wind tunnels were often considerable works of art and craftsmanship. The tunnel designed and built in 1918 at McCook Field was wonderfully shaped in wood. Its 60-inch fan has twenty-four blades, which can propel air through the 14-inch throat at speeds up to 450 mph. In the days of wooden subsonic wind tunnels, the aerofoils tested bore little resemblance to those that were placed in the high-speed tunnels built after World War II. In the jet and space-flight era, the models tested assumed far more exotic shapes. It became possible to create artificial winds of supersonic and hypersonic speeds, and the models resembled winged bullets rather than conventional aircraft. This model was designed by the Air Force Institute of Technology.*

Century The Early Years.) Among those prewar notables who could claim to be both conscientious researchers and competent pilots were Glenn Curtiss, A.V. Roe, Geoffrey de Havilland, Henri Farman, Anthony Fokker and Igor Sikorsky, but many leading aviators preferred to ignore science and make progress solely by trial and error. Louis Blériot, for instance, was notorious for designing, building and crashing aeroplanes, quickly abandoning each unsuccessful machine and moving on to a modified version. In the four years of intense effort preceding his crossing of the English Channel, Blériot was involved in almost fifty crashes, suffering countless broken bones, burns, cuts and bruises. He and his later aircraft were successful, but he was lucky to survive, and his kind of impulsive testing methods were soon consigned to history.

A System Evolves

The first moves toward formalizing a scientific approach to test-flying were made before WWI by Britain's Royal Aircraft Factory at Farnborough. Under the direction of Superintendent Mervyn O'Gorman, a system was introduced that identified various design features to be examined during the testing of each aircraft type. A professional team of scientists and pilots was assembled to check the aircraft's general performance and to ensure that the machine met service specifications before being handed over to the operators. It was a start, but flight-testing remained risky. Given the level of aeronautical engineering wisdom at the time, it is hardly surprising that on occasion aircraft were flown that were barely airworthy and structurally unsound. Since the outer limits of performance envelopes were hazy, pilots sometimes took an aircraft to and beyond them, intent on discovery and guessing at the outcome of their bravado. An airman who flew too fast or too high, or who turned too tightly, might survive and know

A reproduction of the Wright brothers' wind tunnel, a 6-foot-long, 16-inch-square wooden box with a glass viewing-window on top. The metal honeycomb straightened out the air flowing into the tunnel from a large belt-driven fan. Balances measured the lift and drag of model wings inside the tunnel. Scraps of paper are covered with the brothers' calculations. From the National Museum of the United States Air Force.

that he had found a performance edge, but all too often such a breakthrough was marked by his own death.

Once given the task, Farnborough remained at the center of Britain's aeronautical research and development for the rest of the century, maturing in time into the Royal Aircraft Establishment. In the 1920s, military flight-testing was set up on England's east coast, at Martlesham Heath and Felixstowe, under the Aeroplane and Armament Experimental Establishment (A&AEE). In WWII, it moved to a less exposed position at Boscombe Down in the center of the country.

On the other side of the Atlantic, the United States initially found itself left behind in the rush to develop powered flying machines. By 1915, this situation was causing sufficient concern in government circles for Congress to authorize the formation of the National Advisory Committee for Aeronautics (NACA), reorganized as the National Aeronautics and Space Administration — NASA — in 1958. The Committee was enjoined to "supervise and direct the scientific study of the problems of flight," in the process of which the members could "conduct research and experiment in aeronautics." Experimental flight research centers were established for U.S. Army aircraft at McCook Field near Dayton, Ohio, in 1917, and at Langley Field, Virginia, in 1919. The U.S. Navy followed with a similar unit at Anacostia, near Washington, D.C. In later years, as the centers grew and their proximity to cities proved restrictive, the U.S. Navy consolidated its efforts at Patuxent River, Maryland, and McCook's facilities moved first to Wright Field and then embraced the larger Wright-Patterson AFB complex. The massive expansion of the USAAF in WWII made it inevitable that another, more remote, testing area would be needed, and in 1942 a flight-test center was opened near the settlement of Muroc, on Rogers Dry Lake in the Mojave Desert. Eventually known as

Edwards AFB, the Muroc unit grew into a vast complex that became the principal home of flight-testing for both the USAF and NASA.

In other leading aviation countries the trend was similar, with each establishing its own organization for flight-testing. Russia's Central AeroHydrodynamics Institute (abbreviated from the Russian as TsAGI) was founded in Moscow in 1918. In the 1920s and 1930s, TsAGI's projects ranged from prototype aircraft to aero-sleds and torpedo boats. Gradually, TsAGI evolved to concentrate primarily on aerodynamic research, and in 1935 moved to the outskirts of Moscow, expanding into a town that after WWII came to be called Zhukovsky, in honor of TsAGI's founding father. The Gromov Flight Research Institute at Zhukovsky, is one of the largest flight research institutes in the world. In Germany, Rechlin became well known as the testing ground for Hitler's Luftwaffe, and the names of Istres in France and Linköping in Sweden were among those that grew to prominence and gained the respect of the aeronautical research world.

> *"If you are looking for perfect safety you will do well to sit on a fence and watch the birds, but if you really wish to learn you must mount a machine and become acquainted with its tricks by actual trial."*
>
> WILBUR WRIGHT

In addition to the national centers, research facilities of comparable capacity were developed by aircraft manufacturers. Crude though they were in the early days, they grew in capability as the century progressed, contributing enormously to the work of accumulating aeronautical knowledge. Before WWI there were few instances of companies hiring pilots for the specific purpose of testing their machines, and even fewer who had constructed a wind tunnel. With the dawning of the jet era and the development of computer technology, huge corporations formed that were able to employ research technology of staggering sophistication and complexity to produce such aeronautical wonders as the 747, SR-71 and Concorde. Proving the flight characteristics of machines such as these was a task that could be tackled only by aircrew who were both exceptionally competent aviators trained to meet the challenges of their demanding roles.

Training to Test

The origins of the world's first school dedicated to training flight-test professionals date back to WWI. The Experimental Flight formed in 1914 at the Central Flying School at Upavon in Wiltshire comprised the few experienced pilots left in Britain after the departure for France of four fighting squadrons. They were soon applying formal evaluation methods to every new aeroplane produced. Between the wars, air forces and private organizations began issuing flight-testing guides to their pilots, and courses of training for prospective test pilots were prepared. However, not until after the outbreak of WWII was it accepted that experience and flying ability, even when combined with a certain amount of guidance and training by the various organizations concerned, did not necessarily make a good test pilot.

In 1943 a professional Test Pilots' School was formed at Boscombe Down to offer standardized instruction to selected pilots in the special skills so essential in flight-testing. (The name was changed to the Empire Test Pilots School in 1944 in recognition of the Commonwealth students taking the course. From 1949 ETPS adopted the motto "Learn to Test; Test to Learn.") In 1945, the USN and USAF formed their own test pilot schools, and the French were not long after in following suit. These remain the big four schools of the major aviation powers in the West. They are all co-located with flight-test centers and they encourage exchanges of both staff and students with the aim of improving standards within the flight-test profession. There are also two civilian-operated schools, the International Test Pilots School, at Woodford, England, and the National Test Pilot School, at Mojave, California, and test pilot training is undertaken in a number of other countries, including Russia, Germany, Italy, Brazil, India and Japan.

Test pilots and flight-test engineers graduating from these schools go on to define the characteristics, handling and performance of new aircraft and their associated systems, testing them thoroughly so that few uncertainties can remain. They are the aviators who establish safe operational boundaries for the products of the aviation industry, ensuring that by the time an aircraft is given a certificate of airworthiness and is released into service, it is manageable by general squadron or line aircrew and is fully fit for its designed purpose.

BARNES WALLIS

Sir Barnes Wallis was a scientist and engineer who spent most of his career working for Vickers Aircraft. He designed the successful R.100 airship and the Vickers Wellesley and Wellington bombers (both using geodetic construction), but is best remembered for conceiving the bouncing bomb used to destroy the Möhne and Eder dams in Germany in May 1943. Wallis later designed the 6-ton Tallboy and 10-ton Grand Slam bombs, and after WWII developed the idea of swing-wings in his Wild Goose and Swallow variable-geometry aircraft. He is seen (above) holding a model of the Swallow, intended as the basis for an airliner flying nonstop from Europe to Australia in a return journey time of ten hours. In the Swallow he used a flattened profile fuselage blending with the wing and contributing to total lift. The fin was eliminated and all control was provided by the engine pods. These were mounted in pairs toward the tips of the wings, one above and one below the aerofoil. They pivoted about all three axes, providing a constant thrust-line with variations in wing sweep, and served in place of rudder, ailerons and elevators. One supersonic model of the Swallow, 6 feet long, flew in the 1950s and reached speeds over Mach 2.

In the RAF Museum at Hendon, northwest London, is a reconstruction of Barnes Wallis' Brooklands office. Many of his personal papers and belongings are on display. His glasses and his slide rule (the engineer's handheld computer in his day) sit on his diary and a sketch pad. The pilot's logbook is that of Wing Commander Guy Gibson, VC, who led 617 Squadron on the raid against the Ruhr dams. The wider view of the office shows his desk, drafting table, briefcase, jacket and a few of his books.

EUROPEAN TEST AIRCRAFT

In the 1930s, the possibility of powered flight without a propeller was being pursued in several countries. In Italy, Caproni developed the Caproni-Campini N-1 (above), which was said to be a jet aircraft, but was in reality powered by a piston-engine-driven ducted fan and a crude afterburner. On August 27, 1940, the first prototype was tested for 10 minutes over the Taliedo airfield by the celebrated pilot Mario De Bernardi. A second prototype flew on April 11, 1941. At the time, these were recognized by the FAI (Fédération Aéronautique Internationale) as the first jet flights ever made. The nature of the power unit and its dependence on a piston engine were not understood, and the flight of the Heinkel He 178 jet on August 27, 1939, had been kept secret.

The spectacular Nord 1500-02 Griffon II canarded delta high-speed research aircraft of the late 1950s was built around its engines. Inside the fuselage, an Atar turbojet engine was mounted inside a ramjet. The speed of the Griffon was limited by the heating of the airframe, but in June 1959 a Griffon II set a world 100-kilometer closed-circuit speed record.

BELOW Later trials were flown with improved versions, such as the Leduc 022, preserved by the Musée de l'Air et de l'Espace at Le Bourget. The pilot of this extraordinary aircraft sat inside the nosecone of the ramjet intake.

OPPOSITE LEFT AND CENTER The smooth, sculpted lines of the N-1 belie its considerable bulk, but its superficial resemblance to a true jet aircraft is clear. (Top) With the rear fuselage removed for ground runs, the flames issuing from the afterburner — and the noise — were impressive. For all its aerodynamic cleanliness and apparent power, however, the N-1 was not a notable performer. Its top speed was not much more than 200 mph, and it could go no higher than 15,000 feet.

OPPOSITE BOTTOM After WWII, French designers explored supersonic flight in different ways. Test flights of the Leduc 010 ramjet began in 1946, with the aircraft launched from a Sud Est SE-161 Languedoc mothership.

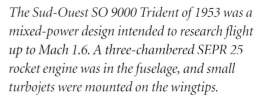

The Sud-Ouest SO 9000 Trident of 1953 was a mixed-power design intended to research flight up to Mach 1.6. A three-chambered SEPR 25 rocket engine was in the fuselage, and small turbojets were mounted on the wingtips.

BUILT FOR SPEED

ABOVE LEFT *The Bell X-1 was designed to investigate the problems of flight at transonic and supersonic speeds. The X-1B at the National Museum of the USAF, Dayton, first flew in October 1954. Its specific mission was research into aerodynamic heating and reaction control systems. The X-1B was carried to above 25,000 feet by a Boeing B-29 before being released. The rockets were then ignited to give their brief surge of power, after which the pilot was left to fly a very inefficient glider.*

TOP RIGHT *In the early 1950s, the Bell X-planes were probing unknowns at the frontiers of flight, and the aeronautical engineers often had to improvise modifications to the aircraft as the research progressed. One such adjustment was an attempt to counter some aileron flutter occurring at about Mach 1. It consisted of plywood wedges glued to the ailerons of the all-metal X-1B.*

RIGHT *The power for the X-1B was provided by a Reaction Motors XLR-11 rocket engine. The four chambers each produced 1,500 pounds of thrust, and could be fired separately or together as required. A pressurized system used gaseous nitrogen to force alcohol into the burners. At full throttle, the fuel of the X-1B lasted four minutes or less.*

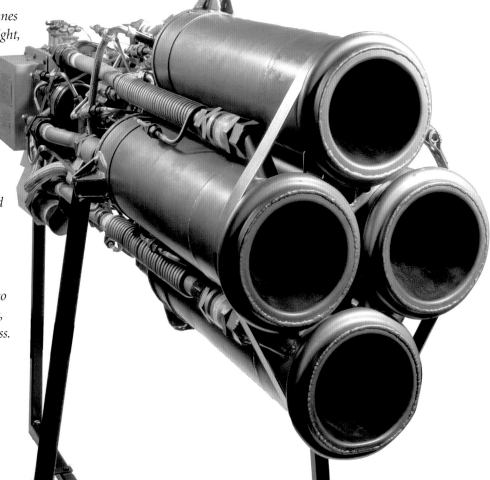

TOP RIGHT *Two Fairey F.D.2s were built. In 1964, by which time Fairey had become part of the British Aircraft corporation, the first one flew as the BAC 221, having had its straight delta wing replaced by an ogival (pointed arch) wing. The BAC 221 was an integral part of the research done to determine the feasibility of building a supersonic transport, and its wing shape and drooped nose were the basis for the design of Concorde. In this photograph of the two little deltas flying together, the difference in wing shape can clearly be seen.*

In the late 1940s, Fairey Aviation began work on a delta-winged aircraft to investigate flight and control at transonic and supersonic speeds. The final design was the Fairey Delta 2, a single-seat, delta-winged aircraft powered by a Rolls-Royce Avon engine with afterburner. The high angle of attack of the delta wing in slow-speed flight led to the provision of a cockpit and nose section that could behinged downward by ten degrees to improve the pilot's forward view during landing, taxiing and takeoff. A similar arrangement was later used on Concorde. Fairey test-pilot Peter Twiss flew the first F.D.2 on its maiden flight on October 6, 1954. On March 10, 1956, flying the second F.D.2, he set a world speed record of 1,132 mph, breaking the old mark by more than 300 mph.

EXPANDING THE ENVELOPE

TOP With the F-100 Super Sabre in production, North American began work on a more advanced version, capable of delivering nuclear weapons at Mach 2. The extensive design changes led to its redesignation from F-100B to F-107A before the first prototype flew. New features included an all-moving vertical fin and a variable area inlet duct which automatically controlled the amount of air fed to the jet engine at high supersonic speeds. The first F-107A went supersonic on its first flight in September 1956, and test flights in the three aircraft built achieved speeds over Mach 2 and an altitude of 69,000 feet. However, because of technical problems the Republic F-105 was selected for the USAF and the F-107 did not go into production. The F-107A on display at the National Museum of the USAF is aircraft F-107A No. 2.

INSET The X-15s were carried to 45,000 feet and Mach 0.83 under the wing of a B-52. The X-15 then dropped away and the rockets were fired.

OPPOSITE The X-15A on display at the National Museum of the USAF is the aircraft flown by Major "Pete" Knight to Mach 6.72 on October 3, 1967. The three-layered windscreen includes a fused silica outer pane and a middle pane of alumino-silicate. The airframe is covered with a skin of nickel alloy steel. A spherical device in the nose is designed to sense angles of attack and sideslip during flight in the upper atmosphere. Around the nose are eight of the twelve small rocket nozzles used to control aircraft attitude above the atmosphere. Two 22-foot-long fuel tanks were alongside the fuselage, one containing anhydrous ammonia, and the other liquid oxygen. The contents of these tanks weighed almost 16 tons, and this was burned by the X-15A in two and a half minutes.

ABOVE Within the atmosphere, the X-15 was controlled with a normal stick in the center of the cockpit. However, there were no ailerons, so both pitch and roll were induced by the all-flying tailplane, the two halves of which could be moved differentially. The small rockets that controlled the aircraft outside the atmosphere were operated by a sidestick hidden from view below the left cockpit rail. On the instrument panel, the dials are almost outnumbered by red warning captions.

OPPOSITE The rear of the X-15 is uncompromisingly blunt. The exhaust cone is on the receiving end of a throttled Thiokol XLR-99 liquid-propellant rocket engine with a rated thrust of 57,000 pounds at 45,000 feet. Above it towers the foot-wide trailing edge of the wedge-section dorsal fin, pivoted for directional control and fitted with split airbrakes. The spherical tank contains helium to pressurize the liquid hydrogen tanks. Underneath is the steel skid used on landing.

VALKYRIE

The North American XB-70A Valkyrie was an experimental delta designed to fly at three times the speed of sound at altitudes above 70,000 feet. The aircraft was intended to investigate the feasibility of building bombers capable of very high speed and long range. It was initially thought that the B-70 would replace the B-52 as the USAF's strategic bomber, but only two were built. They flew research missions between 1964 and 1969. Among the XB-70's design features were a shape to take advantage of the aerodynamic principle known as compression lift, a movable canard, accessibility to electronics equipment in flight, a shirt-sleeve cockpit environment, and encapsulated seats for crew ejection up to the limits of the aircraft's performance. For improved stability at supersonic speeds, the Valkyrie could droop its wingtips as much as 65 degrees.

LEFT The "flying wedge" shape under the fuselage kept boundary layer air from spilling into the intake ducts. An air-intake control system sensed small changes in pressure during flight and adjusted accordingly, decelerating the air from supersonic at the intake duct to ensure a smooth subsonic flow as it entered the engines. The intakes are situated nearly halfway back along the underside of the almost 200 foot long fuselage.

BELOW INSET A retractable visor was used to smooth out the slight bump of the XB-70's cockpit during flight at high Mach numbers. In the cockpit area the fuselage was constructed mainly of titanium. The two-man crew sat on seats that became pressurized ejection capsules in an emergency, so pressure suits were not worn, even at 70,000 feet.

ABOVE The cockpit of the XB-70 was state-of-the-art in the 1960s, neatly organized in impressive ranks of linear instruments, dials and projecting switches. Note the fistful of throttle levers in the center console at lower right, below the rows of engine instruments.

BELOW The XB-70 was powered by six General Electric J-93 turbojet engines, each producing approximately 30,000 pounds of thrust. Here two of the six engine tailpipes can be seen, slightly angled away from each other to avoid excessive turbulence and loss of thrust.

On February 4, 1969, the remaining XB-70 was flown to the United States Air Force Museum (now called the National Museum of USAF), in Dayton, Ohio. These photographs of the last flight of the Valkyrie were made by Dan Patterson, then a sophomore at Colonel White High School. Dan's father, Bill Patterson, called the principal of the school to let him know that he was taking Dan out of school to see this famous and unique bomber make its last landing. The principal argued a bit about missing school. Mr. Patterson told him that Dan "would probably get more education that afternoon than in another school classroom lesson that day." A week later the principal called Mr. Patterson to apologize. It seems that his second-grade daughter had brought home her "Weekly Reader" and the last landing of the XB-70 was the featured story.

TEST PILOTS

Chuck Yeager, AAF WWII ace, USAF, Bell X-1, first to break the sound barrier, with some "Young Eagles."

Peter Twiss, Fleet Air Arm WWII, Fairey FD-2 test pilot, first to exceed 1,000 mph.

Scott Crossfield, NASA, X-1, first to go twice the speed of sound, first to fly X-15.

Fitz Fulton, USAF, long career as project pilot for the B-47, B-52, B-57, B-66, the Mach 2 B-58 and the triple sonic XB-70.

Neil Armstrong, U.S. Navy Korea, NASA test pilot, X-15, astronaut, Gemini 8, *Apollo 11*, first man on Moon.

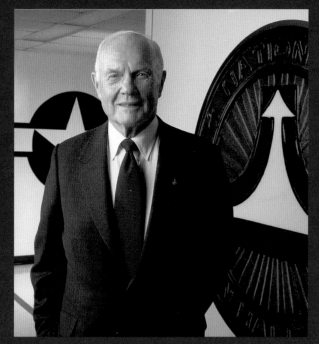

John Glenn, USMC Korea, test pilot, astronaut, first American to orbit Earth, oldest man to orbit.

Art Tomassetti, USMC, current test pilot for Lockheed Joint Strike Fighter (X-35 JSF).

Galina Korchuganova, former Soviet test pilot, test-flew many early MiG jet fighters, and 1966 World Aerobatic Champion.

The Pilots

In the early days of powered flight, and as each new aviation frontier was crossed in later years, the aviators who flew untried aircraft to explore the outer regions of aeronautical research often wrote their names into aviation history, many of them becoming celebrated public figures. Hollywood films dramatized and glamorized their activities, perpetuating the image of handsome daredevils with careless smiles who daily risked their lives. Technological advances have so changed the way the aviation industry produces aircraft and so much aeronautical knowledge has been accumulated that test pilots and engineers are now less likely to be singled out for special attention. Names such as Glenn Curtiss, Igor Sikorsky, Jimmy Doolittle, "Chuck" Yeager, and John Cunningham appeared in newspaper headlines all over the world, but the leading test pilots of the 20th century's last decade were not often featured by the press. The job they did was no less vital to aviation, but opportunities for spectacular "newsworthy" achievement had become almost nonexistent.

WILFRED PARKE

The first man to put himself forward as someone who would be prepared to risk his life by testing aeroplanes designed and built by others was a young British naval officer named Wilfred Parke. In 1911, he took the unprecedented step of advertising in the magazine *Flight* to

proclaim his willingness to fly experimental machines on demand. He took a light-hearted approach in his appeal to possible employers, saying "Why break your aeroplane yourself when we can do it for you?" Eye-catching though the words were, Parke's entrepreneurial flair was not immediately rewarded. It was many months before he was given his first job, and that may have been just as well. At the time he placed his advertisement, he had held a pilot's certificate for only two weeks, and had begun learning to fly just two weeks before that. In 1912, Parke got his chance when he joined Alliott Verdon Roe and began testing the great pioneer's designs, notably the Types F and G, the first enclosed cabin aeroplanes ever built. The Type F was soon shown to be both underpowered and fragile, but the Type G was sturdier and could accommodate two persons. Parke undertook endurance tests lasting three hours in the Type G, but all did not go smoothly. During the landing run after the first, one wheel hit a molehill and the machine was wrecked when it turned over. Parke was saved from injury because he had taken advantage of what was an unusual feature of the cockpit for those days — he was wearing a seat belt.

On August 25, 1912, at the end of the second three-hour trial, he made a lasting contribution to aviation when he found the answer to a much feared and all too often fatal phenomenon, the spin. Descending in a spiral over the airfield on his return, he tried to tighten the turn and stalled. At about 600 feet, the Type G entered a spin and whirled toward the ground. His initial reaction was to pull the stick back and apply rudder *into* the direction of rotation. Noting that these actions only caused the spin to speed up, he consciously reversed the controls, putting the stick forward and applying rudder against the spin. The recovery was immediate and Parke pulled out of the dive only 50 feet from the ground. His detailed analysis of the event was widely disseminated and was instrumental in saving many lives. Four months after this revelation, Parke was dead, destroyed by his own cavalier spirit. He took off from Hendon in a Handley Page monoplane knowing that there were problems with the engine. It failed soon after takeoff, and he tried to turn back. Once again, he stalled in the turn and entered a spin, this time with insufficient height to recover. Besides the legacy of spin recovery (known for a time as "Parke's Dive"), he left a notebook in which were written detailed reports on the characteristics of all of the aircraft he had flown. Their subsequent publication earned Parke the posthumous respect of the aviation community, and secured his place in history as the first pilot to specialize in testing aircraft.

TEDDY BUSK

For all his enthusiasm and his aptitude for flight-testing, Wilfred Parke was essentially an amateur operating by instinct rather than in accordance with an organized system. Scientific flight-testing can trace its origins to another British pilot, Edward "Teddy" Busk, who began his association with aviation at the Royal Aircraft Factory, Farnborough, in 1912. An honors graduate from Cambridge University, he worked at Farnborough initially as a research engineer seeking to design an aeroplane that could maintain stable flight and would therefore be capable of being flown

"hands off." Frustrated by the inadequate reports of the pilots who flew his test profiles in R.E.1s and B.E.2s, Busk took flying lessons with Geoffrey de Havilland, and by the summer of 1913 was flying the tests himself. His meticulous, methodical approach, with precisely flown research flights and carefully recorded results, led to a number of proposals for design modifications.

By the spring of 1914, Busk's ideas had been incorporated into the B.E.2c — staggered wings, a new tail with the rudder swinging from a fixed fin, and ailerons instead of wing-warping. The new design proved to be the world's first truly practical, stable aircraft. Busk had made his point, and in the process established a scientific method for flight-testing that was adopted and built upon by his successors. Busk did not live to see his efforts so richly rewarded. Just six months after the B.E.2c's first flight, he died in the fiery crash of one he was testing. The B.E.2c, in common with many of its contemporaries, had a notoriously leaky fuel system, and it seems likely that a spark from the engine ignited raw fuel in Busk's cockpit. The aircraft burst into flames in the air and, stable to the end, was seen to descend in a steady glide until it hit the ground. Teddy Busk was

twenty-eight and his test-flying career was measured in months, but his contribution to aeronautics was felt throughout the aviation world.

EDDIE ALLEN

When the United States entered WWI in 1917, Eddie Allen was twenty-one years old. He enlisted in the U.S. Army, learned to fly and became a flying instructor. A few months later, he was sent to the United Kingdom to study British flight-testing methods before being assigned to the U.S. Army's flight-test center at McCook Field near Dayton. In 1919, he was one of the first two test pilots taken on by the National Advisory Committee for Aeronautics (NACA), and soon established a reputation for being meticulously thorough in his work. While enjoying his flying, Allen did not neglect his further education, studying aeronautical engineering first at the University of Illinois and then at MIT. He was a freelance test pilot between 1923 and 1925, and from 1925 to 1927 he flew the mail between Cheyenne and Salt Lake City. He joined Boeing Air Transport in 1927 when that company took over the air mail route from Chicago to San Francisco, but his services as a test pilot were increasingly sought, especially by the Boeing Airplane Company.

By the 1930s, Allen was a highly respected independent test pilot and consulting aeronautical engineer, hired at one

time or another by most of the major aircraft manufacturers and by airlines such as Eastern and Pan American. His reputation was such that his presence in the cockpit meant that lower insurance premiums would be charged to cover a first flight. Allen's list of firsts is hard to equal. Among them were the Boeing Model 83 (F4B), Douglas DC-2, Sikorsky S43, Boeing B-17B/C/D/E/F, Boeing XB-15, Boeing XB-29, Curtiss CW-20 (C-46), and Lockheed Model 049 (Constellation). As he gathered experience and prestige, Allen became an advocate for comprehensive, coordinated aeronautical research in the production of any new aircraft. He promoted the idea of involving test pilots from an early stage in the process, rather than calling on them only after the machine was rolled out to fly. On April 26, 1939, Allen was appointed Director of Aerodynamics and Flight Research at Boeing, a position that gave him great influence over the development of the B-17 and B-29, and enabled him to put his ideas into practice by building a flight research facility second to none. One of the biggest challenges of his career was the B-29. Although the first flight was uneventful, the test program did not progress smoothly. The engines in particular gave cause for concern, there being several airborne engine failures and sixteen engine changes on the XB-29 in its first twenty-seven hours of flying.

On December 30, 1942, Allen flew the second XB-29 and was forced to land with two engines on fire and another close to failure. The XB-29 flight made on February 18, 1943, proved to be even worse. Allen took off from Boeing Field and within eight minutes reported that he was returning with an engine fire. The fire appeared to have been extinguished, but as the aircraft was turning on to final approach there was an explosion. Part of the port wing between the engines was blown away and the radio operator was heard to say that the wing was on fire. Dense smoke gushed into the cockpit. Three crew members bailed out but were too low for their parachutes to open. Now beyond control, the XB-29 crashed into a meat-packing plant 3 miles from the runway. Eddie Allen and his crew all died in the accident, as did twenty people in the building.

At the end of WWII, President Truman paid the following tribute: "In the course of a great war such as we have only recently concluded, there are a great many unsung heroes…. Especially this was true in the case of the aircraft

test pilots, the men who took the planes in their experimental stages, tested their potentialities, ironed out their defects and brought in the reports that made it possible to fashion these airplanes into formidable weapons of war. Theirs was the contribution of a scientific objectivity combined with the daring and fearlessness of the pioneer, and the contribution was a magnificent one. They have earned the admiration and the respect of the men who flew the planes that grew out of their efforts and accomplishments and, as a matter of fact, they were really a part of the great Air Force team that bombed the enemy to defeat…. Eddie Allen was outstanding among these men."

MILBURN "MEL" APT

Mel Apt is remembered principally for his fatal flight in the Bell X-2, but he had earned his reputation as a most capable USAF test pilot before that. Although he had no experience of rocket flight, he had been associated with the inertia coupling program flown in the F-100 and he was selected to fly

the X-2 after Pete Everest had departed to attend staff college. Preparation for his X-2 flying was done in an early simulator, and on September 27, 1956, he moved on to his first flight in the real aircraft. This was to be no gentle familiarization flight, but a genuine attempt to fly faster than anyone had done before. Like other X-2 missions, it began with a 230-mph launch from the EB-50D at 31,800 feet. Shortly after release, full thrust was obtained from the rocket motor and the aircraft accelerated rapidly. By the time it passed through 43,000 feet, it was supersonic. Apt followed the planned flight profile precisely to reach a maximum altitude of just over 72,000 feet. He then pushed over and accelerated through Mach 3. Following engine shutdown, Apt was heard to say, "Engine cut; I'm turning." Moments later, the X-2 was rolling violently, and G-forces went from plus 6 to minus 6. Cockpit film later showed Apt being violently thrown about. He reached for the T-handle that would initiate the nose capsule's ejection, and the film's last frame shows him being thrown upward and back in his seat as the capsule was jettisoned at approximately 40,000 feet, some sixty-eight seconds after the engine shut down. The capsule drogue chute deployed normally, but the canopy was jettisoned at a very low altitude. Apt released his lap belt but was unable to jump clear of the capsule and use his seat-pack parachute. His body was found on the desert, partially out of the cockpit, and with the intact but crushed nose capsule lying on its side. Calculations showed that Apt had taken the X-2 to Mach 3.196, equivalent to 2,094 mph at 66,000 feet, the first flight ever to exceed three times the speed of sound.

JACQUELINE AURIOL

Jacqueline Auriol is acclaimed as France's most distinguished woman pilot, but flying was not a major part of her life until after WWII. Born in 1917, she graduated from the university in Nantes and studied art at the École du Louvre in Paris. In 1938, she married Paul Auriol, son of Vincent Auriol, a prominent leader of the Socialist party. During WWII, Madame Auriol, by that time the mother of two sons, evaded Gestapo agents and aided the French Resistance. After the war ended, Vincent Auriol became President of France, and Madame Auriol took up flying, earning her tourist license in 1948. In July 1949, she was severely injured when a seaplane in which she was a passenger crashed into the Seine. Over the next two years, she underwent a series of operations to rebuild her face, but she did not give up flying. Between her last two operations in the United States, she earned her helicopter rating in just four weeks with Bell Aircraft. In 1950, Madame Auriol

qualified as the world's first woman test pilot at the Bretigny Flight Test Centre and became a test pilot for the French government. On May 11, 1951, she set a new women's speed record of 508.8 mph in a de Havilland Vampire. This

began a friendly rivalry with American Jacqueline Cochran, and they traded the women's world speed record for over a decade. Flying a Mystère IV, Madam Auriol became the second woman to fly faster than sound on August 3, 1953, and then, in a Mirage III, the first to exceed Mach 2 in August 1959. She gained the title of "the world's fastest woman" again after recording 1,150 mph in the Mirage IIIC on June 22, 1962, and added the 100-kilometer closed-circuit record of 1,261 mph in the Mirage IIIR on June 14, 1963. Later, she was one of the first pilots to fly the supersonic Concorde. Madame Auriol was awarded the 1952, 1953 and 1955 Harmon International Trophies, the Paul Tissander Diploma in 1953, the 1963 Gold Air Medal, La Grande Medaille de L'Aero Club de France in 1963, and the Legion d'Honneur for her record-setting achievements.

ROLAND BEAMONT

One of Britain's most celebrated aviators, Roland "Bee" Beamont was commissioned in the Royal Air Force just before WWII, and first saw combat as a Hurricane pilot with 87 Squadron in the Battle of France. On May 13, 1940, he achieved the first of his ten aerial victories against manned aircraft, a Dornier 17 bomber, and he downed more enemy aircraft during the Battle of Britain. He flew Hurricane night fighters in the Luftwaffe's winter blitz of 1940–41. In December 1941, he was posted to Hawker Aircraft Company, where he began his career as a test pilot, flying Hurricanes and the new Typhoon. In July 1942, he returned to combat, flying the Typhoon with 56 Squadron, and then took command of 609 Squadron, again with the

and the TSR.2, an advanced supersonic strike and reconnaissance aircraft. Beamont was the first Briton to exceed Mach 1 in level flight and to fly faster than Mach 2 in a British aircraft. He set three Atlantic crossing records in the Canberra and was awarded the Britannia Trophy for the first Atlantic round trip completed in less than a day. The recipient of numerous other aeronautical awards, Beamont flew some 170 different types of aircraft during his long flying career.

BILL BEDFORD

British test pilot Bill Bedford is best known for his pioneering work on the development of practical vertical/short takeoff and landing (V/STOL) aircraft. In 1940 he volunteered for the RAF and served as a fighter pilot, flying the Hawker Hurricane, Republic P-47 Thunderbolt, and P-51

Typhoon, flying moonlight missions against trains in France. Beamont returned to Hawker Aircraft in March 1943, flying advanced models of the Typhoon and the company's newest fighter aircraft, the Tempest. In early 1944 he was given command of 150 Wing, the first operational unit to employ the Tempest V, and on June 8, he shot down a Bf 109G to claim the wing's first aerial victory. During this period, Tempests were used in operations against Germany's V-1 "Buzz Bomb," and Beamont destroyed thirty-two of the 632 flying bombs claimed by 150 Wing. In late 1944, he led the wing to Holland, and there gained his final victory, shooting down an Fw 190. On October 13, while strafing a troop train, he was shot down and taken prisoner of war.

After VE Day, he returned to command the RAF's Air Fighting Development Squadron, but left the service in January 1946 to join Gloster Aircraft Company as an experimental test pilot. At Gloster, he worked on the Meteor IV, and later that year set a British speed record of 616 mph. In May 1947, he became the Chief Test Pilot at English Electric Aircraft and directed test programs in which he conducted first flights on four outstanding aircraft: the Canberra, Britain's first jet bomber; the P.1, Britain's first supersonic aircraft; the Lightning F.1, Britain's first supersonic fighter;

Mustang successively with 605, 135 and 65 Squadrons. He graduated from the Empire Test Pilots' School in 1949 and became a research test pilot at the Aerodynamics Flight of the Royal Aircraft Establishment, Farnborough, participating in supersonic research, the development of powered flight controls, and the spinning characteristics of swept-wing aircraft. For a time he served with the National Gas Turbine Establishment flight-testing jet engines, and then, in 1956, he took over as Chief Test Pilot at Hawker Aircraft, a position he held until 1967. He was the first pilot to fly the V/STOL Hawker P.1127, Kestrel and Harrier, and was instrumental in evolving flight-test techniques for V/STOL aircraft.

Operating in such an unexplored field of aviation gave him some uncomfortable moments, none more so than on December 14, 1961. During a series of flutter tests at high speed and low level, the P.1127 suddenly decelerated and started vibrating. Bedford called for an emergency landing at nearby Yeovilton Naval Air Station. On final approach, at 170 knots and 200 feet, the aircraft rolled to the left uncontrollably. Bedford grabbed the ejection handle between his legs and left the aircraft almost horizontally. He hit the ground in a plowed field just as the parachute fully deployed. Some days later a farmer found the port forward engine nozzle, which had detached in flight. By early 1963, many of the early V/STOL problems were solved, and in February, Bedford accomplished the first fixed-wing V/STOL landing on a ship, touching down on the carrier HMS *Ark Royal* to usher in an era in which small "Harrier carriers" could be considered viable instruments of sea power. During his flying career, Bill Bedford amassed almost 7,000 hours in 150 different types of aircraft. His awards included the Britannia, Segrave and de Havilland trophies, a Queen's Commendation, the Order of the British Empire and the Air Force Cross.

ALBERT BOYD

Born in Rankin, Tennessee, in 1906, Albert Boyd completed primary flying training at March Field, California, in October 1928, and advanced training at Kelly Field, Texas, in February 1929. From 1929 to 1934, he served as a flight instructor at Brooks, Kelly and Randolph Fields near San Antonio, Texas. In June 1935, he graduated from the Air Corps Technical School at Chanute Field, Illinois, where he studied aircraft maintenance and engineering, and then served as an engineering and operations officer. During this period he received his first exposure to the flight-test world, one of his duties being to evaluate the performance of aircraft after they had undergone maintenance or significant modification. In June 1939, he was sent to Hickam Field, Hawaii, where he became chief engineer of the Hawaiian Air Depot. Following the Japanese attack on Pearl Harbor on December 7, 1941, he was commended for "bringing the

Depot back to a higher state of efficiency than enjoyed prior to the attack." He was promoted to full colonel in February 1943 and assigned to the Fairfield Air Depot at Patterson Field, Ohio.

While working in a variety of engineering, maintenance and logistics management capacities, Boyd also managed to maintain his proficiency in the cockpit, remaining current in a wide range of front-line military aircraft. In December 1943, for example, he was rated current in at least twenty-five different types ranging from the B-24 to the P-51. In July 1944, Boyd became deputy commander of the Eighth Air Force Service Command in Europe, and in October 1945, he was appointed as chief of the Flight Test Division at Wright Field, Ohio. Up to this time, military test pilots had generally been confined to limited acceptance tests of aircraft destined for the operational inventory, while NACA (later NASA) and civilian test pilots under contract did most of the serious research and development work. Boyd wanted "his" pilots to be involved in this work, but many then in the Flight Test Division lacked the discipline, patience, objectivity, precision flying skills and love for the job that Boyd believed were necessary prerequisites for effective test-flying. Under his command, only those who met his very exacting standards remained in flight test. Boyd was convinced that, given the ever-increasing complexity of modern combat aircraft, a military test pilot had to have more than just superb flying skills; he would also have to understand all of the systems he was testing and all of the phenomena he was encountering to be able to translate his experiences into the precise language of the engineer and designer.

Often called "the father of modern Air Force flight-testing," Boyd succeeded to a remarkable degree, legitimizing the role of military test pilots in flight research. Always inclined to lead by example, he personally evaluated every aircraft considered for the Air Force inventory and, while doing so, earned high acclaim as a "test pilot's test pilot." At Muroc on June 19, 1947, he returned the world absolute speed record to the United States for the first time in twenty-four years, piloting the Lockheed P-80R to 623.608 mph. He was in command at Muroc in June 1951 when the base was officially designated the USAF Flight Test Center. In 1952, he took over as commander of the Wright Aeronautical Development Center in Ohio, and in July 1955 began his final active duty assignment as the Deputy Commander for Weapons Systems, Headquarters Air Research and Development Command. Throughout his career, he continued to evaluate every U.S., British and French aircraft then under development, and from 1945 through 1957, the USAF did not acquire a single aircraft that had not first earned his personal stamp of approval. At the time of his retirement in late 1957, he had amassed 23,000 flying hours in over 700 types and models of aircraft.

MARION CARL

Marion E. Carl won the Navy Cross for heroism on his first combat mission and was the first U.S. Marine Corps ace. Born in 1915, he earned an engineering degree from Oregon State University in 1938, along with a commission from Army ROTC as a second lieutenant in the Corps of Engineers. Determined to fly for the Marines, he resigned his Army commission so that he could join the Marine aviation cadet program. In December 1939, he won the gold wings of a Naval Aviator and his Marine commission. Soon after Pearl Harbor, he was at Midway Island as a section leader in Marine Fighter Squadron 221 (VMF-221). The

squadron was equipped with a motley collection of aircraft, mostly obsolete F2A Buffalos and a handful of F4F Wildcats. In the first minutes of battle on June 4, 1942, VMF-221 was decimated, but Carl, flying a Wildcat, shot down a Zero to claim his first victory. Soon after the Battle of Midway, he joined VMF-223, part of the legendary "Cactus Air Force" on Guadalcanal. In two months of intense combat, he was credited with 15½ aerial victories, and won his second Navy Cross. On one mission, a Zero attacked him as he was preparing to land. Quickly hand-cranking the landing gear back up, Carl gave chase and shot the Zero down over the Guadalcanal beach.

In 1943, Carl commanded VMF-223, and was withdrawn from combat in November 1944 with 18½ victories. He then moved to the Naval Air Test Center, Patuxent River, Maryland, as a test pilot where, among other projects, he evaluated a captured Me 262. He was the first Marine to land a jet fighter on an aircraft carrier and the first Marine to qualify as a helicopter pilot. On August 25, 1947, he set a world speed record in the Douglas D 558 1 Skystreak (650.6 mph), and six years later he set a world altitude record (83,235 feet) in the Douglas D-558 2 Skyrocket. During the Vietnam War he commanded a Marine brigade and returned to combat, flying missions in both the F-4 and the UH-1 helicopter. One of the most highly decorated Marine aviators, Major General Marion Carl retired in 1973 with more than 14,000 flying hours in some 260 types of aircraft.

VALERY CHKALOV

Valery Chkalov was born on February 9, 1904, in Vasilevo, Tajikistan. He was inspired to try for a flying career when he saw a hydroplane touch down on the Volga. He joined the Red Air Fleet when he was fifteen, and was employed assembling aircraft. Two years later he was selected to attend the military flying school at Yegorevsk and he proved to be a natural, graduating with distinction and joining the Squadron of the Red Banner as a fighter pilot. Talented pilot though he was, he sometimes proved to be undisciplined. Among his exploits, he flew under Trinity Bridge, Leningrad, and bet he could do fifty loops over the city. He actually did 250 — and ten days in the guardhouse. Later he flew through power lines while developing low-level tactics and was sentenced to a year in prison; he served nineteen days before leaving the Red Army. In 1930 he was reinstated and enrolled in the Test Pilot Institute. Later, he admitted: "Only when I had mastered the art of test-flying did I understand that a sober risk has nothing to do with foolhardiness." He tested a series of military aircraft for the Soviet Air Force Scientific Research Institute, among them the Polikarpov U-2 , I-5, R-5; Grigorovich I-1; Tupolev TB-1, TB-3, I-4, R-3, and R-6. His flights in the TB-1 included the "Flying Shelf" trials, when the bomber carried fighters aloft on its wings. In 1933, he left the military once more to become a test pilot at the Mezhinsky Factory. He carried out the first flight and testing of the Polikarpov I-15, I-16, and I-17 fighters, and VIT-1 and VIT-2 antitank aircraft. On May Day 1935, he performed individual aerobatics over Red Square, Moscow, in a red I-16 and received the Order of Lenin from Stalin.

In August 1936, Chkalov began a series of long-distance flights that would make his name known worldwide. After completing a 56-hour flight from Moscow to Udd Island in an ANT-25, he became a Hero of the Soviet Union and then took the aircraft to Paris for the 1936 Aviation Exposition. His June 1937 ANT-25 flight over the North Pole from Moscow to Pearson Field, Washington State, took 63 hours, 16 minutes, and startled the world. He rejoined the military as a colonel and was elected as Deputy to the Supreme Soviet of the USSR from the Volga Region. Chkalov's brilliant career came to an untimely close with his involvement in the Polikarpov I-180 fighter program. The I-180 was inadequately prepared for its flight trials and was rushed to test-flying in 1938 in response to pressure from Moscow. A Soviet fighter to match the Messerschmitt Bf 109 was urgently needed. On December 15, the prototype I-180 was cleared for flying only with landing gear down. Chkalov took off and soon afterward suffered engine failure. He crashed and was killed. The next three prototypes of the I-180 also crashed and claimed the lives of two more pilots. Development of the I-180 was terminated.

SCOTT CROSSFIELD

Born in Berkeley, California, on October 2, 1921, Scott Crossfield had his first flying lessons at the age of twelve, in return for delivering newspapers at Wilmington Airport. He began his engineering training at the University of

Washington in 1940, but interrupted his education to join the U.S. Navy in 1942. Commissioned in 1943 following flight training, he served as a fighter and gunnery instructor before spending six months overseas flying such aircraft as the F6F and F4U fighters. He resumed his engineering studies in 1946 and graduated with a BSc in aeronautical engineering from the University of Washington in 1949. From 1946 to 1950, he was the Chief Operator of the University of Washington's F. K. Kirsten Wind Tunnel, and from 1950 he was an aeronautical research pilot for the National Advisory Committee on Aeronautics. During the next five years, he flew the X-1, X-4, X-5, XF-92A, and D-558-I and -II, accumulating eighty-seven rocket-powered flights in the X-1 and D-558-II aircraft. He made aeronautical history on November 20, 1953 when he passed the aviation milestone of Mach 2 (more than 1,320 mph) in the D-558-II Skyrocket.

From 1955 to 1961, Crossfield was the design specialist, X-15 project pilot, and chief engineering test pilot for North American Aviation in Los Angeles. He was involved in all phases of X-15 specification and design and was also the pilot for the rocket-powered aircraft's first series of demonstration flights. In the process he achieved a maximum speed of Mach 2.97 (1,960 mph) and an altitude of 88,116 feet. On one notable occasion he was in the cockpit for a test run of the rocket engine on the ground when it exploded. His description of the event tended to belittle the danger of what must have been horrifying experience: "It was a pretty violent activity for a moment or two. It was like being inside the sun. It was such a fire outside that it was a very brilliant orange. The fore part of the airplane, which was all that was left, was blown about thirty feet forward, and I was in it. Of course I was pretty safe because I was in a structure that was designed to resist the very high temperatures of reentry flight."

Later, Crossfield served at North American Aviation as System Director responsible for systems test, reliability engineering, and quality assurance on the Hound Dog missile, Paraglider, Apollo Command and Service Module, and the Saturn II Booster, and then from 1966 to 1967 as Technical Director, Research Engineering and Test. In 1967, he joined Eastern Airlines as a division vice president, helping the company develop its technological applications, new aircraft specifications, and flight research programs.

Then from 1974 to 1975, he was Senior Vice President for Hawker Siddeley Aviation, setting up its U.S. subsidiary for design, support and marketing of the HS 146 transport in North America. From 1977 until his retirement in 1993, Scott Crossfield served as technical consultant to the House Committee on Science and Technology, advising committee members on matters relating to civil aviation. Among many awards for his achievements in aviation were the 1960 Harmon International Trophy and the 1961 Collier Trophy, both presented by President John F. Kennedy at the White House.

JOHN CUNNINGHAM

Britain's John Cunningham gained worldwide recognition as a leading Allied night-fighter ace during WWII and later as a civilian test pilot. After joining the Royal Auxiliary Air Force and learning to fly at age eighteen, he began working

for the de Havilland Aircraft Company as a junior test pilot. His unit, 604 Squadron, was mobilized just before England entered the war in 1939, and the following year converted to Bristol Blenheim night fighters. By the end of 1940, 604 Squadron was flying the first radar-equipped Bristol Beaufighters, and Cunningham was developing and perfecting the night-fighting techniques that served the RAF so well for the rest of the war. On November 20, 1940, Cunningham and radar operator John Phillipson achieved the world's first radar-aided aerial victory at night when they shot down a Junkers 88. The nickname "Cat's Eyes Cunningham" (which he disliked) was encouraged by Air Ministry officials anxious to keep the secrets of airborne interception radar for as long as possible. They explained that he ate a lot of carrots to sharpen his already remarkable ability to see in the dark! In 1942, he was given command of a squadron of Mosquito night fighters and in 1944, at the age of twenty-seven, was promoted to the rank of group captain. Of the twenty enemy aircraft he destroyed, Cunningham claimed all but one of them at night; the other was shot down by day in bad weather. The majority of these victories were achieved while flying with radar operator Jimmy Rawnsley; they were the most successful Allied night-fighter team of the war.

As de Havilland's chief test pilot after the war, Cunningham helped to usher in the jet age, flying the experimental D.H.108 Swallow and a series of twin-boomed fighters — the Vampire, Venom, and the much larger D.H.110 Sea Vixen. On March 23, 1948, he flew a Vampire to a new world altitude record of 59,446 feet. Just over a year later, on July 27, he was the pilot for the maiden flight of the de Havilland Comet, the world's first jet airliner. In 1962, he led the flight-testing of the Trident, one of the first of the three-jet airliners. For his outstanding work as a pioneer of jet transports, Cunningham was awarded the Harmon International Trophy for 1955. He retired in 1980 after a lifetime in aviation.

JOHN DERRY

John Derry learned the art of being a test pilot at Supermarine Aviation, under the guiding hand of "Mr. Spitfire," Jeffrey Quill. From 1947, he was involved in testing the later marks of Spitfire and Seafire, and their successors, the Spiteful and the Seafang. A particular interest of his was the loss of control experienced as an aircraft approached the speed of sound, and he carried out research into compressibility in the Seafire 47, reaching speeds close to Mach 0.9 in diving trials. After only ten months at Supermarine, John Cunningham offered Derry a job at de Havilland, where he took over responsibility for testing the dangerous little D.H.108 Swallow, a tailless research aircraft that had already killed Geoffrey de Havilland Jr., the aircraft breaking up during a high-speed dive. In April 1948, Derry used

the Swallow to set a new 100-kilometer closed-circuit record of 605.23 mph, and then went on to continue his research into transonic problems. On one flight, he came close to recreating the de Havilland disaster, with the aircraft pitching violently at high Mach number. Undeterred, he persisted with the trials and, on September 6, 1948, he took the Swallow through a dive from 48,000 feet, pressing on through a series of barely controllable pitching motions until the aircraft was beyond the vertical. With the Machmeter showing 1.04, he found that the controls had no effect, but as he reached the thicker air below 30,000 feet, the Mach number reduced and control returned. The true speed reached was found to be Mach 1.02, and Derry had become the first British airman to exceed the speed of sound, albeit with some difficulty.

John Derry's promise as a test pilot was considerable, but it was not to be fulfilled. In 1952, he began development of the D.H.110, a large twin-boomed fighter that later became the Royal Navy's Sea Vixen. All through the week at that year's Farnborough Air Show, Derry gave a lively demonstration of the new fighter, starting off every day by planting a sonic boom on the crowd. On Saturday, September 6, he boomed the crowd before making a high-speed pass along the runway. He broke left and had completed nearly 270 degrees of a tight turn when the aircraft disintegrated with shocking suddenness, the engines tearing loose and plowing into the crowd, killing twenty-eight and injuring sixty. John Derry and his observer, Tony Richards, died in the crash. In his short test-pilot career, John Derry's achievements had already gained him both the Segrave Trophy and the Gold Medal of the Royal Aero Club.

JIMMY DOOLITTLE

Born in 1896, Jimmy Doolittle earned his pilot's wings in 1918. He is perhaps best known to the world for his exploits in WWII, when he led the first U.S. retaliatory strike against Japan from the aircraft carrier *Hornet* and eventually rose

to command the "Mighty Eighth" Air Force during the combined bomber offensive against Germany. (See *Aviation Century World War II*, Chapter 4, "The Tide Turns.") However, between the wars he had already established his reputation as an exceptionally talented airman. Among other record-breaking feats, in 1922 he became the first to fly across the United States in less than a day, and ten years

later he set the world's record for land-based aircraft at 296 mph in the dangerous little GeeBee R-1. As a racing pilot, he won the 1925 Schneider Trophy, the 1931 Bendix Trophy, and the 1932 Thompson Trophy. (See *Aviation Century The Golden Age*, Chapter 3, "Speed Comes to the Schneider," "The Thompson," and "Point to Point.") All of these were great achievements, but it was as a test pilot that he made some of his most constructive contributions to aviation. He joined the staff at McCook Field in 1923 and undertook exhaustive flight tests of the Fokker PW-7 experimental fighter in 1924. His tests led to the publication of a report, "Accelerations in Flight," that became a standard reference work for both the NACA and the U.S. Army. In 1925 he received a doctorate in aeronautical engineering from MIT, and in 1928 he joined a research program of the Guggenheim Fund for the Promotion of Aeronautics at Mitchel Field, Long Island. By late summer 1929, Doolittle had succeeded in developing a blind-flying instrument panel, and on September 24, Doolittle flew a specially equipped Consolidated NY-2 through a complete flight, from takeoff to landing, on instruments. It was an achievement that had a profound effect on when and how aircraft could be operated. (See *Aviation Century The Golden Age*, Chapter 2, "Jimmy Doolittle and Friends.")

JOE ENGLE

Joe Engle, one of the most experienced aviators ever to become an astronaut, was a key man in the development of the Space Shuttle. Born on August 26, 1932, in Abilene, Kansas, Engle graduated from the University of Kansas in 1955 with a BSc in Aeronautical Engineering. He joined the USAF and earned his pilot's wings in 1958, then flew F-100 Super Sabres at George AFB, California. After graduating from the Air Force Experimental Test Pilot School in 1961 and the Air Force Aerospace Research Pilot School in 1962, Engle became a test pilot in the X-15 aircraft research program at Edwards AFB, California. He piloted the X-15 on sixteen flights and three times reached altitudes of more than 50 miles, thereby qualifying for astronaut wings and becoming the nation's youngest astronaut. Joining NASA in 1966, Engle was the first and only astronaut recruit to have previously flown in space. Assigned to the Apollo program, he served on the support crew for *Apollo 10* and then was named backup lunar module pilot for *Apollo 14*. With the

advent of the Space Shuttle program, Engle became one of four astronauts to conduct the approach and landing tests of this revolutionary vehicle. On November 12, 1981, he returned to space in command of the *Columbia*. It was a highly significant mission, requiring him to fly the Shuttle manually during reentry to explore its handling characteristics. Following this flight, he served as the Deputy Associate Administrator for manned Space Flight at NASA Headquarters, but on August 27, 1985, he returned to space as commander of the Shuttle *Discovery*. It was an action-packed mission, during which the crew captured, repaired, and redeployed the SYNCOM IV-3 satellite, and deployed three new communications satellites. Engle's varied NASA experience later proved invaluable in the *Challenger* accident investigation and in the subsequent Shuttle Improvement Program. He retired from NASA and the USAF in November 1986 and became a major general in the Kansas Air National Guard.

"PETE" EVEREST

Frank K. "Pete" Everest Jr. acquired his private pilot's license in February 1941, while studying engineering at West Virginia University. Accepted into the Aviation Cadet pro-

gram, he earned his commission as a second lieutenant in the Army Air Force in July 1942 and was assigned to the 314th Fighter Squadron. His unit, equipped with the P-40 Warhawk, was assigned to North Africa in January 1943. During this tour, he flew ninety-six combat missions over Africa, Sicily and Italy. He returned to the United States in May 1944 and for a short time was a fighter training instructor. Not content with that role, Everest asked for a return to combat and was assigned to the China-Burma-India Theater, taking command of a P-51 squadron based in Chinkiang in February 1945. Three months later, while he was on a strafing mission against Japanese boats on the Yangtze River, Everest's Mustang was shot down by ground fire. He was captured and spent the remaining months of the war as a prisoner of the Japanese.

After the war, he was sent to Wright Field, Ohio, as a test pilot and flew nearly every aircraft acquired by the Air Force, building experience that later stood him in good stead when, in September 1951, he was appointed Chief of Flight Test Operations at Edwards AFB, California. During his time at Edwards, General Everest tested the X-1, X-2, X-3, X-4, X-5, XF-92 and YB-52. He also took part in test programs for the F-100, F-101, F-102, F-104, F-105, B-52, B-57 and B-66. On October 29, 1953, he established a

world speed record of 755 mph in a YF-100, flying at low level over the dry bed of the Salton Sea in southern California. In December 1954, he accelerated the X-1B to Mach 2.3, and on July 23, 1956, he surpassed that figure in the Bell X-2. Dropped from the B-50 carrier aircraft at 30,000 feet, Everest lit the rockets and achieved Mach 2.87 (1,957 mph) at 68,000 feet, which for a while gave him the title of "The Fastest Man Alive." Pete Everest subsequently commanded a number of USAF squadrons and wings, and served in several senior staff appointments, including Director of Aerospace Safety and Commander, Aerospace Rescue and Recovery Service. Brigadier General Everest retired from the Air Force in 1973. During his career he was recognized repeatedly for his contributions to aviation. He was chosen as one of 1955's "ten outstanding young men" by the U.S. Junior Chamber of Commerce, and a year later the U.S. Chamber of Commerce named him one of the nation's "greatest living Americans." In 1957 he was awarded both the Harmon Trophy and the Octave Chanute Trophy.

ALEKSANDR VASILYEVICH FEDOTOV

Aleksandr Fedotov graduated from military flight school in Stalingrad in 1950 and flew as a squadron pilot and a flying instructor between 1950 and 1957. He attended test pilot school in 1958 and then worked first for Mikoyan and later for the Moscow Aviation Institute. Between 1961 and 1977, he gained eighteen world aviation records, several while flying the MiG-25 and its E-266 variant. On May 17, 1975, he took an E-266 to 25,000 meters (82,000 feet) from a standing start in just 2 minutes and 34 seconds. In 1966, he became a Hero of the Soviet Union, and 1969 he was rewarded with the title Meritious Test Pilot of the Soviet Union. On August 31, 1977, he broke the world altitude record for an aircraft taking off under its own power, reaching 123,524 feet in an E-266. Fedotov performed the maiden flight of the MiG-29 in 1977, and was involved in the MiG-105, the Spiral EPOS (Eksperimentalny Pilotiruyamy Orbitalny Samolyot [Experimental Passenger Orbital Aircraft]) Program. Major General Aleksandr Fedotov and V.S. Zaytsev died in the crash of a MiG-31 on April 4, 1984.

"FITZ" FULTON

One of America's most accomplished test pilots, Fitzhugh L. "Fitz" Fulton accumulated more than 16,000 hours in over 230 aircraft types. After attending Auburn University, he joined the Army as an aviation cadet and earned his

wings in December 1944. Fulton trained in the B-24 Liberator and B-29 Superfortress, but WWII ended before he could enter combat. He converted to the transport role, and in 1948 flew in the Berlin Airlift, completing 225 missions in the C-54 Skymaster. Fulton saw combat in Korea, logging fifty-five missions in the B-26 Invader with the 13th Bombardment Squadron. In 1952, after completing the USAF Experimental Test Pilot School at Edwards AFB, California, he flew the B-29 and B-50 used to launch the Bell X-1 and X-2 rocket planes, and tested a number of bomber, transport, and fighter aircraft. He was the pilot on the first USAF test program for the Mach 2 B-58 Hustler, and in 1962, while Chief of the Bomber Flight Test Section, Fulton piloted a B-58 with a 5,000-kilogram load to an altitude of 85,360 feet. In recognition of that achievement, President Johnson awarded him the Harmon International Aviation Trophy as the world's outstanding aviator for that year. After twenty-three years of service, Fulton retired from the USAF in 1966 and joined the National Aeronautics and Space Administration (NASA) at the Dryden Flight Research Center, Edwards AFB.

As NASA's Chief Test Pilot, he flew the XB-70 Valkyrie and the B-52s that launched the X-15 and the lifting body aircraft. In the mid-1970s, Fulton continued to expand the limits of aeronautical knowledge, flying the YF-12 Blackbird to speeds and altitudes in excess of 2,000 mph and 70,000 feet, and in 1977 he was the project pilot for the Boeing 747 used in the Space Shuttle approach and landing tests. That year, in recognition of his contributions to flight-testing, he was awarded both the Society of Experimental Test Pilots Iven C. Kincheloe Award and NASA's Exceptional Service Medal. Fulton retired from NASA in 1986, but continued test-flying as Flight Operations Director and Chief Research Pilot for Scaled Composites Incorporated. While there, he was the pilot for the first flights of two innovative aircraft, a twin-engine short takeoff and landing turboprop and a twin-engine executive jet.

"TEX" JOHNSTON

A pioneer of the jet age, Alvin "Tex" Johnston became one of America's foremost test pilots. His passion for flying began in 1925 with his first flight in a Hisso-Standard biplane from a pasture near his hometown of Emporia, Kansas. By the time he was nineteen, he had trained as an aircraft and engine mechanic, and earned his pilot's licence. He worked in Inman's Flying Circus and built time flying in a variety of aircraft before buying a Command-Aire biplane and barnstorming around the country. After Pearl Harbor, he became a civilian ferry pilot for the Army Air Force and then, in 1942, went to work for Bell Aircraft's experimental flight-test division. He flew tests on the P-39 Airacobra, XP-63 Kingcobra and on the first U.S. jet, the XP-59 Airacomet. In 1946, he modified a war-surplus P-39 and reached speeds of 430 mph in winning the Thompson Trophy at the National Air Races. Until 1947, Johnston supervised tests of the rocket-powered X-1, and then worked on Bell's helicopter program until mid-1948, when he joined Boeing to become senior test pilot on the XB-47 Stratojet at Wichita. In 1951, he moved to Seattle as project pilot for Boeing's YB-52 Stratofortress. Three years later, he was the pilot for the first

flight of Boeing's Model 367-80, the prototype aircraft that led to the KC-135 Stratotanker and the 707 airliner. It was the first step toward Boeing's domination of the world's air transport market. So confident was Johnston of the Dash 80's handling that, asked to fly by the crowds at the annual Seattle powerboat races, he made a number of passes, startling the spectators by completing several rolls in the process. In the early 1960s, Johnston was Assistant Program Manager for Boeing's X-20 Dyna Soar project, and then worked as Director of the Boeing Atlantic Test Center, before going into business for himself. One of his companies, Aero Spacelines, manufactured the "Guppy," an outsize conversion of the Boeing Stratocruiser designed to haul extremely large and awkwardly shaped cargo, such as ballistic missile bodies or aircraft fuselages.

OLLE KLINKER

Olle Klinker is one of Sweden's most famous pilots and was the first person outside the United States to receive the Society of Experimental Test Pilots' prestigious Doolittle

Award. He joined the Royal Swedish Air Force in 1942 and earned his wings in 1943. After one year of military service, Klinker left the service to study for an MSc in Aeronautical Engineering from the Royal Swedish Institute of Technology. He joined SAAB, the Swedish aircraft company, in 1947 and began his testing career flying the J 21A, a twin-boomed, piston-powered, pusher fighter and the J 21R, a jet-powered version that ushered Sweden into the jet age. During a high-speed dive test on March 28, 1949, the J 2IR's tail began to flutter and then broke away. As the aircraft pitched violently down, the wings were torn off. Klinker tried to eject, but the seat failed, and he escaped only because the fuselage suddenly disintegrated, hurling him clear.

The problems of the J 21R overcome, Klinker went on to serve as the engineering test pilot for most SAAB experimental and fighter designs, including the J 29 Tunnan, a contemporary of the F-86 and MiG-15. He made over 500 flights in the Little Draken, built to test the low-speed characteristics of the double-delta wing, and from 1956 to 1964, developed the J 35 Draken, Sweden's first supersonic fighter. It was followed by the J 37 Viggen canard-winged fighter, an aircraft capable of operating from very short strips on the national highways. In 1968, he became manager of the Flight Test Department of SAAB, and in 1978 he

was named Vice President responsible for all aircraft division operations including ground test, laboratories and simulators. Olle Klinker's numerous awards include the Gold Medal for the most distinguished aviation achievement in Sweden in 1949, presented to him in Stockholm by Jacqueline Cochran. In addition to the Doolittle Award of 1985, he also received SETP's Tenhoff Award in 1968.

JOE KITTINGER

By any standards, Joe Kittinger proved himself to be an exceptional aviator, but his claim to fame in the testing world is anything but conventional. He began his U.S. Air Force career as a fighter pilot, but was then assigned to a series of Air Force high-altitude balloon projects and became a pioneer of the space program, testing pressure suits and parachutes. In 1957, he made the first flight of the Manhigh program, setting a balloon altitude record of 96,000 feet while seated inside a tiny capsule wearing a full pressure suit. His next program was Project Excelsior, which was intended to test man's ability to survive high-altitude bailouts and came close to proving the opposite. His first jump from a balloon at 76,000 feet nearly ended in disaster when a failure of his stabilization chute caused a spin that rendered him unconscious. He was saved by the automatic opening of his parachute and recovered to continue the program. Kittinger's most significant jump occurred in 1960 when he stepped from a balloon at an altitude of 102,800 feet, free-falling to 18,000 feet before opening his parachute and landing in the desert of New Mexico. During the four-and-a-half-minute free fall, he reached a speed exceeding 0.9 Mach and experienced air temperatures down to minus 94 degrees Fahrenheit, setting records that continued to stand beyond the end of the century for the highest ascent in a balloon, the highest parachute jump, the longest free fall, and the fastest speed ever achieved by a man unassisted by machine.

Frustrated at not flying in the Korean War, Kittinger volunteered for three combat tours in Vietnam, and served as commander of the famous 555th "Triple Nickel" Tactical

Fighter Squadron flying F-4s. He downed a MiG-21 before being shot down himself on May 11, 1972, after which he spent eleven months in captivity as a POW. He retired from the USAF as a colonel in 1978. In later years, while working at Martin Marietta Aerospace as an engineer, he was able to devote time to his old love of ballooning. He won the Gordon-Bennett balloon races in 1982, 1984 and 1985, but accomplished his most ambitious feat, a solo balloon crossing of the Atlantic, in 1984, flying from Maine to northern Italy in three and a half days. When he was not competing in balloons, Joe Kittinger lent his considerable energies to the job of Vice President of Flight Operations for Rosie O'Grady's Flying Circus, Orlando, Florida.

"PETE" KNIGHT

William J. "Pete" Knight proved himself in a variety of challenging roles, including those of fighter pilot, test pilot, astronaut, and politician. Born in Nobelsville, Indiana, in 1929, he earned his USAF commission and pilot wings through the Aviation Cadet Program in 1953. As a second lieutenant, Knight won the Allison Trophy racing the F-89 Scorpion in the Dayton National Air Show of 1954. In 1956, he attended the Air Force Institute of Technology, graduating two years later with a degree in aeronautical engineering, and then went on to complete the course at the Air Force Experimental Test Pilot School, Edwards AFB, California. As an Edwards AFB test pilot, Knight was involved in the advanced testing of the F-100 Super Sabre, and in 1960 he was one of five pilots selected for the development of the X-20 Dyna Soar.

After the X-20 was canceled, Knight joined the X-15 test program. On October 3, 1967, he climbed into the cockpit of the X-15A-2 for another flight in a series designed to "push the edge of the envelope." High over the Mojave Desert, his aircraft dropped away from the B-52 and he ignited the rocket engine to begin his climb. As the outboard propellants burned out, he jettisoned the two external fuel tanks and rocketed forward through the thin atmosphere, leveling off at just over 100,000 feet. Boosted by over 140 seconds of engine-burn time, the X-15 accelerated to Mach 6.7 (4,250 miles per hour), the fastest powered flight ever achieved in a manned aircraft other than the Space Shuttle. During this flight, the aircraft surface temperature exceeded 3,000 degrees Fahrenheit. Leaving the

test arena for a while, Knight saw combat in Southeast Asia flying F-100s at Phan Rang AB, from where he flew 253 combat missions. After his Vietnam tour, he was assigned to Wright-Patterson AFB, Ohio, where he served as the Test Director for development of the F-15 Eagle. Following graduation from the Industrial College of the Armed Forces in 1973, Knight returned to Wright-Patterson AFB as the F-4 System Program Office (SPO) Director, and later Director of the Fighter Attack SPO responsible for the development and production of USAF fighter aircraft. In 1979 he returned to Edwards AFB as the Air Force Flight Center Commander, where he served until his retirement from the USAF in 1982. During his distinguished career, Colonel Knight accumulated more than 7,000 flying hours in over 100 types of aircraft. In the years following his retirement, Pete Knight served as Mayor of the City of Palmdale, and as a California State senator.

TONY LE VIER

Tony LeVier was one of aviation's greatest test pilots. Few could equal his active role in the advancement of aviation during a flying career spanning over fifty years. He began flying at age fifteen in 1928, and by 1932 had his commercial license. During the 1930s, he barnstormed, flew charters, instructed, and raced, making a name for himself in 1938 by winning the Greve Trophy Race at Cleveland and

contributions to aviation were not limited to test-flying. As an inventor, LeVier made many significant improvements in aircraft systems. He designed the master caution warning light system, the automatic wing stores release, the first practical afterburner ignition system, the "'hot microphone" intercom system, and he devised the placement of the electric trim switch on top of the control stick. After ten years as Lockheed's chief engineering test pilot, he became Lockheed's Director of Flying Operations, a position he held until shortly before his retirement in 1974. He then became an active aviation consultant and was a founding member of the Society of Experimental Test Pilots. In 1978, LeVier's tremendous contributions to aviation were recognized when he was inducted into the National Aviation Hall of Fame.

JOHN MACREADY

John Arthur Macready graduated from Stanford University in 1912, enlisted in the U.S. Air Service in 1917, and earned his pilot's wings at Rockwell Field, San Diego. While a flight instructor at the Army Pilot School at Brooks Field, Texas, he authored a book, *The All Through System of Flying*

the Pacific International Air Race at Oakland. World War II then brought new flying opportunities. After jobs with Douglas Aircraft, Mid-Continent Airlines, and General Motors, LeVier joined Lockheed Aircraft in April 1941. At first, he ferried Lockheed Hudson bombers built for the Royal Air Force, but soon worked his way into the Engineering Flight Test Department and remained there for thirty-two years. He conducted a compressibility dive program, improving the P-38 Lightning and helping to pave the way for future high-speed and supersonic flight. His skill with the P-38 led to an assignment as a special research test pilot with the USAAF in the United Kingdom. To improve the combat effectiveness of the P-38, he conducted lectures, flight tests, and demonstration flights at all Eighth Air Force P-38 bases. He then returned to Lockheed and helped the United States enter the jet age.

On June 10, 1944, LeVier took off from Muroc Field in the XP-80A, known as the "Gray Ghost" and the predecessor to America's first production jet aircraft. It was not a happy experience, bedeviled as it was by a faulty tachometer and by asymmetric flaps. It took all of LeVier's considerable skill to get the aircraft down in one piece. He went on to make successful first flights in nineteen other aircraft including the T-33, F-94, XF-104, and U-2. During his flying career, he flew more than 250 types of aircraft, but his

Instruction, which became the basic manual for student pilots in the early years of U.S. military aviation. After WWI, he was assigned to the Air Service Experimental Test Center at McCook Field, near Dayton, Ohio, and became one of the elite first group of engineering test pilots. One of his projects was testing turbo-superchargers, and for the next six years, Macready flew all the tests, routinely climbing higher and higher in the open-cockpit LUSAC-11 biplane. In the course of these tests, he set several world altitude records, the highest being 34,508 feet, an achievement for which he was awarded the Mackay Trophy for 1921. These flights, made at great personal risk, significantly advanced the knowledge of high-altitude physiology.

In 1922, John Macready joined Oakley Kelly in an attempt fly the coffin-shaped Fokker T-2 across the continent nonstop. On their first attempt, they took off from Rockwell Field, San Diego, but could not coax the heavily laden T-2 over the hills to the west. Not wishing to waste the occasion, they settled down to break the world's endurance record. They landed over 35 hours later, having surpassed the record by almost nine hours. After modifying the aircraft at McCook Field, they tried for endurance again in April 1923, and set a new world mark of 36 hours, 4 minutes, 34 seconds. The following month, they took off on another transcontinental flight, this time going in the opposite direction, from Roosevelt Field on Long Island. A little less than 27 hours later, they touched down in San Diego, exhausted but jubilant after the first nonstop coast-to-coast flight. For these various achievements, Macready and Kelly were awarded the Mackay Trophy for the years 1922 and 1923, Macready becoming the only pilot to be so honored three times. Besides such memorable performances, Macready also represented the Air Service in the Pulitzer races, made the first emergency parachute jump at night, was the second man to fly in a pressurized cabin, the first pilot to demonstrate crop-dusting, and a pioneer of U.S. aerial photographic survey. He left the Air Service in 1926, but continued to promote aviation by participating in exhibition and racing events. During WWII, he was recalled to active duty, commanded several Army Air Force groups, and served as inspector general for the Twelfth Air Force in North Africa. He retired from active duty in 1948 and in 1976 was invested in the International Aerospace Hall of Fame.

RUDI OPITZ

Before WWII, Rudi Opitz garnered most of his flying time in gliders. In 1934, when he was twenty-four years old, he built his own glider, and soon afterward he was established as an instructor at Germany's premier gliding center, the

Wasserkuppe. By the mid-1930s he was involved in test-flying the gliders and tailless aircraft designed by Dr. Alexander Lippisch, and was in the cockpit of the prototype Messerschmitt Bf 110 for its first flight in 1936. Opitz joined the Luftwaffe at the beginning of the war and served initially as a glider pilot. In this capacity he took part in the brilliantly successful commando raid on the Belgian fortress of Eben Emael in May 1940. Meanwhile Dr. Lippisch had been engaged to work on the development of a rocket-propelled tailless fighter, a design that by 1939 had been given the designation Messerschmitt Me 163. Opitz joined the project in the autumn of 1941 and continued to fly the dangerous little aircraft until the end of the war, surviving a number of near fatal crashes. It was estimated that on one occasion he had experienced an impact of 20 G while recovering an Me 163 with a failed landing skid, severely damaging his spine and putting him in hospital for three months. On another flight, while Opitz was testing an Me 163B at full rocket power, it accelerated so rapidly that it exceeded the limiting Mach number before he could shut off the motor. Control of the aircraft became difficult and it entered a steep dive from which Opitz recovered only a few feet above the Baltic. After landing, it was found that most of the rudder had been torn off, and that a speed of 702 mph had been achieved. In the years after WWII, Opitz worked as an engineer and test pilot at Wright Field, Ohio, and then completed his test-flying career with the Avco-Lycoming Company before retiring to live in Connecticut.

HANNA REITSCH

Hanna Reitsch was born in Hirschburg, Germany, in 1912. When she was a twenty-year-old medical student she took up gliding, and the experience changed her life, setting her on her way to becoming one of the leading women aviators of the 20th century. Her remarkable abilities were soon demonstrated by her success in competition, and she added to her reputation by being one of the first people to cross the Alps in a glider. She became a test pilot for the German Institute for Glider Research and was involved in promotional tours to Africa and South America. On progressing to powered aircraft, she showed that she was truly exceptional, proving herself capable of flying any aircraft with great competence. In 1938 she astonished audiences in Berlin's huge Deutschland Halle by flying the Focke-Achgelis Fw 61 helicopter inside the building. (See "Power to the Rotor," Chapter 1.) From then on, there was no flying task that the diminutive (5-foot, 88-pound) Reitsch could not be asked to do. Among the aircraft she test flew during WWII were the huge Me 321 Gigant, the hazardous Me 163 rocket fighter, and a piloted version of the V-1 flying bomb. In the last days of the Third Reich, when most of Berlin had

already been occupied by the Russians, she undertook a desperate flight in a Fieseler Storch that took General von Greim to see Hitler in the "Fuhrerbunker." With the aircraft hit by ground fire and the General wounded, she managed to land the aircraft on a street cratered by shell-holes. Two days later, she took the Storch out again; it was the last aircraft to leave the city before it finally fell to the Soviet Army. During her career in aviation, Hanna Reitsch set more than forty altitude and endurance records in gliders and powered aircraft, and she was the only woman ever to be awarded the Iron Cross and Luftwaffe Diamond Clasp.

JEAN MARIE SAGET

Fascinated by flying from an early age, Jean Marie Saget was eleven years old when German forces invaded France. His enthusiasm for aircraft survived the war years, after which he attended the Air Force Academy at Salon. He completed his flying training in the United States and, in May 1952, was posted to No. 2 Wing of the Armée de l'Air's Fighter Command, flying the Dassault Ouragan. In 1953, he won an air race flying between Paris and Cannes, a feat that earned him the offer of a job from Marcel Dassault. On May 1, 1955, with a total of 950 hours in his logbook, he left the Armée de l'Air and became a company pilot. In the years that followed he gained experience in a variety of aircraft, including the Nord 1100 and the Mystère II and IV, before attending the test pilots' course at Brétigny. Now fully qualified as a test pilot, Saget took on the high-altitude trials of the Mirage IIIA, and on February 3, 1960, registered Mach 2 at 70,000 feet, at which height the engine stalled and was relit on the descent. On a later flight he took the IIIA to 88,500 feet.

During the 1960s, Saget was involved in testing the Mirage V, F1, and G fighters. The Mirage G, a variable geometry aircraft, achieved its maximum sweep of 70 degrees in flight less than a week after its first flight on November 18, 1967, and exceeded Mach 2 within two months. On July 1, 1971, Saget was appointed Dassault's Chief Pilot. In 1978, while in Egypt to give demonstrations of the Alpha Jet, he lost both engines on long final approach. After his Egyptian copilot had ejected, he found himself too low to eject safely and was fortunate to survive the subsequent crash with broken ribs and a fractured cheekbone. His rescuers inadvertently pulled the ejection

Mirage jet fighters at Le Bourget.

seat handle in releasing him from the cockpit, and Saget was lucky that the firing mechanism had been damaged in the crash and the charge had been expended through the bottom of the cockpit. By March 1979, he was back in the cockpit, testing the Super Mirage 4000 and taking it to Mach 1.6 on its first flight. Saget's enthusiasm for the 4000 knew no bounds. He delighted in the aircraft's ability to take him effortlessly through a vertical 8 from takeoff, and to hold 4 G in the transonic range at 40,000 feet. In 1982, he logged his 10,000th flying hour, and had the remarkable experience of celebrating by leading a formation of eight aircraft, each of which had a member of his family at the controls. After suffering another engine failure on finals in a Mirage 2000 and surviving the subsequent ejection, Saget stopped testing military combat aircraft in 1985, but did not retire completely, continuing to enjoy his flying in aircraft such as the Falcon executive jet series.

PETER TWISS

Peter Twiss became an airman trainee in the Royal Navy just after the outbreak of WWII. In his first four years as a naval pilot, he flew Fairey Fulmars from carriers escorting the Malta convoys and Seafires during the Allied invasion of North Africa. For a while, he endured the long, anxious hours of being a Hurricat pilot on the CAM ships, waiting to be rocket-launched to intercept the Luftwaffe Condors that stalked the convoys, knowing that the only way back was to ditch alongside a friendly ship. (See *Aviation Century*

World War II, Chapter 5, "The Maritime War.") In 1943, Twiss undertook intruder operations against German airfields at night, and it was then that he was introduced to the fascination of test-flying. Much new night-fighting equipment was being tried out on the operational squadrons, and he was intrigued by the process. He got the chance to fly his first jet aircraft during a visit to the United States in 1944, and that stood him in good stead for his postwar career. In 1946, Twiss joined Fairey Aviation as a test pilot, and completed projects with a number of the company's aircraft, including the Gannet ASW aircraft and the forty-eight-seat Rotodyne VTOL airliner. Then in 1954 the Fairey Delta 2 supersonic research aircraft was produced. On the FD-2's fourteenth flight, Twiss suffered an engine failure and had

to recover to base without power from 30,000 feet. Only the nosewheel lowered when he selected gear down, and he had to land without airbrakes, touching down at well over 200 mph. He walked away from the accident, but the FD-2 was grounded for a year. Once the Delta was flying again, it was decided to attack the world air-speed record, and on March 10, 1956, Twiss raised the mark to more than 1,000 mph for the first time, averaging 1,132 mph over a measured course. By 1959, Fairey had been bought by Westlands and his testing career was over, but Peter Twiss had more flying to do. In a move to the other end of the air-speed scale, he flew the Fairey Swordfish for the epic 1960 movie *Sink the Bismarck*, and in his later years became an accomplished glider pilot.

FRITZ WENDEL

Fritz Wendel joined Willi Messerschmitt's team at the Bayerische Flugzeugwerke in 1935, at first employed only as a production test pilot, flying license-built Heinkel 45 biplanes as they emerged from the factory. In due course, he graduated to Bf 109s and was appointed as the company's chief test pilot at the age of twenty-four. His name jumped into the world's headlines in 1939 with his startling performance in what was described for German propaganda purposes as a Messerschmitt Bf 109R. In fact he flew an aircraft that bore little resemblance to the Luftwaffe fighter. It was actually an Me 209, an aircraft built for the specific pur-

The fuselage of the Messerschmitt Me 209V1, photographed in 2003 by Dan Patterson at the Muzeum Lotnictwa Polskiego (Polish Aviation Museum), Krakow, Poland. The Me 209 was an experimental aircraft built primarily for the propaganda value of capturing the world speed record. On April 26, 1939, Fritz Wendel recorded 469.22 mph, a record that would stand for thirty years. Hitler's propaganda ministry announced that the record had been achieved using a Messerschmitt Bf 109R, implying that its performance was similar to that of the Luftwaffe's front-line fighter. Fritz Wendel was not impressed by the machine, referring to it as "a vicious little brute."

pose of capturing the world's air-speed record. Very small and powered by a special engine that could deliver 2,300 horsepower for short periods, it was described by Wendel as a "winged horror" and "a brute." On April 4, 1939, he walked away from an Me 209 after it had been reduced to a "heap of twisted metal" when the engine seized during a training flight, but on April 26 he flew another one to a world record speed of 469.22 mph, a mark for piston-engined aircraft that stood for over thirty years. Recalling the Me 209 years later, Wendel said, "Its flying characteristics still make me shudder." He continued to test Messerschmitt's aircraft throughout WWII, flying such diverse types as the Me 261 Adolfine long-range aircraft, originally designed to carry the Olympic Fire to Tokyo in 1940, and every model of the Bf 109, including an advanced nosewheel version designated Me 309. He was forced to abandon aircraft twice, once when the starboard elevator broke away from an Me 210, and again after the port wing flew off a Bf 109H during a dive to 500 mph. Wendel's supreme achievement was his development testing of the Me 262, first with the assistance of a nose-mounted piston engine, and then with two Jumo 004 turbojets. On July 18, 1942, he flew the purely jet-powered Me 262 for the first time and "it flew beautifully." Testing the Me 262, he said "was not work to me, it was a pleasure."

ROBERT MICHAEL "BOB" WHITE

Bob White earned his pilot's wings in February 1944 and joined the 355th Fighter Group in England five months later, flying P-51 Mustangs. In February 1945, on his fifty-second combat mission, he was shot down by antiaircraft fire over Germany. Recalled to active duty in response to the Korean War, he elected to remain in the USAF and attended the Experimental Test Pilot School at Edwards Air Force Base, graduating in January 1955. Staying on at Edwards, he evaluated advanced models of the F-86K Sabre, F-89H Scorpion, F-102 Delta Dart and F-105B Thunderchief. White's career changed dramatically when he was designated the Air Force's primary pilot for the X-15 program in 1958. After the aircraft's 57,000-pound thrust engine was installed, he flew it to a speed of 2,275 mph in February 1961, and over the next eight months he became the first man to exceed Mach 4, Mach 5 and Mach 6. On July 17, 1962, he took the X-15 to a record-setting altitude of

314,750 feet, more than 59 miles above the Earth's surface. This qualified him for astronaut wings. President John F. Kennedy later conferred the Collier Trophy jointly to White and three of his fellow X-15 pilots — NASA's Joseph Walker, Commander Forrest S. Peterson of the U.S. Navy, and North American Aviation test pilot Scott Crossfield. White was awarded his rating as a Command Pilot Astronaut by the USAF's Chief of Staff, General Curtis E. LeMay, and he also received NASA's Distinguished Service Medal and the Harmon International Trophy for the year's most outstanding contribution to aviation. Added to these was an award from his peers — the Society of Experimental Test Pilot's Iven C. Kincheloe Award.

Returning to more conventional duties, White completed tours of duty in Germany, commanding the 53rd Tactical Fighter Squadron, and Thailand, from where he flew seventy combat missions over North Vietnam in the F-105. He returned to research and development in June 1968, going back to Wright-Patterson Air Force Base as director of the Aeronautical Systems Division's F-15 Systems Program Office. Now a full colonel, he was responsible for managing the development and production planning of the F-15 Eagle. Two years later he assumed command of the Air Force Flight

Test Center at Edwards AFB. White's responsibilities included testing the A-7D and C-5A Galaxy, and system evaluations of the F-111 and FB-111A. During his command, evaluation began of a number of other aircraft — the F-15, A-10 and E-3A AWACS. In addition to his other duties, White completed the Naval Test Parachutist course and was awarded his parachutist's wings in October 1971. He served at the Flight Test Center until October 1972, and then became Commandant, Air Force Reserve Officer's Training Corps. In February 1975, he won his second star and in March was appointed Chief of Staff of the Fourth Allied Tactical Air Force. Bob White retired from active duty with the Air Force as a major general in February 1981.

CHUCK YEAGER

Most widely known as the first man recorded as traveling at a speed faster than sound in 1947, Chuck Yeager has made immense contributions to aviation during a flying career that has covered more than fifty years. A fighter pilot who scored thirteen aerial victories in just sixty-four combat missions in the P-51 Mustang, he went on after WWII to become perhaps the most experienced test pilot of the 20th century. In the months immediately following the end of the war, Yeager participated in an evaluation of captured German and Japanese aircraft, and flew test projects in first-generation jets such as the P-80 and P-84 at Wright Field. These assignments led to his selection to fly the Bell X-1, and to his successful penetration of the "sound barrier" in October 1947.

During the next two years, Yeager flew the X-1 over forty times, reaching speeds of more than 1,000 mph and heights above 70,000 feet. In December 1953 he flew the Bell X-1A to Mach 2.44 at 80,000 feet and nearly paid the price for taking the aircraft into regions where it proved to be unstable. As it reached its maximum speed, the X-1A suddenly tumbled out of control and fell for over 50,000 feet, subjecting Yeager to massive and rapidly changing G-forces — positive, negative and lateral. He eventually managed to get the aircraft into a spin from which he could recover and land on Rogers Dry Lake near Muroc. When he was on final approach, he said, with feeling, "Boy! I'm not going to do that again." However, there were to be other occasions when an aircraft would come close to giving him his last flight. The NF-104 was a version of Lockheed's

Starfighter used for high-altitude, zero-G training. On December 12, 1963, while Commandant of the Air Force Aerospace Research Pilot School at Edwards AFB, Yeager zoomed an NF-104 up to 104,000 feet, aiming to let it fly a ballistic curve over the top and fall into a dive, as he had done successfully on previous flights. This time, the aircraft pitched up, failed to respond to thrusters in the nose, and entered an irrecoverable flat spin. Yeager ejected below 10,000 feet, but his rocket-powered seat hit him hard as it separated, the red hot rocket pack striking him in the head and setting the seals round the helmet of his pressure suit on fire. By the time he reached the desert, his face was badly burned, condemning him to many months of painful recuperation. Among his later appointments, Yeager commanded fighter wings in Southeast Asia and the United States, and was Director of the Air Force Inspection and Safety Center before retiring from the USAF as a Brigadier General in 1975. He continued to serve as a consulting test pilot for many years, and has brought his considerable abilities to bear on well over 200 aircraft types. His many civilian honors and awards include the Collier, Mackay, and Harmon Trophies, a special peacetime Medal of Honor, and the Medal of Freedom.

JAN ZURAKOWSKI

Janusz Zurakowski was born in Ryzawka, Russia, of Polish parents, on September 12, 1914. After the Bolshevik revolution in 1921, the family immigrated to Poland. By 1932 he was a glider pilot, and in 1934 he joined the Polish Air Force. He attended the Polish Air Force Officers' School in Deblin, was awarded his wings in 1935, and was commissioned as an officer in the Polish Air Force in 1937. His first posting was to 161 Fighter Squadron in Lwow, but in March 1939 he became a flight instructor at the Central Flying School in Deblin flying the PZL P.7 fighter. He was heavily involved in the brief campaign against the Luftwaffe in September 1939, and, when Poland fell, escaped through Rumania and made his way eventually to Britain, where he joined the RAF to continue the fight against Hitler's Third Reich. By the time the Battle of Britain began he was with 234 Squadron flying the Spitfire 1. During August and September he was frequently in action as one of "The Few," shooting down two Bf 109s and a Bf 110 while himself being shot down once and having to crash-land on another occasion. Between October 1940 and March 1944, Zurakowski served with a number of squadrons, including several entirely manned by Poles, steadily gaining more responsibility first as a flight commander and then as squadron commander. In July 1943, he was promoted to Deputy Wing Leader of the Polish No. 1 Fighter Wing stationed at Northolt, and led the Wing on forty-six combat sorties, escorting USAAF bombers on daylight raids against Germany as well as flying fighter sweeps over occupied Europe. For repeated courage in the face of the enemy, he was awarded Poland's highest medal for valor, the Virtuti Militari.

In March 1944 Zurakowski's career took a decisive turn when he was posted to the Empire Test Pilot's School. On completing the course, he joined the staff of the Aircraft and Armament Experimental Establishment (A&AEE) and for the next two years was occupied in testing an array of

British and American aircraft, including early RAF jets such as the Vampire. In 1947, he left the RAF to join Gloster Aircraft, where he tested various marks of Meteor and the Javelin all-weather delta-winged fighter. He became famous for his sensational displays in the Meteor, for which he had perfected a maneuver known as the "Zurabatic Cartwheel." In 1952, he left Gloster's and joined Avro Canada in Malton, Ontario, as chief development test pilot. An early project was the CF-100 Canuck, the first Canadian indigenous jet fighter, an aircraft designed for a top speed of Mach 0.85. On December 18, 1952, flying a CF-100 Mk.4, Zurakowski forced the aircraft beyond Mach 1, becoming the first person to exceed the speed of sound in a straight-wing pure-jet aircraft without rocket power. This event was commemorated in 1996 by the Canadian Mint when they issued a special edition $20 silver piece depicting a pair of CF-100s and a gold cameo of Janusz Zurakowski. During the 1950s, Avro pursued the development of a supersonic interceptor, the CF-105 Arrow. Before it was canceled by the Canadian government in 1959, Zurakowski had demonstrated that it was a remarkable aircraft with great potential, reaching speeds close to Mach 2 at heights up to 50,000 feet. In September 1958, Zurakowski retired from test-flying at the age of forty-four. His many honors include the McKee Trophy and a place in Canada's Aviation Hall of Fame. The main building of the Canadian Flight Test Centre at Cold Lake, Alberta, bears his name.

AND MANY MORE.....

Any listing of test pilots is bound to be incomplete, and this one leaves out hundreds who richly deserve to be mentioned for their contributions to aviation. The distinguished pilots included here stand as a few representatives of a brave profession, honoring those of many nations.

Shorty Schroeder McCook Field, high-altitude research
Harold Harris McCook Field; Caterpillar Club Member No. 1 after the breakup of a Loening PW-2A
Roland Rohlfs Curtiss post-WWI; world records of 163 mph and 34,610 feet in 1918/19
Gene Barksdale McCook Field; killed testing an experimental Douglas O-2 observation aircraft
Bill McAvoy NACA; multiple types, from autogyros to P-61s

Mutt Summers Vickers Wellington; Supermarine Spitfire
John Lankester Parker Short flying boats; Stirling four-engined bomber
Jimmy Collins Freelance; killed dive-testing Curtiss XF3F
Harald Penrose Westland Wapiti, Pterodactyl, Wyvern, helicopters
Lloyd Child P-40 and other Curtiss aircraft, WWII
Jeffrey Quill and *Alex Henshaw* Supermarine Spitfire development
George Bulman Hawker; biplane fighters and Hurricane
Erich Warsitz Heinkel; first jet flight in He 178
Karl Baur Testing of all Messerschmitt prototypes
Lukas Schmid Messerschmitt; Bf 109 dive-testing to 500 mph
Fritz Schäfer Heinkel: He 280 jet; He 177 four-engined bomber
Ronald Harker Rolls-Royce: Merlin/Mustang development
Geoffrey de Havilland Jr. D.H. aircraft; killed in the D.H.108 Swallow
Mike Daunt Gloster; E28/39 and Meteor
Bernard Lynch Martin Baker; ejection-seat testing
Eric "Winkle" Brown Royal Navy and RAE Farnborough; over 400 types tested
Mike Lithgow Supermarine, BAC; killed in a BAC One-Eleven super stall
Neville Duke Hawker jet aircraft, particularly the Hunter; world record 728 mph, 1963
Stepan Mikoyan MiG jet fighters
George Welch North American; F-86, F-100; killed in F-100 inertia coupling
Brian Trubshaw Concorde; 11,000 hours in more than 100 types
André Turcat Concorde; testing for Nord and Aerospatiale
Joe Walker NASA; killed in F-104/XB-70 collision
John Moore North American Vigilante; Flex-deck no-wheel landing program
Iven Kincheloe USAF; first man to fly above 100,000 feet, killed in an F-104 crash
Neil Armstrong (NASA; 11,000 hours in over 200 types of jets, rockets, helicopters and gliders)
Bill Bridgeman Douglas; Skyrocket and X-3
Jack Woolams Bell; P-59 and X-1; killed in P-39 during Thompson Trophy practice
….and many more.

BIBLIOGRAPHY

Allen, Oliver E. *The Airline Builders*. Alexandria, VA: Time-Life Books, 1981

Anderton, David A. *History of the U.S. Air Force*. New York: Military Press, 1981

Angelucci, Enzo. *World Encyclopedia of Civil Aircraft*. New York: Crown Publishers, 1982

Angelucci, Enzo. *Rand McNally Encyclopedia of Military Aircraft*. New York: Military Press, 1983

Apple, Nick, and Gene Gurney. *The Air Force Museum*. Dayton, Ohio: Central Printing, 1991

Armitage, Michael. *The Royal Air Force*. London: Arms & Armour Press, 1993

Baker, David. *Flight and Flying: A Chronology*. New York: Facts on File, 1994

Baldry, Dennis, ed. *The Hamlyn History of Aviation*. London: Hamlyn, 1996

Bauer, Eugene E. *Boeing in Peace & War*. Enumclaw, WA: TABA Publishing, 1991

Bauer, Eugene E. *Boeing, the First Century*. Enumclaw, WA: TABA Publishing, 2000

Bickers, Richard Townshend. *A Century of Manned Flight*. Broadstone, U.K.: CLB, 1998

Biddle, Wayne. *Barons of the Sky*. New York: Simon & Schuster, 1991

Bonds, Ray, ed. *The Story of Aviation*. New York, Barnes & Noble, 1997

Botting, Douglas. *The Giant Airships*. Alexandria, VA: Time-Life Books, 1981

Bowyer, Chaz. *History of the RAF*. London: Hamlyn, 1982

Bowyer, Chaz. *The Age of the Biplane*. London: Hamlyn, 1981

Bowyer, Chaz, and Michael Turner. *Royal Air Force*. Feltham, U.K.: Temple Press, 1983

Boyd, Alexander. *The Soviet Air Force since 1918*. New York: Stein & Day, 1977

Boyne, Walter J. *The Leading Edge*. New York: Stewart, Tabori & Chang, 1986

Boyne, Walter J. *The Smithsonian Book of Flight*. Washington, DC: Smithsonian Books, 1987

Boyne, Walter J., and Donald S. Lopez, eds. *Vertical Flight*. Washington, DC: Smithsonian Institution Press, 1984

Brown, David, Christopher Shores and Kenneth Macksey. *Air Warfare*. Enfield, U.K.: Guinness Superlatives, 1976

Bryan, C.D.B. *The National Air & Space Museum*. New York: Harry N. Abrams, Inc., 1980

Burge, C.G., ed. *Encyclopaedia of Aviation*. London: Pitman, 1935

Cacutt, Len, ed. *Classics of the Air*. New York: Exeter Books, 1988

Chant, Christopher. *20th Century War Machines (Air)*. London: Chancellor Press, 1999

Chant, Christopher. *The History of Aviation*. London: Tiger Books International, 1998

Chant, Christopher. *Pioneers of Aviation*. Rochester, U.K.: Grange Books, 2001

Chesnau, Roger. *Aircraft Carriers of the World*. Annapolis, MD: Naval Institute Press, 1984

Chilstrom, Ken, and Penn Leary. *Test-Flying at Old Wright Field*. Omaha, NB: Westchester House, 1993

Christienne, Charles, and Pierre Lissarrague. *Histoire de L'Aviation Militaire Francaise*. Paris: Charles-Lavauzelle, 1980

Cooksley, Peter G. *Air Warfare*. London: Arms & Armour Press, 1997

Cooling, Benjamin Franklin, ed. *Close Air Support*. Washington, DC: Office of Air Force History, 1990

Davies, R.E.G. *Fallacies and Fantasies*. McLean, VA: Paladwr Press, 1994

Dick, Ron, and Dan Patterson. *American Eagles*. Charlottesville, VA: Howell Press, 1997

Divone, Louis, and Judene. *Wings of History*. Oakton, VA: Oakton Hills Publications, 1989

Donald, David, ed. *The Classic Civil Aircraft Guide*. Edison, NJ: Chartwell Books, 1999

Ellis, Ken. *Wrecks & Relics*. Leicester, U.K.: Midland Publishing, 1998

Endres, Günter. *Major Airlines of the World*. Shrewsbury, U.K.: Airlife, 1996

Friedman, Norman. *U.S. Aircraft Carriers.* Annapolis, MD: Naval Institute Press, 1983

Friedman, Norman. *British Carrier Aviation.* Annapolis, MD: Naval Institute Press, 1988

Fritzsche, Peter. *A Nation of Fliers.* Cambridge, MA: Harvard University Press, 1992

Gibbs-Smith, Charles H. *Aviation: An Historical Survey.* London: Science Museum, 1985

Gildemeister, Jerry. *Avian Dreamers.* Union, OR: Bear Wallow, 1991

Green, Geoff. *British Aerospace.* Wotton under Edge, U.K.: Geoff Green, 1988

Green, William. *Warplanes of the Third Reich.* New York: Galahad Books, 1986

Greenwood, John T., ed. *Milestones of Aviation.* New York: Hugh Lauter Levin Associates, 1989

Gunston, Bill. *The Development of Piston Aero Engines.* Yeovil, U.K.: Patrick Stephens Ltd., 1993

Gunston, Bill, ed. *Chronicle of Aviation.* London: Chronicle Communications, 1992

Gurney, Gene. *Test Pilots.* New York: Franklin Watts, 1962

Hallion, Richard P. *Legacy of Flight.* Seattle, WA: University of Washington Press, 1977

Hallion, Richard P. *On the Frontier.* Washington, DC: NASA, 1984

Hallion, Richard P. *Test Pilots.* Washington, DC: Smithsonian Institution Press, 1988

Harrison, James P. *Mastering the Sky.* New York: Sarpedon, 1996

Hengi, B.I. *Airlines Remembered.* Leicester, U.K.: Midland Publishing, 2000

Hengi, B.I. *Airlines Worldwide.* Leicester, U.K.: Midland Publishing, 2000

Heppenheimer, T.A. *A Brief History of Flight.* New York: John Wiley & Sons, 2001

Heppenheimer, T.A. *Turbulent Skies.* New York: John Wiley & Sons, 1995

Hudson, Kenneth, and Julian Pettifer. *Diamonds in the Sky.* London: The Bodley Head, 1979

Jackson, Robert. *The Sky Their Frontier.* Shrewsbury, U.K.: Airlife, 1983

Jarrett, Philip, ed. *Biplane to Monoplane.* London: Putnam, 1997

Jarrett, Philip, ed. *Modern Air Transport.* London: Putnam, 2000

Josephy, Alvin M. *The American Heritage History of Flight.* New York: American Heritage Publishing, 1962

Kasmann, Ferdinand C.W. *World Speed Record Aircraft.* London: Putnam, 1990

Knott, Richard C. *The American Flying Boat.* Annapolis, MD: Naval Institute Press, 1979

Larson, George. *The Blimp Book.* Mill Valley, CA: Squarebooks, 1977

Leary, William M., ed. *From Airships to Airbus (Vols 1 & 2).* Washington, DC: Smithsonian Institution Press, 1995

Marriott, Leo. *80 Years of Civil Aviation.* Edison, NJ: Chartwell Books, 1997

McKay, Stuart. *Tiger Moth.* New York: Orion, 1988

Middleton, Donald. *Tests of Character.* Shrewsbury, U.K.: Airlife, 1995

Millbrooke, Anne. *Aviation History.* Englewood, CO: Jeppesen Sanderson, 1999

Miller, Richard. *Without Visible Means of Support.* Los Angeles, CA: Parker & Son, 1967

Mondey, David, ed. *Aviation.* London: Octopus Books, 1980

Moolman, Valerie. *Women Aloft.* Alexandria, VA: Time-Life Books, 1981

Moore, John. *The Wrong Stuff.* North Branch, MN: Specialty Press, 1997

Morrison, Steven A., and Clifford Winston. *The Evolution of the Airline Industry.* Washington, DC: Brookings Institution, 1995

Norris, Guy, and Mark Wagner. *Boeing 777.* Osceola, WI: Motorbooks International, 1996

Novosel, Michael. *Dustoff.* Novato, CA: Presidio Press, 1999

Nowara, H.J., and G.R. Duval. *Russian Civil and Military Aircraft.* London: Fountain Press, 1971

Oakes, Claudia, ed. *Aircraft of the National Air & Space Museum.* Washington, DC: Smithsonian Institution Press, 1981

Owen, David. *Lighter than Air.* Edison, NJ: Chartwell Books, 1999

Pattillo, Donald M. *A History in the Making.* New York: McGraw-Hill, 1998

Penrose, Harald. *Adventure with Fate.* Shrewsbury, U.K.: Airlife, 1984

Penrose, Harald. *Airymouse*. Shrewsbury, U.K.: Airlife, 1982

Penrose, Harald. *Cloud Cuckooland*. Shrewsbury, U.K.: Airlife, 1981

Prentice, Colin W. *Monino*. Shrewsbury, U.K.: Airlife, 1997

Rabinowitz, Harold. *Conquer the Sky*. New York: Metro Books, 1996

Rawlings, John D.R. *The History of the Royal Air Force*. Feltham, UK: Temple Press, 1984

Redding, Robert, and Bill Yenne. *Boeing, Planemaker to the World*. Greenwich, CT: Bison Books, 1983

Sabbach, Karl. *Twenty-First Century Jet*. New York: Scribner, 1996

Sampson, Anthony. *Empires of the Sky*. New York: Random House, 1984

Serling, Robert J. *The Jet Age*. Alexandria, VA: Time-Life Books, 1982

Sharpe, Mike. *Air Disasters*. London: Brown Partworks, 1998

Shute, Neville. *Slide Rule*. Kingswood, U.K.: Windmill Press, 1954

Simpson, Rod. *Commercial Aircraft and Airliners*. Shrewsbury, U.K.: Airlife, 1999

Smith, Herschel. *A History of Aircraft Piston Engines*. Manhattan, KS: Sunflower University Press, 1986

Späte, Wolfgang. *Test Pilots*. Bromley, U.K.: Independent Books, 1995

Sturtivant, Ray. *British Naval Aviation*. Annapolis, MD: Naval Institute Press, 1990

Szurovy, Geza. *Executive Jets*. Osceola, WI: MBI Publishing, 1998

Taylor, John W.R., Michael Taylor and David Mondey. *Air Facts & Feats*. Enfield, U.K.: Guinness Superlatives, 1977

Taylor, John W.R., and Kenneth Munson. *History of Aviation*. New York: Crown Publishers, 1972

Taylor, John W.R., and Susan Young. *Passenger Aircraft and Airlines*. London: Marshall Cavendish Publications, 1975

Taylor, Michael J.H. *Great Moments in Aviation*. London: Prion, 1989

Taylor, Michael J.H. *The World's Commercial Airlines*. London: Regency House, 1997

Thetford, Owen. *Aircraft of the Royal Air Force*. London: Putnam, 1988

Toland, John. *The Great Dirigibles*. New York: Dover Publications, 1972

Twiss, Peter. *Faster than the Sun*. London: Grub Street, 2000

van der Kooij, Otger. *European Wrecks & Relics*. Leicester, U.K.: Midland Publishing, 1998

van der Linden, F. Robert. *Aircraft of the National Air & Space Museum*. Washington, DC: Smithsonian Institution Press, 1998

Wohl, Robert. *Aviation and the Western Imagination*. New Haven, CT: Yale University Press, 1994

Young, Warren R. *The Helicopters*. Alexandria, VA: Time-Life Books, 1982

BOOKS BY CORPORATIONS, MUSEUMS AND OTHER ORGANIZATIONS

Ad Inexplorata. Edwards AFB, CA: Air Force Flight Test Center History Office, *1996*

Dateline Lockheed. Burbank, CA: Lockheed Corporate Communications, 1982

Forty Years On… London: Handley Page Ltd., 1949

National Museum of Naval Aviation. Pensacola, FL: Naval Aviation Foundation, 1996

Pedigree of Champions: Boeing since 1916. Seattle, WA: The Boeing Company, 1977

The Pratt & Whitney Aircraft Story. Hartford, CT: Pratt & Whitney Aircraft, 1950

United States Air Force Museum. Wright-Patterson AFB, OH: Air Force Museum Foundation, 1997

Young, James O. *Meeting the Challenge of Supersonic Flight*. Edwards AFB, CA: Air Force Flight Test Center, 1997

ANNUAL PUBLICATIONS

Aviation Year Book. New York: Aeronautical Chamber of Commerce of America

Jane's All the World's Aircraft. London: Jane's Yearbooks

Jane's Fighting Ships. London: Jane's Yearbooks

MAGAZINES

Aeroplane Monthly. London: IPC Media Ltd.

Flypast. Stamford, U.K.: Key Publishing

Air International. Stamford, U.K.: Key Publishing

Air & Space Smithsonian. Washington, DC: Smithsonian Business Ventures

Flight Journal. Ridgefield, CT: Air Age Inc.

INDEX BY SUBJECT

Note: Page numbers in bold indicate an illustration.

SHIPS

GENERAL INDEX

Note: Page numbers in bold indicate an illustration.